Photograph by Celia Bartram

Dear ESL/EFL colleagues,

I once met a teacher who had recently used one of my texts in her class. At the end of the term, one of her students said to her, "Thank you for teaching me the secrets of English."

I still smile when I think of that comment. Of course, we know there are no "secrets," but I think I understand what the student meant—that it's sometimes helpful to understand what's going on underneath the surface of a language. A second language can seem so dizzying and random. A little information about its patterns can help students make sense of it and give them a foundation for language growth.

The first book in the Azar series was published in 1981. It was the blue book, *Understanding and Using English Grammar,* which grew out of many years of creating my own materials for my own classes. I then wrote two other texts, the red and the black, creating *The Azar Grammar Series.*

All of the texts have undergone revisions over the years with many evolutionary changes, especially in the use of more interactive and communicative activities. But throughout this time, the original vision remains as stated in the very first book: the goal is the development of all usage skills from a grammar base by giving clear grammar information and employing a variety of practice modes, from controlled response to open communicative interaction.

When I published the first book, I hoped maybe a few other teachers might find the textbook useful, too. In all honesty, I never imagined there were so many teachers like myself who found a grammar-based skills approach to be effective and appropriate for their students. It turns out we are legion.

During the naturalist approach heyday in the 80s and into the 90s, when advocates of zero grammar held sway, grammar instruction largely disappeared from school curricula for native speakers of English. But because of teacher support for grammar-based materials like mine, grammar teaching did not disappear from curricula for second language learners.

Because of you, grammar is today a viable and vigorous component in the ESL/EFL classroom—much to our students' benefit. A great deal of current research shows that many if not most of our students benefit greatly from a grammar component blended with other approaches in a well-balanced program of second language instruction. Together we have served our students well.

My hat is off to you.

Betty S. Azar

Betty Azar
Whidbey Island, Washington
2006

BASIC

ENGLISH GRAMMAR

Third Edition

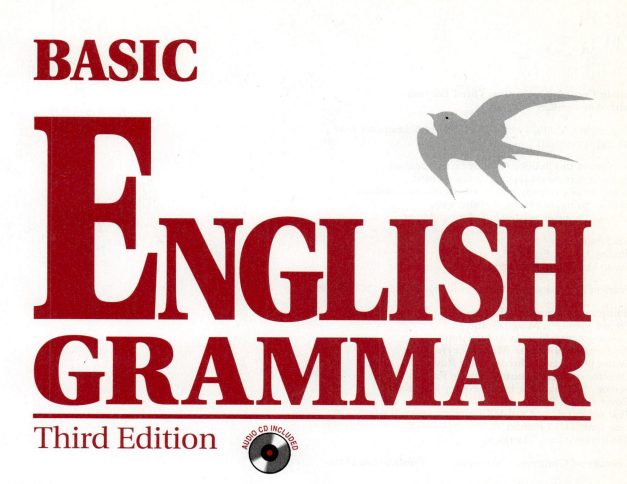

AUDIO CD INCLUDED

with Answer Key

PEARSON
Longman

Betty Schrampfer Azar
Stacy A. Hagen

Basic English Grammar, Third Edition
with Answer Key

Azar Associates
Shelley Hartle, Editor
Susan Van Etten, Manager

Pearson Education, 10 Bank Street, White Plains, NY 10606

Editorial manager: Pam Fishman
Project manager: Margo Grant
Development editor: Janet Johnston
Production supervisor: Melissa Leyva
Senior production editor: Robert Ruvo
Director of manufacturing: Patrice Fraccio
Senior manufacturing buyer: Nancy Flaggman
Cover design: Pat Wosczyk
Text composition: Carlisle Communications, Ltd.
Text font: 11/13 Plantin
Illustrations: Don Martinetti

Library of Congress Cataloging-in-Publication Data

Azar, Betty Schrampfer, 1941-
  Basic English grammar / Betty Schrampfer Azar.-- 3rd ed.
    p. cm.
  ISBN 0-13-184937-9 (pbk.) -- ISBN 0-13-184412-1 (pbk.) -- ISBN
0-13-195734-1 (pbk.) -- ISBN 0-13-195733-3 (pbk.) -- ISBN
0-13-195436-9
(pbk.) -- ISBN 0-13-195350-8 (pbk.) -- ISBN 0-13-184939-5 (pbk.) -- ISBN
0-13-184940-9 (pbk.)
  1. English language--Textbooks for foreign speakers. 2. English
language--Grammar--Problems, exercises, etc. I. Title.
  PE1128.A96 2005
  428.2'4--dc22
                                                    2005014671

ISBN: 0-13-184937-9
6 7 8 9 10–CRK–09 08 07

ISBN: 0-13-195734-1 (International Edition with audio CDs)
6 7 8 9 10–CRK–09 08 07

ISBN: 0-13-195436-9 (International Edition)
3 4 5 6 7 8 9 10–CRK–09 08 07 06

CONTENTS

Preface to the Third Edition

Basic English Grammar is a beginning level ESL/EFL developmental skills text in which grammar serves as the springboard for expanding learners' abilities in speaking, writing, listening, and reading. It uses a grammar-based approach integrated with communicative methodologies. Starting from a foundation of understanding form and meaning, students engage in meaningful communication about real actions, real things, and their own real lives in the classroom context.

Teaching grammar is the art of helping students look at how the language works and engaging them in activities that enhance language acquisition in all skill areas. The direct teaching of grammar to academically oriented adults and young adults is one component of a well-balanced program of second language instruction and can, much to students' benefit, be integrated into curricula that are otherwise content/context-based or task-based.

This third edition has the same basic approach as earlier editions, with new material throughout. It has

- student-friendly grammar charts with clear information that is easily understood by beginning students.
- numerous exercises to give students lots of practice.
- more illustrations to help students learn vocabulary, understand contexts, and engage in communicative language tasks.
- reorganized chapters with expanded practice for high-frequency structures.
- the option of a student text with or without an answer key in the back.

In addition, the new edition has a greater variety of practice modes, including

- greatly increased speaking practice through extensive use of interactive pair and group work.
- the addition of numerous listening exercises, accompanied by audio CDs, with listening scripts included in the back of the book.
- more activities that provide real communication opportunities.

A new *Workbook* accompanies the student text to provide additional self-study practice. A *Test Bank* is also available.

HOW TO USE THIS TEXT

GRAMMAR CHARTS

The grammar charts present the target structure by way of example and explanation. Teachers can introduce this material in a variety of ways:

a. Present the examples in the chart, perhaps highlighting them on the board. Add additional examples, relating them to students' experience as much as possible. For example, when presenting simple present tense, talk about what students do every day: come to school, study English, etc.

b. Elicit target structures from students by asking questions. (For example, for simple past tense, ask: What did you do last night?) Proceed to selected examples in the chart.

c. Instead of beginning with a chart, begin with the first exercise after the chart, and as you work through it with students, present the information in the chart or refer to examples in the chart.

d. Assign a chart for homework; students bring questions to class. This works best with a more advanced class.

e. Some charts have a preview exercise or pretest. Begin with these, and use them as a guide to decide what areas to focus on. When working through the chart, you can refer to the examples in these exercises.

With all of the above, the explanations on the right side of the chart are most effective when recast by the teacher, not read word for word. Keep the discussion focus on the examples. Students by and large learn from examples and lots of practice, not from explanations. In the charts, the explanations focus attention on what students should be noticing in the examples and the exercises.

FIRST EXERCISE AFTER A CHART

In most cases, this exercise includes an example of each item shown in the chart. Students can do the exercise together as a class, and the teacher can refer to chart examples where necessary. More advanced classes can complete it as homework. The teacher can use this exercise as a guide to see how well students understand the basics of the target structure(s).

SENTENCE PRACTICE

These exercises can be assigned as either oral or written practice, depending on the ability and needs of the class. Many of them can also be done as homework or seatwork.

LET'S TALK

Each "Let's Talk" activity is designated as one of the following: pairwork, small group, class activity, or interview. These exercises encourage students to talk about their ideas, their everyday lives, and the world around them. Examples for each are given so that students can easily transition into the activity, whether it be student- or teacher-led.

LISTENING

Listening exercises for both form and meaning give exposure to and practice with spoken English. Listening scripts for teacher use are in the back of the book. Two audio CDs also accompany the text. Many of the exercises also introduce students to common features of reduced speech.

Teachers may want to play or read aloud some listening scripts one time in their entirety before asking students to write, so they have some familiarity with the overall context. Other exercises can be done sentence by sentence.

WRITING

As students gain confidence in using the target structures, they are encouraged to express their ideas in paragraphs and other writing formats. To help students generate ideas, some of these tasks are combined with "Let's Talk" activities.

When correcting student writing, teachers may want to focus primarily on the structures taught in the chapter.

REVIEW EXERCISES

All chapters finish with review exercises; some are cumulative reviews that include material from previous chapters, so students can incorporate previous grammar with more recently taught structures.

Each chapter review contains an error-correction exercise. Students can practice their editing skills by correcting errors commonly found in beginning students' speaking and writing.

ANSWER KEY

The text is available with or without an answer key in the back. If the answer key is used, homework can be corrected as a class or, if appropriate, students can correct it at home and bring questions to class. In some cases, the teacher may want to collect the assignments written on a separate piece of paper, correct them, and then highlight common problems in class.

For more teaching suggestions and supplementary material, please refer to the accompanying *Teacher's Guide*.

Acknowledgment

Janet Johnston was the finest editor an author could ever hope to work with. Wielding pencils of many colors (with purple seeming to be her personal favorite), she cheerfully held her authors to account for every single word they wrote. She saw the Azar Series through thousands of pages of manuscript and proof for more than fifteen years. Each published page bears the seal of her high standards and keen eye. Her delight in the process of shaping text was contagious and her technical expertise extraordinary, making all of us who worked with her enthusiastically reach for our highest level of professionalism. They simply don't make editors like Janet anymore. Working with her has been a privilege and a joy. As we grieve her untimely death from breast cancer, we will deeply miss her good, sweet friendship as well as her editorial wizardry. Simply stated, Janet Johnston was, and will always remain, the best of the best.

Betty Azar
Stacy Hagen
Shelley Hartle
Sue Van Etten

☐ **EXERCISE 1. Let's talk: class activity.**

Directions: Ask your classmates their names. Write their first names in the spaces below. You can also ask them what city or country they are from.

FIRST NAME	CITY OR COUNTRY

Directions: Listen to the sentences. Write the words you hear.

Paulo _____*is a student*_____ from Brazil. Marie _____
　　　　　　　　　　¹　　　　　　　　　　　　　　　　　　　　　²

student from France. _____ the classroom. Today
　　　　　　　　　　　　　　　³

_____ exciting day. _____ the first day of school, but they
　　　⁴　　　　　　　　　　　　　⁵

_____ nervous. _____ to be here. Mrs. Brown
　　⁶　　　　　　　　　　　　⁷

_____ the teacher. She _____ in the classroom right now.
　　⁸　　　　　　　　　　　　　　⁹

_____ late today.
　　¹⁰

1-1　NOUN + *IS* + NOUN: SINGULAR

NOUN + IS + NOUN	
(a) ***Canada*** **is** a ***country.***	*Singular* means "one." In (a): *Canada* = a singular noun 　　　　　*is* = a singular verb 　　　*country* = a singular noun
(b) Mexico is ***a*** country.	***A*** frequently comes in front of singular nouns. In (b): ***a*** comes in front of the singular noun *country.* ***A*** is called an "article."
(c) ***A*** cat is ***an*** animal.	***A*** and ***an*** have the same meaning. They are both articles. ***A*** is used in front of words that begin with consonants: *b, c, d, f, g, etc.* 　Examples: *a bed, a cat, a dog, a friend, a girl* ***An*** is used in front of words that begin with *a, e, i,* and *o.*★ 　Examples: *an animal, an ear, an island, an office*

★***An*** is sometimes used in front of words that begin with *u.* See Chart 7-2, p. 183.
Vowels = a, e, i, o, u.
Consonants = b, c, d, f, g, h, j, k, l, m, n, p, q, r, s, t, v, w, x, y, z.

□ **EXERCISE 3. Sentence practice.**

Directions: Complete the sentences. Use an article (***a*** or ***an***).

1. ___*A*___ horse is ___*an*___ animal.

2. English is _____ language.

3. Tokyo is _____ city.

4. Australia is _____ country.

5. Red is _____ color.

6. _____ dictionary is _____ book.

7. _____ hotel is _____ building.

8. _____ bear is _____ animal.

9. _____ bee is _____ insect.

10. _____ ant is _____ insect.

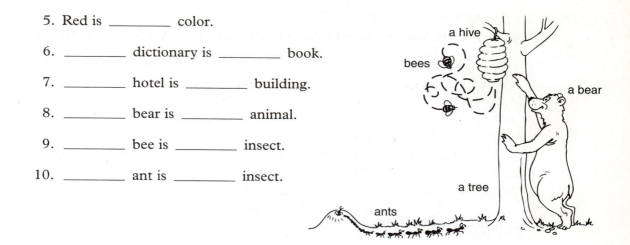

☐ **EXERCISE 4.** Sentence practice.

Directions: Complete the sentences. Use *a* or *an* and the words in the list.

animal	country	language
city	insect	sport

1. Arabic is ____*a language*____.

2. Rome is ____*a city*____.

3. A cat is ____*an animal*____.

4. Tennis is _____.

5. Chicago is _____.

6. Spanish is _____.

7. Mexico is _____.

8. A cow is _____.

9. A fly is _____.

10. Baseball is _____.

11. China is _____.

12. Russian is _____.

Directions: Work in small groups. Choose a leader. Only the leader's book is open.

Example: a language
> LEADER: Name a language.
> SPEAKER A: English is a language.
> SPEAKER B: French is a language.
> SPEAKER C: Arabic is a language.
> LEADER: Japanese is a language.
> SPEAKER A: Spanish is a language.
> SPEAKER B: Etc.

(Continue until no one can name another language.)

1. an animal
2. a sport
3. an insect
4. a color
5. a country
6. a city

1-2 NOUN + *ARE* + NOUN: PLURAL

NOUN + *ARE* + NOUN
(a) **Cats   are   animals.**
	Plural means "two, three, or more."
	    Cats = a plural noun
	    are = a plural verb
	    animals = a plural noun

(b) SINGULAR: a cat, an animal PLURAL: *cats, animals*	Plural nouns end in **-s**. *A* and **an** are used only with singular nouns.
(c) SINGULAR: a ci**t**y, a count**r**y PLURAL: ci**ties**, count**ries**	Some singular nouns that end in **-y** have a special plural form: They omit the **-y** and add **-ies**.★
NOUN *and* NOUN + *ARE* + NOUN (d) **Canada and China are countries.** (e) **Dogs and cats are animals.**	Two nouns connected by **and** are followed by **are**. In (d): *Canada* is a singular noun. *China* is a singular noun. They are connected by **and**. Together they are plural, i.e., "more than one."

★See Chart 3-6, p. 63, for more information about adding **-s/-es** to words that end in **-y**.

□ **EXERCISE 6.** Sentence practice.

Directions: Change the singular sentences to plural sentences.

SINGULAR		PLURAL
1. An ant is an insect.	→	*Ants are insects.*
2. A computer is a machine.	→	_____

SINGULAR		PLURAL
3. A dictionary is a book.	→	_____
4. A chicken is a bird.	→	_____
5. A rose is a flower.	→	_____
6. A carrot is a vegetable.	→	_____
7. A rabbit is an animal.	→	_____

roses   chickens   a rabbit   a carrot

8. Egypt is a country.
   Indonesia is a country. → _____

9. Winter is a season.
   Summer is a season. → _____

☐ **EXERCISE 7. Game.**

Directions: Work in small groups. Close your books for this activity. Your teacher will say the beginning of a sentence. As a group, write the complete sentence. In the end, the group who completes the most sentences correctly wins the game.

Example:
TEACHER *(book open):* Spanish . . . .
GROUP *(books closed):* Spanish is a language.

1. A bear . . . .
2. An ant . . . .
3. London . . . .
4. Spring . . . .
5. A carrot . . . .
6. September and October . . . .
7. Mexico and Canada . . . .
8. A dictionary . . . .
9. Chickens . . . .
10. China . . . .
11. Winter and summer . . . .
12. Arabic . . . .
13. A computer . . . .
14. A fly . . . .

☐ **EXERCISE 8. Listening.**

Directions: Listen to the sentences. Circle *yes* or *no*.

Example: Cows are animals. (yes)   no
Horses are insects.   yes   (no)

1. yes no	4. yes no	7. yes no
2. yes no	5. yes no	8. yes no
3. yes no	6. yes no	9. yes no

☐ **EXERCISE 9. Let's talk: pairwork.**

Directions: Your partner will ask you to name something. Answer in a complete sentence. You can look at your book before you speak. When you speak, look at your partner.

Example:

Partner A	Partner B
1. a country	1. two countries
2. an insect	2. a season

PARTNER A: Name a country.
PARTNER B: Brazil is a country.
PARTNER A: Yes, Brazil is a country. Your turn now.

PARTNER B: Name two countries.
PARTNER A: Italy and China are countries.
PARTNER B: Yes, Italy and China are countries. Your turn now.

PARTNER A: Name an insect.
PARTNER B: A bee is an insect.
PARTNER A: Yes, a bee is an insect. Your turn now.

PARTNER B: Name a season.
PARTNER A: Etc.

Remember: You can look at your book before you speak. When you speak, look at your partner.

Partner A	Partner B
1. a language	1. two cities
2. two languages	2. an island
3. a city	3. two countries in Asia
4. an animal	4. a vegetable
5. two seasons	5. a street in this city

1-3 PRONOUN + *BE* + NOUN

		SINGULAR					PLURAL			
PRONOUN	+	*BE*	+	NOUN		PRONOUN	+	*BE*	+	NOUN
(a) *I*		*am*		a student.		(f) *We*		*are*		students.
(b) *You*		*are*		a student.		(g) *You*		*are*		students.
(c) *She*		*is*		a student.		(h) *They*		*are*		students.
(d) *He*		*is*		a student.						
(e) *It*		*is*		a country.						

I
you
he
she } = pronouns
it
we
they

am
is } = forms of *be*
are

(i) Rita is in my class. *She* is a student.	Pronouns refer to nouns.
(j) Tom is in my class. *He* is a student.	In (i): *she* (feminine) = Rita.
(k) Rita and Tom are in my class. *They* are students.	In (j): *he* (masculine) = Tom.
	In (k): *they* = Rita and Tom.

☐ **EXERCISE 10. Sentence practice.**

Directions: Complete the sentences. Use a verb *(am, is,* or *are)*. Use a noun *(a student* or *students)*.

1. We ___are students___ .

2. I _____ .

3. Rita _____ .

4. Rita and Tom _____ .

5. You *(one person)* _____ .

6. You *(two persons)* _____ .

☐ **EXERCISE 11. Let's talk: class activity.**

Directions: Close your books. Complete the sentences with *a form of **be*** + ***a student/students***. Point to the student or students as you name them.

Example:
TEACHER: *(name of a student in the class)* Yoko . . . .
STUDENT: *(The student points to Yoko.)* Yoko is a student.

1. *(name of a student)*
2. *(name of a student)* and *(name of a student)*
3. I
4. *(name of a student)* and I
5. We
6. *(name of a student)*
7. *(name of a student)* and *(name of a student)*
8. They
9. You
10. *(name of a student)* and *(name of a student)* and *(name of a student)*

1-4 CONTRACTIONS WITH *BE*

	PRONOUN + BE → CONTRACTION		
AM	*I* + *am* → **I'm**	(a) **I'm** a student.	

IS	*she* + *is* → **she's**	(b) **She's** a student.	
	he + *is* → **he's**	(c) **He's** a student.	
	it + *is* → **it's**	(d) **It's** a city.	

ARE	*you* + *are* → **you're**	(e) **You're** a student.	
	we + *are* → **we're**	(f) **We're** students.	
	they + *are* → **they're**	(g) **They're** students.	

When people speak, they often push two words together. *A contraction =* two words that are pushed together.

Contractions of a *subject pronoun* + *be* are used in both speaking and writing.

PUNCTUATION: The mark in the middle of a contraction is called an "apostrophe" (').★

---

*★NOTE: Write an apostrophe above the line. Do not write an apostrophe on the line.

CORRECT: _____*I'm a student*_____ .

INCORRECT: _____*I,m a student*_____ .

☐ EXERCISE 12. Sentence practice.

Directions: Complete the sentences. Use contractions *(pronoun + **be**)*.

1. *Sara* is a student. _____*She's*_____ in my class.

2. *Jim* is a student. _____ in my class.

3. I have *one brother*. _____ twenty years old.

4. I have *two sisters*. _____ students.

5. I have *a dictionary*. _____ on my desk.

6. I like *my classmates*. _____ friendly.

7. I have *three books*. _____ on my desk.

8. *My brother* is twenty-six years old. _____ married.

9. *My sister* is twenty-one years old. _____ single.

10. *Yoko and Ali* are students. _____ in my class.

11. I like *my books*. _____ interesting.

12. I like *grammar*. _____ easy.

13. *Kate and I* live in an apartment. _____ roommates.

14. We live in *an apartment*. _____ on Pine Street.

15. *I* go to school. _____ a student.

16. I know *you*. _____ in my English class.

☐ **EXERCISE 13. Listening.**

Directions: Listen to the sentences. Write the contractions you hear. Use the words in the list.

Example:
You will hear: You are in class. You're a student.
You will write: _____*You're*_____ a student.

I'm	*She's*	*We're*
You're	*He's*	*They're*
	It's	

1. _____ very nice.

2. _____ in the classroom.

3. _____ late.

4. _____ a teacher.

5. _____ her friend.

6. _____ in the same class.

7. _____ young.

8. _____ very big.

9. _____ very friendly.

10. _____ fun.

☐ **EXERCISE 14. Listening.**

Directions: Complete the sentences with the words you hear. Some of them will be contractions.

SPEAKER A: Hello. My name _____ Mrs. Brown.
                      1

_____ the new teacher.
    2

SPEAKER B: Hi. My name _____ Paulo, and
                      3

this _____ Marie.
      4

_____ in your class.
    5

SPEAKER A: _____ nice to meet you.
                6

SPEAKER B: _____ happy to meet you too.
                7

SPEAKER A: _____ time for class. Please take a seat.
                8

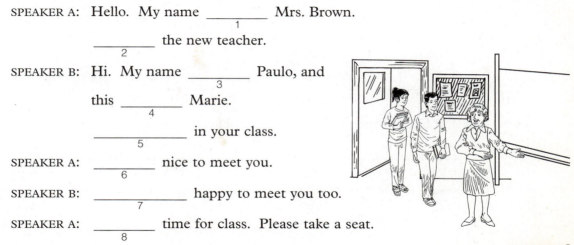

1-5 NEGATIVE WITH *BE*

	CONTRACTIONS	*Not* makes a sentence negative.
(a) I ***am not*** a teacher.	**I'*m not***	
(b) You ***are not*** a teacher.	you***'re not*** / you ***aren't***	CONTRACTIONS:
(c) She ***is not*** a teacher.	she***'s not*** / she ***isn't***	***Be*** and ***not*** can be contracted.
(d) He ***is not*** a teacher.	he***'s not*** / he ***isn't***	Note that "I am" has only one
(e) It ***is not*** a city.	it***'s not*** / it ***isn't***	contraction with ***be***, as in (a), but
(f) We ***are not*** teachers.	we***'re not*** / we ***aren't***	there are two contractions with ***be***
(g) You ***are not*** teachers.	you***'re not*** / you ***aren't***	for (b) through (g).
(h) They ***are not*** teachers.	they***'re not*** / they ***aren't***	

☐ **EXERCISE 15. Sentence practice.**

Directions: Write sentences using *is, isn't, are,* and *aren't* and the given information.

Examples: Africa \ city . . . It \ continent

→ _____ *Africa isn't a city. It's a continent.* _____

Baghdad and Chicago \ city . . . They \ continent

→ _____ *Baghdad and Chicago are cities. They aren't continents.* _____

1. Canada \ country . . . It \ city

_____

2. Jakarta \ country . . . It \ city

_____

3. Beijing and London \ city . . . They \ country

_____

4. Asia \ country . . . It \ continent

_____

5. Asia and South America \ continent . . . They \ country

_____

☐ **EXERCISE 16. Sentence practice.**

PART I.

Directions: Write the name of the person next to his or her job.

artist   ___*Jim*___   gardener   _____

bus driver   _____   doctor   _____

police officer   _____   photographer   _____

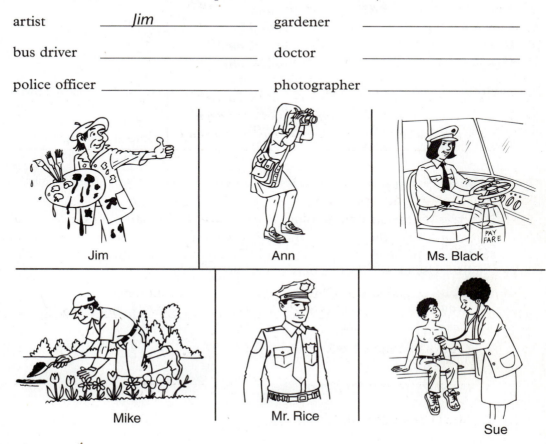

Jim   Ann   Ms. Black

Mike   Mr. Rice   Sue

PART II.

Directions: Complete the sentences with the correct information.

1. Ann ___*isn't*___ a gardener. She ___*'s a photographer*___ .

2. Mike ___*is*___ a gardener. He _____ an artist.

3. Jim _____ a bus driver. He _____ .

4. Sue _____ a photographer. She _____ .

5. Mr. Rice _____ a police officer. He _____ .

6. Ms. Black isn't a _____ . She _____ .

7. I'm not a _____ . I'm a _____ .

1-6 *BE* + ADJECTIVE

	NOUN	+	*BE*	+	ADJECTIVE
(a)	A ball		is		***round.***
(b)	Balls		are		***round.***
(c)	Mary		is		***intelligent.***
(d)	Mary and Tom		are		***intelligent.***

	PRONOUN	+	*BE*	+	ADJECTIVE
(e)	I		am		***hungry.***
(f)	She		is		***young.***
(g)	They		are		***happy.***

round
intelligent
hungry } = adjectives
young
happy

Adjectives often follow a form of ***be*** *(am, is, are).* Adjectives describe or give information about a noun or pronoun that comes at the beginning of a sentence.★

★The noun or pronoun that comes at the beginning of a sentence is called a "subject." See Chart 6-1, p. 158.

☐ EXERCISE 17. Sentence practice.

Directions: Find the adjective in the first sentence. Then complete the second sentence with ***be*** + *an adjective* that has an opposite meaning. Use the adjectives in the list. Use each adjective only once.

beautiful	expensive	noisy	short
clean	fast	old	tall
easy	✓happy	poor	

1. I'm not sad. I ___'m happy___ .

2. Mr. Thomas isn't rich.   He _____ .

3. My hair isn't long. It _____ .

4. My clothes aren't dirty. They _____ .

5. Flowers aren't ugly. They _____ .

6. Cars aren't cheap. They _____ .

7. Airplanes aren't slow. They _____ .

8. Grammar isn't difficult. It _____ .

9. My sister isn't short. She _____ .

10. My grandparents aren't young. They _____ .

11. The classroom isn't quiet. It _____ .

□ EXERCISE 18. Sentence practice.

Directions: Write sentences using *is* or *are* and an adjective from the list. Use each adjective only once.

cold	funny	round	sweet
dangerous	✓hot	small/little	wet
dry	important	sour	
flat	large/big	square	

1. Fire _____*is hot*_____ .

2. Ice and snow _____ .

3. A box _____ .

4. Balls and oranges _____ .

5. Sugar _____ .

6. An elephant _____ , but a

   mouse _____ .

7. A rain forest _____ , but a

   desert _____ .

8. A joke _____ .

9. Good health _____ .

10. Guns aren't safe. They _____ .

11. A coin _____ small, round, and _____ .

12. A lemon _____ .

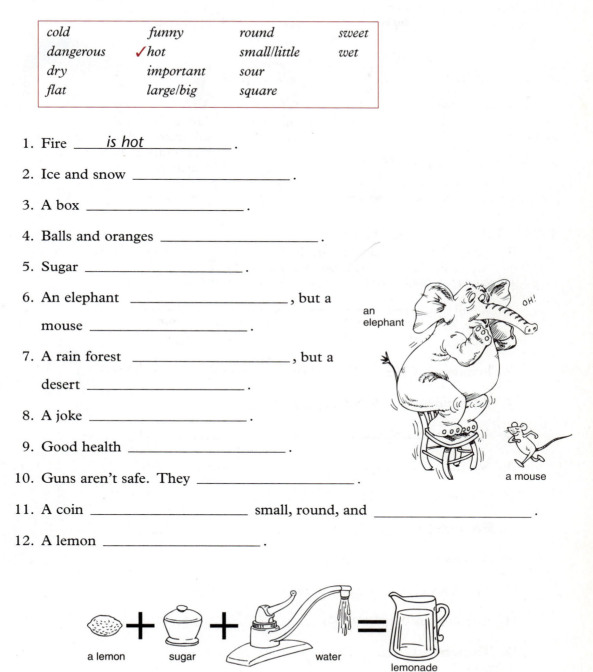

an elephant

a mouse

a lemon   sugar   water   lemonade

Directions: Complete the drawings by making the faces **happy**, **angry**, **sad**, or **nervous**. Then show your drawings to your partner. Your partner will identify the emotions in your drawings.

□ EXERCISE 20. Sentence practice.

Directions: Complete the sentences. Use *is, isn't, are,* or *aren't*.

1. A ball _____*isn't*_____ square.

2. Balls _____*are*_____ round.

3. Lemons _____*are*_____ yellow.

4. Ripe bananas _____*are*_____ yellow too.

bananas

5. A lemon _____*is*_____ sweet. It _____*is*_____ sour.

6. My pen _____*is*_____ heavy. It _____*is*_____ light.

7. This room _____ dark. It _____ light.

a turtle

8. My classmates _____ friendly.

9. A turtle _____ slow.

10. Airplanes _____ slow. They _____ fast.

11. The floor in the classroom _____ clean. It _____ dirty.

12. The weather _____ cold today.

13. The sun _____ bright today.

14. My shoes _____ comfortable.

□ **EXERCISE 21. Let's talk: pairwork.**

Directions: Work with a partner. Take turns making two sentences for each picture. Use the given adjectives. You can look at your book before you speak. When you speak, look at your partner.

Example: The girl . . . happy/sad
PARTNER A: The girl isn't happy. She's sad.
            Your turn now.

Example: The flower . . . beautiful/ugly
PARTNER B: The flower is beautiful. It isn't ugly.
            Your turn now.

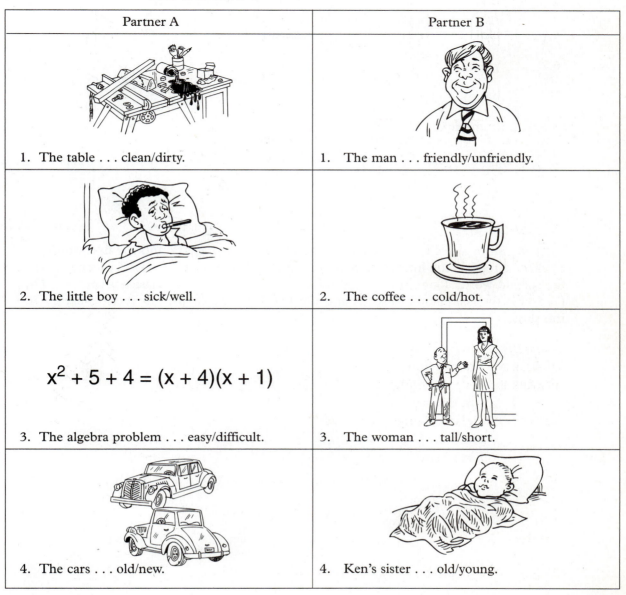

Partner A	Partner B
1. The table . . . clean/dirty.	1. The man . . . friendly/unfriendly.
2. The little boy . . . sick/well.	2. The coffee . . . cold/hot.
3. The algebra problem . . . easy/difficult. $x^2 + 5 + 4 = (x + 4)(x + 1)$	3. The woman . . . tall/short.
4. The cars . . . old/new.	4. Ken's sister . . . old/young.

☐ **EXERCISE 22. Let's talk: game.**

Directions: Practice using adjectives.

PART I. Look at the words. Check (✓) all the words you know. Your teacher will explain the words you don't know.

1. ____ hungry		11. ____ angry
2. ____ thirsty		12. ____ nervous
3. ____ sleepy		13. ____ quiet
4. ____ tired		14. ____ lazy
5. ____ old		15. ____ hardworking
6. ____ young		16. ____ famous
7. ____ happy		17. ____ sick
8. ____ homesick		18. ____ healthy
9. ____ married		19. ____ friendly
10. ____ single		20. ____ shy

PART II. Sit in a circle. Speaker 1 makes a sentence using **"I"** and the first word. Speaker 2 repeats the information about Speaker 1 and makes a new sentence using the second word. Continue around the circle until everyone in class has spoken. The teacher is the last person to speak and must repeat the information about everyone in the class.

Example:
SPEAKER A: I'm not hungry.
SPEAKER B: He's not hungry.
            I'm thirsty.
SPEAKER C: He's not hungry.
            She's thirsty.
            I'm sleepy.

☐ EXERCISE 23. Let's talk: pairwork.

Directions: Check (✓) each adjective that describes this city/town (the city or town where you are studying now). When you finish, compare your work with a partner. Do you and your partner have checks beside the same adjectives? Report to the class on things you disagree about.

1. ____ big		11. ____ noisy
2. ____ small		12. ____ quiet
3. ____ clean		13. ____ crowded
4. ____ dirty		14. ____ not crowded
5. ____ friendly		15. ____ hot
6. ____ unfriendly		16. ____ cold
7. ____ safe		17. ____ warm
8. ____ dangerous		18. ____ cool
9. ____ beautiful		19. ____ expensive
10. ____ ugly		20. ____ inexpensive/cheap

☐ EXERCISE 24. Let's talk: game.

Directions: Sit in small groups. Close your books for this activity. Your teacher will ask you to name things. As a group, make a list. The teacher will give you only a short time to make the list. Share the list with the rest of your class. The group that makes the longest list gets a point. The group with the most points at the end of the game is the winner.

Example: round
TEACHER: Name something that is round.
GROUP A's LIST: a ball, an orange, the world
GROUP B's LIST: a baseball, a basketball, a soccer ball
GROUP C's LIST: a ball, a head, an orange, the world, the sun, a planet
Result: Group 3 wins a point.

1. hot	6. flat	11. beautiful
2. square	7. little	12. expensive
3. sweet	8. important	13. cheap
4. sour	9. cold	14. free
5. large	10. funny	15. delicious

1-7 *BE* + A PLACE

(a) Maria is **here**. (b) Bob is **at the library**.	In (a): *here* = a place. In (b): *at the library* = a place. **Be** is often followed by *a place*.
(c) Maria is { **here**. **there**. **downstairs**. **upstairs**. **inside**. **outside**. **downtown**.	A place may be one word, as in the examples in (c).
PREPOSITION + NOUN (d) Bob is { **at** **the library**. **on** **the bus**. **in** **his room**. **at** **work**. **next to** **Maria**.	A place may be a prepositional phrase *(preposition + noun)*, as in (d).

SOME COMMON PREPOSITIONS

above	*between*	*next to*
at	*from*	*on*
behind	*in*	*under*

□ **EXERCISE 25. Sentence practice.**

Directions: Complete the sentences with prepositions that describe the pictures. Use each preposition only once.

above	*between*	*next to*	*under*
behind	✓*in*	*on*	

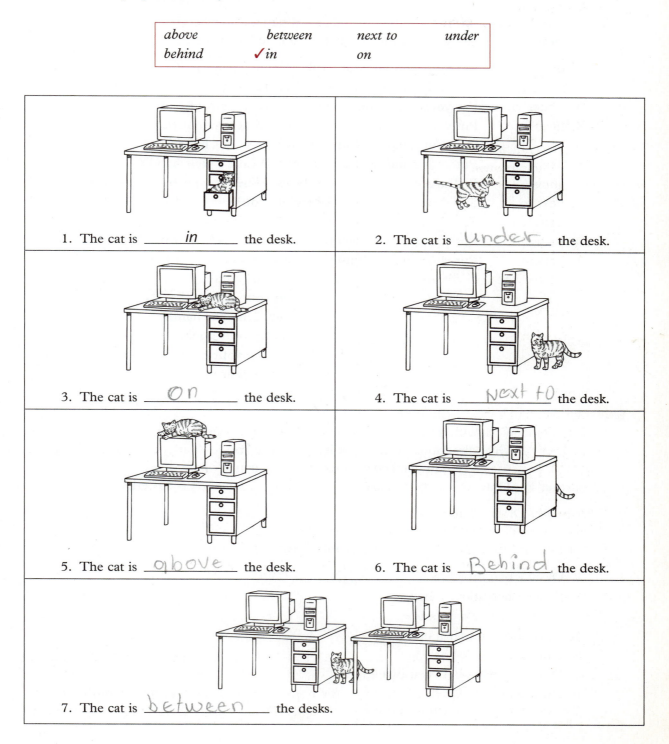

1. The cat is _____*in*_____ the desk.

2. The cat is _____Under_____ the desk.

3. The cat is _____On_____ the desk.

4. The cat is _____Next to_____ the desk.

5. The cat is _____above_____ the desk.

6. The cat is _____Behind_____ the desk.

7. The cat is _____between_____ the desks.

□ EXERCISE 26. Let's talk: class activity.

Directions: Close your books. Practice using prepositions of place.

Example: under
TEACHER: Put your hand under your chair. Where is your hand?
STUDENT: My hand is under my chair. OR: It's under my chair.

1. on	Put your pen on your book. Where is your pen?
2. in	Put your pen in your book. Where's your pen?
3. under	Put your pen under your book. Where's your pen?
4. next to	Put your pen next to your book. Where's your pen?
5. on	Put your hand on your ear. Where's your hand?
6. next to	Put your hand next to your ear. Where's your hand?
7. above	Put your hand above your head. Where's your hand?
8. next to	Stand next to (. . .). Where are you?
9. between	Stand between (. . .) and (. . .). Where are you?
10. between	Put your pen between two books. Where's your pen?
11. behind	Put your hand behind your head. Where's your hand?

12. Follow these directions: Put your pen . . . in your hand.

. . . on your arm.
. . . between your hands.
. . . under your book.
. . . next to your book.
. . . above your book.

□ EXERCISE 27. Let's talk: pairwork.

Directions: Work with a partner. Give and follow directions.
Partner A: Give directions. Your book is open. You can look at your book before you speak. When you speak, look at your partner.
Partner B: Draw the pictures Partner A describes. Your book is closed.

Example: Draw a ball on a box.
PARTNER A *(book open):* Draw a ball on a box.
PARTNER B *(book closed):* *(Draw the picture Partner A described.)*

1. Draw a ball on a box.
2. Draw a ball above a box.
3. Draw a ball next to a box.
4. Draw a ball under a box.
5. Draw a ball in a box.
6. Draw a banana between two apples.
7. Draw a house. Draw a bird above the house. Draw a car next to the house. Draw a cat between the car and the house.

8. Draw a flower. Draw a tree next to the flower. Draw a bird above the tree. Draw a turtle under the flower.

Switch roles.
Partner A: Close your book.
Partner B: Open your book. Your turn to talk now.

9. Draw a circle next to a triangle.
10. Draw a circle in a triangle.
11. Draw a circle above a triangle.
12. Draw a triangle between two circles.
13. Draw a circle under a triangle.
14. Draw an apple on a banana. Draw an apple above a banana.
15. Draw a tree. Draw bananas in the trees. Draw a person next to the tree. Draw a dog between the person and the tree.
16. Draw a cloud. Draw a bird under the cloud. Draw a bird above the cloud. Draw a bird in the cloud.

1-8 SUMMARY: BASIC SENTENCE PATTERNS WITH *BE*

	SUBJECT +	*BE* +	NOUN	The noun or pronoun that comes at the beginning of a sentence is called the "subject."
(a)	I	am	*a student.*	
	SUBJECT +	*BE* +	ADJECTIVE	*Be* is a "verb." Almost all English sentences have a subject and a verb.
(b)	He	is	*intelligent.*	
	SUBJECT +	*BE* +	A PLACE	Notice in the examples: There are three basic completions for sentences that begin with a *subject + the verb **be**:*
(c)	We	are	*in class.*	• *a noun,* as in (a)
(d)	She	is	*upstairs.*	• *an adjective,* as in (b)
				• *an expression of place,*★ as in (c) and (d)

★An expression of place can be a *preposition + noun,* or it can be one word.

☐ EXERCISE 28. Sentence practice.

   Directions: Write the form of *be (am, is,* or *are)* that is used in each sentence. Then write the grammar structure that follows *be*.

		BE	+	COMPLETION
1.	We're students.	*are*	+	*a noun*
2.	Anna is in Rome.	*is*	+	*a place*
3.	I'm hungry.	*am*	+	*an adjective*

	BE	+	COMPLETION

4. Dogs are animals.   _____ + _____

5. Jack is at home.   _____ + _____

6. He's sick.   _____ + _____

7. They're artists.   _____ + _____

8. I'm in class.   _____ + _____

9. Gina is upstairs.   _____ + _____

10. Joe's pockets are empty.   _____ + _____

☐ EXERCISE 29. Listening.

Directions: **Is** and **are** are often contracted with nouns in spoken English. Listen to the sentences. Practice saying them yourself.

1. Grammar is easy.
   → "Grammar's easy."
2. My name is John.
3. My books are on the table.
4. My brother is 21 years old.
5. The weather is cold today.
6. The windows are open.
7. My money is in my wallet.
8. Mr. Smith is a teacher.
9. Mrs. Lee is at home now.
10. The sun is bright today.
11. Tom is at home right now.
12. My roommates are from Chicago.
13. My sister is a student in high school.

☐ EXERCISE 30. Listening.

Directions: Listen to the sentences. Circle the completions you hear.

Example: My friend _____ from Korea.
     A. is   (B.)'s   C. Ø⋆

1. The test _____ easy.
        A. is   B. 's   C. Ø

2. My notebook _____ on the table.
        A. is   B. 's   C. Ø

3. My notebooks _____ on the table.
        A. are   B. 're   C. Ø

_____
⋆ Ø = nothing

4. Sue _____ a student.
    A. is   B. 's   C. Ø

5. The weather _____ warm today.
    A. is   B. 's   C. Ø

6. The windows _____ open.
    A. are   B. 're   C. Ø

7. My parents _____ from Cuba.
    A. are   B. 're   C. Ø

8. My cousins _____ from Cuba, too.
    A. are   B. 're   C. Ø

9. My _____ on my desk.
    A. book's   B. books're   C. Ø

10. The _____ in class.
    A. teacher's   B. teachers're   C. Ø

☐ **EXERCISE 31. Sentence review.**

Directions: Complete the sentences. Use *is* or *are*. Then exchange papers and correct each other's sentences.

1. _____ an animal.

2. _____ here.

3. _____ languages.

4. _____ not cheap.

5. _____ friendly.

6. _____ not expensive.

7. _____ an insect.

8. _____ countries.

9. _____ not from Canada.

10. _____ noisy.

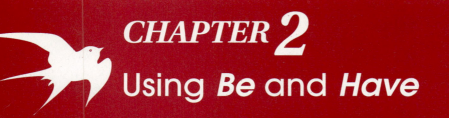

CHAPTER 2
Using *Be* and *Have*

☐ **EXERCISE 1. Preview: listening.**

Directions: Listen to the questions. Circle *yes* or *no*.

Example: Is Africa a continent? (yes)   no

1. yes	no	4. yes	no	7. yes	no
2. yes	no	5. yes	no	8. yes	no
3. yes	no	6. yes	no	9. yes	no

2-1 YES/NO QUESTIONS WITH *BE*

QUESTION	STATEMENT	In a question, ***be*** comes in front of the subject.
BE + SUBJECT (a) ***Is Anna*** a student? (b) ***Are they*** at home?	SUBJECT + *BE* ***Anna is*** a student. ***They are*** at home.	PUNCTUATION: A question ends with a question mark (?). A statement ends with a period (.).

☐ **EXERCISE 2. Question practice.**

Directions: Make questions for the given answers.

1. A: _____*Is Mrs. Lee a teacher?*_____

   B: Yes, Mrs. Lee is a teacher.

2. A: _____

   B: Yes, the sun is a ball of fire.

3. A: _____

   B: Yes, carrots are vegetables.

4. A: _____

   B: Yes, chickens are birds.

5. A: _____

   B: Yes, Mr. Wu is here today.

6. A: _____

   B: Yes, Sue and Mike are here today.

7. A: _____

   B: Yes, English grammar is fun.

8. A: _____

   B: Yes, I am ready for the next grammar chart.

2-2 SHORT ANSWERS TO YES/NO QUESTIONS

QUESTION		SHORT ANSWER	
(a) *Is Anna* a student?	→	Yes, *she is*.	Spoken contractions are not used in short answers that begin with *yes*.
	→	No, *she's not*.	In (a): *INCORRECT: Yes, she's.*
	→	No, *she isn't*.	
(b) *Are they* at home?	→	Yes, *they are*.	
	→	No, *they aren't*.	In (b): *INCORRECT: Yes, they're.*
(c) *Are you* ready?	→	Yes, *I am*.	
	→	No, *I'm not*.★	In (c): *INCORRECT: Yes, I'm.*

★*Am* and *not* are not contracted.

☐ EXERCISE 3. Question practice.

   Directions: Make questions and give short answers.

   1. A: _____*Are you tired?*_____

      B: _____*No, I'm not.*_____ (I'm not tired.)

   2. A: _____*Is Anna in your class?*_____

      B: _____*Yes, she is.*_____ (Anna is in my class.)

   3. A: _____

      B: _____ (I'm not homesick.)

   4. A: _____

      B: _____ (Bob is homesick.)

5. A: _____

   B: _____ (Sue isn't here today.)

6. A: _____

   B: _____ (The students in this class are intelligent.)

7. A: _____

   B: _____ (The chairs in this room aren't comfortable.)

8. A: _____

   B: _____ (I'm not married.)

9. A: _____

   B: _____ (Tom and I are roommates.)

10. A: _____

   B: _____ (A butterfly is not a bird.)

☐ **EXERCISE 4. Let's talk: find someone who . . . .**

Directions: Walk around the room. Ask your classmates questions. Find someone who can answer *yes* to each question. Write down his/her name. Use ***Are you . . . ?***

Example:
SPEAKER A: Are you hungry?
SPEAKER B: No, I'm not.
SPEAKER A: *(Ask another student.)* Are you hungry?
SPEAKER C: Yes, I am. *(Write down his/her name.)*
            (Now ask another student a different question.)

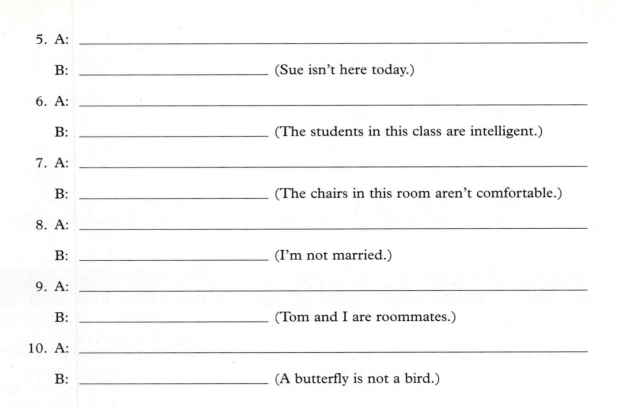

	First name
1. hungry	
2. sleepy	
3. thirsty	
4. married	
5. a parent	
6. single	
7. happy	

	First name
8. tired	
9. nervous	
10. friendly	
11. lazy	
12. cold	
13. comfortable	
14. from *(name of country)*	

□ **EXERCISE 5. Let's talk: pairwork.**

Directions: Work with a partner. Ask and answer questions. You can look at your book before you speak. When you speak, look at your partner.

Example: turtles: fast/slow
PARTNER A: Are turtles fast?
PARTNER B: No, they aren't.
PARTNER A: Your turn now.
            OR
PARTNER A: Are turtles slow?
PARTNER B: Yes, they are.
PARTNER A: Your turn now.

Partner A	Partner B
1. a mouse: big/little	1. diamonds: expensive/cheap
2. lemons: sweet/sour	2. your grammar book: light/heavy
3. the world: flat/round	3. butterflies: beautiful/ugly
4. the weather: cool today/warm today	4. English grammar: easy/difficult
5. your dictionary: with you/at home	5. dolphins: intelligent/dumb
6. your shoes: comfortable/uncomfortable	6. the floor in this room: clean/dirty

□ **EXERCISE 6. Question practice.**

Directions: Complete the conversations with your own words.

1. A: _____*Are*_____ you a student at this school?

   B: Yes, _____.

   A: _____ you from _____?

   B: No, _____ from _____.

2. A: Are you a/an _____?

   B: No, _____ not. I'm a/an _____.

3. A: Are _____ expensive?

   B: Yes, _____.

   A: Is _____ expensive?

   B: No, _____.

4. A: _____ countries in Asia?

   B: Yes, _____ are.

   A: _____ a country in South America?

   B: Yes, _____ is.

   A: _____ a country in Africa?

   B: No, _____ not. It's a country in _____.

2-3 QUESTIONS WITH *BE:* USING *WHERE*

Where asks about place. *Where* comes at the beginning of the question, in front of *be*.

QUESTION	SHORT ANSWER + (LONG ANSWER)
BE + SUBJECT	
(a) *Is* *the book* on the table? →	Yes, *it is*. *(The book is on the table.)*
(b) *Are* *the books* on the table? →	Yes, *they are*. *(The books are on the table.)*
WHERE + *BE* + SUBJECT	
(c) *Where* *is* *the book*? →	*On the table*. *(The book is on the table.)*
(d) *Where* *are* *the books*? →	*On the table*. *(The books are on the table.)*

☐ EXERCISE 7. Question practice.
   Directions: Make questions.

   1. A: _____*Is Kate at home?*_____

      B: Yes, she is. (Kate is at home.)

   2. A: _____*Where is Kate?*_____

      B: At home. (Kate is at home.)

   3. A: _____

      B: Yes, it is. (Cairo is in Egypt.)

   4. A: _____

      B: In Egypt. (Cairo is in Egypt.)

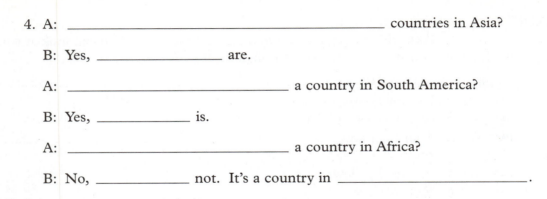

Cairo ★

Nile River

Egypt

5. A: _____

   B: Yes, they are. (The students are in class today.)

6. A: _____

   B: In class. (The students are in class today.)

7. A: _____

   B: On Main Street. (The post office is on Main Street.)

8. A: _____

   B: Yes, it is. (The train station is on Grand Avenue.)

9. A: _____

   B: Over there. (The bus stop is over there.)

10. A: _____

    B: At the zoo. (Sue and Ken are at the zoo today.)

☐ EXERCISE 8. Let's talk: pairwork.

   Directions: Work with a partner. Ask questions. Use **where**. You can look at your book before you speak. When you speak, look at your partner.

   Example:
   PARTNER A: Where is your pen?
   PARTNER B: It's in my hand. *(or any other true answer)*
   PARTNER A: Your turn now.

Partner A	Partner B
1. your dictionary	1. your notebooks
2. your money	2. your wallet
3. your books	3. your glasses or sunglasses
4. your coat	4. your family
5. your pencil	5. your apartment
6. *(name of a classmate)*	6. *(names of two classmates)*
7. your hometown	7. your hometown
8. *(name of a city in the world)*	8. *(name of a country in the world)*

2-4 USING *HAVE* AND *HAS*

SINGULAR	PLURAL	
(a) *I* **have** a pen.	(f) *We* **have** pens.	$\left.\begin{array}{l} I \\ you \\ we \\ they \end{array}\right\}$ + **have**
(b) *You* **have** a pen.	(g) *You* **have** pens.	
(c) *She* **has** a pen.	(h) *They* **have** pens.	$\left.\begin{array}{l} she \\ he \\ it \end{array}\right\}$ + **has**
(d) *He* **has** a pen.		
(e) *It* **has** blue ink.		

☐ EXERCISE 9. Sentence practice.

Directions: Complete the sentences. Use **have** and **has**.

1. We _____*have*_____ grammar books.

2. I _____ a dictionary.

3. Kate _____ a blue pen. She _____ a blue notebook too.

4. You _____ a pen in your pocket.

5. Bob _____ a notebook on his desk.

6. Anna and Bob _____ notebooks. They _____ pens too.

7. Samir is a student in our class. He _____ a red grammar book.

8. I _____ a grammar book. It _____ a red cover.

9. You and I are students. We _____ books on our desks.

10. Mike _____ a wallet in his pocket. Sara _____ a wallet in her purse.

11. Nadia isn't in class today because she _____ the flu.

12. Mr. and Mrs. Johnson _____ two daughters.

13. Ducks _____ feathers.

14. A duck _____ a beak.

Directions: Complete the sentences with **have** or **has** and words from the list.

backaches	*a headache*	*a stomachache*
a cold	*a sore throat*	*toothaches*
a fever		

1. Mr. Wu _____.

2. The patients _____.

3. I _____.   101°

4. Mrs. Ramirez _____.

5. You _____.   Achoo!

6. The workers _____.

7. Olga _____.

Directions: Complete this conversation with a partner. You can look at your book before you speak. When you speak, look at your partner.

Partner A: How _____?

Partner B: Not so good. _____.

Partner A: That's too bad. Your turn now.

Example:

1. Jim? . . . a toothache

2. Susan? . . . a stomachache

PARTNER A: How's Jim?

PARTNER B: Not so good. He has a toothache.

PARTNER A: That's too bad. Your turn now.

PARTNER B: How's Susan?

PARTNER A: Not so good. She has a stomachache.

PARTNER B: That's too bad. Your turn now.

1. you? . . . a headache   5. your parents? . . . colds

2. you? . . . a sore tooth   6. the patients? . . . stomachaches

3. your mother? . . . a sore back   7. your little brother? . . . a sore throat

4. Mr. Lee? . . . a backache   8. Mrs. Wood? . . . a fever

☐ EXERCISE 12. Listening.

Directions: Listen to the sentences. Circle the verbs you hear.

Example: Anna _____ boots. (has) have

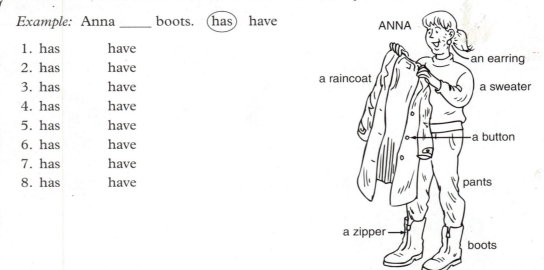

ANNA

an earring

a raincoat

a sweater

a button

pants

a zipper

boots

1. has   have
2. has   have
3. has   have
4. has   have
5. has   have
6. has   have
7. has   have
8. has   have

☐ EXERCISE 13. Let's talk: find someone who . . . .

Directions: Walk around the room. Ask your classmates questions. Try to find people who can answer *yes* to the questions. Write down their names. Use **Do you have . . . ?**

Example: . . . car?

SPEAKER A: Do you have a car?

SPEAKER B: Yes, I have a car. OR No, I don't have a car.

(You can also give additional information: I have a sports car.)

	First name		First name
1. brothers and sisters?		5. a job?	
2. children?		6. a favorite sport?	
3. pets?		7. a favorite movie star?	
4. hobbies?		8. a favorite movie?	

2-5 USING *MY, YOUR, HIS, HER, OUR, THEIR*

SINGULAR	PLURAL	SUBJECT FORM	POSSESSIVE FORM

(a) **I** have a book.
My book is red.

(b) **You** have a book.
Your book is red.

(c) **She** has a book.
Her book is red.

(d) **He** has a book.
His book is red.

(e) **We** have books.
Our books are red.

(f) **You** have books.
Your books are red.

(g) **They** have books.
Their books are red.

SUBJECT FORM		POSSESSIVE FORM
I	→	*my*
you	→	*your*
she	→	*her*
he	→	*his*
we	→	*our*
they	→	*their*

I *possess* a book. = I *have* a book. = It is *my* book.

My, our, her, his, our, and *their* are called "possessive adjectives." They come in front of nouns.

☐ **EXERCISE 14. Sentence practice.**

Directions: Complete the sentences with the correct possessive adjectives.

1. You're next. It's _____ turn.

2. Sue's next. It's _____ turn.

3. John and Jane are next. It's _____ turn.

4. My aunt is next. It's _____ turn.

5. I'm next. It's _____ turn.

6. The children are next. It's _____ turn.

7. You and Sam are next. It's _____ turn.

8. Marcos and I are next. It's _____ turn.

9. Bill's next. It's _____ turn.

10. Mrs. Brown is next. It's _____ turn.

☐ **EXERCISE 15. Sentence practice.**

Directions: Complete the sentences with the information on the ID cards.

What information do you know about this person from his ID card?

John B. Palmer

1. _____ last name is _____.

2. _____ first name is _____.

3. _____ middle initial is _____.

What information do the ID cards give you about Don and Kathy Johnson?

4. _____ zip code is

_____ .

5. _____ area code is

_____ .

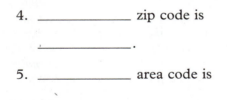

April

Sun.	Mon.	Tues.	Wed.	Thurs.	Fri.	Sat.
				1	2	3
4	5	6	7	8	9	10
11	12	13	14	15	16	17
18	19	20	21	22	23	24
25	26	27	28	29	30	

What do you know about Dr. Nelson?

6. _____ birthdate is _____ .

7. _____ birthday is _____ .

8. _____ middle name is _____ .

Write about yourself.

9. _____ first name is _____ .

10. _____ last name is _____ .

11. _____ middle name is _____ .

12. _____ middle initial is _____ .

13. _____ area code is _____ .

14. _____ phone number is _____ .

15. _____ zip code is _____ .

Directions: Work with a partner. Look at the vocabulary. Put a check (✓) beside the words you know. Ask your partner about the ones you don't know. Your teacher can help you. The pictures below and on the next page illustrate clothing and jewelry.

VOCABULARY CHECKLIST		
Colors	**Clothes**	**Jewelry**
__ black	__ belt	__ bracelet
__ blue, dark blue, light blue	__ blouse	__ earrings
__ blue green	__ boots	__ necklace
__ brown, dark brown, light brown	__ coat	__ ring
__ gold	__ dress	__ watch/wristwatch
__ gray, dark gray, light gray	__ gloves	
__ green, dark green, light green	__ hat	
__ orange	__ jacket	
__ pink	__ jeans	
__ purple	__ pants	
__ red	__ sandals	
__ silver	__ shirt	
__ tan, beige	__ shoes	
__ white	__ skirt	
__ yellow	__ socks	
	__ suit	
	__ sweater	
	__ tie, necktie	
	__ T-shirt	

a hard hat

a T-shirt

an ax(e)

a jacket

gloves

a belt

jeans

boots

an earring

a blouse

a sweater

a ring

a skirt

sandals

a hat

a shirt

a tie

a watch

a coat
pants } a suit

a briefcase

shoes

a necklace

a purse

a dress

heels

☐ EXERCISE 17. Sentence practice.

Directions: Complete the sentences with ***my, your, her, his, our,*** or ***their***.

1. Rita is wearing a blouse. _____*Her*_____ blouse is light blue.

2. Tom is wearing a shirt. _____ shirt is yellow and brown.

3. I am wearing jeans. _____ jeans are blue.

4. Bob and Tom are wearing boots. _____ boots are brown.

5. Sue and you are wearing dresses. _____ dresses are red.

6. Ann and I are wearing sweaters. _____ sweaters are green.

7. You are wearing shoes. _____ shoes are dark brown.

8. Sue is wearing a skirt. _____ skirt is black.

9. John is wearing a belt. _____ belt is white.

10. Sue and Ann are wearing socks. _____ socks are dark gray.

11. Tom is wearing pants. _____ pants are dark blue.

12. I am wearing earrings. _____ earrings are gold.

☐ EXERCISE 18. Let's talk: class activity.

Directions: Your teacher will ask you questions about people and their clothing. Then describe an article of clothing/jewelry and its color. Use this pattern: *possessive adjective* + *noun* + ***is/are*** + *color*. Close your book for this activity.

Examples:
TEACHER: Look at Ali. Tell me about his shirt. What color is his shirt?
STUDENT: His shirt is blue.

TEACHER: Look at Rosa. What is this?
STUDENT: A sweater.
TEACHER: Tell me about her sweater. What color is it?
STUDENT: Her sweater is red.

TEACHER: Look at me. What am I touching?
STUDENT: Your shoes.
TEACHER: Tell me about the color.
STUDENT: Your shoes are brown.

☐ EXERCISE 19. Sentence practice.

Directions: Complete the sentences. Use ***have*** or ***has***. Use ***my, your, her, his, our,*** or ***their***.

1. I ____*have*____ a book. ____*My*____ book is interesting.

2. Bob _____ a backpack. _____ backpack is green.

3. You _____ a raincoat. _____ raincoat is brown.

4. Kate _____ a raincoat. _____ raincoat is red.

5. Ann and Jim are married. They _____ a baby. _____ baby is six months old.

6. Ken and Sue _____ a daughter. _____ daughter is ten years old.

7. John and I _____ a son. _____ son is seven years old.

8. I _____ a brother. _____ brother is sixteen.

9. We _____ grammar books. _____ grammar books are red.

10. Tom and you _____ backpacks. _____ backpacks are brown.

11. Ann _____ a dictionary. _____ dictionary is red.

12. Mike _____ a car. _____ car is blue.

2-6 USING *THIS* AND *THAT*

(a) I have a book in my hand. **This book** is red. (b) I see a book on your desk. **That book** is blue. (c) **This** is my book. (d) **That** is your book.	*this* book = the book is near me. *that* book = the book is not near me.
(e) **That's** her book.	CONTRACTION: *that is = that's*
(f) **This is** *("This's")* her book.	In spoken English, *this is* is usually pronounced as *"this's."* It is not used in writing.

☐ **EXERCISE 20. Sentence completion.**
   Directions: Complete the sentences with **this** or **that**.

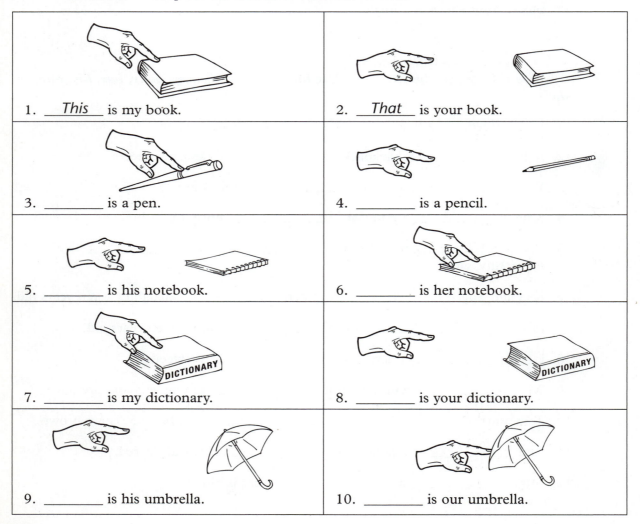

1. ___This___ is my book.

2. ___That___ is your book.

3. _____ is a pen.

4. _____ is a pencil.

5. _____ is his notebook.

6. _____ is her notebook.

7. _____ is my dictionary.

8. _____ is your dictionary.

9. _____ is his umbrella.

10. _____ is our umbrella.

☐ EXERCISE 21. Let's talk: pairwork.

Directions: Work with a partner. Use **this** and **that**. Touch and point to things in the classroom.

Example: red \ yellow
PARTNER A *(book open):* red \ yellow
PARTNER B *(book closed):* This (book) is red. That (shirt) is yellow.
(Partner B touches a red book and points to a yellow shirt.)

1. red \ blue
2. red \ green
3. red \ yellow
4. blue \ black
5. white \ black
6. orange \ green

Switch roles.
PARTNER A: Close your book.
PARTNER B: Open your book. Your turn to talk now.

7. red \ pink
8. dark blue \ light blue
9. black \ gray
10. gold \ silver
11. dark brown \ tan
12. purple \ red

☐ EXERCISE 22. Listening.

Directions: Listen to the sentences. Circle the words you hear.

Example: _____ is my pen. (This) That

1. This   That
2. This   That
3. This   That
4. This   That
5. this   that
6. This   That
7. this   that
8. this   that
9. This   That
10. This   That

2-7 USING *THESE* AND *THOSE*

		SINGULAR		PLURAL
(a) My books are on my desk. ***These*** are my books.		*this*	→	*these*
(b) Your books are on your desk. ***Those*** are your books.		*that*	→	*those*

☐ **EXERCISE 23. Sentence practice.**

Directions: Complete the sentences with ***these*** or ***those***.

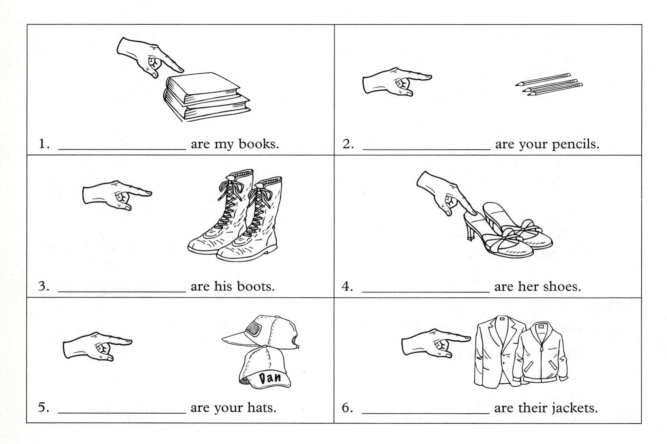

1. _____ are my books.

2. _____ are your pencils.

3. _____ are his boots.

4. _____ are her shoes.

5. _____ are your hats.

6. _____ are their jackets.

☐ **EXERCISE 24. Sentence practice.**

Directions: Complete the sentences. Use the words in parentheses.

1. *(This, These)* _____*These*_____ books belong to me. *(That, Those)*

_____*That*_____ book belongs to Kate.

2. *(This, These)* _____ coat is black. *(That, Those)*

_____ coats are tan.

3. (*This, These*) _____ earrings are gold. (*That, Those*)

_____ earrings are silver.

4. (*This, These*) _____ pencil belongs to Alex.

(*That, Those*) _____ pencil belongs to Olga.

5. (*This, These*) _____ sunglasses belong to me.

(*That, Those*) _____ sunglasses belong to you.

6. (*This, These*) _____ exercise is easy. (*That, Those*)

_____ exercises are hard.

7. Students are sitting at (*this, these*) _____ desks, but

(*that, those*) _____ desks are empty.

8. (*This, These*) _____ book is on my desk. (*That, Those*)

_____ books are on your desk.

□ **EXERCISE 25. Let's talk: pairwork.**

Directions: Work with a partner. Use ***this***, ***that***, ***these***, or ***those***. Touch and point to things in the classroom.

Example:
PARTNER A (*book open*): book
PARTNER B (*book closed*): This is my book. That is your book.

PARTNER A (*book open*): books
PARTNER B (*book closed*): These are my books. Those are your books.

1. notebook	4. dictionary
2. coat	5. purse
3. coats	6. glasses

Switch roles.
Partner A: Close your book.
Partner B: Open your book. Your turn to talk now.

7. notebooks	10. pens
8. shoes	11. pen
9. wallet	12. desk

2-8 ASKING QUESTIONS WITH *WHAT* AND *WHO* + *BE*

(a) **What is** this (thing)?	It's a pen.	**What** asks about things.
(b) **Who is** that (man)?	That's Mr. Lee.	**Who** asks about people.
(c) **What are** those (things)?	They're pens.	
(d) **Who are** they?	They're Mr. and Mrs. Lee.	Note: In questions with **what** and **who**,
		• **is** is followed by a singular word.
		• **are** is followed by a plural word.
(e) **What's** this?		CONTRACTIONS
(f) **Who's** that man?		*what is = what's*
		who is = who's

□ EXERCISE 26. Sentence practice.

    Directions: Complete the questions with **what** or **who** and **is** or **are**.

    1. A: _____*Who is*_____ that woman?

       B: She's my sister. Her name is Sonya.

    2. A: _____ those things?

       B: They're ballpoint pens.

    3. A: _____ that?

       B: That's Ms. Walenski.

    4. A: _____ this?

       B: That's my new notebook.

    5. A: Look at those people over there. _____ they?

       B: I'm not sure, but I think they're new students from Thailand.

    6. A: _____ your name?

       B: Anita.

    7. A: _____ your grammar teacher?

       B: Mr. Cook.

    8. A: _____ your favorite teachers?

       B: Mr. Cook and Ms. Rosenberg.

9. A: _____ a rabbit?

   B: It's a small furry animal with big ears.

10. A: _____ bats?

    B: They're animals that can fly. They're not birds.

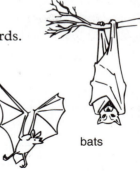
bats

□ EXERCISE 27. Let's talk: pairwork.
   Directions: Work with a partner. Talk about things and people in the classroom. You can look at your book before you speak. When you speak, look at your partner.

   Example: What's this?
   PARTNER A *(book open):* What's this? *(indicating a book)*
   PARTNER B *(book closed):* This is your grammar book.

   PARTNER A *(book open):* Who's that? *(indicating a classmate)*
   PARTNER B *(book closed):* That's Ivan.

   1. What's this?
   2. Who's that?
   3. What's that?
   4. What are these?
   5. Who's this?
   6. What are those?

   Switch roles.
   PARTNER A: Close your book.
   PARTNER B: Open your book. Your turn to ask questions. Use new people and things in your questions.

   7. Who's this?
   8. What's this?
   9. What are those?
   10. What's that?
   11. Who's that?
   12. What are these?

□ EXERCISE 28. Let's talk: pairwork.

Directions: Work with a partner.

PART I. Write the names of the parts of the body on the illustration. Use the words in the list.

ankle	*ear*	*foot*	*leg*	*shoulder*
arm	*elbow*	*hand*	*mouth*	*side*
back	*eye*	*head*	*neck*	*teeth*
chest	*fingers*	*knee*	*nose*	*toes*

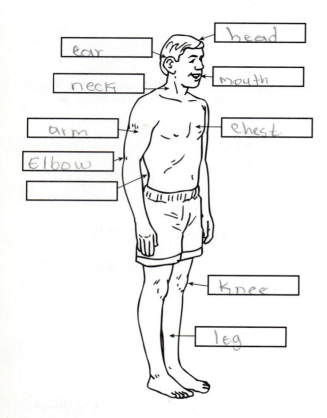

ear
neck
arm
Elbow
head
mouth
chest
knee
leg

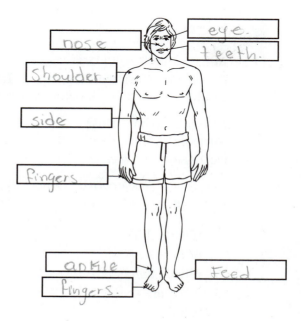

nose
eye.
teeth.
Shoulder.
side
fingers
ankle
fingers.
Feed

PART II. With your partner, take turns asking questions with *this*, *that*, *these*, and *those*.

Note: Both partners can ask about both pictures.

Example:
PARTNER A: What is this?
PARTNER B: This is his leg.

PARTNER B: What are those?
PARTNER A: Those are his fingers.

☐ **EXERCISE 29.** Let's talk: class activity.

EXERCISE 29. Let's talk: class activity.

Directions: Close your books for this activity. Your teacher will ask questions. Answer with ***this, that, these,*** and ***those.***

Example: hand
TEACHER: What is this? *(The teacher indicates her or his hand.)*
STUDENT: That is your hand.
      OR
TEACHER: What is that? *(The teacher indicates a student's hand.)*
STUDENT: This is my hand.

1. nose	6. knee
2. eyes	7. foot
3. arm	8. shoulder
4. elbow	9. fingers
5. legs	10. ears

☐ **EXERCISE 30.** Let's talk: pairwork.

Directions: Ask your partner questions about the picture on p. 46. Use ***What's this?*** ***What's that?*** ***What are these?*** ***What are those?***
Partner A: Use the list below to point out items on the picture.
Partner B: Look at the picture on p. 46 and name the items your partner points to.

Example: apples
PARTNER A: What are these? *(pointing to apples in the picture)*
PARTNER B: These are apples.

Example: tree
PARTNER A: What's this? *(touching a tree in the picture)*
PARTNER B: This is a tree.

1. apples	4. ears	7. clouds	10. bat
2. fence	5. apple tree	8. dog	11. trees
3. log	6. cow	9. egg	12. turtle

Switch roles.
Partner B: Use the list to point out items on the picture.
Partner A: Look at the picture on p. 46 and name the items your partner points to.

13. animals	16. bee	19. beehive	22. wings
14. grass	17. fences	20. bird	23. tree
15. birds	18. bees	21. chicken	24. hill

□ EXERCISE 31. Chapter review: error analysis.
    Directions: Correct the errors.

        are
1. We ~~is~~ students.

2. I no hungry.

3. I am student. He is teacher.

4. Yoko not here. She at school.

5. I'm from Mexico. Where you are from?

6. Roberto he is a student in your class?

7. Those pictures are beautifuls.

8. This is you dictionary. It not my dictionary.

9. Mr. Lee have a brown coat.

10. They are n't here today.

11. This books are expensive.

12. Cuba is a island.

□ EXERCISE 32. Chapter review.
    Directions: Circle the correct completion.

    Example: Those _____ expensive.
        A. book is   (B.) books are   C. books is

1. Ann _____ a grammar book.
    A. have   B. is   C. has

2. This floor _____.
    A. dirty is   B. dirty   C. is dirty

3. _____ yellow.
    A. A banana are   B. A banana is   C. Bananas is

4. BOB: _____ is your apartment?
   ANN: It's on Forest Street.
   A. What   B. Where   C. Who

5. Mike is _____ engineer.
   A. a   B. an   C. on

6. Give this to Ann. It is _____ dictionary.
   A. she   B. an   C. her

7. YOKO: _____ these?
   GINA: My art books. I'm taking an art history course.
   A. What is   B. Who are   C. What are

8. TOM: Are you hungry?
   SUE: Yes, _____.
   A. I'm   B. I'm not   C. I am

9. _____ books are really expensive.
   A. Those   B. They   C. This

10. TINA: _____ that?
    JIM: That's Paul Carter.
    A. Who's   B. What's   C. Where's

11. That is _____.
    A. a mistakes   B. mistakes   C. a mistake

12. PAUL: _____ in your class?
    ERIC: No.
    A. Mr. Kim   B. Is Mr. Kim   C. Mr. Kim is he

☐ EXERCISE 33. Chapter review.
   Directions: Complete the sentences with *am, is,* or *are.* Use *not* if necessary.

   1. Lemons _____ vegetables.

   2. A lemon _____ a kind of fruit.

   3. I _____ from the United States.

   4. We _____ human beings.

   5. Eggs _____ oval.

   6. Chickens _____ birds, but bats _____ birds.

7. Salt _____ sweet. Sugar _____ sweet.

8. Soccer _____ a sport.

9. Soccer and basketball _____ sports.

10. Africa _____ a country. It _____ a continent.

□ EXERCISE 34. Chapter review.

Directions: Complete the conversations.

1. A: Where _____ your book?

   B: Yoko _____ it.

   A: Where _____ your notebooks?

   B: Ali and Roberto _____ my notebooks.

2. A: _____ this?

   B: It _____ picture of my family.

   A: _____ this?

   B: That's _____ father.

   A: _____ they?
   B: My brother and sister.

3. A: What's _____?
   B: I don't know. Ask someone else.

   A: What's _____?

   B: It's _____.

4. A: _____ an animal?
   B: Yes.

   A: _____ animals?
   B: Yes.

   A: _____ an insect?
   B: No, it's not. It's an animal too.

5. A: Where _____?

   B: He's _____.

   A: Where _____?

   B: They're _____.

6. A: _____ turtle?

   B: Just a minute. Let me look in my dictionary. Okay. A turtle is a reptile.

   A: _____ reptile?

   B: _____ animal that has cold blood.

   A: _____ snake a reptile too?

   B: Yes. _____ reptiles too.

□ EXERCISE 35. Review: pairwork.

Directions: Work with a partner. Give directions using the given prepositions. You can look at your book. When you speak, look at your partner.

Example: in
PARTNER A: Put your pen in your pocket.
PARTNER B: *(Partner B puts her/his pen in her/his pocket.)*
PARTNER A: Your turn now.

Partner A	Partner B
1. in	1. in
2. on	2. between
3. above	3. behind
4. under	4. above
5. between	5. on
6. next to	6. next to
7. behind	7. under

□ **EXERCISE 36. Activity: let's talk.**

Directions: Do one or more of these activities. In each activity, ask **What's this?** **What's that? What are these? What are those?** and any other questions you want to ask.

ACTIVITY 1. Pairwork.
Use a blank sheet of paper. Draw a simple picture of an outdoor scene: for example, things you can see in a park, on a city street, in the country, at a marketplace. Show your picture to a partner and answer questions about it.

Sample drawing:

ACTIVITY 2. Group work.
Volunteers can draw pictures of outdoor scenes on the chalkboard, and the class will ask questions about the pictures.

ACTIVITY 3. Pairwork or group work.
Bring to class pictures without people in them: postcards, photographs, magazine ads, etc. Show them to a partner or the class and answer questions about them. Your teacher will help answer questions about vocabulary.

ACTIVITY 4. Pairwork or group work.
Draw the floor plan of your dream house. Show where the kitchen is, the bedrooms, etc. Show the drawing to a partner or the class and answer questions about it.

□ **EXERCISE 37. Chapter review.**

Directions: Complete the sentences in this composition by Carlos.

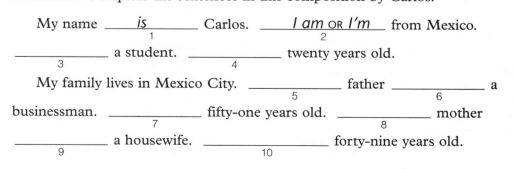

My name ____*is*____ Carlos. ____*I am* OR *I'm*____ from Mexico.
                    1   2

_____ a student. _____ twenty years old.
       3   4

My family lives in Mexico City. _____ father _____ a
                                         5   6

businessman. _____ fifty-one years old. _____ mother
                    7   8

_____ a housewife. _____ forty-nine years old.
       9   10

I _____ two sisters and one brother. The names of my sisters
        11

_____ Rosa and Patricia. Rosa _____ a teacher.
        12   13

_____ twenty-eight years old. Patricia _____ a student.
        14   15

_____ eighteen years old. The name of _____ brother
        16   17

_____ Pedro. _____ an engineer. He is married. He
        18   19

_____ two children.
        20

    I live in a dormitory. _____ a tall building on Pine Street. My address
                                        21

_____ 3225 Pine St. I live with my roommate. _____ name is Bob.
        22   23

_____ from Chicago. _____ nineteen years old.
        24   25

    I like my classes. _____ interesting. I like _____
                                    26   27

classmates. _____ friendly.
                28

☐ **EXERCISE 38. Review.**

Directions: Write a composition by completing the sentences. (Use your own paper.)
Note: A sentence begins with a capital letter (a big letter), and a sentence ends with a
period (.)★

    My name _____. I _____ from _____. _____ a student.

_____ years old.

    My family lives in _____. _____ father _____ years old. _____

mother _____ years old.

    I have _____ sister(s) and _____ brother(s). The name(s) of my sister(s)

_____. _____ is a/an _____. _____ years old.

    (Write about each sister.) The name(s) of my brother(s) _____. _____

is a _____. _____ years old. *(Write about each brother.)*

    I live in *(a dormitory, a house, an apartment)* _____. My address _____. I

live with _____. _____ name(s) _____.

    I like _____ classes. _____ are _____ and _____. I like _____

classmates. They _____.

_____

★In British English, a period is called a "full stop."

CHAPTER 3
Using the Simple Present

3-1 FORM AND BASIC MEANING OF THE SIMPLE PRESENT TENSE

	SINGULAR	PLURAL
1st PERSON	I *talk*	we *talk*
2nd PERSON	you *talk*	you *talk*
3rd PERSON	she *talks* he *talks* it *rains*	they *talk*

Notice: The verb after *she, he, it* (3rd person singular) has a final *-s: talks.*

(a) I *eat* breakfast **every morning**.
(b) Olga *speaks* English **every day**.
(c) We *sleep* **every night**.
(d) They *go* to the beach **every weekend**.

The simple present tense expresses habits.
In (a): Eating breakfast is a habit, a usual activity. *Every morning* = Monday morning, Tuesday morning, Wednesday morning, Thursday morning, Friday morning, Saturday morning, and Sunday morning.

She wakes up every morning at 7:00.

He shaves every morning.

☐ **EXERCISE 1. Let's talk: pairwork.**

Directions: Work with a partner.

PART I. What do you do every morning? On the left is a list of habits.
Check (✓) <u>your</u> habits every morning. Put them in order. What do you do first,
second, third, etc.? Write them on the lines.

HABITS		MY HABITS EVERY MORNING
___✓___	eat breakfast	1. *The alarm clock rings.*
_____	go to class	2. <u>*I turn off the alarm clock.*</u>
_____	put on my clothes	3. _____
_____	drink a cup of coffee/tea	4. _____
_____	shave	5. _____
_____	put on my make-up	6. _____
___✓___	take a shower/bath	7. _____
___✓___	get up	8. _____
_____	pick up my books	9. _____
___✓___	walk to the bathroom	10. _____
_____	watch TV	11. _____
___✓___	look in the mirror	12. _____
___✓___	turn off the alarm clock	13. _____
_____	go to the kitchen/the cafeteria	14. _____
_____	brush/comb my hair	15. _____
_____	say good-bye to my roommate/ wife/husband/parents/partner/etc.	16. _____
___✓___	brush my teeth	
_____	do exercises	
___✓___	wash my face	

PART II. Tell a partner about your habits every morning. Close your book.

□ **EXERCISE 2. Listening.**

Directions: Listen to the sentences and circle the verbs you hear.

1. (wake)	wakes		6. watch	watches
2. wake	wakes		7. take	takes
3. get	gets		8. take	takes
4. go	goes		9. take	takes
5. do	does		10. talk	talks

□ **EXERCISE 3. Sentence practice.**

Directions: Choose the correct completions.

1. My mother and father _____*eat*_____ breakfast at 7:00 every day.

                         eat   eats

2. My mother _____ tea with her breakfast.

              drink   drinks

3. I _____ a bath every morning.

        take   takes

4. My sister _____ a shower.

          take   takes

5. I _____ English with my friends.

      study   studies

6. We _____ to school together every morning.

       walk   walks

7. Class _____ at 9:00 every day.

       begin   begins

8. It _____ at 12:00 for lunch.

       stop   stops

9. We _____ in the cafeteria.

       eat   eats

10. My friends and I _____ home at 3:00 every afternoon.

         go   goes

3-2 USING FREQUENCY ADVERBS: *ALWAYS, USUALLY, OFTEN, SOMETIMES, SELDOM, RARELY, NEVER*

100%	*always*	(a) **Bob *always* eats** breakfast.
90%–99%	*usually*	(b) **Mary *usually* eats** breakfast.
75%–90%	*often*	(c) **They *often* watch** TV at night.
25%–75%	*sometimes*	(d) **Tom *sometimes* watches** TV.
5%–10%	*seldom*	(e) **I *seldom* watch** TV.
1%–10%	*rarely*	(f) **I *rarely* drink** milk.
0%	*never*	(g) **I *never* eat** paper.

$$\text{SUBJECT} + \left\{ \begin{array}{l} always \\ usually \\ often \\ sometimes \\ seldom \\ rarely \\ never \end{array} \right\} + \text{VERB}$$

The words in this list are called "frequency adverbs." They come between the subject and the simple present verb.★

★Some frequency adverbs can also come at the beginning or at the end of a sentence. For example:
   Sometimes *I get up at seven.* *I **sometimes** get up at seven.* *I get up at seven* ***sometimes***.
   Also: See Chart 3-4, p. 59, for the use of frequency adverbs with *be*.

☐ EXERCISE 4. Sentence practice.
   Directions: Complete the sentences in the chart. Use each frequency adverb once.

✓*always* *often* *never* *rarely* *seldom* *sometimes* *usually*

	Sun.	Mon.	Tues.	Wed.	Thurs.	Fri.	Sat.
1. Ann ___*always*___ drinks tea with lunch.	☕	☕	☕	☕	☕	☕	☕
2. Bob _____ drinks tea with lunch.		☕	☕	☕	☕	☕	☕
3. Maria _____ drinks tea with lunch.			☕	☕	☕	☕	☕
4. Gary _____ drinks tea with lunch.					☕	☕	☕
5. Ali _____ drinks tea with lunch.						☕	☕
6. Sonya _____ drinks tea with lunch.							☕
7. Joe _____ drinks tea with lunch.							

□ EXERCISE 5. Sentence practice.

Directions: Write **S** over the subject and **V** over the verb in each sentence. Then rewrite the sentences, adding the *italicized* frequency adverbs.

                            S V

1. *always*   I eat breakfast in the morning.

                      I always eat breakfast _____ in the morning.

2. *never*   I eat carrots for breakfast.

                     _____ for breakfast.

3. *seldom*   I watch TV in the morning.

                     _____ in the morning.

4. *sometimes*   I have tea with dinner.

                     _____ with dinner.

5. *usually*   Sonya eats lunch at the cafeteria.

                     _____ at the cafeteria.

6. *rarely*   Joe drinks tea.

                     _____

7. *often*   We listen to music after dinner.

                     _____ after dinner.

8. *always*   The students speak English in the classroom.

                     _____ in the classroom.

□ EXERCISE 6. Let's talk: class activity.

Directions: Your teacher will ask you to talk about your morning, afternoon, and evening activities. Close your books for this activity.

TEACHER: Tell me something you . . .

1. always do in the morning.
2. never do in the morning.
3. sometimes do in the morning.
4. usually do in the afternoon.
5. seldom do in the afternoon.

6. never do in the afternoon.
7. often do in the evening.
8. sometimes do in the evening.
9. rarely do in the evening.
10. sometimes do on weekends.

3-3 OTHER FREQUENCY EXPRESSIONS

(a) I drink tea	**once** *a day*. **twice** *a day*. **three times** *a day*. **four times** *a day*. **etc.**	We can express frequency by saying how many times something happens *a day*. *a week*. *a month*. *a year*.
(b) I see my grandparents **three times** *a week*. (c) I see my aunt **once** *a month*. (d) I see my cousin Sam **twice** *a year*.		
(e) I see my roommate **every** *morning*. I pay my bills **every** *month*. I see my doctor **every** *year*.		*Every* is singular. The noun that follows (e.g., *morning*) must be singular. *INCORRECT: every mornings*

□ EXERCISE 7. Sentence practice.

Directions: How often do the people in the chart take the bus? Use the chart to complete the sentences.

	Sun.	Mon.	Tues.	Wed.	Thurs.	Fri.	Sat.
Hamid	🚌	🚌	🚌	🚌	🚌	🚌	🚌
Anna							🚌
Yoko						🚌	🚌
Marco		🚌	🚌	🚌	🚌	🚌	🚌
Joe			🚌	🚌	🚌	🚌	🚌
Mr. Wu							
Mrs. Cook					🚌	🚌	🚌

1. Hamid takes the bus _____*seven times*_____ a week. That means he

_____*always*_____ takes the bus.

2. Anna takes the bus _____ a week. That means she

_____ takes the bus.

3. Yoko takes the bus _____ a week. That means she

_____ takes the bus.

4. Marco takes the bus _____ a week. That means he

_____ takes the bus.

5. Joe takes the bus _____ a week. That means he

_____ takes the bus.

6. Mr. Wu _____ takes the bus.

7. Mrs. Cook takes the bus _____ a week. That means she

_____ takes the bus.

☐ **EXERCISE 8. Listening.**

Directions: Listen to the sentences and circle the words you hear.

1. (morning)   mornings   5. day   days

2. year   years   6. time   times

3. year   years   7. night   nights

4. day   days   8. month   months

3-4 USING FREQUENCY ADVERBS WITH *BE*

SUBJECT + *BE* + FREQUENCY ADVERB	Frequency adverbs follow *am, is, are* (the simple forms of *be*).
Tom + *is* + { *always* *usually* *often* *sometimes* *seldom* *rarely* *never* } + late for class.	
SUBJECT + FREQUENCY ADVERB + OTHER SIMPLE PRESENT VERBS	Frequency adverbs come before all simple present verbs except *be*.
Tom + { *always* *usually* *often* *sometimes* *seldom* *rarely* *never* } + *comes* late.	

Directions: Add the frequency adverbs to the sentences.

1. *always*   Ann is on time for class. → *Ann is always on time for class.*
2. *always*   Ann comes to class on time. → *Ann always comes to class on time.*
3. *often*   Maria is late for class.
4. *often*   Maria comes to class late.
5. *never*   It snows in my hometown.
6. *never*   It is very cold in my hometown.
7. *usually*   Bob is at home in the evening.
8. *usually*   Bob stays at home in the evening.
9. *seldom*   Tom studies at the library in the evening.
10. *seldom*   His classmates are at the library in the evening.
11. *sometimes* I skip breakfast.
12. *rarely*   I have time for a big breakfast.
13. *usually* I am very hungry by lunchtime.
14. *never*   Sue drinks coffee.

☐ EXERCISE 10. Let's talk: class activity.

Directions: Talk about what your classmates do in the evening.

PART I. Check (✓) the boxes to describe your activities after 5:00 P.M.

	always	usually	often	sometimes	seldom	rarely	never
1. eat dinner							
2. go to a movie							
3. go shopping							
4. go swimming							
5. spend time with my friends							
6. be at home							
7. listen to music							
8. watch videos or DVDs							
9. speak English							
10. send e-mails							
11. surf the Internet							
12. drink coffee after 9:00							
13. be in bed at ten o'clock							
14. go to bed late							

PART II. Exchange books with a partner. Your partner will tell the class two things about your evening.

Example: (Carlos) is usually at home. He sometimes sends e-mails.
(Olga) sometimes drinks coffee after 9:00. She usually goes to bed late.

☐ **EXERCISE 11. Paragraph practice.**

Directions: Write about a typical day in your life, from the time you get up in the morning until you go to bed. Use the following words to show the order of your activities: ***then, next, at . . . o'clock, after that, later.***

Example: I usually get up at seven-thirty. I shave, brush my teeth, and take a shower. Then I put on my clothes and go to the student cafeteria for breakfast. After that I go back to my room. I sometimes watch the news on TV. At 8:15, I leave the dormitory. I go to class. My class begins at 8:30. I'm in class from 8:30 to 11:30. After that I eat lunch. I usually have a sandwich and a cup of tea for lunch. (Continue until you complete your day.)

3-5 SPELLING AND PRONUNCIATION OF FINAL -ES

			SPELLING	PRONUNCIATION	
-sh	(a)	push →	*pushes*	*push/əz/*	Ending of verb: **-sh, -ch, -ss, -x.**
-ch	(b)	teach →	*teaches*	*teach/əz/*	Spelling: add **-es.**
-ss	(c)	kiss →	*kisses*	*kiss/əz/*	Pronunciation: /əz/.
-x	(d)	fix →	*fixes*	*fix/əz/*	

☐ **EXERCISE 12. Sentence practice.**

Directions: Use the verbs in *italics* to complete the sentences.

1. *brush*   Alice _____*brushes*_____ her hair every morning.

2. *teach*   Alex _____ English.

3. *fix*   Jason _____ his breakfast every morning. He makes eggs and toast.

4. *drink*   Sonya _____ tea every afternoon.

5. *watch*   Joon Kee often _____ television at night.

6. *kiss*   Peter always _____ his children goodnight.

7. *wear*   Tina usually _____ jeans to class.

8. *wash*   Eric seldom _____ dishes.

9. *walk*   Jenny _____ her dog twice each day.

10. *stretch,*   When Jack gets up in the morning, he _____ and
    yawn
    _____ .

☐ EXERCISE 13. Listening.

Directions: Listen to the sentences and circle the verbs you hear.

1. teach	(teaches)	6. watch	watches
2. teach	teaches	7. brush	brushes
3. fix	fixes	8. brush	brushes
4. fix	fixes	9. wash	washes
5. watch	watches	10. wash	washes

☐ EXERCISE 14. Verb form practice.

Directions: Complete the sentences. Use the words in the list and add *-s* or *-es*.
Then practice reading the story aloud (with a partner or in small groups).

brush	*get*	*take*	*wash*
cook	✓ *leave*	*turn*	*watch*
fall	*read*	*sit*	

Laura ____*leaves*____ her office every night at 5:00 and _____ on

a bus to go home. She has a regular schedule every evening. She _____

dinner and then _____ down to eat at 6:00. After she _____

the dishes, she _____ on the TV. She usually _____ the

news and then a movie. At 9:00, she _____ a shower. She always

_____ her teeth after her shower. Then she picks up a book

and _____ in bed for a while. She usually _____ asleep

before 10:00.

3-6 ADDING FINAL -S/-ES TO WORDS THAT END IN -Y

(a) *cry* → *cries* *try* → *tries*	End of verb: Spelling:	consonant + *-y*. change *y* to *i*, add *-es*.
(b) *pay* → *pays* *enjoy* → *enjoys*	End of verb: Spelling:	vowel + *-y*. add *-s*.

☐ EXERCISE 15. Spelling practice.

Directions: Complete the chart with the correct form of each verb.

1. I try.	He _____ .
2. We study.	She _____ .
3. They say.	It _____ .
4. You worry.	My mother _____ .
5. We fly.	A bird _____ .
6. I stay awake.	Paul _____ awake.
7. I enjoy games.	Ann _____ games.
8. Students buy books.	My brother _____ books.
9. We pay bills.	Gina _____ bills.
10. I play music. ♪♪	My friend _____ music.

☐ EXERCISE 16. Sentence practice.

Directions: Use the words in *italics* to complete the sentences.

1. *pay, always*   Boris _____*always pays*_____ his bills on time.

2. *cry, seldom*   Our baby _____ at night.

3. *study*   Paul _____ at the library every day.

4. *stay, usually*   Laura _____ home at night.

5. *fly*   Kunio is a pilot. He _____ a plane.

a plane

6. *carry, always*   Carol _____ her books to class.

7. *buy, seldom*   Ann _____ new clothes.

8. *worry*   Tina is a good student, but she _____ about her grades.

9. *enjoy*   Ron _____ good food.

3-7   IRREGULAR SINGULAR VERBS: *HAS, DOES, GOES*

(a) I **have** a book. (b) He **has** a book.	she he } + **has** /hæz/ it	**Have, do,** and **go** have irregular forms for third person singular: have → has do → does go → goes
(c) I **do** my work. (d) She **does** her work.	she he } + **does** /dəz/ it	
(e) They **go** to school. (f) She **goes** to school.	she he } + **goes** /gowz/ it	

☐ EXERCISE 17. Sentence practice.
   Directions: Use the given verbs to complete the sentences.

   1. *do*   Pierre always _____*does*_____ his homework.

   2. *do*   We always _____*do*_____ our homework.

   3. *have*   Yoko and Hamid _____ their books.

   4. *have*   Mrs. Chang _____ a car.

   5. *go*   Andy _____ to school every day.

6. *have* Jessica _____ a snack every night around ten.

7. *do* Sara seldom _____ her homework.

8. *do* We _____ exercises in class every day.

9. *go, go* Roberto _____ downtown every weekend. He and his wife

_____ shopping.

10. *go* My friends often _____ to the beach.

□ **EXERCISE 18. Listening.**

Directions: Listen to the story. Complete the sentences with *is*, *has*, *does*, or *goes*.

Marco ____*is*____ a student. He ____*has*____ an unusual schedule. All of
       1   2

his classes are at night. His first class _____ at 6:00 P.M. every day. He
                                 3

_____ a break from 7:30 to 8:00. Then he _____ classes from 8:00
    4   5

to 10:00.

He leaves school and _____ home at 10:00. After he _____
                         6   7

dinner, he watches TV. Then he _____ his homework from midnight to 3:00
                                8

or 4:00 in the morning.

Marco _____ his own computer at home. When he finishes his
          9

homework, he usually goes on the Internet. He usually stays at his computer until the

sun comes up. Then he _____ a few exercises, _____ breakfast, and
                       10   11

_____ to bed. He sleeps all day. Marco thinks his schedule _____
   12   13

great, but his friends think it _____ strange.
                             14

	SPELLING	PRONUNCIATION	
(a)	rub → *rubs* ride → *rides* smile → *smiles* dream → *dreams* run → *runs* wear → *wears* drive → *drives* see → *sees* snow → *snows*	rub/z/ ride/z/ smile/z/ dream/z/ run/z/ wear/z/ drive/z/ see/z/ snows/z/	To form a simple present verb in 3rd person singular, you usually add only **-s**, as in (a) and (b). In (a): **-s** is pronounced /z/. The final sounds in (a) are "voiced."★ Voiced sounds make your vocal cords vibrate. The sound /b/ is a voiced sound.
(b)	drink → *drinks* sleep → *sleeps* write → *writes* laugh → *laughs*	drink/s/ sleep/s/ write/s/ laugh/s/	In (b): **-s** is pronounced /s/. The final sounds in (b) are "voiceless."★ Your vocal cords do NOT vibrate with voiceless sounds. You push air through your teeth and lips. The sound /p/ is a voiceless sound.
(c)	push → *pushes* teach → *teaches* kiss → *kisses* fix → *fixes*	push/əz/ teach/əz/ kiss/əz/ fix/əz/	End of verb: **-sh, -ch, -ss, -x** Spelling: add **-es** Pronunciation: /əz/
(d)	cry → *cries* study → *studies*	cry/z/ study/z/	End of verb: consonant + **-y** Spelling: change **y** to **i**, add **-es**
(e)	pay → *pays* buy → *buys*	pay/z/ buy/z/	End of verb: vowel + **-y** Spelling: change **y** to **i**, add **-es**
(f)	have → **has** go → **goes** do → **does**	/hæz/ /gowz/ /dəz/	The 3rd person singular forms of *have, go,* and *do* are irregular.

★Voiced sounds = b, d, g, l, m, n, r, v, y, and all the vowels: a, e, i, o, u.
 Voiceless sounds = f, h, k, p, s, t, th as in *think*.

□ EXERCISE 19. Let's talk: class activity.

Directions: Talk about everyday activities using the given verbs. Close your book.

Example:
   TEACHER: eat
SPEAKER A: I eat breakfast every morning.
   TEACHER: What does *(Speaker A)* do every morning?
SPEAKER B: She/He eats breakfast.

1. eat	4. brush	7. get up	10. do	13. put on
2. go	5. have	8. watch	11. listen to	14. carry
3. drink	6. study	9. speak	12. wash	15. kiss

Directions: Complete the sentences. Use the words in parentheses. Use the simple present tense. Pay special attention to singular and plural and to the spelling of final *-s/-es*.

1. The students *(ask, often)* _____ *often ask* _____ questions in class.

2. Pablo *(study, usually)* _____ at the library every

   evening.

3. Olga *(bite)* _____ her fingernails when she is nervous.

4. Donna *(cash)* _____ a check at the bank once a week.

5. Sometimes I *(worry)* _____ about my grades at school. Sonya

   (worry, never) _____ about her grades. She *(study)*

   _____ hard.

6. Ms. Jones and Mr. Anderson *(teach)* _____ at the local high school.

   Ms. Jones *(teach)* _____ math.

7. Birds *(fly)* _____. They *(have)* _____ wings.

8. A bird *(fly)* _____. It *(have)* _____ wings.

9. Jason *(do, always)* _____ his homework. He *(go, never)*

   _____ to bed until his homework is finished.

10. Mr. Cook *(say, always)*★ _____ hello to his neighbor in the

    morning.

11. Ms. Chu *(pay, always)*★ _____ attention in class. She

    (answer) _____ questions. She *(listen)* _____

    to the teacher. She *(ask)* _____ questions.

_____

★ Pronunciation of **says** = /sɛz/. Pronunciation of **pays** = /peyz/.

12. Sam *(enjoy)* _____ cooking. He *(try, often)* _____

_____ new recipes. He *(like)* _____ to have company for

dinner. He *(invite)* _____ me to dinner once a month. When I

arrive, I *(go)* _____ to the kitchen and *(watch)* _____ him

cook. He usually *(have)* _____

three or four pots on the stove. He *(watch)*

_____ the pots carefully.

He *(make)* _____ a big

mess in the kitchen when he cooks.

After dinner, he *(wash)* _____

all the dishes and *(clean)* _____ the kitchen. I *(cook, never)*

_____. It *(be)* _____ too much trouble. But my

friend Sam *(love)* _____ to cook.

☐ **EXERCISE 21.** Let's talk: pairwork.

Directions: Work with a partner. Use frequency words like **sometimes, rarely,** etc.

PART I. Billy, Jenny, and Peter do many things in their evenings. How often do they
do the things in the list? Pay attention to final **-s**.

Example: Billy rarely/seldom does homework.

	BILLY	JENNY	PETER
do homework	once a week	6 days a week	every day
surf the Internet	every day	once a week	once a month
watch TV	3–4 days a week	3–4 days a week	3–4 days a week
read for pleasure	5 days a week	5 days a week	5 days a week
try to go to bed early	once a week	5 nights a week	6 nights a week

PART II. For homework, write ten sentences about the activities of Billy, Jenny, and
Peter.

□ EXERCISE 22. Let's talk and write: pairwork.

Directions: Work with a partner.

Partner A: Tell Partner B five to ten things you do every morning. You can look at the list you made for Exercise 1.

Partner B: Take notes while Partner A is talking. (You will use these notes later to write a paragraph about Partner A's usual morning habits.)

Switch roles.

Partner B: Tell Partner A five to ten things you do every morning.

Partner A: Take notes while Partner B is talking.

When you finish talking, write a paragraph about your partner's daily morning activities. Pay special attention to the use of final *-s/-es*. Show your paragraph to your partner, who will look at your use of final *-s/-es*.

3-9 THE SIMPLE PRESENT: NEGATIVE

(a) **I**	*do not*	drink coffee.	NEGATIVE: $\left.\begin{array}{l} I \\ We \\ You \\ They \end{array}\right\}$ + **do not** + *main verb*
We	*do not*	drink coffee.	
You	*do not*	drink coffee.	
They	*do not*	drink coffee.	
(b) **She**	*does not*	drink coffee.	$\left.\begin{array}{l} She \\ He \\ It \end{array}\right\}$ + **does not** + *main verb*
He	*does not*	drink coffee.	
It	*does not*	drink coffee.	

Do and *does* are called "helping verbs."

Notice in (b): In 3rd person singular, there is no *-s* on the main verb; the final *-s* is part of *does*.

INCORRECT: She does not drinks coffee.

(c) I **don't** drink tea. They **don't** have a car.	CONTRACTIONS: **do not** = **don't** **does not** = **doesn't**
(d) He **doesn't** drink tea. Mary **doesn't** have a car.	People usually use contractions when they speak. People often use contractions when they write.

□ EXERCISE 23. Sentence practice.

Directions: Use the words in *italics* to make negative sentences. Use contractions.

1. *like, not*   Ingrid _____ *doesn't like* _____ tea.

2. *like, not*   I _____ *don't like* _____ tea.

3. *know, not*   Mary and Jim are strangers. Mary _____ Jim.

4. *need, not*   It's a nice day today. You _____

your umbrella.

5. *snow, not*   It _____ in Bangkok in the winter.

an umbrella

6. *speak, not*   I _____ French.

7. *be, not*   I _____ hungry.

8. *live, not*   Butterflies _____ long.

9. *have, not*   A butterfly _____ a long life.

10. *be, not*   A butterfly _____ large.

11. *be, not*   Butterflies _____ large.

a butterfly

12. *have, not*   We _____ class every day.

13. *have, not*   This city _____ nice weather in the summer.

14. *be, not*   It _____ cold today.

15. *rain, not*   It _____ every day.

☐ **EXERCISE 24. Let's talk: pairwork.**

Directions: Work with a partner. Make two sentences about each picture.

Example:
PARTNER A: Ann takes showers. She doesn't take baths. Your turn now.
PARTNER B: Omar has a dog. He doesn't have a cat. Your turn now.

YES   NO

   1. (Ann \ take)
                               showers
                               baths

	YES		NO

<table>
<tr><td></td><td>YES</td><td></td><td>NO</td></tr>
</table>

 2. (Omar \ have)
a cat
a dog

 3. (I \ drink)
tea
coffee

 4. (Rob and Ed \ live)
an apartment
a house

 5. (Becky \ drive)
a new car
an old car

 6. (I \ play)
soccer
tennis

7. (Mr. Davis \ teach)
English
French

 8. (we \ use)
typewriters
computers

 9. (Alex \ watch)
news reports
old movies

 10. (Marco \ study)
history
physics

□ **EXERCISE 25. Let's talk: game.**

Directions: Sit in a circle. Choose any of the verbs in the list. Make sentences with **not**.

have	*like*	*need*	*play*	*read*	*speak*

Example: like
SPEAKER A: I don't like bananas.
SPEAKER B: *(Speaker A)* doesn't like bananas. I don't have a dog.
SPEAKER C: *(Speaker A)* doesn't like bananas. *(Speaker B)* doesn't have a dog.
          I don't play baseball.

Continue around the circle, each time repeating the information of your classmates before saying your sentence. If you have trouble, your classmates can help you. Your teacher will be the last one to speak.

□ **EXERCISE 26. Sentence practice.**

Directions: Use verbs from the list to complete the sentences. Make all of the sentences negative by using **does not** or **do not**. You can use contractions **(doesn't/don't)**. Some verbs may be used more than one time.

do	*go*	*shave*
drink	*make*	*smoke*
eat	*put on*	*speak*

1. Bob _____ *doesn't go* _____ to school every day.

2. My roommates are from Japan. They _____ Spanish.

3. Roberto has a beard. He _____ in the morning.

4. We _____ to class on Sunday.

5. Sally is healthy. She _____ cigarettes.

6. Jane and Alex always have lunch at home. They _____ at the cafeteria.

7. Sometimes I _____ my homework in the evening. I watch TV instead.

8. My sister likes tea, but she _____ coffee.

9. Hamid is a careful writer. He _____ mistakes in spelling when he writes.

10. I'm lazy. I _____ exercises in the morning.

11. Sometimes Ann _____ her shoes when she goes outside.

□ **EXERCISE 27. Let's talk: class activity.**

Directions: Use the given words to make truthful sentences.

Example: Grass \ blue.
SPEAKER A: Grass isn't blue.
SPEAKER B: Grass is green.

Example: Dogs \ tails.
SPEAKER C: Dogs have tails.
SPEAKER D: People* don't have tails.

1. A restaurant \ sell shoes.
2. A restaurant \ serve food.
3. People \ wear clothes.
4. Animals \ wear clothes.
5. A child \ need love, food, care, and toys.
6. A child \ need a driver's license.
7. Refrigerators \ hot inside.
8. Refrigerators \ cold inside.
9. A cat \ have whiskers.

10. A bird \ have whiskers.
11. Doctors \ take care of sick people.
12. Doctors in my country \ be expensive.
13. A bus \ carry people from one place to another.
14. It \ be cold today.
15. English \ be an easy language to learn.
16. People in this city \ be friendly.
17. It \ rain a lot in this city.

whiskers

_____

*People is a plural noun. It takes a plural verb.

3-10 THE SIMPLE PRESENT: YES/NO QUESTIONS

DO/DOES + SUBJECT + MAIN VERB	QUESTION FORMS, SIMPLE PRESENT
(a) **Do** *I* *like* coffee? (b) **Do** *you* *like* coffee? (c) **Do** *we* *like* coffee? (d) **Do** *they* *like* coffee?	**Do I** **Do you** } + *main verb* (simple form) **Do we** **Do they** **Does she** **Does he** } + *main verb* (simple form) **Does it**
(e) **Does** *she* *like* coffee? (f) **Does** *he* *like* coffee? (g) **Does** *it* *taste* good?	Notice in (e): The main verb in the question does not have a final *-s*. The final *-s* is part of **does**. *INCORRECT: Does she likes coffee?*
(h) **Are you** a student? *INCORRECT: Do you be a student?*	When the main verb is a form of **be, do** is NOT used. See Chart 2-1, p. 24, for question forms with **be**.

QUESTION	SHORT ANSWER	
(i) *Do* you *like* tea?	→ Yes, I **do**. No, I **don't**.	**Do, don't, does,** and **doesn't** are used in the short answers to yes/no questions in the simple present.
(j) *Does* Bob *like* tea?	→ Yes, he **does**. No, he **doesn't**.	

☐ EXERCISE 28. Question practice.

Directions: Make questions. Give short answers.

1. A: <u>   Do you like tea?   </u>

   B: <u>   Yes, I do.   </u> (I like tea.)

2. A: <u>   Do you like coffee?   </u>

   B: <u>   No, I don't.   </u> (I don't like coffee.)

3. A: <u>   </u>

   B: <u>   </u> (I don't speak Chinese.)

4. A: <u>   </u>

   B: <u>   </u> (Ann speaks Italian.)

5. A: _____

   B: _____ (Ann and Tom don't speak Arabic.)

6. A: _____

   B: _____ (I do exercises every morning.)

7. A: _____

   B: _____ (Sue has a cold.)

8. A: _____

   B: _____ (Jim doesn't do his homework every day.)

9. A: _____

   B: _____ (It rains a lot in April.)

10. A: _____

    B: _____ (Frogs don't have tails.)

☐ **EXERCISE 29. Interview and question practice: pairwork.**

Directions: Work with a partner. Ask and answer questions.

PART I. Ask each other about the following activities. Check (✓) the correct box.
You can look at your book before you speak. When you speak, look at your partner.

Example: drive a car
PARTNER A: Do you drive a car?
PARTNER B: No, I don't. Do you drive a car?
PARTNER A: Yes, I do.

	yes	no			yes	no
1. live in an apartment	☐	☐	6. dream in English		☐	☐
2. go to movie theaters	☐	☐	7. have a cell phone		☐	☐
3. play tennis	☐	☐	8. like vegetables		☐	☐
4. enjoy sports on TV	☐	☐	9. eat red meat		☐	☐
5. read newspapers every day	☐	☐	10. like chocolate		☐	☐

PART II. Write five sentences about your partner. Write five sentences about yourself.

□ **EXERCISE 30. Let's talk: pairwork.**

Directions: Work with a partner. Ask and answer questions.

PART I. Take turns making questions and giving short answers. Use the **names of your classmates** in the questions. Note: This is speaking practice. Do not write the answers yet.

Example:

PARTNER A: _____

PARTNER B: _____ (He is in class today.)

PARTNER A: Is Ali in class today?
PARTNER B: Yes, he is.

Example:

PARTNER B: _____

PARTNER A: _____ (She doesn't speak Spanish.)

PARTNER B: Does Yoko speak Spanish?
PARTNER A: No, she doesn't.

1. Partner A: _____

   Partner B: _____ (He speaks English in class every day.)

2. Partner B: _____

   Partner A: _____ (She comes to class every day.)

3. Partner A: _____

   Partner B: _____ (They're in class today.)

4. Partner B: _____

   Partner A: _____ (She sits in the same seat every day.)

5. Partner A: _____

   Partner B: _____ (He wears jeans every day.)

6. Partner B: _____

   Partner A: _____ (They aren't from Australia.)

7. Partner A: _____

   Partner B: _____ (They don't have dictionaries on

   their desks.)

8. Partner B: _____

   Partner A: _____ (They speak English.)

PART II. Now write the questions and answers in your book.

☐ EXERCISE 31. Let's talk: pairwork.

Directions: Work with a partner to make conversations. Begin your answers with *no*.

Example: children \ walk to school every day
PARTNER A: Do the children walk to school every day?
SPEAKER B: No, they don't. They take the bus.
PARTNER A: Your turn now.

1. the students \ come to class at 10:00

2. Amy \ watch TV in the mornings

3. Luis \ write letters

4. Beth \ drive a car

5. the workers \ wear shoes

6. Joe \ have a cat

students

Amy

Luis

Beth

a worker

Joe

THE SIMPLE PRESENT: ASKING INFORMATION QUESTIONS WITH *WHERE*

(WHERE) + *DO*/ + SUBJECT + MAIN DOES VERB				SHORT ANSWER	(a) = a yes/no question (b) = an information question ***Where*** asks for information about a place.
(a)	***Do***	they	***live*** in Miami? →	***Yes,*** they do. ***No,*** they don't.	
(b) ***Where***	***do***	they	***live?***	→ ***In Miami.***	The form of yes/no questions and information questions is the same: ***Do/Does*** + *subject* + *main verb*
(c)	***Does***	Gina	***live*** in Rome? →	***Yes,*** she does. ***No,*** she doesn't.	
(d) Where	***does***	Gina	***live?***	→ ***In Rome.***	

☐ **EXERCISE 32. Question practice.**

Directions: Make questions.

1. A: _____*Does Jean eat lunch at the cafeteria every day?*_____

   B: Yes, she does. (Jean eats lunch at the cafeteria every day.)

2. A: _____*Where does Jean eat lunch every day?*_____

   B: At the cafeteria. (Jean eats lunch at the cafeteria every day.)

3. A: _____

   B: At the post office. (Peter works at the post office.)

4. A: _____

   B: Yes, he does. (Peter works at the post office.)

5. A: _____

   B: Yes, I do. (I live in an apartment.)

6. A: _____

   B: In an apartment. (I live in an apartment.)

7. A: _____

   B: At a restaurant. (Bill eats dinner at a restaurant every day.)

8. A: _____

   B: In the front row. (I sit in the front row during class.)

9. A: _____

   B: At the University of Toronto. (Jessica goes to school at the University of Toronto.)

10. A: _____

    B: On my desk. (My book is on my desk.)

11. A: _____

    B: To class. (I go to class every morning.)

12. A: _____

    B: In class. (The students are in class right now.)

13. A: _____

    B: In Australia. (Kangaroos live in Australia.)

☐ **EXERCISE 33. Let's talk: pairwork.**

Directions: Work with a partner.
Partner A: Ask your partner questions using **where**.
             Your book is open.
Partner B: Answer the questions. Your book is closed.

Example: live
PARTNER A *(book open):*   Where do you live?
PARTNER B *(book closed):* *(free response)*

1. live
2. eat lunch every day
3. go after class
4. study at night
5. go to school
6. buy school supplies

Switch roles.
Partner A: Close your book.
Partner B: Open your book. Your turn to ask questions now.

7. buy your clothes
8. go on weekends
9. sit during class
10. eat dinner
11. do your homework
12. go on vacation

3-12 THE SIMPLE PRESENT: ASKING INFORMATION QUESTIONS WITH *WHEN* AND *WHAT TIME*

Q-WORD* +	DO/ DOES	+ SUBJECT +	MAIN VERB			SHORT ANSWER	*When* and *what time* ask for information about time.
(a) **When**	do	you	go	to class?	→	**At nine o'clock.**	
(b) **What time**	do	you	go	to class?	→	**At nine o'clock.**	
(c) **When**	does	Anna	eat	dinner?	→	**At six** P.M.	
(d) **What time**	does	Anna	eat	dinner?	→	**At six** P.M.	

(e) **What time** do you **usually** go to class?	The frequency adverb usually comes immediately after the subject in a question: *Q-word* + **does/do** + *subject* + **usually** + *main verb*

*A "Q-Word" is "a question word." *Where, when, what, what time, who,* and *why* are examples of question words.

EXERCISE 34. Question practice.

Directions: Make questions.

1. A: _____*When/What time do you eat breakfast?*_____
   B: At 7:30. (I eat breakfast at 7:30 in the morning.)

2. A: _____*When/What time do you usually eat breakfast?*_____
   B: At 7:00. (I usually eat breakfast at 7:00.)

3. A: _____
   B: At 6:45. (I get up at 6:45.)

4. A: _____
   B: At 6:30. (Maria usually gets up at 6:30.)

5. A: _____
   B: At 8:15. (The movie starts at 8:15.)

6. A: _____
   B: Around 11:00. (I usually go to bed around 11:00.)

7. A: _____
   B: At half-past twelve. (I usually eat lunch at half-past twelve.)

8. A: _____
   B: At 5:30. (The restaurant opens at 5:30.)

9. A: _____

    B: At 9:05. (The train leaves at 9:05.)

10. A: _____

    B: Between 6:30 and 8:00. (I usually eat dinner between 6:30 and 8:00.)

11. A: _____

    B: At eight fifteen. (My classes begin at eight fifteen.)

12. A: _____

    B: At 10:00 P.M. (The library closes at 10:00 P.M. on Saturday.)

□ **EXERCISE 35. Let's talk: class interview.**

    Directions: Ask and answer questions.

    PART I. Walk around the room. Ask a question using ***when*** or ***what time***. Write the answer and your classmate's name. Then ask another classmate a different question.

    Example: eat breakfast
    SPEAKER A: When/What time do you eat breakfast?
    SPEAKER B: I usually eat breakfast around seven o'clock.

	Name	Answer
SPEAKER A: *(write)*	*Yoko*	*7 A.M.*

	Name	Answer
1. wake up	_____	_____
2. usually get up	_____	_____
3. eat breakfast	_____	_____
4. leave home in the morning	_____	_____
5. usually get to class	_____	_____
6. eat lunch	_____	_____
7. get home from school	_____	_____
8. have dinner	_____	_____
9. usually study in the evening	_____	_____
10. go to bed	_____	_____

    PART II. Tell the class about a few of the answers you got.

□ EXERCISE 36. Interview and paragraph practice.

> *Directions:* Interview someone (a friend, a roommate, a classmate, etc.) about her/his daily schedule. Use the information from the interview to write a paragraph.
>
> *Some questions you might want to ask during the interview:*
>
> What do you do every morning?   What time do you . . . ?
> What do you do every afternoon? When do you . . . ?
> What do you do every evening?   Where do you . . . ?

3-13 SUMMARY: INFORMATION QUESTIONS WITH *BE* AND *DO*

Q-WORD	+ *BE*	+ SUBJECT		LONG ANSWER
(a) Where	*is*	Thailand?	→	Thailand *is* in Southeast Asia.
(b) Where	*are*	your books?	→	My books *are* on my desk.
(c) When	*is*	the concert?	→	The concert *is* on April 3rd.
(d) What	*is*	your name?	→	My name *is* Yoko.
(e) What time	*is*	it?	→	It *is* ten-thirty.

Q-WORD	+ *DO*	+ SUBJECT	+ MAIN VERB	LONG ANSWER
(f) Where	*do*	you	*live?*	→ I *live* in Los Angeles.
(g) What time	*does*	the plane	*arrive?*	→ The plane *arrives* at six-fifteen.
(h) What	*do*	monkeys	*eat?*	→ Monkeys *eat* fruit, plants, and insects.
(i) When	*does*	Bob	*study?*	→ Bob *studies* in the evenings.

NOTICE: In questions with *be* as the main and only verb, the subject follows *be*. In simple present questions with verbs other than *be*, the subject comes between *do/does* and the main verb.

□ EXERCISE 37. Question practice.

> *Directions:* Complete the questions in the written conversations. Use *is*, *are*, *does*, or *do*.

CONVERSATION ONE

A: What time _____*does*_____ the movie start?
                   1

B: Seven-fifteen. _____ you want to go with us?
                         2

A: Yes. What time _____ it now?
                          3

B: Almost seven o'clock. _____ you ready to leave?
                                4

A: Yes, let's go.

CONVERSATION TWO

A: Where _____ my keys to the car?
   ₅

B: I don't know. Where _____ you usually keep them?
   ₆

A: In my purse. But they're not there.
B: Are you sure?

A: Yes. _____ you see them?
   ₇

B: No. _____ they in one of your pockets?
   ₈

A: I don't think so.

B: _____ your husband have them?
   ₉

A: No. He has his own set of car keys.
B: Well, I hope you find them.
A: Thanks.

CONVERSATION THREE

A: _____ you go to school?
   ₁₀

B: Yes.

A: _____ your brother go to school too?
   ₁₁

B: No. He quit school last semester. He has a job now.

A: _____ it a good job?
   ₁₂

B: Not really.

A: Where _____ he work?
   ₁₃

B: At a restaurant. He washes dishes.

A: _____ he live with you?
   ₁₄

B: No, he lives with my parents.

A: _____ your parents unhappy that he quit school?
   ₁₅

B: They're very unhappy about it.

A: _____ they want him to return to school?
   ₁₆

B: Of course. They have many dreams for him and his future.

☐ EXERCISE 38. Let's talk: small group activity.

Directions: Work in small groups. Complete the sentences with *is, are, do,* or *does*.
Circle if the answer is *yes* or *no*. Discuss your answers with your classmates. If you
don't know the answer, guess.

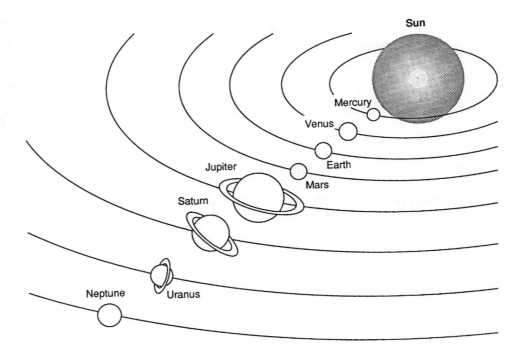

1. ___Does___ the moon go around the earth?   yes   no

2. _____ the sun go around the earth?   yes   no

3. _____ the planets go around the sun?   yes   no

4. _____ the sun a planet?   yes   no

5. _____ stars planets?   yes   no

6. _____ Venus hot?   yes   no

7. _____ Neptune easy to see?   yes   no

8. _____ Jupiter windy?   yes   no

9. _____ Venus and Mars go around the sun?   yes   no

10. _____ Saturn and Uranus have moons?   yes   no

Directions: Complete the questions and answers with your own words.

1. A: Do _____?
   B: No, I don't.

2. A: Where are _____?
   B: I don't know.

3. A: What time does _____?
   B: _____.

4. A: When do _____?
   B: _____.

5. A: Is _____?
   B: _____.

6. A: What is _____?
   B: _____.

7. A: Are _____?
   B: _____.

8. A: What are _____?
   B: _____.

9. A: What do _____?
   B: _____.

10. A: What does _____?
    B: _____.

□ EXERCISE 40. Chapter review.

Directions: Add *-s* or *-es* where necessary.

ABDUL AND PABLO

s (lives = live + /z/)

(1) My friend Abdul live⌃ in an apartment near school. (2) He walk to school almost every day. (3) Sometimes he catch a bus, especially if it's cold and rainy outside. (4) Abdul share the apartment with Pablo. (5) Pablo come from Venezuela.

(6) Abdul and Pablo go to the same school. (7) They take English classes.

(8) Abdul speak Arabic as his first language, and Pablo speak Spanish. (9) They communicate in English. (10) Sometimes Abdul try to teach Pablo to speak a little Arabic, and Pablo give Abdul Spanish lessons. (11) They laugh a lot during the Arabic and Spanish lessons. (12) Abdul enjoy having Pablo as his roommate, but he miss his family back in Saudi Arabia.

□ EXERCISE 41. Chapter review: pairwork.
Directions: Work with a partner.

PART I.
Partner A: Ask Partner B five questions about things s/he has and doesn't have (for example, a car, a computer, a pet, children, a TV set, a briefcase, etc.). Take notes.
Partner B: Answer the questions.

Example:
PARTNER A: Do you have a car?
PARTNER B: No.
PARTNER A: Do you have a computer?
PARTNER B: Yes, but it's not here. It's in my country.
Etc.

Switch roles. (Partner B now asks five questions.)

PART II.
Partner B: Ask Partner A five questions about things s/he likes and doesn't like (for example, kinds of food and drink, music, movies, books, etc.)
Partner A: Answer the questions.

Example:
PARTNER B: Do you like pizza?
PARTNER A: Yes.
PARTNER B: Do you like the music of *(name of a group or singer)?*
PARTNER A: No, I don't.
Etc.

PART III. Write about your partner. The vocabulary on the next page can help you.
- Give a physical description.
- Write about things this person has and doesn't have.
- Write about things this person likes and doesn't like.

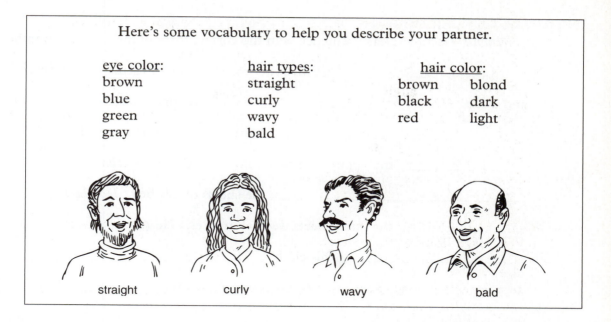

Here's some vocabulary to help you describe your partner.

eye color:	hair types:	hair color:	
brown	straight	brown	blond
blue	curly	black	dark
green	wavy	red	light
gray	bald		

straight   curly   wavy   bald

□ EXERCISE 42. Chapter review: question practice.

Directions: Complete the questions and answers with the words in parentheses. Use the simple present of the verbs.

A: *(you, study)* _____ a lot?
                          1

B: I *(study)* _____ at least three hours every night. My roommate
                    2

(study) _____ at least five hours. She's very serious about her
              3

education. How about you? *(you, spend)* _____ a lot of
                                                    4

time studying?

A: No, I don't. I *(spend)* _____ as little time as possible. I
                                5

(like, not) _____ to study.
                  6

B: Then why *(you, be)* _____ a student?
                              7

A: My parents *(want)* _____ me to go to school. I *(want, not)*
                            8

_____ to be here.
        9

B: In that case, I *(think)* _____ that you should drop out of
                                10

school and find a job until you decide what you want to do with your life.

□ EXERCISE 43. Chapter review.

Directions: Complete each sentence with the correct form of the verb in parentheses.

I *(have)* _____ two roommates. One of them, Sam, is always neat

            1

and clean. He *(wash)* _____ his clothes once a week. *(you, know)*

                       2

_____ Matt, my other roommate? He *(be)*

            3

_____ the opposite of Sam. For example, Matt *(change, not)*

    4

_____ the sheets on his bed. He *(keep)*

        5

_____ the same sheets week after week. He *(wash, never)*

   6

_____ his clothes. He *(wear)* _____ the same

    7   8

dirty jeans every day. Sam's side of the room *(be, always)* _____

                                            9

neat, and Matt's side *(be, always)* _____ a mess. As my mother

                            10

always *(say)* _____, it *(take)* _____ all kinds of people to

           11   12

make a world.

Sam's side   Matt's side

□ EXERCISE 44. Chapter review: let's talk.

Directions: Work with a partner.

PART I. Complete the conversations.

1. PARTNER A: Do you ____?

   PARTNER B: Yes, I do. How about you? Do you ____?

   PARTNER A: ____.

2. PARTNER B: Are you ____?

   PARTNER A: Yes, I am. How about you? Are you ____?

   PARTNER B: ____.

3. PARTNER A: ____ you usually ____ in the morning?

   PARTNER B: ____.

   PARTNER A: When ____?

   PARTNER B: ____.

4. PARTNER B: _____?
   PARTNER A: Yes, I do.
   PARTNER B: _____?
   PARTNER A: No, he doesn't.
   PARTNER B: _____?
   PARTNER A: Yes, I am.
   PARTNER B: _____?
   PARTNER A: No, he isn't.

PART II. Share one or two of your dialogues with the class.

□ EXERCISE 45. Chapter review.
   Directions: Make questions. Use your own words.

1. A: _____?
   B: No, I don't.

2. A: _____?
   B: Yes, I am.

3. A: _____?
   B: In an apartment.

4. A: _____?
   B: Six-thirty.

5. A: _____?
   B: Monday.

6. A: _____?
   B: At home.

7. A: _____?
   B: No, he doesn't.

8. A: _____?
   B: No, she isn't.

9. A: _____?
   B: South of the United States.

10. A: _____?
    B: Yes, it is.

11. A: _____?
    B: Yes, they do.

12. A: _____?

   B: In Southeast Asia.

13. A: _____?

   B: Hot in the summer.

14. A: _____?

   B: September.

15. A: _____?

   B: Yes, I do.

□ **EXERCISE 46. Chapter review: let's talk.**

Directions: Which lifestyle do you like the most? Ask your teacher questions to get more information about them. Then decide which you like best and explain why.

Example:
SPEAKER A: Where does Peter live?
TEACHER: On a boat.
SPEAKER B: What does Kathy do?
TEACHER: She teaches skiing.
SPEAKER C: Where does Ron work?
TEACHER: At a jewelry store.
SPEAKER D: What pets does Lisa have?
TEACHER: She has a snake.

Continue asking questions until your chart is complete.

Name	Where does she/he live?	What does he/she do?	Where does she/he work?	What pets does he/she have?
PETER	*on a boat*			
KATHY		*teaches skiing*		
RON			*at a jewelry store*	
LISA				*a snake*
JACK				

□ EXERCISE 47. Chapter review: error analysis.

Directions: Correct the errors.

       lives

1. Yoko ~~live~~ in Japan.

2. Ann comes usually to class on time.

3. Peter use his cell phone often.

4. Amy carry a notebook computer to work every day.

5. She enjoy her job.

6. I no know Joe.

7. Mike don't like milk. He never drink it.

8. Tina doesn't speaks Chinese. She speakes Spanish.

9. You a student?

10. Does your roommate sleeps with the window open?

11. A: Do you like strong coffee?

    B: Yes, I like.

12. Where your parents live?

13. What time is your English class begins?

14. Olga isn't need a car. She have a bicycle.

15. Do Pablo does his homework every day?

CHAPTER 4
Using the Present Progressive

4-1 *BE* + *-ING:* THE PRESENT PROGRESSIVE TENSE

am + *-ing*	(a) I ***am sitting*** in class right now.	In (a): When I say this sentence, I am in class. I am sitting. I am not standing. The action (sitting) is happening right now, and I am saying the sentence at the same time.
is + *-ing*	(b) Rita ***is sitting*** in class right now.	
are + *-ing*	(c) You ***are sitting*** in class right now.	
		am, **is**, **are** = helping verbs ***sitting*** = *the main verb*
		am, ***is***, ***are*** + ***-ing*** = the present progressive tense★

★The present progressive is also called the "present continuous" or the "continuous present."

☐ **EXERCISE 1. Let's talk: class activity.**

Directions: Your teacher will perform and describe some actions. Listen for the form of the verb. Answer questions about these actions.

Example: read
TEACHER: *(pantomimes reading)* I am reading. What am I doing?
STUDENT: You are reading.

1. write
2. sit
3. stand
4. count
5. wave
6. look at the ceiling

☐ **EXERCISE 2. Let's talk: pairwork.**

Directions: Work with a partner. What are the animals in the following pictures doing?
Partner A: Choose any picture and describe the activity. Use the present progressive (***is*** + ***-ing***).
Partner B: Point to the picture described by your partner.

Example: horse

PARTNER A: The horse is sleeping.

PARTNER B: *(points to the horse in the picture)*

PARTNER A: Your turn now.

Animals		Actions	
bird	*mouse*	*drink a cup of tea*	*play the piano*
cat	*horse*	*drive a car*	*read a newspaper*
dog	*monkey*	*eat a carrot*	*sleep*
elephant	*rabbit*	*sing*	*take a bath*
giraffe	*tiger*	*paint a picture*	*talk on the phone*

☐ EXERCISE 3. Let's talk: class activity.

Directions: Answer questions about what you are wearing today and what your classmates are wearing. Use the present progressive (*am/is/are* + *wearing*).

Example:
  TEACHER: Rosa, what are you wearing today?
  SPEAKER A: I'm wearing a white blouse and a blue skirt.
  TEACHER: What is Jin Won wearing?
  SPEAKER A: He's wearing jeans and a sweatshirt.
  TEACHER: What color is his sweatshirt?
  SPEAKER A: It's gray with red letters.
  TEACHER: What else is Jin Won wearing?
  SPEAKER B: He's wearing sneakers, white socks, and a wristwatch.
Etc.

☐ EXERCISE 4. Let's talk: pairwork.

Directions: Work with a partner. Identify who is wearing particular articles of clothing. If no one is wearing that piece of clothing, say "no one."

Example:
PARTNER A: brown shoes
PARTNER B: Marco is wearing brown shoes. OR
          Marco and Abdul are wearing brown shoes. OR
          No one is wearing brown shoes.
PARTNER A: Your turn now.

Partner A	Partner B
1. a T-shirt	1. a white shirt
2. blue jeans	2. a skirt (or dress)
3. earrings	3. a necklace
4. boots	4. running shoes
5. pants	5. a belt

☐ EXERCISE 5. Let's talk: class activity.

Directions: Act out the directions the teacher gives you. Describe the actions using the present progressive. Continue the action during the description. Close your books for this activity.

Example: Smile.
  TEACHER: *(Student A),* please smile. What are you doing?
  SPEAKER A: I'm smiling.

TEACHER: *(Speaker A)* and *(Speaker B)*, please smile. *(Speaker A)*, what are you and *(Speaker B)* doing?

SPEAKER A: We're smiling.

TEACHER: *(Speaker C)*, what are *(Speaker A and Speaker B)* doing?

SPEAKER C: They're smiling.

TEACHER: *(Speaker A)*, please smile. *(Speaker B)*, what is *(Speaker A)* doing?

SPEAKER B: He/She is smiling.

1. Stand up.
2. Sit down.
3. Stand in the middle of the room.
4. Sit in the middle of the room.
5. Stand in the back of the room.
6. Stand between (. . .) and (. . .).
7. Touch the floor.
8. Touch the ceiling.
9. Touch your toes.
10. Open/Close the door/window.
11. Speak in your native language.
12. Shake hands with (. . .).
13. Stand up and turn around in a circle.
14. Hold your book above your head.
15. Hold up your right hand.
16. Hold up your left hand.
17. Touch your right ear with your left hand.
18. Clap your hands.

□ EXERCISE 6. Let's talk: pairwork.

Directions: Work with a partner. Look around your classroom. Make sentences about people in the room. Use their names. You can use the verbs in the list to help you.

Example: the name of a student near you

PARTNER A: Maria is sitting near me.

PARTNER B: Yes. And she is talking to Po.

PARTNER A: Your turn now.

daydream	read	stand	watch
help	sit	talk	wear
listen	speak English	think in English	write

Partner A	Partner B
1. the name of the teacher	1. the name of a student near the door
2. the names of two classmates near you	2. the names of two classmates on the other side of the room
3. the name of a classmate	3. the names of three classmates
4. yourself *(Use "I.")*	4. yourself and your partner

□ **EXERCISE 7. Listening.**

Directions: Read the story. Then listen to each sentence and look at the picture of Tony. Circle the correct answers. Compare your answers with your classmates' answers.

Tony is not a serious student. He is lazy. He doesn't go to class much. He likes to sit in the cafeteria. Sometimes he sits alone, and sometimes he visits with friends from his country. He is in the cafeteria right now. What is he doing?

Example: Tony is talking on his cell phone. (yes) no

1. yes	no	6. yes	no
2. yes	no	7. yes	no
3. yes	no	8. yes	no
4. yes	no	9. yes	no
5. yes	no	10. yes	no

□ **EXERCISE 8. Pretest.**

Directions: Write the **-ing** form for the following words.

1. smile _____ *smiling* _____

2. ride _____

3. run _____

4. stop _____

5. rain _____

6. sleep _____

7. push _____

8. count _____

9. fix _____   fix

10. write _____

11. grow _____

12. wait _____

4-2 SPELLING OF -ING

	END OF VERB → -ING FORM
Rule 1	A CONSONANT★ + -e → DROP THE -e and ADD -ing smi**le** → smil**ing** wri**te** → writ**ing**
Rule 2	ONE VOWEL★ + ONE CONSONANT → DOUBLE THE CONSONANT and ADD -ing★★ s**it** → s**itting** r**un** → r**unning**
Rule 3	TWO VOWELS + ONE CONSONANT → ADD -ing; DO NOT DOUBLE THE CONSONANT r**ead** → r**eading** r**ain** → r**aining**
Rule 4	TWO CONSONANTS → ADD -ing; DO NOT DOUBLE THE CONSONANT sta**nd** → sta**nding** pu**sh** → pu**shing**

★Vowels = *a, e, i, o, u.*   Consonants = *b, c, d, f, g, h, j, k, l, m, n, p, q, r, s, t, v, w, x, y, z.*
★★Exception to Rule 2: Do not double *w, x,* and *y.*   *snow* → *snowing   fix* → *fixing   say* → *saying*

☐ EXERCISE 9. Spelling practice.

Directions: Write the **-ing** forms for the following words.

1. take   <u>   *taking*   </u>

2. come   _____

3. dream   _____

4. bite   _____

5. hit   _____

6. join   _____

7. hurt   _____

8. plan   _____

9. dine   _____

10. snow   _____

11. study   _____

12. warn   _____

□ EXERCISE 10. Spelling practice.

Directions: Your teacher will say a sentence. Write the word that ends in *-ing*.
Close your book for this activity.

Example: wave
TEACHER: I'm waving.
STUDENTS: *waving*

1. smile	9. eat
2. fly	10. run
3. laugh	11. sing
4. sit	12. read
5. stand	13. drink
6. sleep	14. sneeze
7. clap	15. cry
8. write	16. cut a piece of paper

□ EXERCISE 11. Let's talk: class activity.

Directions: Practice using the present progressive to describe actions. Your teacher
will give directions. One student acts out the directions, and another describes it.

Example: erase the board
  TEACHER: *(Student A),* please erase the board.
STUDENT A: *(erases the board)*
  TEACHER: What is *(Student A)* doing?
STUDENT B: He/She is erasing the board.

1. draw a picture on the board	11. tear a piece of paper
2. clap your hands	12. sing, hum, or whistle
3. walk around the room	13. sleep
4. wave at *(name of a student)*	14. snore
5. sign your name on the board	15. stand up and stretch
6. count your fingers out loud	16. sneeze
7. hit your desk with your hand	17. cough
8. carry your book on the top of your head to the front of the room	18. chew gum
9. bite your finger	19. hold your grammar book between your ankles
10. look at the ceiling	20. *(two students)* throw and catch *(something in the room)*

4-3 THE PRESENT PROGRESSIVE: NEGATIVES

(a) I **am not** sleeping. I am awake. (b) Ben **isn't** listening. He's daydreaming. (c) Mr. and Mrs. Brown **aren't** watching TV. They're reading.	Present progressive negative: *am* *is* $\Big\}$ + *not* + *-ing* *are*

Ben   Mr. and Mrs. Brown

☐ **EXERCISE 12. Sentence practice.**

Directions: Use the present progressive to make two sentences about each situation, one negative and one affirmative.

Example: Nancy: standing up /sitting down

Written: *Nancy isn't standing up.*

                She's sitting down.

1.

Otto: watching the news / talking on the phone

Otto isn't _____

He's _____

2.

Anita: listening to music / playing the piano

Anita _____

She's _____

3.

Sophia: reading a magazine / reading a book

Sophia _____

She's _____

4.

The birds: flying / sitting on a telephone wire

The birds _____

They're _____

□ **EXERCISE 13. Let's talk: pairwork.**

   Directions: Work with a partner. Make sentences about your classmates' activities right now. In the first sentence, describe what is not true. In the second sentence, describe what is true.

   Example:

Partner A	Partner B
1. not wearing a white shirt	1. not sitting near us

PARTNER A: Toshi is not wearing a white shirt. He's wearing a blue shirt. Your turn now.

PARTNER B: Olga is not sitting near us. She's sitting near the teacher. Your turn now.

Partner A	Partner B
1. not standing up	1. not writing
2. not holding a piece of chalk	2. not looking out the window
3. not talking to *(name of a classmate)*	3. not sitting on the floor
4. not wearing T-shirts	4. not standing next to each other *(names of classmates)*

□ **EXERCISE 14. Sentence practice.**

   Directions: Write the names of people you know. Write two sentences about each person. Write about
   (1) what they are doing right now and
   (2) what they are not doing right now.
   Use your own paper. Share a few of your sentences with the class.

   Example: your neighbor
   → *Mrs. Martinez is working at her office right now.*
   → *She is not working in her garden.*

   1. someone in your family
   2. the leader of your country
   3. your favorite actor, writer, or sports star
   4. a friend from childhood

4-4 THE PRESENT PROGRESSIVE: QUESTIONS

	QUESTION	→	SHORT ANSWER (+ LONG ANSWER)
	BE + SUBJECT + *-ING*		
(a)	**Is** Mary **sleeping?**	→ Yes, ***she is***. (She's sleeping.)
		→ No, ***she's not***. (She's not sleeping.)
		→ No, ***she isn't***. (She isn't sleeping.)
(b)	**Are** you **watching** TV?	→ Yes, ***I am***. (I'm watching TV.)
		→ No, ***I'm not***. (I'm not watching TV.)

	Q-WORD + *BE* + SUBJECT + *-ING*		
(c)	**Where** **is** Mary **sleeping?**	→ ***In bed***. (She's sleeping in bed.)
(d)	**What** **is** Ted **watching?**	→ ***A movie***. (Ted is watching a movie).
(e)	**Why** **are** you **watching** TV?	→ ***Because I like this program***. (I'm watching TV because I like this program.)

□ **EXERCISE 15. Question practice.**

Directions: Make questions.

1. ____*Is the teacher helping*_____ students?
   Yes, she is. (The teacher is helping students.)

2. _____?
   Yes, he is. (John is riding a bicycle.)

3. _____?
   No, I'm not. (I'm not sleeping.)

4. _____ TV?
   No, they aren't. (The students aren't watching TV.)

5. _____ outside?
   No, it isn't. (It isn't raining outside.)

a bicycle

□ **EXERCISE 16. Let's talk: pairwork.**

Directions: Work with a partner. You and your partner have different pictures.
Ask and answer questions about your partner's picture.
Partner A: Look at the pictures in Exercise 2, p. 93.
Partner B: Look at the pictures below. Find the differences.

Example:
PARTNER A: Is the rabbit eating a carrot in your picture?
PARTNER B: No, it isn't. It's eating an ice-cream cone.
PARTNER A: Your turn now.

Partner A	Partner B
1. Is the rabbit . . . ?	1. Is the elephant . . . ?
2. Is the cat . . . ?	2. Is the tiger . . . ?
3. Is the giraffe . . . ?	3. Is the monkey . . . ?
4. Is the horse . . . ?	4. Is the bird . . . ?
5. Is the dog . . . ?	5. Is the mouse . . . ?

☐ EXERCISE 17. Let's talk: small groups.

Directions: Work in small groups. Ask yes/no questions using the present progressive. Use the verbs in the list. Ask two questions for each verb: ***Are you ... ?*** and ***Is (name of a group member) ... ?*** Take turns asking questions.

Example: write
SPEAKER A: Are you writing?
SPEAKER B: Yes, I am. OR No, I'm not.
SPEAKER A: Is *(Speaker B)* writing?
SPEAKER C: Yes, she/he is. OR No, she's/he's not.
SPEAKER A: Your turn now, *(Speaker B)*.

1. sit
2. stand
3. smile
4. answer questions
5. sleep
6. speak English
7. look out the window
8. write in your/her/his book
9. talk to *(name of a classmate)*
10. ask me a question

☐ EXERCISE 18. Question practice.

Directions: Create questions with ***where, why,*** and ***what.***

1. A: _____*What are you reading?*_____
   B: My grammar book. (I'm reading my grammar book.)

2. A: _____
   B: Because we're doing an exercise. (I'm reading my grammar book because we're doing an exercise.)

3. A: _____
   B: A sentence in my grammar book. (I'm writing a sentence in my grammar book.)

4. A: _____
   B: In the back of the room. (Seung is sitting in the back of the room.)

5. A: _____
   B: In an apartment. (I'm living in an apartment.)

6. A: _____
   B: Jeans and a sweatshirt. (Roberto is wearing jeans and a sweatshirt today.)

7. A: _____
   B: Because I'm happy. (I'm smiling because I'm happy.)

□ **EXERCISE 19. Question practice.**

Directions: Make questions. Give short answers to yes/no questions.

1. A: What _____ *are you writing?* _____
   B: A letter. (I'm writing a letter.)

2. A: _____ *Is Ali reading a book?* _____

   B: No, _____ *he isn't/he's not.* _____ (Ali isn't reading a book.)

3. A: _____

   B: Yes, _____ (Anna is eating lunch.)

4. A: Where _____
   B: At the Red Bird Cafe. (She's eating lunch at the Red Bird Cafe.)

5. A: _____

   B: No, _____ (Mike isn't drinking a cup of coffee.)

6. A: What _____
   B: A cup of tea. (He's drinking a cup of tea.)

7. A: _____

   B: No, _____ (The girls aren't playing in the street.)

8. A: Where _____

    B: In the park. (They're playing in the park.)

9. A: Why _____

    B: Because they don't have school today. (They're playing in the park because they don't have school today.)

4-5   THE SIMPLE PRESENT vs. THE PRESENT PROGRESSIVE

STATEMENTS (a) I **sit** in class *every day.* (b) I **am sitting** in class *right now.* (c) The teacher **writes** on the board *every day.* (d) The teacher **is writing** on the board *right now.*	• The SIMPLE PRESENT expresses habits or usual activities, as in (a), (c), and (e). • The PRESENT PROGRESSIVE expresses actions that are happening right now, while the speaker is speaking, as in (b), (d), and (f).
QUESTIONS (e) **Do** you **sit** in class every day? (f) **Are** you **sitting** in class right now? (g) **Does** the teacher **write** on the board every day? (h) **Is** the teacher **writing** on the board right now?	• The SIMPLE PRESENT uses **do** and **does** as helping verbs in questions. • The PRESENT PROGRESSIVE uses **am, is,** and **are** in questions.
NEGATIVES (i) I **don't sit** in class every day. (j) I**'m not sitting** in class right now. (k) The teacher **doesn't write** on the board every day. (l) The teacher **isn't writing** on the board right now.	• The SIMPLE PRESENT uses **do** and **does** as helping verbs in negatives. • The PRESENT PROGRESSIVE uses **am, is,** and **are** in negatives.

□ **EXERCISE 20. Sentence practice.**

Directions: Complete the sentences with the words in parentheses.

1. Ahmed *(talk)* _____*talks*_____ to his classmates every day in class. Right now

   he *(talk)* _____ to Yoko. He *(talk, not)* _____

   _____ to his friend Omar right now.

2. It *(rain)* _____ a lot in this city, but it *(rain, not)* _____

   _____ right now. The sun *(shine)* _____.

   (it, rain) _____ a lot in your hometown?

3. Hans and Anna *(sit)* _____ next to each other in class every day, so they

   often *(help)* _____ each other with their grammar exercises. Right now

   Anna *(help)* _____ Hans with an exercise on present verb

   tenses.

4. Roberto *(cook)* _____ his own dinner every evening. Right now he is

   in his kitchen. He *(cook)* _____ rice and beans. *(he, cook)*

   _____ meat for his dinner tonight too? No, he is a

   vegetarian. He *(eat, not)* _____ meat. *(you, eat)* _____

   _____ meat? *(you, be)* _____ a vegetarian?

□ **EXERCISE 21. Listening.**

Directions: Listen to the sentences. Circle the correct completions.

Examples: John sleeps late . . . .   now   (every day)
            John is sleeping . . . .   (now)   every day

1. now	every day		5. now	every day
2. now	every day		6. now	every day
3. now	every day		7. now	every day
4. now	every day		8. now	every day

□ **EXERCISE 22. Let's talk: pairwork.**

Directions: Work with a partner. Take turns asking and answering questions about Anna's activities. Use the present progressive and the simple present.

Example: read a newspaper
PARTNER A: Is Anna reading a newspaper?
PARTNER B: Yes, she is.
PARTNER A: Does she read a newspaper every day?
PARTNER B: Yes, she does.
PARTNER A: Your turn now.

drink tea	*ride her bicycle*	*talk on the phone*
listen to music	*say "hello" to her neighbor*	*watch TV*
play tennis	*swim*	
play the guitar	*take a walk*	

□ **EXERCISE 23. Sentence practice.**

Directions: Complete the sentences. Use words from the list.

am	*is*	*are*	*do*	*does*

1. _____ you ready? The bus _____ leaving right now.

2. _____ you have enough money for the bus?

3. Oh, no. It _____ raining again. _____ it rain often in this city?

4. Excuse me, what time _____ you have?

5. No one is here. _____ I early or late?

6. I _____ looking for the registration office. _____ you know

   where it is?

7. When _____ the registration office close?

8. Where _____ your school?

9. Where _____ you live?

10. _____ your classmates live near you?

□ EXERCISE 24. Question practice.

    Directions: Complete the sentences with the words in parentheses.

1. A: Tom is on the phone.
   B: *(he, talk)* _____*Is he talking*___ to his wife?
   A: Yes.
   B: *(he, talk)* ____*Does he talk*_____ to her often?
   A: Yes, he *(talk)* _____*talks*_____to her every day during his lunch break.

2. A: I *(walk)* _____ to school every day. I *(take, not)* _____
      _____ the bus. *(you, take)* _____ the bus?
   B: No, I don't.

3. A: Anna is in the hallway.
   B: *(she, talk)* _____ to her friends?
   A: No, she isn't. She *(run)* _____ to her next class.

4. A: I *(read)* _____ the newspaper every day.
   B: How about your grammar book? *(you, read)* _____
      your grammar book every day?
   A: No, I don't. I *(read, not)* _____ my grammar book
      every day.

5. A: What *(you, read)* _____ right now?
   B: I *(read)* _____ my grammar book.

6. A: (you, want) _____ your coat?

   B: Yes.

   A: (be, this) _____ your coat?

   B: No, my coat (hang) _____ in the closet.

☐ **EXERCISE 25. Listening.**

Directions: Listen to each conversation. Complete the sentences with the words you hear.

Example:

You will hear: Is Ann here today?

You will write: _____*Is*_____ Ann here today?

You will hear: No. She's working at her uncle's bakery today.

You will write: No. _____*She's working*_____ at her uncle's bakery today.

1. A: _____ Tom _____ a black hat?

   B: Yes.

   A: _____ it every day?

   B: No.

   A: _____ it right now?

   B: I _____. Why do you care about Tom's hat?

   A: I found a hat in my apartment. Someone left it there. I _____ that it belongs to Tom.

2. A: _____ animals _____?

   B: I don't know. I suppose so. Animals _____ very different from human beings in lots of ways.

   A: Look at my dog. She _____. Her eyes _____ closed. At the same time, she _____ and _____ her head and her front legs. I _____ sure that she _____ right now. I'm sure that animals _____.

Directions: Listen to the conversation. Complete the sentences with the words you hear.

Example:

You will hear: Are you doing an exercise?

You will write: _____*Are you doing*_____ an exercise?

You will hear: Yes, I am.

You will write: Yes, _____*I am*_____.

SPEAKER A: What are you doing? _____ on your English paper?

SPEAKER B: No, _____. _____ an e-mail to my sister.

SPEAKER A: _____ to her often?

SPEAKER B: Yes, but I _____ a lot of e-mails to anyone else.

SPEAKER A: _____ to you often?

SPEAKER B: Yes. I _____ an e-mail from her several times a week.

How about you? _____ a lot of e-mails?

SPEAKER A: Yes. I _____ to send e-mails to friends all over the world.

4-6 NONACTION VERBS NOT USED IN THE PRESENT PROGRESSIVE

(a) I'm hungry *right now*. I *want* an apple. *INCORRECT: I am wanting an apple.* (b) I *hear* a siren. *Do* you *hear* it too? *INCORRECT: I'm hearing a siren. Are you hearing it too?*	Some verbs are NOT used in the present progressive. They are called "nonaction verbs." In (a): *Want* is a nonaction verb. *Want* expresses a physical or emotional need, not an action. In (b): *Hear* is a nonaction verb. *Hear* expresses a sensory experience, not an action.

NONACTION VERBS

dislike	*hear*	*believe*
hate	*see*	*know*
like	*smell*	*think* (meaning *believe*)★
love	*taste*	*understand*
need		
want		

★Sometimes *think* is used in progressive tenses. See Chart 4-8, p. 117, for a discussion of *think about* and *think that*.

□ EXERCISE 27. Sentence practice.

Directions: Use the words in parentheses to complete the sentences. Use the simple present or the present progressive.

1. Alice is in her room right now. She *(read)* _____*is reading*_____ a book. She *(like)*

   _____*likes*_____ the book.

2. It *(snow)* _____ right now. It's beautiful! I *(like)*

   _____ this weather.

3. I *(know)* _____ Jessica Jones. She's in my class.

4. The teacher *(talk)* _____ to us right now. I *(understand)*

   _____ everything she's saying.

5. Mike is at a restaurant right now. He *(eat)* _____ dinner.

   He *(like)* _____ the food. It *(taste)* _____ good.

6. Sniff-sniff. I *(smell)* _____ gas. *(you, smell)* _____

   _____ it too?

7. Jason *(tell)* _____ us a story right now. I *(believe)*

   _____ his story. I *(think)* _____ that his story is true.

8. Ugh! Someone *(smoke)* _____ a cigar. It *(smell)*

   _____ terrible! I *(hate)* _____ cigars.

9. Look at Mr. Allen. He *(hold)* _____ a kitten in his hand.

   He *(love)* _____ the kitten. Mr. Allen *(smile)*

   _____ .

□ EXERCISE 28. Let's talk: interview.

Directions: Ask two students each question. Write their answers in the chart. Share some of their answers with the class.

Question	Student A	Student B
1. What \ you \ like?		
2. What \ babies \ around the world \ like?		
3. What \ you \ want?		
4. What \ children around the world \ want?		
5. What \ you \ love?		
6. What \ teenagers around the world \ love?		
7. What \ you \ dislike or hate?		
8. What \ people around the world \ dislike or hate?		
9. What \ you \ need?		
10. What \ elderly people around the world \ need?		

4-7   SEE, LOOK AT, WATCH, HEAR, AND LISTEN TO

SEE, LOOK AT, and *WATCH* (a) I **see** many things in this room.	In (a): **see** = a nonaction verb. Seeing happens because my eyes are open. Seeing is a physical reaction, not a planned action.
(b) I'**m looking** at the clock. I want to know the time.	In (b): **look at** = an action verb. Looking is a planned or purposeful action. Looking happens for a reason.
(c) Bob **is watching** TV.	In (c): **watch** = an action verb. I *watch* something for a long time, but I *look at* something for a short time.
HEAR and *LISTEN TO* (d) I'm in my apartment. I'm trying to study. I **hear** music from the next apartment. The music is loud.	In (d): **hear** = a nonaction verb. Hearing is an unplanned act. It expresses a physical reaction.
(e) I'm in my apartment. I'm studying. I have a tape recorder. I'**m listening to** music. I like to listen to music when I study.	In (e): **listen (to)** = an action verb. Listening happens for a purpose.

☐ EXERCISE 29. Let's talk: class activity.

Directions: Your teacher will ask you questions. Your book is closed.

Example:
TEACHER: Look at the floor. What do you see?
SPEAKER: I see shoes/dirt/etc.

1. What do you see in this room? Now look at something. What are you looking at?

2. Turn to p. 103 of this book. What do you see? Now look at one thing on that page. What are you looking at?

3. Look at the chalkboard. What do you see?

4. What programs do you like to watch on TV?

5. What sports do you like to watch?

6. What animals do you like to watch when you go to the zoo?

7. What do you hear at night in the place where you live?

8. What do you listen to when you go to a concert?

9. What do you listen to when you are at home?

Directions: Complete the sentences with the words in parentheses. Use the simple present or the present progressive.

1. I *(sit)* _____*am sitting*_____ in class right now. I *(sit, always)*

    _____*always sit*_____ in the same seat every day.

2. Ali *(speak)* _____ Arabic, but right now he *(speak)*

    _____ English.

3. Right now we *(do)* _____ an exercise in class. We *(do)*

    _____ exercises in class every day.

4. I'm in class now. I *(look)* _____ at my classmates. Kim

    (write) _____ in his book. Francisco *(look)* _____

    _____ out the window. Yoko *(bite)* _____

    _____ her pencil. Abdullah *(smile)* _____.

    Maria *(sleep)* _____. Jung-Po *(chew)* _____

    _____ gum.

5. The person on the bench in the picture on p. 116 is Barbara. She's an accountant.

    She *(work)* _____ for the government. She *(have)* _____ an

    hour for lunch every day. She *(eat, often)* _____ lunch in

    the park. She *(bring, usually)* _____ a sandwich and

    some fruit with her to the park. She *(sit, usually)* _____

    on a bench, but sometimes she *(sit)* _____ on the grass. While she's at the

    park, she *(watch)* _____ people and animals. She *(watch)*

    _____ joggers and squirrels. She *(relax)* _____

    when she eats at the park.

6. Right now I (look) _____ at a picture of Barbara. She (be, not)

_____ at home in the picture. She (be) _____ at the park.

She (sit) _____ on a bench. She (eat) _____

_____ her lunch. A jogger (run) _____

on a path through the park. A squirrel (sit) _____ on the

ground in front of Barbara. The squirrel (eat) _____ a nut.

Barbara (watch) _____ the squirrel. She (watch, always)

_____ squirrels when she eats lunch in the park.

Some ducks (swim) _____ in the pond in the picture,

and some birds (fly) _____ in the sky. A police officer

(ride) _____ a horse. He (ride) _____ a

horse through the park every day. Near Barbara, a family (have) _____

_____ a picnic. They (go) _____ on a picnic every

week.

4-8 THINK ABOUT AND THINK THAT

(a) I **think** THINK + ABOUT about + A NOUN **my family** every day. (b) I **am thinking** about **grammar** right now.	In (a): Ideas about my family are in my mind every day. In (b) My mind is busy now. Ideas about grammar are in my mind right now.
(c) I **think** THINK + THAT that + A STATEMENT **Sue is lazy.** (d) Sue **thinks** that **I am lazy.** (e) I **think** that **the weather is nice.**	In (c): In my opinion, Sue is lazy. I believe that Sue is lazy. People use **think that** when they want to say (to state) their beliefs. The present progressive is often used with **think about**. The present progressive is almost never used with **think that**. INCORRECT: *I am thinking that Sue is lazy.*
(f) I **think that** Mike is a nice person. (g) I **think** Mike is a nice person.	(f) and (g) have the same meaning. People often omit **that** after **think**, especially in speaking.

☐ **EXERCISE 31. Sentence practice.**

Directions: Use **I think (that)** to give your opinion. Share a few of your opinions with the class.

1. English grammar is easy / hard / fun / interesting. ___*I think (that)*___

   ___*English grammar is*_____

2. People in this city are friendly / unfriendly / kind / cold.

   _____

3. The food at *(name of a place)* is delicious / terrible / good / excellent / awful.

   _____

4. Baseball / football / soccer / golf is interesting / boring / confusing / etc.

   _____

☐ **EXERCISE 32. Sentence practice.**

Directions: Make sentences.

PART I. Complete the sentences with your own words.

1. I think that the weather today is _____

2. I think my classmates are _____

3. Right now I'm thinking about _____

4. In my opinion, English grammar is _____

5. In my opinion, soccer is _____

6. I think that my parents are _____

7. I think this school _____

8. I think about _____

9. I think that _____

10. In my opinion, _____

PART II. Share a few of your completions with the class.

☐ **EXERCISE 33. Let's talk: small groups.**

Directions: Work in small groups. Take turns stating an opinion about each of the following topics.

Example: books
Response: I think that *War and Peace* is an excellent novel. OR
           In my opinion, *War and Peace* is an excellent novel.

1. this city

2. your English classes

3. music

4. movies

5. cars

6. the food in this country

7. the weather in this area

8. a current local, national, or international news story

☐ **EXERCISE 34. Chapter review.**

Directions: Choose the correct completions.

1. Anita and Pablo _____ TV right now.
   A. watch   B. watching   C. are watching

2. "_____ you writing a letter to your parents?"
   "No. I'm studying."
   A. Do   B. Are   C. Don't

3. I _____ like to write letters.
   A. no   B. am not   C. don't

4. "Jack has six telephones in his apartment."
   "I _____ you. No one needs six telephones in one apartment."
   A. am believe   B. am not believing C. don't believe

5. When I want to know the time, I _____ a clock.
   A. see   B. look at   C. watch

6. "Do you know Fatima?"
   "Yes, I do. I _____ she is a very nice person."
   A. am thinking   B. thinking   C. think

7. Where _____ John? Upstairs or downstairs?
   A. does   B. is   C. lives

8. Oh no. Ron _____. He is allergic to cats.
   A. is sneezing   B. doesn't sneeze   C. sneezes

9. The teacher often _____ on time.
   A. doesn't start B. isn't starting   C. don't start

10. "You look sad."
    "Yes, I _____ about my family back in my country. I miss them."
    A. think   B. am thinking   C. thinking

☐ **EXERCISE 35. Chapter review: error analysis.**

Directions: Correct the errors.

1. It's rainning today. I no like the rain.

2. I like New York City. I am thinking that it is a wonderful city.

3. Does Abdul be sleeping right now?

4. Why you are going downtown today?

5. I'm listening you.

6. Are you hearing a noise outside the window?

7. Kunio at a restaurant right now. He usually eat at home, but today he eatting dinner at a restaurant.

8. I am liking flowers. They are smelling good.

9. Alex is siting at his desk. He writting a letter.

10. Where do they are sitting today?

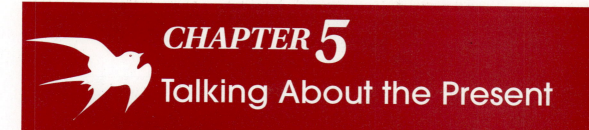

CHAPTER 5
Talking About the Present

☐ **EXERCISE 1.   Preview: listening.**

🎧 *Directions:* Write the answers to the questions.

Example:

You will hear: What time is it?

You will write: It's _____ *10:10 A.M. / around ten o'clock / etc.* _____ .

1. It's _____ .

2. It's _____ .

3. It's _____ .

4. It's _____ .

5. It's _____ .

5-1   USING *IT* TO TALK ABOUT TIME

QUESTION		ANSWER	
(a) What day is it?	→	*It's* Monday.	In English, people use *it* to express (to talk about) time.
(b) What month is it?	→	*It's* September.	
(c) What year is it?	→	*It's* 2 _____ .	
(d) What's the date today?	→	*It's* September 15th.	
	→	*It's* the 15th of September.	
(e) What time is it?	→	*It's* 9:00.★	
	→	*It's* nine.	
	→	*It's* nine o'clock.	
	→	*It's* nine (o'clock) A.M.	

★American English uses a colon (two dots) between the hour and the minutes: 9:00 A.M. British English uses one dot: 9.00 A.M.

Directions: Make questions. Begin each question with ***What***.

1. A: _____*What day is it?*_____

   B: It's Tuesday.

2. A: _____

   B: It's March 14th.

3. A: _____

   B: Ten-thirty.

4. A: _____

   B: March.

5. A: _____

   B: It's six-fifteen.

6. A: _____

   B: Wednesday.

7. A: _____

   B: The 1st of April, 2 _____.

8. A: _____

   B: It's two thousand and _____.

9. A: _____

   B: It's seven A.M.

Sun	Mon	Tues	Wed	Thurs	Fri	Sat
				1	2	3
4	5	6	7	8	9	10
11	12	13	14	15	16	17
18	19	20	21	22	23	24
25	26	27	28	29	30	31

a calendar page

5-2 PREPOSITIONS OF TIME

at	(a) We have class *at* one o'clock. (b) I have an appointment with the doctor *at* 3:00. (c) We sleep *at* night.	*at* + a specific time on the clock. *at* + *night*
in	(d) My birthday is *in* October. (e) I was born *in* 1989. (f) We have class *in* the morning. (g) Bob has class *in* the afternoon. (h) I study *in* the evening.	*in* + a specific month *in* + a specific year *in* + *the morning* *in* + *the afternoon* *in* + *the evening*
on	(i) I have class *on* Monday. (j) I was born *on* October 31, 1991.	*on* + a specific day of the week *on* + a specific date
from ... to	(k) We have class *from* 1:00 *to* 2:00.	*from* (a specific time) *to* (a specific time)

□ **EXERCISE 3. Sentence practice.**

Directions: Complete the sentences with prepositions of time.

1. We have class ___*at*___ ten o'clock.

2. We have class _____ ten _____ eleven.

3. I have class _____ the morning, and I work _____ the afternoon.

4. I study _____ the evening.

5. I sleep _____ night.

6. I was born _____ May.

7. I was born _____ 1988.

8. I was born _____ May 21.

9. I was born _____ May 21, 1988.

10. The post office isn't open _____ Sundays.

11. The post office is open _____ 8:00 A.M. _____ 5:00 P.M. Monday through Saturday.

12. The post office closes _____ 5:00 P.M.

☐ EXERCISE 4. Listening and sentence practice.

Directions: Identify the people in the pictures.

PART I. Listen to each description. Write the name of the person who is described.

Example:
You will hear: I was born on June 2, 1986. I go to class in the morning.
           My name is _____.
You will write: ___*Lisa*___

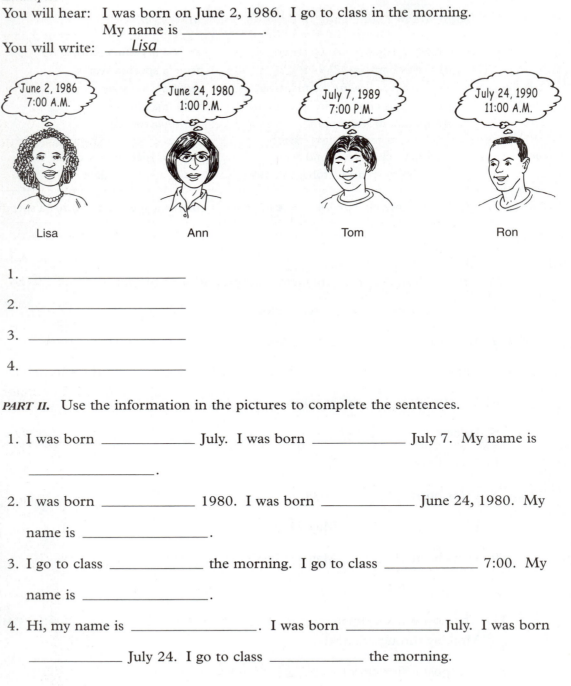

1. _____

2. _____

3. _____

4. _____

PART II. Use the information in the pictures to complete the sentences.

1. I was born _____ July. I was born _____ July 7. My name is

   _____.

2. I was born _____ 1980. I was born _____ June 24, 1980. My

   name is _____.

3. I go to class _____ the morning. I go to class _____ 7:00. My

   name is _____.

4. Hi, my name is _____. I was born _____ July. I was born

   _____ July 24. I go to class _____ the morning.

5-3 USING *IT* TO TALK ABOUT THE WEATHER

(a) *It's* sunny today. (b) *It's* hot and humid today. (c) *It's* a nice day today.	In English, people usually use *it* when they talk about the weather.
(d) *What's the weather like* in Istanbul in January? (e) *How's the weather* in Moscow in the summer?	People commonly ask about the weather by saying *What's the weather like?* OR *How's the weather?*

☐ EXERCISE 5. Let's talk: pairwork.

Directions: How's the weather today? Circle *yes* or *no*. Share your answers with a partner. Do your answers agree? Report to the class.

1. hot	yes	no	8. sunny	yes	no
2. warm	yes	no	9. nice	yes	no
3. cool	yes	no	10. clear	yes	no
4. chilly	yes	no	11. partly cloudy	yes	no
5. cold	yes	no	12. humid★	yes	no
6. freezing	yes	no	13. windy	yes	no
7. below freezing	yes	no	14. stormy	yes	no

☐ EXERCISE 6. Let's talk: small groups.

Directions: Change the Fahrenheit (F) temperatures to Celsius (C) by choosing temperatures from the list. Then describe the temperature in words.

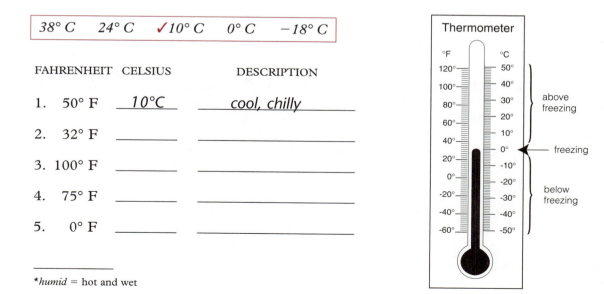

> *38° C   24° C   ✓10° C   0° C   −18° C*

FAHRENHEIT	CELSIUS	DESCRIPTION
1. 50° F	_10°C_	_cool, chilly_
2. 32° F	_____	_____
3. 100° F	_____	_____
4. 75° F	_____	_____
5. 0° F	_____	_____

──────────
★*humid* = hot and wet

□ EXERCISE 7. Let's talk: small groups.

Directions: Work in small groups. Read the chart and follow the instructions.

"Approximate" means "close but not exact." Here is a fast way to get an **approximate** number when you convert from one temperature system to another.*

- To change **Celsius to Fahrenheit**: DOUBLE THE CELSIUS NUMBER AND ADD 30.

  Examples: 12°C × 2 = 24 + 30 = 54°F. (Exact numbers: 12°C = 53.6°F.)
  20°C × 2 = 40 + 30 = 70°F. (Exact numbers: 20°C = 68°F.)
  35°C × 2 = 70 + 30 = 100°F. (Exact numbers: 35°C = 95°F.)

- To change **Fahrenheit to Celsius**: SUBTRACT 30 FROM THE FAHRENHEIT NUMBER AND THEN DIVIDE BY 2.

  Examples: 60°F − 30 = 30 ÷ 2 = 15°C. (Exact numbers: 60°F = 15.6°C.)
  80°F − 30 = 50 ÷ 2 = 25°C. (Exact numbers: 80°F = 26.7°C.)
  90°F − 30 = 60 ÷ 2 = 30°C. (Exact numbers: 90°F = 32.2°C.)

---

*To get exact numbers, use these formulas: C = 5/9 (°F − 32) OR F = 9/5 (°C) + 32.

Change the following from Celsius to Fahrenheit and Fahrenheit to Celsius. Calculate the **approximate** numbers.

1. 22°C → *22°C = approximately 74°F (22°C x 2 = 44 + 30 = 74°F)*

2.   2°C → _____

3. 30°C → _____

4. 10°C → _____

5. 16°C → _____

6. 45°F → _____

7. 70°F → _____

8. 58°F → _____

9. 100°F → _____

10. 20°F → _____

□ EXERCISE 8. Interview and paragraph practice.

Directions: Find out information about your classmates' hometowns. Use the information to write a report. Ask questions about *the name of the hometown, its location, its population, its weather and average temperature in a particular month (of your choosing)*.

Example:
SPEAKER A: What's your hometown?
SPEAKER B: Athens.
SPEAKER A: Where is it located?
SPEAKER B: In southeastern Greece near the Aegean Sea.
SPEAKER A: What's the population of Athens?
SPEAKER B: Almost four million.
SPEAKER A: What's the weather like in Athens in May?
SPEAKER B: It's mild. Sometimes it's a little rainy.
SPEAKER A: What's the average temperature in May?
SPEAKER B: The average temperature is around 21° Celsius.

Chart for recording information about three of your classmates' hometowns.

Name	Spyros			
Hometown	Athens			
Location	SE Greece			
Population	almost 4 million			
Weather	mild in May, around 21°C, in the mid-seventies Fahrenheit			

5-4 THERE + BE

THERE + BE + SUBJECT + PLACE
(a) **There**   **is**   **a bird**   in the tree.
(b) **There**   **are**   **four birds** in the tree.
	There + be is used to say that something exists in a particular place.
	Notice: The subject follows **be**:
	   there + is + singular noun
	   there + are + plural noun

(c) **There's** a bird in the tree.
(d) **There're** four birds in the tree.
	CONTRACTIONS:
	   there + is = there's
	   there + are = there're

☐ EXERCISE 9. Sentence practice.

Directions: Complete the sentences with **is** or **are**. Then circle *yes* or *no*. Compare your answers with your classmates' answers.

1. There _____*is*_____ a butterfly in this picture.   (yes)   no

2. There _____*are*_____ two trees in this picture.   yes   (no)

3. There _____ a bird in this picture.   yes   no

4. There _____ seven flowers in this picture.   yes   no

5. There _____ a grammar book on my desk.   yes   no

6. There _____ many grammar books in this room.   yes   no

7. There _____ comfortable chairs in this classroom.   yes   no

8. There _____ a nice view from the classroom window.   yes   no

9. There _____ interesting places to visit in this area.   yes   no

10. There _____ a good place to eat near school.   yes   no

11. There _____ fun activities to do on weekends in this area.   yes   no

12. There _____ difficult words in this exercise.   yes   no

☐ EXERCISE 10. Let's talk: pairwork.

Directions: Work with a partner. Complete the sentences with the words in the list or your own words. When you speak, look at your partner.

a book	*a map*	*a notebook*
some books	*some papers*	*some notebooks*
tall buildings	*a park*	*some restaurants*
a bulletin board	*a pen*	*a sink*
a calendar	*a pencil*	*many stores*
some chairs	*a pencil sharpener*	*several students*
a chalkboard	*many people*	*a teacher*
a clock	*a picture*	*a whiteboard*
a coffee shop	*some pictures*	*a window*
some desks	*a post office*	*some windows*
some light switches		

1. PARTNER A: There is . . . on this desk.
   PARTNER B: There are . . . on that desk.

2. PARTNER A: There are . . . on that wall.
   PARTNER B: There is . . . on this wall.

3. PARTNER A: There are . . . in this room.
   PARTNER B: There is also . . . in this room.

4. PARTNER A: There is . . . near our school.
   PARTNER B: There are also . . . near our school.

☐ EXERCISE 11. Let's talk: small groups.

Directions: Work in small groups. After everybody puts two or three objects (e.g., a coin, some keys, a pen, a dictionary) on a table in the classroom, describe the items on the table. Use ***There is . . . .*** and ***There are . . . .***

Examples:
SPEAKER A: There are three dictionaries on the table.
SPEAKER B: There are some keys on the table.
SPEAKER C: There is a pencil sharpener on the table.

☐ **EXERCISE 12. Listening.**

Directions: Listen to each sentence. Circle the word you hear. Note: You will hear contractions for *There is* and *There are*.

Example: _____ several windows in this room.   There's   (There're)

1. There's	There're	5. There's	There're
2. There's	There're	6. There's	There're
3. There's	There're	7. There's	There're
4. There's	There're	8. There's	There're

☐ **EXERCISE 13. Let's talk: small groups.**

Directions: Work in small groups. Choose a leader. Take turns making sentences. Begin your sentence with **There**.

Example:
     LEADER: . . . in this building.
SPEAKER A: There are five floors in this building.
SPEAKER B: There are many classrooms in this building.
SPEAKER C: There are stairs in this building.
     LEADER: There is an elevator in this building.
Etc.

1. . . . in my home.
2. . . . in this city.
3. . . . in my country.
4. . . . in the world.
5. . . . in the universe.

5-5   *THERE + BE:* YES/NO QUESTIONS

	QUESTION					SHORT ANSWER
	BE +	*THERE* +	SUBJECT			
(a) **Is**		**there**	**any juice**	in the refrigerator?	→	Yes, **there is**.
					→	No, **there isn't**.
(b) **Are**		**there**	**any eggs**	in the refrigerator?	→	Yes, **there are**.
					→	No, **there aren't**.

☐ EXERCISE 14. Let's talk: pairwork.

Directions: Work with a partner. Ask questions about the contents of the refrigerator in the picture. Use the nouns in the list in your questions.
Use **Is there . . . ?** or **Are there . . . ?**

Example:

PARTNER A: Is there any cheese in the refrigerator?
PARTNER B: Yes, there is.
PARTNER A: Your turn now.
PARTNER B: Are there any onions in the refrigerator?
PARTNER A: No, there aren't.
PARTNER B: Your turn now.

Partner A	Partner B
1. cheese	1. onions
2. eggs	2. strawberries
3. bread	3. oranges
4. apples	4. orange juice
5. butter	5. fruit
6. potatoes	6. flour
7. vegetables	7. pickles

☐ EXERCISE 15. Let's talk: small groups.

Directions: Work in small groups. Take turns asking and answering questions using **there + be.** Ask questions about this city. Use **Is there . . . ?** or **Are there . . . ?** If the answer is "I don't know," ask someone else.

Example: a zoo

SPEAKER A: Is there a zoo in *(name of this city)?*
SPEAKER B: Yes, there is. / No, there isn't.
SPEAKER B: *(to Speaker C)* Is there an airport near *(name of this city)?*
SPEAKER C: I don't know.
SPEAKER B: *(to Speaker D)* Is there an airport near *(name of this city)?*
SPEAKER D: Yes, there is. / No, there isn't.
Etc.

1. a zoo
2. an airport
3. any lakes
4. any good restaurants
5. a good Chinese restaurant
6. an art museum
7. an aquarium
8. any interesting bookstores
9. a subway system
10. any public swimming pools
11. a good public transportation system
12. any movie theaters

□ **EXERCISE 16.** Let's talk: class activity.

Directions: Solve the puzzle. Teacher's Note: Use the grid on p. 509 of the *Answer Key* to answer your students' questions.

The Johnson family needs to decide where to stay for their summer vacation. They want a hotel that has everything in the list below. Your teacher has information about several hotels. Ask her/him questions using the list. Then write *yes* or *no* in the correct column of the chart. Which hotel has everything that the Johnsons want?

Example:
SPEAKER A: Is there a swimming pool at Hotel 1?
  TEACHER: Yes, there is.
SPEAKER B: Are there tennis courts at Hotel 3?
  TEACHER: Yes, there are.
SPEAKER C: Are there ocean-view rooms at Hotel 5?
  TEACHER: Yes, there are.

LIST	
a beach	*a swimming pool*
horses to ride	*tennis courts*
ocean-view rooms	

CHART					
	a swimming pool	a beach	tennis courts	horses	ocean-view rooms
HOTEL 1	*yes*				
HOTEL 2		*yes*			
HOTEL 3			*yes*		
HOTEL 4				*yes*	
HOTEL 5					*yes*

5-6 THERE + BE: ASKING QUESTIONS WITH HOW MANY

QUESTION	SHORT ANSWER
HOW MANY + SUBJECT + *ARE* + *THERE* + PLACE (a) **How many chapters are there** in this book? →	Sixteen. (There are 16 chapters in this book.)
(b) **How many provinces are there** in Canada? →	Ten. (There are ten provinces in Canada.)
(c) How many **words** do you see? *INCORRECT:* How many word do you see?	Notice: The noun that follows **how many** is plural.

☐ **EXERCISE 17. Let's talk: class activity.**

Directions: Ask and answer questions about this room. Use **How many** and the given words.

Example: desks
SPEAKER A: How many desks are there in this room?
SPEAKER B: Thirty-two. OR There are thirty-two desks in this room.
SPEAKER A: That's right. OR No, I count thirty-three desks.

1. windows
2. desks
3. students
4. teachers
5. women
6. men
7. grammar books
8. dictionaries

☐ **EXERCISE 18. Let's talk: pairwork.**

Directions: Work with a partner. Ask questions with **How many**.

Example: days in a week
PARTNER A: How many days are there in a week?
PARTNER B: Seven. OR There are seven days in a week.
PARTNER A: Right. There are seven days in a week. Your turn now.

Partner A
1. chapters in this book
2. doors in this room
3. floors in this building
4. states in the United States (50)
5. countries in North America (3)

Partner B
1. pages in this book
2. people in this room
3. letters in the English alphabet (26)
4. provinces in Canada (10)
5. continents in the world (7)

5-7 PREPOSITIONS OF PLACE

(a) My book is **on** my desk.	In (a): *on* = a preposition *my desk* = object of the preposition *on my desk* = a prepositional phrase
(b) Tom lives **in** *the United States.* He lives **in** *New York City.* (c) He lives **on** *Hill Street.* (d) He lives **at** *4472 Hill Street.*	A person lives: **in** a country and **in** a city **on** a street, avenue, road, etc. **at** a street address (See Chart 12-9, p. 374, for more information about using **in** and **at**.)

Note: Prepositions of place are also called "prepositions of location."

☐ **EXERCISE 19. Sentence practice.**

Directions: Complete the sentences with **in, on,** or **at**.

Write about Pablo.

Pablo
5541 Lake Street
Toronto, Canada

1. Pablo lives _____ Canada.

2. He lives _____ Toronto.

3. He lives _____ Lake Street.

4. He lives _____ 5541 Lake Street

   _____ Toronto, Canada.

Write about Dr. Lee.

5. Dr. Lee lives on _____.

6. He lives in _____.

7. He lives at _____.

Dr. H.K. Lee
342 First Street
Miami, Florida

Write about yourself.

8. I live _____.
   (name of country)

9. I live _____.
   (name of city)

10. I live _____.
    (name of street)

11. I live _____.
    (street address)

5-8 SOME PREPOSITIONS OF PLACE: A LIST

above	*beside*	*in back of*	*in the middle of*	*on*
around	*between*	*in the back of*	*inside*	*on top of*
at	*far (away) from*	*in front of*	*near*	*outside*
behind	*in*	*in the front of*	*next to*	*under*
below				

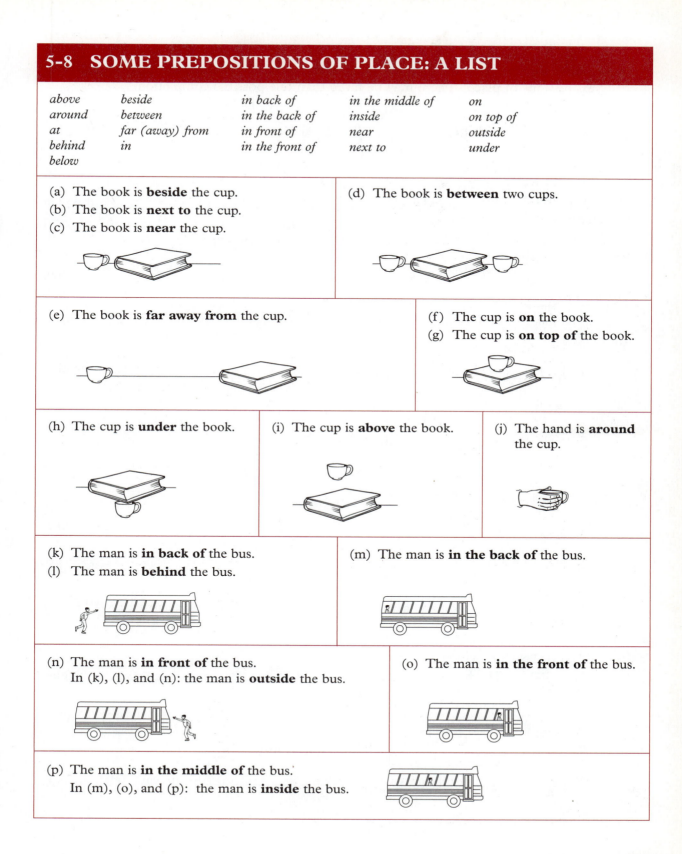

(a) The book is **beside** the cup.
(b) The book is **next to** the cup.
(c) The book is **near** the cup.

(d) The book is **between** two cups.

(e) The book is **far away from** the cup.

(f) The cup is **on** the book.
(g) The cup is **on top of** the book.

(h) The cup is **under** the book.

(i) The cup is **above** the book.

(j) The hand is **around** the cup.

(k) The man is **in back of** the bus.
(l) The man is **behind** the bus.

(m) The man is **in the back of** the bus.

(n) The man is **in front of** the bus.
   In (k), (l), and (n): the man is **outside** the bus.

(o) The man is **in the front of** the bus.

(p) The man is **in the middle of** the bus.
   In (m), (o), and (p): the man is **inside** the bus.

☐ **EXERCISE 20. Sentence practice.**

Directions: Describe the pictures by completing the sentences with prepositional expressions of place. There may be more than one possible completion.

1. The apple is ___*on, on top of*___ the plate.

2. The apple is _____ the plate.

3. The apple is _____ the plate.

4. The apple is _____ the glass.

5. The apple isn't near the glass. It is _____ _____ the glass.

6. The apple is _____ the glass.

7. The apple is _____ two glasses.

8. The hand is _____ the glass.

9. The dog isn't inside the car. The dog is _____ the car.

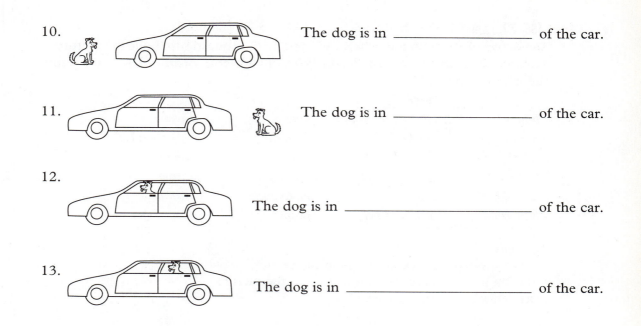

10. The dog is in _____ of the car.

11. The dog is in _____ of the car.

12. The dog is in _____ of the car.

13. The dog is in _____ of the car.

□ **EXERCISE 21. Let's talk: pairwork.**

Directions: Work with a partner. Choose a small object (a pen, pencil, coin, etc.). Give and follow directions. You can look at your book before you speak. When you speak, look at your partner.
Partner A: Give your partner directions. Your book is open.
Partner B: Follow the directions. Your book is closed.

Example: (a small object such as a coin)
PARTNER A *(book open):* Put it on top of the desk.
PARTNER B *(book closed): (Partner B puts the coin on top of the desk.)*

1. Put it on your head.
2. Put it above your head.
3. Put it between your fingers.
4. Put it near me.

5. Put it far away from me.
6. Put it under your book.
7. Put it below your knee.
8. Put it in the middle of your grammar book.

Switch roles.
Partner A: Close your book.
Partner B: Open your book. Your turn to give directions.

9. Put it inside your grammar book.
10. Put it next to your grammar book.
11. Put it on top of your grammar book.
12. Put it in front of me.

13. Put it behind me.
14. Put it in back of your back.
15. Put it in the back of your grammar book.
16. Put your hand around it.

☐ **EXERCISE 22. Let's talk: pairwork.**

Directions: Work with a partner. Ask and answer questions about the picture. Practice using *Is there/Are there*, *Where*, and *How many*. Use the vocabulary in the list to help you.

bikes	*cars*	*flowers*	*a picnic bench*
a bird	*chickens*	*a guitar*	*a picnic table*
a boat	*clouds*	*hills*	*rabbits*
boots	*dogs*	*a knife*	*a river*
a bridge	*a fish*	*motorcycles*	*a train*
butterflies	*a fishing pole*	*people*	*trees*

Example:
PARTNER A: **Are there** any dogs in the picture?
PARTNER B: No, there aren't any dogs in the picture.
PARTNER A: Your turn to ask.

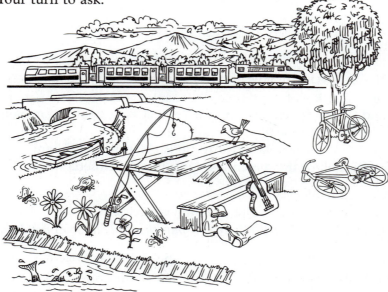

☐ **EXERCISE 23. Listening.**

Directions: Listen to the sentences about the picture in Exercise 22. Circle the correct answers.

Example: The bike is in the water.   yes   (no)

1. yes	no	6. yes	no	11. yes	no
2. yes	no	7. yes	no	12. yes	no
3. yes	no	8. yes	no	13. yes	no
4. yes	no	9. yes	no	14. yes	no
5. yes	no	10. yes	no	15. yes	no

□ **EXERCISE 24. Review: Chapters 4 and 5.**

Directions: Talk about the picture below. Use the vocabulary in the list to help you answer the questions.

burn	*a bowl*	*meat*
eat dinner	*a bowl of salad*	*a piece of meat*
have a steak for dinner	*a candle*	*a plate*
hold a knife and a fork	*a cup*	*a restaurant*
	a cup of coffee	*a saucer*
	a fork	*a spoon*
	a glass	*a steak*
	a glass of water	*a table*
	a knife	*a waiter*
	a vase of flowers	

PART I. Work in pairs or as a class. Answer the questions. (Alternate questions if working in pairs.)

1. What is Mary doing?
2. What do you see on the table?
3. What is Mary holding in her right hand? in her left hand?
4. What is in the bowl?
5. What is on the plate?
6. What is in the cup?
7. What is burning?
8. Is Mary eating breakfast?
9. Is Mary at home? Where is she?
10. What is she cutting?

PART II. Complete the sentences.

11. Mary is sitting _____ a table.

12. There is a candle _____ the table.

13. There is coffee _____ the cup.

14. Mary _____ holding a knife _____

    her right hand.

15. She's _____ a restaurant.

16. She _____ at home.

17. She _____ eating breakfast.

□ EXERCISE 25. Review: Chapters 4 and 5.

Directions: Talk about the picture below. Use the vocabulary in the list to help you answer the questions.

read a book	the circulation desk
study at the library	a librarian
take notes	a shelf (singular)
	shelves (plural)*

PART I. Work in pairs or as a class. Answer the questions. (Alternate questions if working in pairs.)

1. What is John doing?
2. What do you see in the picture?
3. Is John at home? Where is he?

4. Is John reading a newspaper?
5. Where is the librarian standing?
6. Is John right-handed or left-handed?

PART II. Complete the sentences.

7. John is studying _____ the library.

8. He is sitting _____ a table.

9. He is sitting _____ a chair.

10. His legs are _____ the table.

11. There are books _____ the shelves.

12. John is writing _____ a piece of paper.

13. He's taking notes _____ a piece of paper.

14. He _____ reading a newspaper.

15. The librarian _____

   standing _____

   the circulation desk.

16. Another student is sitting

   _____ John.

_____

*See Chart 6-5, p. 173, for information about nouns with irregular plural forms.

Directions: Talk about the picture. Use the vocabulary in the list to help you answer the questions.

the date	a bank	first name / given name
sign a check	cash	middle initial
sign her name	a check	last name / family name / surname
write a check★		name and address

PART I. Work in pairs or as a class. Answer the questions. (Alternate questions if working in pairs.)

1. What is Mary doing?
2. What is Mary's address?
3. What is Mary's full name?
4. What is Mary's middle initial?
5. What is Mary's last name?
6. How much money does Mary want?

7. What is in the upper-left corner of the check?
8. What is in the lower-left corner of the check?
9. What is the name of the bank?

PART II. Complete the sentences.

10. Mary is writing a _____.

11. She is signing _____ name.

12. The name _____ the bank is First National Bank.

13. Mary lives _____ 3471 Tree Street.

14. Mary lives _____ Chicago, Illinois.

15. Mary's name and address are _____ the upper-left corner _____ the check.

_____

★*Check* (American English) is spelled *cheque* in British and Canadian English. The pronunciation of *check* and *cheque* is the same.

☐ **EXERCISE 27. Review: Chapters 4 and 5.**

Directions: Talk about the picture below. Use the vocabulary in the list to help you answer the questions.

cash a check	a bank teller	a man (singular)
stand in line	a counter	men (plural)★
	a line	people (plural)★
		a woman (singular)
		women (plural)★

PART I. Work in pairs or as a class. Answer the questions. (Alternate questions if working in pairs.)

1. What is Mary doing?
2. Is Mary at a store? Where is she?
3. What do you see in the picture?
4. Who is standing behind Mary, a man or a woman?
5. Who is standing at the end of the line, a man or a woman?

6. How many men are there in the picture?
7. How many women are there in the picture?
8. How many people are there in the picture?
9. How many people are standing in line?

PART II. Complete the sentences.

10. Mary is _____ a bank.

11. Four people _____ standing in line.

12. Mary is standing _____ the counter.

13. The bank teller is standing _____ the counter.

14. A woman _____ standing _____ Mary.

15. Mary _____ standing _____

    the end _____ the line.

16. A man _____ standing _____

    the end _____ the line.

17. A businessman _____

    standing _____ the woman

    in the dress and the young man with the beard.

_____

★See Chart 6-5, p. 173, for information about nouns with irregular plural forms.

5-9 *NEED* AND *WANT* + A NOUN OR AN INFINITIVE

		VERB	+	NOUN
(a)	We	*need*		*food*.
(b)	I	*want*		*a sandwich*.
		VERB	+	INFINITIVE
(c)	We	*need*		*to eat*.
(d)	I	*want*		*to eat* a sandwich.

Need is stronger than *want*. *Need* gives the idea that something is very important.

Need and *want* are followed by a noun or by an infinitive.

An infinitive = *to* + *the simple form of a verb.*★

★The simple form of a verb = a verb without *-s, -ed*, or *-ing*. Examples of the simple form of a verb: *come, help, answer, write.* Examples of infinitives: *to come, to help, to answer, to write.*

☐ EXERCISE 28. Sentence practice.
Directions: Add *to* where necessary.

1. I want some water. *(no change)*

2. I want ⌄ drink some water.
        to

3. Linda wants go to the bookstore.

4. Linda wants a new dictionary.

5. I need make a telephone call.

6. I need a telephone.

7. Do you want go to the movie with us?

8. Do you need a new notebook?

☐ EXERCISE 29. Let's talk: class activity.
Directions: Your teacher will ask you questions using *need* and *want*. Think about your day tomorrow. Close your book for this activity.

Example:

TEACHER:	What do you need to do tomorrow morning?
STUDENT A:	I need to go to school at 8:00.
TEACHER:	*(to Student B)* What do you need to do?
STUDENT B:	I need to eat breakfast.
TEACHER:	*(to Student C)* What does *(Student B)* need to do?
STUDENT C:	He/She needs to eat breakfast.

What do you . . .

1. need to do tomorrow morning?
2. want to do tomorrow morning?
3. need to do in the afternoon tomorrow?
4. want to do in the afternoon?
5. want to do in the evening?
6. need to do tomorrow evening?

□ EXERCISE 30. Sentence practice.

Directions: Use the words in the list or your own words to complete the sentences. Use an infinitive (*to* + verb) in each sentence. Some words can be used more than once.

buy	*go*	*pay*	*walk*
call	*listen to*	*play*	*wash*
cash	*marry*	*take*	*watch*
do			

1. Anna is sleepy. She wants _____*to go*_____ to bed.

2. I want _____ downtown today because I need _____

   a new coat.

3. Mike wants _____ TV. There's a good program on Channel 5.

4. Do you want _____ soccer with us at the park this afternoon?

5. I need _____ Jennifer on the phone.

6. I want _____ to the bank because I need _____ a check.

7. James doesn't want _____ his homework tonight.

8. My clothes are dirty. I need _____ them.

9. John loves Mary. He wants _____ her.

10. Helen needs _____ an English course.

11. Where do you want _____ for lunch?

12. Do you want _____ some music on the radio?

13. It's a nice day. I don't want _____
the bus home today. I want _____
home instead.

14. David's desk is full of overdue bills. He needs
_____ his bills.

☐ EXERCISE 31. Listening.

Directions: Listen to the conversations and complete the sentences.

Example:

You will hear: Do you want to go downtown this afternoon?
You will write: ___*Do you want to go*___ downtown this afternoon?
You will hear: Yes, I do. I need to buy a winter coat.
You will write: Yes, I do. ___*I need to buy*___ a winter coat.

1. A: Where _____ for dinner tonight?
   B: Rossini's Restaurant.

2. A: What time _____ to the airport?
   B: Around five. My plane leaves at seven.

3. A: Jean _____ to the baseball game.
   B: Why not?
   A: Because _____ for a test.

4. A: I'm getting tired. _____ a break for a few
   minutes.
   B: Okay. Let's take a break. We can finish the work later.

5. A: _____ to class on Friday.
   B: Why not?
   A: It's a holiday.

6. A: Peter _____ to his
   apartment.
   B: Why?
   A: Because _____ his
   clothes before he goes to the party.

7. A: Where _____ for your vacation?

   B: _____ Niagara Falls, Quebec, and Montreal.

8. A: May I see your dictionary? _____ a word.
   B: Of course. Here it is.
   A: Thanks.

9. A: _____ with us to the park?

   B: Sure. Thanks. _____ some exercise.

5-10 WOULD LIKE

(a) I'm thirsty. I **want** a glass of water. (b) I'm thirsty. I **would like** a glass of water.	(a) and (b) have the same meaning, but **would like** is usually more polite than **want**. *I would like* is a nice way of saying *I want*.

(c) **I would like**
   You would like
   She would like
   He would like   a glass of water.
   We would like
   They would like
	Notice in (c):
	There is no final **-s** on **would**.
	There is no final **-s** on **like**.

(d) CONTRACTIONS
   I'd = **I would**
   you'd = **you would**
   she'd = **she would**
   he'd = **he would**
   we'd = **we would**
   they'd = **they would**
	Would is often contracted with pronouns in both speaking and writing.
	In speaking, **would** is usually contracted with nouns too.
	WRITTEN: Tom would like to come.
	SPOKEN: "Tom'd like to come."

WOULD LIKE + INFINITIVE (e) I **would like** **to eat** a sandwich.	Notice in (e): **would like** can be followed by an infinitive.
WOULD + SUBJECT + *LIKE* (f) **Would** you **like** some tea?	In a question, **would** comes before the subject.
(g) Yes, I **would**. (I would like some tea.)	**Would** is used alone in short answers to questions with **would like**. It is not contracted in short answers.

Directions: Make sentences.

PART I. Change the sentences by using *would like*.

1. **Tony wants** a cup of coffee.

   →   <u>Tony would like OR Tony'd like</u>   a cup of coffee.

2. **He wants** some sugar in his coffee.

   →   <u>He would like OR He'd like</u>   some sugar in his coffee.

3. **Ahmed and Anita want** some coffee too.

   → _____ some coffee too.

4. **They want** some sugar in their coffee too.

   → _____ some sugar in their coffee too.

5. A: **Do you want** a cup of coffee?
   B: Yes, **I do**. Thank you.

   → A: _____ a cup of coffee?

   B: Yes, _____. Thank you.

6. **I want to thank** you for your kindness and hospitality.

   → _____ you for your kindness and hospitality.

7. **My friends want to thank** you too.

   → _____ you too.

8. A: **Does Robert want to ride** with us?
   B: Yes, **he does**.

   → A: _____ with us?

   B: Yes, _____.

👀 **PART II.** Listen to the sentences for contractions with *would*. Practice repeating them.

□ EXERCISE 33. Let's talk: class activity.

Directions: Your teacher will ask you questions. Close your book for this activity.

1. Who's hungry right now? (. . .), are you hungry? What would you like?
2. Who's thirsty? (. . .), are you thirsty? What would you like?
3. Who's sleepy? What would you like to do?
4. What would you like to do this weekend?
5. What would you like to do after class today?
6. What would you like to have for dinner tonight?
7. What countries would you like to visit?
8. What cities would you like to visit in *(the United States, Canada, etc.)?*
9. What languages would you like to learn?
10. You listened to your classmates. What would they like to do? Do you remember what they said?
11. Pretend that you are a host at a party at your home and your classmates are your guests. Ask them what they would like to eat or drink.
12. Think of something fun to do tonight or this weekend. Using *would you like,* invite a classmate to join you.

5-11 *WOULD LIKE* vs. *LIKE*

(a) I ***would like to go*** to the zoo.	In (a): *I would like to go to the zoo* means *I want to go to the zoo.*
(b) I ***like to go*** to the zoo.	In (b): *I like to go to the zoo* means *I enjoy the zoo.*
	Would like indicates that I want to do something now or in the future.
	Like indicates that I always, usually, or often enjoy something.

□ EXERCISE 34. Listening.

Directions: Listen to the sentences and circle the verbs you hear. Some sentences have contractions.

Example: I _____ some tea.   like   ('d like)

1. like	'd like		6. likes	'd like
2. like	'd like		7. like	'd like
3. like	'd like		8. like	'd like
4. likes	'd like		9. like	'd like
5. like	'd like		10. like	'd like

☐ EXERCISE 35. Let's talk: class activity.

Directions: Discuss possible completions for the sentences. Use your own words.

1. I need to _____ every day.

2. I want to _____ today.

3. I like to _____ every day.

4. I would like to _____ today.

5. I don't like to _____ every day.

6. I don't want to _____ today.

7. Do you like to _____ ?

8. Would you like to _____ ?

9. I need to _____ and _____ today.

10. _____ would you like to _____ this evening?

☐ EXERCISE 36. Let's talk: pairwork.

Directions: Work in pairs. Ask and answer questions. Look at your partner when you speak.

Example:
PARTNER A: Do you like apples?
PARTNER B: Yes, I do. OR No, I don't.
PARTNER A: Would you like an apple right now?
PARTNER B: Yes, I would. OR Yes, thank you. OR No, but thank you for asking.
PARTNER A: Your turn now.

Partner A	Partner B
1. Do you like coffee ? Would you like a cup of coffee?	1. Do you like chocolate? Would you like some chocolate right now?
2. Do you like to go to movies? Would you like to go to a movie with me later today?	2. Do you like to go shopping? Would you like to go shopping with me later today?
3. What do you like to do on weekends? What would you like to do this weekend?	3. What do you like to do in your free time? What would you like to do in your free time tomorrow?
4. What do you need to do this evening? What would you like to do this evening?	4. Do you like to travel? What countries would you like to visit?

☐ EXERCISE 37. Review: Chapters 4 and 5.

Directions: Talk about the picture below. Use the vocabulary in the list to help you answer the questions.

cook	a kitchen	bread
cook dinner	a list/a grocery list	butter
make dinner	a pepper shaker	coffee
taste (food)	a pot	an egg
	a refrigerator	pepper
	a salt shaker	salt
	a stove	

PART I. Work in pairs or as a class. Answer the questions. (Alternate questions if working in pairs.)

1. What is John doing?
2. What do you see in the picture?
3. Where is John?
4. Is John tasting his dinner?
5. Is John a good cook?

6. Where is the refrigerator?
7. What is on the refrigerator?
8. Is the food on the stove hot or cold?
9. Is the food in the refrigerator hot or cold?

PART II. Complete the sentences.

10. John is making dinner. He's _____ the kitchen.

11. There is a pot _____ the stove.

12. The stove is _____ the refrigerator.

13. There is a grocery list _____ the refrigerator door.

14. John needs _____ to the grocery store.

15. A salt shaker and a pepper shaker are _____ the stove.

16. There is hot food _____ top _____

    the stove.

17. There is cold food _____ the

    refrigerator.

□ **EXERCISE 38. Review: Chapters 4 and 5.**

Directions: Talk about the picture below. Use the vocabulary in the list to help you answer the questions.

sing	*a cat*	*a living room*
sit on a sofa	*a dog*	*a rug*
sleep	*a fish*	*a singer*
swim	*a fishbowl*	*a sofa*
watch TV/television	*a floor*	*a TV set/a television set*
	a lamp	

PART I. Work in pairs or as a class. Answer the questions. (Alternate questions if working in pairs.)

1. What are John and Mary doing?
2. What do you see in the picture?
3. Are John and Mary in the kitchen? Where are they?
4. Where is the lamp?
5. Where is the rug?
6. Where is the dog?
7. Where is the cat?

8. Is the cat walking? What is the cat doing?
9. What is the dog doing?
10. What is on top of the TV set?
11. Is the fish watching TV?
12. What is on the TV screen? What are John and Mary watching?

PART II. Complete the sentences.

13. John and Mary _____ watching TV. They like _____ watch TV.

14. They _____ sitting _____ a sofa.

15. They _____ sleeping.

16. There is a rug _____ the floor.

17. A dog _____ sleeping _____ the rug.

18. A cat _____ sleeping _____

    the sofa.

☐ **EXERCISE 41. Let's talk: pairwork.**

Directions: Work with a partner. Bring to class one or two pictures of your country (or any interesting picture). Ask your partner to describe the picture(s).

☐ **EXERCISE 42. Paragraph practice.**

Directions: Choose one of the pictures your classmates brought to class. Describe the picture in a paragraph.

☐ **EXERCISE 43. Chapter review.**

Directions: Circle the correct completions.

1. Jack lives _____ China.
   - (A.) in
   - B. at
   - C. on

2. I need _____ a new notebook.
   - A. buy
   - B. to buy
   - C. buying

3. "_____ a cup of tea?"
   "Yes, thank you."
   - A. Would you like
   - B. Do you like
   - C. Are you like

4. There _____ twenty-two desks in this room.
   - A. be
   - B. is
   - C. are

5. Pilots sit _____ an airplane.
   - A. in front of
   - B. in the front of
   - C. front of

6. I live _____ 6601 Fourth Avenue.
   - A. in
   - B. on
   - C. at

7. The students _____ do their homework.
   - A. don't want
   - B. aren't wanting
   - C. don't want to

8. _____ a TV in Jane's bedroom?
   - A. Are there
   - B. There
   - C. Is there

☐ **EXERCISE 44. Chapter review: error analysis.**

Directions: Correct the errors.

1. Do you want go downtown with me?

2. There's many problems in big cities today.

3. I'd like see a movie tonight.

4. We are needing to find a new apartment soon.

5. Mr. Rice woulds likes to have a cup of tea.

6. How many students there are in your class?

7. Yoko and Ivan are study grammar right now. They want learn English.

8. I am like to leave now. How about you?

9. Please put the chair in middle the room.

10. The teacher needs to checking our homework now.

☐ EXERCISE 45. Review: Chapters 4 and 5.
   Directions: Complete the sentences with your own words. Use your own paper.

   1. I need _____ because _____.

   2. I want _____ because _____.

   3. I would like _____.

   4. Would you like _____?

   5. Do you like _____?

   6. There is _____.

   7. There are _____.

   8. I'm listening to _____, but I also hear _____.

   9. I'm looking at _____, but I also see _____.

   10. I'm thinking about _____.

   11. I think that _____.

   12. In my opinion, _____.

   13. How many _____ are there _____?

   14. Is there _____?

   15. Are there _____?

□ **EXERCISE 46. Review: Chapters 1 → 5.**

Directions: Complete the sentences. Use the words in parentheses. Use the simple present or the present progressive. Use an infinitive where necessary.

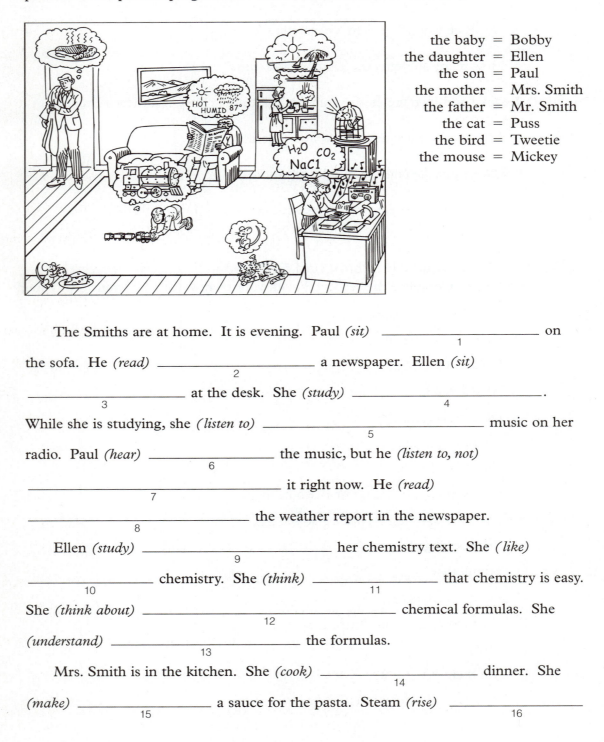

the baby	=	Bobby
the daughter	=	Ellen
the son	=	Paul
the mother	=	Mrs. Smith
the father	=	Mr. Smith
the cat	=	Puss
the bird	=	Tweetie
the mouse	=	Mickey

The Smiths are at home. It is evening. Paul *(sit)* _____ on

the sofa. He *(read)* _____ a newspaper. Ellen *(sit)*

_____ at the desk. She *(study)* _____.

While she is studying, she *(listen to)* _____ music on her

radio. Paul *(hear)* _____ the music, but he *(listen to, not)*

_____ it right now. He *(read)*

_____ the weather report in the newspaper.

Ellen *(study)* _____ her chemistry text. She *(like)*

_____ chemistry. She *(think)* _____ that chemistry is easy.

She *(think about)* _____ chemical formulas. She

(understand) _____ the formulas.

Mrs. Smith is in the kitchen. She *(cook)* _____ dinner. She

(make) _____ a sauce for the pasta. Steam *(rise)* _____

from the pot on the stove. Mrs. Smith *(like, not)* _____ 17 to cook, but she *(know)* _____ 18 that her family has to eat good food. While she *(make)* _____ 19 dinner, Mrs. Smith *(think about)* _____ 20 a vacation on the beach. Sometimes Mrs. Smith *(get)* _____ 21 tired of cooking all the time, but she *(love)* _____ 22 her family very much and *(want)* _____ 23 to *(take)* _____ 24 care of their health.

Mr. Smith *(stand)* _____ 25 near the front door. He *(take off)* _____ 26 his coat. Under his coat, he *(wear)* _____ 27 a suit. Mr. Smith is happy to be home. He *(think about)* _____ 28 dinner. After dinner, he *(want)* _____ 29 *(watch)* _____ 30 television. He *(need)* _____ 31 *(go)* _____ 32 to bed early tonight because he has a busy day at work tomorrow.

In the corner of the living room, a mouse *(eat)* _____ 33 a piece of cheese. The mouse *(think)* _____ 34 that the cheese *(taste)* _____ 35 good.

Puss *(see, not)* _____ 36 the mouse. She *(smell, not)* _____ 37 the mouse. Puss *(sleep)* _____ 38 . She *(dream about)* _____ 39 a mouse.

Bobby is in the middle of the living room. He *(play)* _____ 40 with a toy train. He *(see, not)* _____ 41 the mouse because he *(look at)* _____ 42 his toy train. The bird, Tweetie, *(sing)* _____ 43 . Bobby *(listen to, not)* _____ 44 the bird. He is busy with his train.

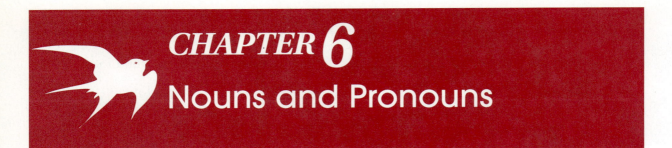

CHAPTER 6
Nouns and Pronouns

☐ **EXERCISE 1. Let's talk: small groups.**

Directions: Work in small groups. Name things that belong to each category. Make lists. Compare your lists with other groups' lists. All of the words you use in this exercise are called nouns.

1. Name clothing you see in this room. *(shirt)*
2. Name kinds of fruit. *(apple)*
3. Name things you drink. *(coffee)*
4. Name parts of the body. *(head)*
5. Name kinds of animals. *(horse)*
6. Name cities in the United States and Canada.★ *(New York, Montreal, etc.)*
7. Name languages.★ *(English)*
8. Name school subjects. *(history)*

6-1 NOUNS: SUBJECTS AND OBJECTS

(a)	NOUN **Birds** | fly. | subject verb	A NOUN is used as the **subject** of a sentence. A NOUN is used as the **object** of a verb.★ In (a): *Birds* is a NOUN. It is used as the subject of the sentence. In (b): *pen* is a NOUN. It has the article *a* in front of it; *a pen* is used as the object of the verb *is holding*.
(b)	NOUN NOUN **John** | is holding | **a pen**. | subject verb object	
(c)	NOUN NOUN **Birds** | fly | in | the **sky**. | subject verb prep. object of prep.	A NOUN is also used as the **object of a preposition.** In (c): *in* is a **preposition** (prep.). The noun *sky* (with the article *the* in front) is the OBJECT of the preposition *in*. Some common prepositions: *about, across, at, between, by, for, from, in, of, on, to, with.*
(d)	NOUN NOUN NOUN **John** | is holding | **a pen** | in | his **hand**. | subject verb object prep. object of prep.	

★Some verbs are followed by an object. These verbs are called transitive verbs (*v.t.* in a dictionary). Some verbs are not followed by an object. These verbs are called intransitive verbs (*v.i.* in a dictionary).

★ The names of cities and languages begin with capital letters.

☐ EXERCISE 2. Noun practice.

Directions: Check (✓) the words that are nouns.

1. _____ eat   7. _____ think
2. _____ dog   8. _____ mathematics
3. _____ beautiful   9. _____ flowers
4. _____ have   10. _____ juice
5. _____ eyes   11. _____ Paris
6. _____ English   12. _____ wonderful

☐ EXERCISE 3. Sentence practice.

Directions: Describe the grammatical structure of the sentences as shown in items 1 and 2. Then identify each noun. Is the noun used as
   • the subject of the sentence?
   • the object of the verb?
   • the object of a preposition?

1. Marie studies chemistry.

Marie	studies	chemistry	(none)	(none)
subject	verb	object of verb	preposition	object of prep.

→ *Marie = a noun, subject of the sentence*
   chemistry = a noun, object of the verb "studies"

2. The children are playing in the park.

The children	are playing	(none)	in	the park
subject	verb	object of verb	preposition	object of prep.

→ *children = a noun, subject of the sentence*
   park = a noun, object of the preposition "in"

3. Children like candy.

subject	verb	object of verb	preposition	object of prep.

4. The teacher is erasing the board with her hand.

subject	verb	object of verb	preposition	object of prep.

5. Mike lives in Africa.

| subject | verb | object of verb | preposition | object of prep. |

6. The sun is shining.

| subject | verb | object of verb | preposition | object of prep. |

7. Robert is reading a book about butterflies.

| subject | verb | object of verb | preposition | object of prep. |

8. Tom and Ann live with their parents.

| subject | verb | object of verb | preposition | object of prep. |

9. Monkeys eat fruit and insects.

| subject | verb | object of verb | preposition | object of prep. |

10. Mary and Bob help Sue with her homework.

| subject | verb | object of verb | preposition | object of prep. |

11. Ships sail across the ocean.

| subject | verb | object of verb | preposition | object of prep. |

12. Water contains hydrogen and oxygen.

| subject | verb | object of verb | preposition | object of prep. |

6-2 ADJECTIVE + NOUN

(a) I don't like **cold** weather.
               adj. + noun
(b) Alex is a **happy** child.
          adj. + noun
(c) The **hungry** boy has a **fresh** apple.
    adj. + noun   adj. + noun
	An adjective (adj.) describes a noun. In grammar, we say that adjectives "modify" nouns. The word "modify" means "change a little." Adjectives give a little different meaning to a noun: *cold weather, hot weather, nice weather, bad weather.*
	Adjectives come in front of nouns.

(d) The *weather* *is* **cold**. noun + be + adj.	Reminder: An adjective can also follow **be**; the adjective describes the subject of the sentence. (See Chart 1-6, p. 12.)

COMMON ADJECTIVES

beautiful – ugly	good – bad	angry	hungry
big – little	happy – sad	bright	important
big – small	large – small	busy	intelligent
boring – interesting	long – short	delicious	kind
cheap – expensive	noisy – quiet	exciting	lazy
clean – dirty	old – new	famous	nervous
cold – hot	old – young	favorite	nice
dangerous – safe	poor – rich	free	ripe
dry – wet	sour – sweet	fresh	serious
easy – hard	strong – weak	healthy	wonderful
easy – difficult		honest	

☐ EXERCISE 4. Sentence practice.
    Directions: Find the adjectives and nouns.

1. Jim has an expensive bicycle.
   → *Jim = a noun; expensive = an adjective; bicycle = a noun*

2. My sister has a beautiful house.

3. We often eat at an Italian restaurant.

4. Maria sings her favorite songs in the shower.

5. Olga likes American hamburgers.

6. You like sour apples, but I like sweet fruit.

7. Political leaders make important decisions.

8. Heavy traffic creates noisy streets.

9. Poverty causes serious problems in the world.

10. Young people have interesting ideas about modern music.

☐ **EXERCISE 5.** Let's talk: small groups.

Directions: Work in small groups. Take turns adding adjectives to the sentences. Use any adjectives that make sense. Think of at least three possible adjectives to complete each sentence.

1. I don't like _____*cold / hot / wet / rainy / bad / etc.*_____ weather.

2. Do you like _____ food?

3. I admire _____ people.

4. _____ people make me angry.

5. Pollution is a/an _____ problem in the modern world.

6. I had a/an _____ experience yesterday.

7. I don't like _____ cities.

8. I had a/an _____ dinner last night.

☐ **EXERCISE 6.** Sentence practice.

Directions: Find each noun. Is the noun used as
- the subject of the sentence?
- the object of the verb?
- the object of a preposition?

1. <u>Bob</u> and his <u>wife</u> like <u>coffee</u> with their <u>breakfast.</u>
   → *Bob = a noun, subject of the sentence*
   wife = a noun, subject of the sentence
   coffee = a noun, object of the verb "like"
   breakfast = a noun, object of the preposition "with"

2. Jack doesn't have a radio in his car.

3. Monkeys and apes have thumbs.

4. Does Janet work in a large office?

5. Scientists don't agree on the origin of the earth.

a chimpanzee

6. Egypt has hot summers and mild winters.

7. Many Vietnamese farmers live in small villages near their fields.

8. Large cities face many serious problems.

9. These problems include poverty, pollution, and crime.

10. An hour consists of 60 minutes. Does a day consist of 1440 minutes?

□ EXERCISE 7. Let's talk: small groups.
Directions: Work in groups. When you are done, you will have a list of adjectives for different countries.

PART I. Complete each sentence with the name of a country and the appropriate adjective.

1. Food from _____ China _____ is _____ Chinese _____ food.

2. Food from _____ Mexico _____ is _____ food.

3. Food from _____ is _____ food.

4. Food from _____ is _____ food.

5. Food from _____ is _____ food.

6. Food from _____ is _____ food.

7. Food from _____ is _____ food.

8. Food from _____ is _____ food.

PART II. What is the favorite ethnic food in your group? Give an example of this kind of food.

Example: Favorite ethnic food?
GROUP A: Italian
Example: An example of Italian food?
GROUP A: spaghetti

Favorite ethnic food in our group: _____

An example of this kind of food: _____

PART III. Find out the most popular ethnic food in other groups too.

PART IV. Working as a class, make a list of adjectives of nationality.

6-3 SUBJECT PRONOUNS AND OBJECT PRONOUNS

SUBJECT PRONOUNS	OBJECT PRONOUNS	SUBJECT	—	OBJECT
(a) *I* speak English.	(b) Bob knows *me*.	*I*	—	*me*
(c) *You* speak English.	(d) Bob knows *you*.	*you*	—	*you*
(e) *She* speaks English.	(f) Bob knows *her*.	*she*	—	*her*
(g) *He* speaks English.	(h) Bob knows *him*.	*he*	—	*him*
(i) *It* starts at 8:00.	(j) Bob knows *it*.	*it*	—	*it*
(k) *We* speak English.	(l) Bob talks to *us*.	*we*	—	*us*
(m) *You* speak English.	(n) Bob talks to *you*.	*you*	—	*you*
(o) *They* speak English.	(p) Bob talks to *them*.	*they*	—	*them*

(q) I know *Tony*. *He* is a friendly person.	A pronoun has the same meaning as a noun. In (q): *he* has the same meaning as *Tony*. In (r): *him* has the same meaning as *Tony*. In grammar, we say that a pronoun "refers to" a noun. The pronouns *he* and *him* refer to the noun *Tony*.
(r) I like *Tony*. I know *him* well.	
(s) I have *a red book*. *It* is on my desk.	Sometimes a pronoun refers to a "noun phrase." In (s): *it* refers to the whole phrase *a red book*.

☐ EXERCISE 8. Sentence practice.

Directions: Complete the sentences. Use pronouns (*I, me, he, him,* etc.).

1. John loves Mary. _____He_____ loves _____her_____ very much.

2. Mary loves John. _____ loves _____ very much.

3. Mary and John love their daughter, Anna. _____ love _____ very much.

4. Mary and John love their son, Tom. _____ love _____ very much.

5. Tom loves his little sister, Anna. _____ loves _____ very much.

6. Mary loves her children. _____ loves _____ very much.

7. John loves his children. _____ loves _____ very much.

8. Mary and John love Tom and Anna. _____ love _____ very much.

□ **EXERCISE 9. Sentence practice.**

Directions: Complete the sentences. Use pronouns (***I, me, he, him,** etc.*).

1. Rita has a book. _____*She*_____ bought _____*it*_____ last week.

2. I know the new students, but Tony doesn't know _____ yet.

3. I wrote a letter, but I can't send _____ because I don't have a stamp.

4. Tom is in Canada. _____ is studying at a university.

5. Bill lives in my dorm. I eat breakfast with _____ every morning.

6. Ann is my neighbor. I talk to _____ every day. _____ and _____ have interesting conversations.

7. I have two pictures on my bedroom wall. I like _____. _____ are beautiful.

8. Ann and I have a dinner invitation. Mr. and Mrs. Brown want _____ to come to dinner at their house.

9. Judy has a new car. _____ is a Toyota.

10. My husband and I have a new car. _____ got _____ last month.

□ **EXERCISE 10. Let's talk: find someone who . . . .**

Directions: Interview your classmates. Find someone who can answer *yes* to a question. Then ask the follow-up question using the appropriate object pronoun.

Example:
SPEAKER A: Do you send e-mails?
SPEAKER B: No, I don't.
SPEAKER A: *(Ask another student.)* Do you send e-mails?
SPEAKER C: Yes, I do.
SPEAKER A: When do you send **them**?
SPEAKER C: I send **them** in the evenings.

1. Do you do your homework?
   When do you . . . ?

2. Do you visit friends?
   When do you . . . ?

3. Do you read newspapers or magazines?
   When do you . . . ?

4. Do you talk to *(name of female classmate)*?
   When do you . . . ?

5. Do you watch TV?
   When do you . . . ?

6. Do you buy groceries?
   When do you . . . ?

7. Do you wear boots?
   When do you . . . ?

8. Do you use a computer?
   When do you . . . ?

□ **EXERCISE 11.   Sentence practice.**

   Directions: Complete the sentences. Use pronouns.

   1. A: Do you know Kate and Jim?

      B: Yes, _____I_____ do. I live near _____them_____.

   2. A: Is the chemical formula for water H_3O?

      B: No, _____ isn't. _____ is H_2O.

   3. A: Would Judy and you like to come to the movie with us?

      B: Yes, _____ would. Judy and _____ would enjoy going to

      the movie with _____.

   4. A: Do Mr. and Mrs. Kelly live in the city?

      B: No, _____ don't. _____ live in the suburbs. I visited

      _____ last month.

   5. A: Do you know how to spell "Mississippi"?

      B: Sure! I can spell _____. _____ is easy to spell.

   6. A: Is Paul Cook in your class?

      B: Yes, _____ is. I sit next to _____.

□ **EXERCISE 12.   Listening practice.**

   Directions: Listen to the sentences. Note that the "h" in ***her*** and ***him*** is often
   dropped in spoken English. The "th" in ***them*** can also be dropped. Discuss the
   pronunciation changes.

   1. Sara knows Joe. She knows him very well.
   2. Where does Shelley live? Do you have her address?
   3. There's Sam. Let's go talk to him.
   4. There's Bill and Julie. Let's go talk to them.
   5. The teacher is speaking with Lisa because she doesn't have her homework.
   6. I need to see our airline tickets. Do you have them?

Directions: Listen to each conversation and complete the sentences.

Example:
You will hear: How is Mr. Adams doing?
You will write: How _____*is*_____ Mr. Adams doing?
You will hear: Great! I see him every week at the office.
You will write: Great! I see _____*him*_____ every week at the office.

1. A: Yoko and _____ downtown this afternoon. Do

    you want to come _____?

  B: I don't think so, but thanks anyway. Chris and _____

    to the library. _____ study for our test.

2. A: Hi, Ann. How do you like your new apartment?

  B: _____ very nice.

  A: Do you have a roommate?

  B: Yes. Maria Hall is my roommate. Do you _____?

    _____ Miami.

  A: No, I don't _____. Do you get along _____?

  B: Yes, _____ living together. You must _____

    _____ sometime. Maybe _____ can come over for

    dinner soon.

  A: Thanks. _____ that.

3. A: Do George and Mike come over to your house often?

  B: Yes, _____. I invite _____

    to my house often. We like to play cards.

  A: Who usually wins your card games?

  B: Mike. _____ a really good
    card player. We can't beat

    _____.

6-4 NOUNS: SINGULAR AND PLURAL

SINGULAR	PLURAL	
(a) **one pen** **one apple** **one cup** **one elephant**	**two pens** **three apples** **four cups** **five elephants**	To make the plural form of most nouns, add **-s**.
(b) **baby** **city**	**babies** **cities**	End of noun: *consonant* + **-y** Plural form: change **y** to **i**, add **-es**.
(c) **boy** **key**	**boys** **keys**	End of noun: *vowel* + **-y** Plural form: add **-s**.
(d) **wife** **thief**	**wives** **thieves**	End of noun: **-fe** or **-f** Plural form: change **f** to **v**, add **-es**.
(e) **dish** **match** **class** **box**	**dishes** **matches** **classes** **boxes**	End of noun: **-sh, -ch, -ss, -x** Plural form: add **-es**. Pronunciation: /əz/
(f) **tomato** **potato** **zoo** **radio**	**tomatoes** **potatoes** **zoos** **radios**	End of noun: *consonant* + **-o** Plural form: add **-es**. End of noun: *vowel* + **-o** Plural form: add **-s**.

☐ EXERCISE 14. Sentence practice.

Directions: Complete the sentences. Use the plural form of the words in the lists. Use each word only once.

LIST A.

baby	cowboy	lady
✓ boy	dictionary	party
city	key	tray
country		

1. Mr. and Mrs. Parker have one daughter and two sons. They have one girl and two _____*boys*_____ .

2. The students in my class come from many _____ .

3. Women give birth to _____ .

4. My money and my _____ are in my pocket.

5. I know the names of many _____ in the United States and Canada.

6. I like to go to _____ because I like to meet and talk to people.

7. People carry their food on _____ in a cafeteria.

8. We always use our _____ when we write compositions.

9. Good evening, _____ and gentlemen.

10. _____ ride horses.

LIST B.

knife	*life*	*wife*
leaf	*thief*	

11. It is fall. The _____ are falling from the trees.

12. Sue and Ann are married. They have husbands.

They are _____.

13. We all have some problems in our _____.

14. Police officers catch _____.

15. Please put the _____, forks, and spoons

on the table.

LIST C.

bush	glass	sandwich	tomato
class	match	sex	zoo
dish	potato	tax	

16. Bob drinks eight _____ of water every day.

17. There are two _____: male and female.

18. Please put the _____ and the silverware on the table.

19. All citizens pay money to the government every year. They pay their

_____.

20. I can see trees and _____ outside the window.

21. I want to light the candles. I need some _____.

22. When I make a salad, I use lettuce and _____.

23. Sometimes Sue has a hamburger and French-fried

_____ for dinner.

24. We often eat _____ for lunch.

25. Mehmet is a student. He likes his _____.

26. Some animals live all of their lives in _____.

☐ **EXERCISE 15. Pronunciation practice.**

Directions: Listen to the pronunciation of final **-s/-es**. Practice saying the words.

GROUP A. Final **-s** is pronounced /z/ after voiced sounds.*

1. taxicabs
2. beds
3. dogs
4. balls
5. rooms
6. coins
7. years
8. lives
9. trees
10. cities
11. boys
12. days

_____

* For more information on voiced sounds, see Chart 3-8, p. 66.

GROUP B. Final **-s** is pronounced /s/ after voiceless sounds.★

13. books   16. groups
14. desks   17. cats
15. cups   18. students

GROUP C. Final **-s/-es** is pronounced /əz/.

- after "s" sounds: 19. classes
                         20. glasses
                         21. horses
                         22. places
                         23. sentences

- after "z" sounds: 24. sizes
                         25. exercises
                         26. noises

- after "sh" sounds: 27. dishes
                         28. bushes

- after "ch" sounds: 29. matches
                         30. sandwiches

- after "ge/dge" sounds: 31. pages
                         32. oranges
                         33. bridges

□ EXERCISE 16. Listening.

Directions: Listen to each word. Circle the noun you hear.

1. toy   (toys)
2. table   tables
3. face   faces
4. hat   hats
5. office   offices
6. box   boxes
7. package   packages
8. chair   chairs
9. edge   edges
10. top   tops

★ For more information on voiceless sounds, see Chart 3-8, p. 66.

☐ **EXERCISE 17. Listening.**

Directions: Listen to each sentence. Circle the noun you hear.

1. desk   (desks)
2. place   places
3. sandwich   sandwiches
4. sentence   sentences
5. apple   apples

6. exercise   exercises
7. piece   pieces
8. rose   roses
9. bush   bushes
10. college   colleges

☐ **EXERCISE 18. Pronunciation practice.**

Directions: Find the plural noun(s) in each sentence. Pronounce the noun(s). Then read the sentences aloud.

1. The students are carrying books and backpacks.

2. Department stores sell many sizes of clothes.

3. The weather is terrible. It's raining cats and dogs.★

4. The teachers have their offices in this building.

5. Engineers build bridges.

6. At the zoo you can see tigers, monkeys, birds, elephants, bears, and snakes.

7. People have two ears, two eyes, two arms, two hands, two legs, and two feet.

8. Square tables and rectangular tables have four edges.

9. My dictionary has 350 pages.

10. I like apples, bananas, strawberries, and peaches.

11. My apartment has cockroaches in the kitchen.

_____

★ The idiom "raining cats and dogs" means "raining very hard."

6-5 NOUNS: IRREGULAR PLURAL FORMS

	SINGULAR	PLURAL	EXAMPLES
(a)	*child*	**children**	Mr. Smith has one *child*. Mr. Cook has two **children**.
(b)	*foot*	**feet**	I have a right *foot* and a left *foot*. I have two **feet**.
(c)	*man*	**men**	I see a *man* on the street. I see two **men** on the street.
(d)	*mouse*	**mice**	My cat sees a *mouse*. Cats like to catch **mice**.
(e)	*tooth*	**teeth**	My *tooth* hurts. My **teeth** are white.
(f)	*woman*	**women**	There's one *woman* in our class. There are ten **women** in your class.
(g)	*sheep*	**sheep**	Annie drew a picture of one *sheep*. Tommy drew a picture of two **sheep**. one sheep two sheep
(h)	*fish*	**fish**	Bob has an aquarium. He has one *fish*. Sue has an aquarium. She has seven **fish**. seven fish one fish
(h)	*(none)*★	**people**	There are fifteen **people** in this room. (Notice: *People* does not have a final *-s*.)

★**People** is always plural. It has no singular form.

☐ EXERCISE 19. Game.

> *Directions:* Work in groups or individually. The object of the game on p. 174 is to fill in each list with nouns. If possible, write one noun that begins with each letter of the alphabet. The nouns must belong to the category of the list. When you finish your lists, count the number of nouns you have. That is your score. Who has the highest score?

	List 1 Things in nature	List 2 Things you eat and drink	List 3 Animals and insects	List 4 Things for sale at *(name of a local store)*
A	air			
B	bushes			
C				
D				
E	earth			
F	fish			
G	grass			
H				
I	ice			
J				
K				
L	leaves			
M				
N				
O	ocean			
P	plants			
Q				
R	rain			
S	stars			
T	trees			
U				
V				
W	water			
X				
Y				
Z				
	Score: ___13___	Score: _____	Score: _____	Score: _____

☐ **EXERCISE 20. Let's talk: class activity.**

Directions: Your teacher will say a noun. You say the plural form with **two**. Close your books for this activity.

Example:
TEACHER: one child
STUDENTS: two children

1. one child
2. one woman
3. one tooth
4. one foot
5. one man
6. one mouse
7. one fish
8. one page
9. one place
10. one banana
11. one child
12. one desk

13. one sentence
14. one man
15. one orange
16. one foot
17. one knife
18. one sex
19. one girl
20. one exercise
21. one tooth
22. one woman
23. one boy and
    one woman

☐ **EXERCISE 21. Review.**

Directions: Fill in the grammatical structure of the sentences. Item 1 has been completed for you.

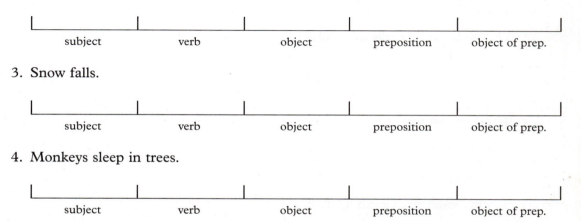

1. Mr. Cook is living in a hotel.

Mr. Cook	*is living*	*(none)*	*in*	*a hotel*
subject	verb	object	preposition	object of prep.

2. Anita carries her books in her backpack.

subject	verb	object	preposition	object of prep.

3. Snow falls.

subject	verb	object	preposition	object of prep.

4. Monkeys sleep in trees.

subject	verb	object	preposition	object of prep.

5. The teacher is writing words on the chalkboard.

subject	verb	object	preposition	object of prep.

6. I like apples.

subject	verb	object	preposition	object of prep.

☐ EXERCISE 22. Review.

Directions: A *complete sentence* has a subject and a verb. An *incomplete sentence* is a group of words that does not have a subject and a verb.

If the words are a complete sentence, change the first letter to a capital letter (a big letter) and add final punctuation (a period or a question mark). If the words are an incomplete sentence, write "*Inc.*" to mean "*Incomplete.*"

1. monkeys like bananas → *Mmonkeys like bananas.*

2. in my garden → *Inc.*

3. do you like sour apples → *Do you like sour apples?*

4. this class ends at two o'clock

5. teaches English

6. my mother works

7. in an office

8. my mother works in an office

9. does your brother have a job

10. does not work

11. rain falls

12. my sister lives in an apartment

13. has a roommate

14. the apartment has two bedrooms

15. a small kitchen and a big living room

16. on the third floor

□ **EXERCISE 23. Review.**

Directions: Circle the correct completions.

1. My sister and I live together. Our parents often call _____ on the telephone.
   (A.) us   B. them   C. we   D. they

2. Tom has a broken leg. I visit _____ every day.
   A. he   B. him   C. them   D. it

3. Sue and I are good friends. _____ spend a lot of time together.
   A. They   B. You   C. We   D. She

4. Our children enjoy the zoo. We often take _____ to the zoo.
   A. it   B. they   C. them   D. him

5. Mary drives an old car. She takes good care of _____.
   A. her   B. them   C. it   D. him

6. Jack and _____ don't know Mr. Wu.
   A. I   B. me   C. us   D. them

7. Ms. Gray is a lawyer in Chicago. Do you know _____?
   A. them   B. it   C. him   D. her

8. Ahmed lives near Yoko and _____.
   A. I   B. me   C. him   D. her

9. My sister and a friend are visiting me. _____ are visiting here for two days.
   A. She   B. They   C. We   D. Them

10. Do _____ have the correct time?
    A. you   B. them   C. him   D. her

□ **EXERCISE 24. Chapter review: error analysis.**

    Directions: Correct the errors.

    1. Omar a car has. → *Omar has a car.*

    2. Our teacher gives tests difficult.

    3. Alex helps Mike and I.

    4. Babys cry.

    5. Mike and Tom in an apartment live.

    6. There are seven woman in this class.

    7. There are nineteen peoples in my class.

    8. Olga and Ivan has three childrens.

    9. There is twenty classroom in this building.

    10. Mr. Jones is our teacher. I like her very much.

CHAPTER 7
Count and Noncount Nouns

□ **EXERCISE 1. Preview: noun practice.**

Directions: Describe the pictures. Add **-s** to the ends of the words if necessary. Otherwise, write an "x."

Picture	Description
	1. one ring __*X*__
	2. two ring __*s*__
	3. three ring __*s*__
	4. some jewelry __*X*__
	5. two letter _____
	6. one postcard _____
	7. some mail _____

Picture	Description
	8. one sofa _____
	9. two table _____
	10. some chair _____
	11. some furniture _____
	12. a lot of car _____
	13. a lot of traffic _____
	14. a lot of money _____
	15. a lot of coin _____

7-1 NOUNS: COUNT AND NONCOUNT

	SINGULAR	PLURAL	
COUNT NOUN	*a book* *one book*	*books* *two books* *some books* *a lot of books*	**A COUNT NOUN**
NONCOUNT NOUN	*mail* *some mail* *a lot of mail*	(no plural form)	**A NONCOUNT NOUN**

A COUNT NOUN

SINGULAR: ***a*** + *noun* ***one*** + *noun*	PLURAL: *noun* + ***-s***

A NONCOUNT NOUN

SINGULAR: Do not use *a*. Do not use *one*.	PLURAL: A noncount noun does not have a plural form.

COMMON NONCOUNT NOUNS

advice	*mail*	*bread*	*pepper*
furniture	*money*	*cheese*	*rice*
help	*music*	*coffee*	*salt*
homework	*traffic*	*food*	*soup*
information	*vocabulary*	*fruit*	*sugar*
jewelry	*weather*	*meat*	*tea*
luck	*work*	*milk*	*water*

☐ **EXERCISE 2. Noun practice.**

Directions: Look at the *italicized* words. <u>Underline</u> the noun. Is it count or noncount?

1. He sits on *a chair*.	(count)	noncount
2. He sits on *furniture*.	count	(noncount)
3. She has *a coin*.	count	noncount
4. She has *some money*.	count	noncount
5. The street is full of *traffic*.	count	noncount
6. There are *a lot of cars* in the street.	count	noncount
7. I know *a fact* about bees.	count	noncount
8. I have *some information* about bees.	count	noncount
9. The teacher gives us *homework*.	count	noncount
10. We have *an assignment*.	count	noncount
11. I like *music*.	count	noncount
12. Would you like *some coffee*?	count	noncount
13. Our school has *a library*.	count	noncount

14. We are learning new *vocabulary* every day.	count	noncount
15. I need *some advice.*	count	noncount
16. Tom has *a good job.*	count	noncount
17. He likes *his work.*	count	noncount
18. Maria wears *a lot of bracelets.*	count	noncount

□ EXERCISE 3. Let's talk: small groups.

Directions: Work in small groups. List the noncount nouns. Then find the count nouns that are close in meaning. Use ***a/an*** with the count nouns.

advice	*furniture*	*money*
assignment	*homework*	*music*
bracelet	*information*	*song*
cloud	*jewelry*	*suggestion*
coin	*job*	*weather*
desk	✓ *letter*	*work*
fact	✓ *mail*	

	NONCOUNT	COUNT
1.	*mail*	*a letter*
2.		
3.		
4.		
5.		
6.		
7.		
8.		
9.		
10.		

Directions: Most nouns are count nouns. Complete the sentences by naming things you see in the classroom.

1. I see a . . . .
2. I see a . . . .
3. I see a . . . .   and a . . . .
4. I see two . . . .

5. I see five . . . .
6. I see some . . . .
7. I see a lot of . . . .
8. I see many . . . .

7-2 USING *AN* vs. *A*

(a) ***A*** *dog* is ***an*** *animal.*	***A*** and ***an*** are used in front of singular count nouns. In (a): *dog* and *animal* are singular count nouns.
(b) I work in ***an*** *office.* (c) Mr. Lee is ***an*** *old man.*	Use ***an*** in front of words that begin with the vowels ***a, e, i,*** and ***o***: *an apartment, an elephant, an idea, an ocean.* In (c): Notice that ***an*** is used because the adjective *(old)* begins with a vowel and comes in front of a singular count noun *(man)*.
(d) I have ***an*** *uncle.* COMPARE (e) He works at ***a*** *university.*	Use ***an*** if a word that begins with "*u*" has a vowel sound: *an uncle, an ugly picture.* Use ***a*** if a word that begins with "*u*" has a /yu/ sound: *a university, a usual event.*
(f) I need ***an*** *hour* to finish my work. COMPARE (g) I live in ***a*** *house.* He lives in ***a*** *hotel.*	In some words that begin with "*h*," the "*h*" is not pronounced. Instead, the word begins with a vowel sound and ***an*** is used: *an hour, an honor.* In most words that begin with "*h*," the "*h*" is pronounced. Use ***a*** if the "*h*" is pronounced.

□ EXERCISE 5. Sentence practice.

Directions: Complete the sentences. Use ***a*** or ***an***.

1. Bob is eating _____ apple.

2. Tom is eating _____ banana.

3. Alice works in _____ office.

4. I have _____ idea.

5. I have _____ good idea.

6. Sue is taking _____ class.

7. Sue is taking _____ easy class.

8. Cuba is _____ island near the United States.

9. _____ hour has sixty minutes.

10. _____ healthy person gets regular exercise.

11. _____ horse has a long nose.

12. Maria is _____ honest worker.

13. Mark needs _____ math tutor.

14. _____ university is _____ educational institution.

15. Ann has _____ unusual job.

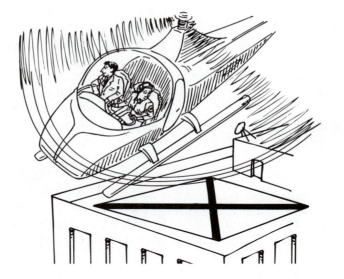

□ EXERCISE 6. Listening.

Directions: Listen to each sentence. Circle the word you hear.

1. a	(an)		6. a	an
2. a	an		7. a	an
3. a	an		8. a	an
4. a	an		9. a	an
5. a	an		10. a	an

7-3 USING A/AN vs. SOME

(a) I have **a** pen.	**A/An** is used in front of **singular** count nouns. In (a): The word *pen* is a singular count noun.
(b) I have **some** pens.	**Some** is used in front of **plural** count nouns. In (b): The word *pens* is a plural count noun.
(c) I have **some** rice.	**Some** is used in front of noncount nouns.* In (c): The word *rice* is a noncount noun.

*Reminder: Noncount nouns do not have a plural form. Noncount nouns are grammatically singular.

□ EXERCISE 7. Noun practice.

Directions: Look at the noun and circle the correct word (*a, an,* or *some*). Then decide if the noun is singular count, plural count, or noncount.

					sing. count	pl. count	noncount
1.	a	an	(some)	letters		✓	
2.	a	an	(some)	mail			✓
3.	(a)	an	some	letter	✓		
4.	a	an	some	table			
5.	a	an	some	tables			
6.	a	an	some	furniture			
7.	a	an	some	car			
8.	a	an	some	automobiles			
9.	a	an	some	buses			
10.	a	an	some	traffic			
11.	a	an	some	advice			
12.	a	an	some	egg			

□ EXERCISE 8. Sentence practice.

Directions: Use *a/an* or *some* with the count nouns in these sentences. Are the nouns singular or plural?

1. Bob has _____*a*_____ book on his desk. → *book = a singular count noun*

2. Bob has _____*some*_____ books on his desk. → *books = a plural count noun*

3. I see _____ desk in this room.

4. I see _____ desks in this room.

5. I'm hungry. I would like _____ apple.

6. The children are hungry. They would like _____ apples.

7. We are doing _____ exercise in class.

8. We are doing _____ exercises in class.

☐ EXERCISE 9. Sentence practice.

Directions: Use *a, an,* or *some* with the nouns in these sentences. Are they singular count nouns or noncount nouns?

1. I need _____*some*_____ money. → *money = a noncount noun*

2. I need _____*a*_____ dollar. → *dollar = a singular count noun*

3. Alice has _____ mail in her mailbox.

4. Alice has _____ letter in her mailbox.

5. I'm hungry. I would like _____ fruit.

6. I would like _____ apple.

7. Jane is hungry. She would like _____ food.

8. She would like _____ sandwich.

9. I'd like to have _____ soup with my sandwich.

10. I'm thirsty. I'd like _____ water.

an apple   a pear   some grapes
a banana
an orange

☐ EXERCISE 10. Let's talk: small groups.

Directions: Work in small groups. Complete the lists with nouns. You may use adjectives with the nouns. Share some of your answers with the class.

1. Things you can see in an apartment.

a _____

an _____

some _____ (plural noun)

some _____ (singular noun)

2. Things you can see in a classroom.

a _____

an _____

some _____ (plural noun)

some _____ (singular noun)

3. Things you can see outdoors.

a _____

an _____

some _____ (plural noun)

some _____ (singular noun)

☐ **EXERCISE 11. Sentence practice.**

Directions: Use **a/an** or **some** with the nouns in these sentences.

1. Sonya is wearing ____*some*____ silver jewelry. She's wearing

    ____*a*____ necklace and ____*some*____ earrings.

2. I'm busy. I have _____ homework to do.

3. Jane is very busy. She has _____ work to do.

4. Jane has _____ job. She is _____ teacher.

5. We have _____ table, _____ sofa, and _____ chairs in

    our living room.

6. We have _____ furniture in our living room.

7. Susan has a CD player. She is listening to _____ music.

8. I'm hungry. I would like _____ orange.

9. The children are hungry. They would like _____ oranges. They would

    like _____ fruit.

10. I need _____ information about the bus schedule.

11. I'm confused. I need _____ advice.

12. I'm looking out the window. I see _____ cars, _____ bus, and

_____ trucks on the street. I see _____ traffic.

□ **EXERCISE 12. Let's talk: pairwork.**

Directions: Work with a partner.
Partner A: Your book is open to this page. Use *a, an,* or *some* with the given word.
Partner B: Your book is open to p. 515. Help Partner A with the correct response if
        necessary.

Example: desk
PARTNER A: a desk
PARTNER B: Right.

Example: desks
PARTNER A: a desks
PARTNER B: Again?
PARTNER A: some desks
PARTNER B: Right.

1. apple	6. flower	11. rice
2. apples	7. man	12. advice
3. child	8. old man	13. hour
4. children	9. men	14. horse
5. music	10. island	15. food

Switch roles.

Partner B: Your book is open to this page. Use *a, an,* or *some* with the given word.
Partner A: Your book is open to p. 515. Help Partner B with the correct response if
        necessary.

16. animal	21. homework	26. university
17. animals	22. orange	27. uncle
18. chair	23. bananas	28. people
19. chairs	24. banana	29. house
20. furniture	25. fruit	30. bread

□ **EXERCISE 13. Sentence practice.**

Directions: Use the word in *italics* to complete the sentence. Add *-s* to a count noun (or give the irregular plural form). Do not add *-s* to a noncount noun.

1. *money*   I need some _____money_____ .

2. *desk*   I see some _____desks_____ in this room.

3. *man*   Some _____men_____ are working in the street.

4. *music*   I want to listen to some _____ .

5. *flower*   Andy wants to buy some _____ for his girlfriend.

6. *information*   I need some _____ .

7. *jewelry*   Fred wants to buy some _____ .

8. *child*   Some _____ are playing in the park.

9. *homework*   I can't go to the movie because I have some _____ to do.

10. *advice*   Could you please give me some _____ ?

11. *suggestion*   I have some _____ for you.

12. *help*   I need some _____ with my homework.

13. *sandwich*   We're hungry. We want to make some _____ .

14. *animal*   I see some _____ in the picture.

15. *banana*   The monkeys are hungry. They would like some _____ .

16. *fruit*   I'm hungry. I would like some _____ .

17. *weather*   We're having some hot _____ right now.

18. *picture*   I have some _____ of my family in my wallet.

19. *rice, bean*   I usually have some _____ and

                   _____ for dinner.

□ EXERCISE 14. Sentence practice.
   Directions: Change the *italicized* noun to its plural form if possible, changing **a** to
   some. Make other changes in the sentence as necessary.

   1. There is *a chair* in this room. PLURAL FORM → *There are some chairs in this room.*

   2. There is *some furniture* in this room. PLURAL FORM → *(none)*

   3. I have *a coin* in my pocket.

   4. I have *some money* in my wallet.

   5. There's *a lot of traffic* on Main Street.

   6. There's *a car* on Main Street.

   7. Our teacher assigns *a lot of homework*.

   8. I like rock *music*.

   9. Hong Kong has *a lot of hot weather*.

   10. I need *some information* and *some advice* from you.

   11. There's *a dictionary* on the shelf.

   12. I hope you do well on your exam. Good *luck!*

   13. Here is *a flower* from my garden.

   14. Be careful! There's *some water* on the floor.

   15. I need *an apple* for the fruit salad.

   16. The soup needs *a potato* and *some salt*.

7-4 MEASUREMENTS WITH NONCOUNT NOUNS

(a) I'd like **some** water.	Units of measure are used with noncount nouns to express a specific quantity. For example: *a glass of, a cup of, a piece of.*
(b) I'd like **a glass of** water.	In (a): *some water* = an unspecific quantity.
(c) I'd like **a cup of** coffee.	In (b): *a glass of water* = a specific quantity.
(d) I'd like **a piece of** fruit.	

COMMON EXPRESSIONS OF MEASURE

a bag of rice   *a bunch of bananas*   *a jar of pickles*
a bar of soap   *a can of corn★*   *a loaf of bread*
a bottle of olive oil *a carton of milk*   *a piece of cheese*
a bowl of cereal   *a glass of water*   *a sheet of paper*
a box of candy   *a head of lettuce*   *a tube of toothpaste*

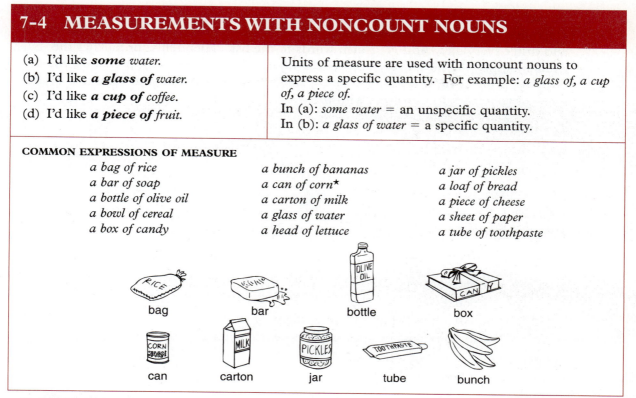

bag   bar   bottle   box

can   carton   jar   tube   bunch

*In British English: *a tin of corn.*

☐ EXERCISE 15. Noun practice.

Directions: Complete the phrases. You are hungry and thirsty. What would you like?
Use **a piece of, a cup of, a glass of, a bowl of.**

1. _____a cup of / a glass of_____ tea

2. _____ bread

3. _____ water

4. _____ coffee

5. _____ cheese

6. _____ soup

7. _____ meat

8. _____ wine

9. _____ fruit

10. _____ rice

□ EXERCISE 16. Let's talk: pairwork.

Directions: Work in pairs. Look at the list of food and drink. Check (✓) what you eat and drink every day. Add your own words to the list. Then tell your partner the usual <u>quantity</u> you have every day. Use *a piece of, two pieces of, a cup of, three cups of, a glass of, a bowl of*, or *one, two, a, some*, etc., in your answers. Share a few of your partner's answers with the class.

Example:

___✓___ egg

_____ banana

_____ coffee

___✓___ fruit

___*ice cream*___

___*orange juice*___

PARTNER A: I have one egg every day.
I usually eat two pieces of fruit.
I like a bowl of ice cream at night.
I drink a glass of orange juice every morning.

List of food and drinks.

_____ egg	_____ rice
_____ soup	_____ ice cream
_____ fruit	_____ water
_____ bread	_____ chicken
_____ banana	_____ cheese
_____ apples	_____ tea

_____   _____

_____   _____

_____   _____

□ EXERCISE 17. Sentence practice.

Directions: Complete the sentences with nouns.

1. I'm going to the store. I need to buy a carton of ___*orange juice / milk / etc.*___

2. I also need a tube of _____ and two bars of

   _____ .

3. I need to find a can of _____ and a jar of _____.

4. I need to get a loaf of _____ and a box of _____.

5. I would like a head of _____ if it looks fresh.

6. Finally, I would like a couple of bottles of _____ and a jar of _____.

□ EXERCISE 18. Review.

Directions: Make a list of everything in the picture by completing the sentence *I see* .... Try to use numbers (e.g., *three* spoons) or other units of measure (e.g., *a box of candy).* Use *a* for singular count nouns (e.g., *a fly).*

Example: I see three spoons, a box of candy, a fly, etc.

□ EXERCISE 19. Review: pairwork.

Directions: Work in pairs. Pretend that tomorrow you are moving into a new apartment together. What do you need? Ask each other questions.

In writing, list the things you need and indicate quantity *(two, some, a lot of, a little, etc.).* List twenty to thirty things. Be sure to write down the quantity. You are completing this sentence: *We need ....*

Example: We need . . .
PARTNER A: a sofa and two beds.
PARTNER B: a can opener.
PARTNER A: some spaghetti.
PARTNER B: a little fruit.
PARTNER A: some bookcases.
Etc.

□ **EXERCISE 20. Let's talk: pairwork.**

> *Directions:* Work with a partner.
>
> Partner A: Your book is open to this page. Complete the sentences by using ***a, an,*** or ***some*** with the nouns.
>
> Partner B: Your book is open to p. 515. Help Partner A with the correct responses if necessary.

1. I'm hungry. I'd like . . .
   a. food.
   b. apple.
   c. sandwich.
   d. bowl of soup.

2. I'm thirsty. I'd like . . .
   a. glass of milk.
   b. water.
   c. cup of tea.

3. I'm sick. I need . . .
   a. medicine.
   b. ambulance.

4. I'm cold. I need . . .
   a. coat.
   b. hat.
   c. warm clothes.
   d. heat.

5. I'm tired. I need . . .
   a. sleep.
   b. break.
   c. relaxing vacation.

Switch roles.

> Partner B: Your book is open to this page. Complete the sentences by using ***a, an,*** or ***some*** with the nouns.
>
> Partner A: Your book is open to p. 515. Help Partner B with the correct responses if necessary.

6. I'm hungry. I'd like . . .
   a. snack.
   b. fruit.
   c. orange.
   d. piece of chicken.

7. I'm thirsty. I'd like . . .
   a. juice.
   b. bottle of water.
   c. glass of ice tea.

8. I'm sick. I need . . .
   a. doctor.
   b. help.

9. I'm cold. I need . . .
   a. boots.
   b. blanket.
   c. hot bath.
   d. gloves.

10. I'm tired. I need . . .
   a. strong coffee.
   b. break.
   c. vacation.
   d. nap.

7-5 USING *MANY, MUCH, A FEW, A LITTLE*

(a) I don't get *many* letters.	In (a): *many* is used with PLURAL COUNT nouns.
(b) I don't get *much* mail.	In (b): *much* is used with NONCOUNT nouns.
(c) Ann gets *a few* letters.	In (c): *a few* is used with PLURAL COUNT nouns.
(d) Tom gets *a little* mail.	In (d): *a little* is used with NONCOUNT nouns.

☐ **EXERCISE 21. Sentence practice.**

Directions: Change *a lot of* to *many* or *much* in these sentences.

1. Tom has a lot of problems. → *Tom has many problems.*

2. I don't have a lot of money. → *I don't have much money.*

3. I want to visit a lot of cities in the United States and Canada.

4. I don't put a lot of sugar in my coffee.

5. I have a lot of questions to ask you.

6. Sue and John have a small apartment. They don't have a lot of furniture.

7. You can see a lot of people at the zoo on Sunday.

8. Dick doesn't get a lot of mail because he doesn't write a lot of letters.

9. Chicago has a lot of skyscrapers. Montreal has a lot of tall buildings too.

10. Mary is lazy. She doesn't do a lot of work.

11. I don't drink a lot of coffee.

12. Jeff is a friendly person. He has a lot of friends.

13. Do you usually buy a lot of fruit at the market?

14. Does Andy drink a lot of coffee?

15. Do you write a lot of letters?

☐ **EXERCISE 22. Sentence practice.**

Directions: Complete the questions with *many* or *much*.

1. How _____*much*_____ money do you have in your wallet?

2. How _____*many*_____ roommates do you have?

3. How _____ languages do you speak?

4. How _____ homework does your teacher usually assign?

5. How _____ tea do you drink in a day?

6. How _____ sugar do you put in your tea?

7. How _____ sentences are there in this exercise?

8. How _____ water do you need to cook rice?

☐ **EXERCISE 23. Let's talk: pairwork.**

Directions: Work with a partner.

Partner A: Your book is open to this page. Make questions with ***how many*** or ***how much*** and ***are there*** or ***is there***.

Partner B: Help Partner A if necessary.

Example: students in this room
PARTNER A: How many students is there in this room?
PARTNER B: Please try again.
PARTNER A: How many students are there in this room?
PARTNER B: Right.

Example: coffee in that pot
PARTNER A: How much coffee is there in that pot?
PARTNER B: Right.

1. restaurants in *(name of this city)*
2. desks in this room
3. furniture in this room
4. letters in your mailbox today
5. mail in your mailbox today

Switch roles.

Partner B: Your book is open to this page. Make questions with ***how many*** or ***how much*** and ***are there*** or ***is there***.

Partner A: Help Partner B if necessary.

6. chicken in your refrigerator
7. bridges in *(name of this city)*
8. traffic on the street right now
9. cars in the street outside the window
10. people in this room

□ **EXERCISE 24. Sentence practice.**

   Directions: Change *some* to *a few* or *a little*. Use *a few* with count nouns. Use *a little* with noncount nouns. (See Chart 7-5, p. 195.)

   1. I need some paper. → *I need a little paper.*

   2. I usually add some salt to my food.

   3. I have some questions to ask you.

   4. Bob needs some help. He has some problems. He needs some advice.

   5. I need to buy some clothes.

   6. I have some homework to do tonight.

   7. I usually get some mail every day.

   8. I usually get some letters every day.

   9. When I'm hungry in the evening, I usually eat some cheese.

   10. We usually do some oral exercises in class every day.

□ **EXERCISE 25. Let's talk: pairwork.**

   Directions: Work with a partner. Take turns asking and answering questions. Use the words from your list. Remember, you can look at your book before you speak. When you speak, look at your partner.
   Partner A: How *much/many* . . . would you like?
   Partner B: I'd like *a little/a few,* please. Thanks.

   Example: chicken
   PARTNER A: How **much chicken** would you like?
   PARTNER B: I'd like **a little,** please. Thanks.
   PARTNER A: Your turn now.

   Example: pencil
   PARTNER B: How **many pencils** would you like?
   PARTNER A: I'd like **a few,** please.
   PARTNER B: Your turn now.

Partner A	Partner B
1. pen	1. salt
2. tea	2. banana
3. rice	3. soup
4. apple	4. coffee
5. money	5. assignment
6. help	6. cheese
7. toy	7. book

□ EXERCISE 26. Sentence review.

    Directions: Complete the sentences with these words. If necessary, use the plural form.

bush	glass	✓ match	strawberry
centimeter	homework	page	thief
dish	inch	paper	tray
edge	information	piece	valley
fish	knife	sex	weather
foot	leaf	size	woman

1. I want to light a candle. I need some _____*matches*_____.

2. _____ fall from the trees in autumn.

3. There are two _____: male and female.

4. There are some _____, forks, and spoons on the table.

5. I want to take the bus downtown, but I don't know the bus schedule. I need some

    _____ about the bus schedule.

6. I want to write a letter. I have a pen, but I need some _____.

7. Plates and bowls are called _____.

8. Married _____ are called wives.

9. There are a lot of trees and _____ in the park.

10. Bob is studying. He has a lot of _____ to do.

11. My dictionary has 437 _____.

12. This puzzle has 200 _____.

13. A piece of paper has four _____.

14. Mountains are high, and _____
    are low.

15. When the temperature is around 35°C (77°F), I'm comfortable. But I don't like

    very hot _____.

16. _____ steal things: money, jewelry, cars, etc.

17. _____ are small, red, sweet, and delicious.

18. People carry their food on _____ at a cafeteria.

19. Sweaters in a store often have four _____: small, medium, large, and extra large.

20. In some countries, people use cups for their tea. In other countries, they usually use _____ for their tea.

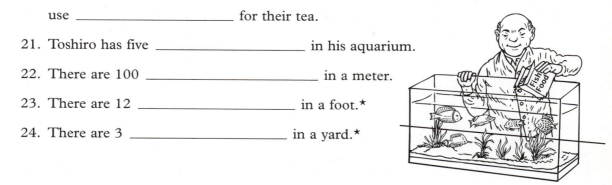

21. Toshiro has five _____ in his aquarium.

22. There are 100 _____ in a meter.

23. There are 12 _____ in a foot.★

24. There are 3 _____ in a yard.★

7-6 USING *THE*

(a) A: Where's David? 　　B: He's in ***the*** *kitchen*.	A speaker uses ***the*** when the speaker and the listener have the same thing or person in mind. ***The*** shows that a noun is specific. In (a): Both A and B have the same kitchen in mind. In (b): When B says "the apple," both A and B have the same apple in mind.
(b) A: I have two pieces of fruit for us, an apple and a banana. Which do you want? 　　B: I'd like ***the*** *apple,* thank you.	
(c) A: It's a nice summer day today. ***The*** *sky* is blue. ***The*** *sun* is hot. 　　B: Yes, I really like summer.	In (c): Both A and B are thinking of the same sky (there is only one sky for them to think of) and the same sun (there is only one sun for them to think of).
(d) Mike has *a pen* and *a pencil.* ***The*** *pen* is blue. ***The*** *pencil* is yellow.	***The*** is used with 　• singular count nouns, as in (d). 　• plural count nouns, as in (e). 　• noncount nouns, as in (f). In other words, ***the*** is used with each of the three kinds of nouns.
(e) Mike has ***some*** *pens and pencils.* ***The*** *pens* are blue. ***The*** *pencils* are yellow.	
(f) Mike has ***some*** *rice* and ***some*** *cheese.* ***The*** *rice* is white. ***The*** *cheese* is yellow.	Notice in the examples: the speaker is using ***the*** for the **second** mention of a noun. When the speaker mentions a noun for a second time, both the speaker and listener are now thinking about the same thing. 　　First mention:　　I have ***a*** *pen.* 　　Second mention: ***The*** *pen* is blue.

_____

★1 inch = 2.54 centimeters. 1 foot = 30.48 centimeters. 1 yard = 0.91 meters.

□ **EXERCISE 27. Sentence practice.**

Directions: Complete the sentences with *the* or *a/an*.

1. I have _____*a*_____ notebook and _____ grammar book. _____ notebook is brown. _____ grammar book is red.

2. Right now Pablo is sitting in class. He's sitting between _____ woman and _____ man. _____ woman is Graciela. _____ man is Mustafa.

3. Susan is wearing _____ ring and _____ necklace. _____ ring is on her left hand.

4. Tony and Sara are waiting for their plane to depart. Tony is reading _____ magazine. Sara is reading _____ newspaper. When Sara finishes _____ newspaper and Tony finishes _____ magazine, they will trade.

5. In the picture below, there are four figures: _____ circle, _____ triangle, _____ square, and _____ rectangle. _____ circle is next to _____ triangle. _____ square is between _____ triangle and _____ rectangle.

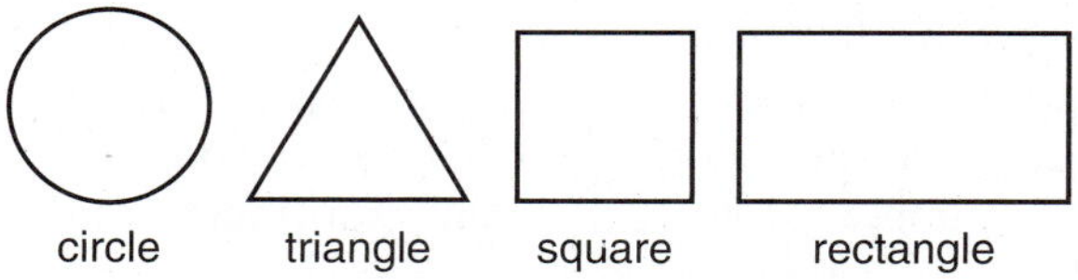

circle   triangle   square   rectangle

6. Linda and Anne live in _____ apartment in _____ old building. They like _____ apartment because it is big. _____ building is very old. It was built more than one hundred years ago.

7. I gave my friend _____ card and _____ flower for her birthday. _____ card wished her "Happy Birthday." She liked both _____ card and _____ flower.

8. We stayed at _____ hotel in New York. _____ hotel was expensive.

Directions: Work with a partner. Read the sentences aloud and complete them with ***the*** or ***a/an***. Then change roles. When you have finished speaking, write the answers.

A: Look at the picture below. What do you see?

B: I see _____ chair, _____ desk, _____ window, _____
                  1   2   3   4

    plant.

A: Where is _____ chair?
                   5

B: _____ chair is under _____ window.
       6   7

A: Where is _____ plant?
                   8

B: _____ plant is beside _____ chair.
       9   10

A: Do you see any people?

B: Yes. I see _____ man and _____ woman. _____ man is
                     11   12   13

    standing. _____ woman is sitting down.
                14

A: Do you see any animals?

B: Yes. I see _____ dog, _____ cat, and _____ bird in
                     15   16   17

    _____ cage.
      18

A: What is _____ dog doing?
               19

B: It's sleeping.

A: How about _____ cat?
                 20

B: _____ cat is watching
      21

    _____ bird.
      22

□ **EXERCISE 29. Review.**

Directions: Complete the sentences with **the** or **a/an**.

1. A: I need to go shopping. I need to buy _____ coat.

   B: I'll go with you. I need to get _____ umbrella.

   A: Okay. Great! When should we go?

2. A: Hi! Come in!

   B: Hi! _____ weather is terrible today! It's cold and wet outside.

   A: Well, it's warm in here.

   B: What should I do with my coat and umbrella?

   A: You can put _____ coat in that closet. I'll take _____ umbrella

   and put it in _____ kitchen where it can dry.

3. My cousin Jane has _____ good job. She works in _____ office. She

   uses _____ computer.

4. A: How much longer do you need to use _____ computer?

   B: Why?

   A: I need to use it too.

   B: Just five more minutes, then you can have it.

5. A: I need _____ stamp for this letter. Do you have one?

   B: Yes. Here.

   A: Thanks.

6. A: Would you like _____ egg for breakfast?

   B: No thanks. I'll just have _____ glass of juice

   and some toast.

some toast

a toaster

7. A: Do you see my pen? I can't find it.

   B: There it is. It's on _____ floor.

   A: Oh. I see it. Thanks.

8. A: Be sure to look at _____ moon tonight.

   B: Why?

   A: _____ moon is full now, and it's beautiful.

9. A: Can I call you tonight?

   B: No. I don't have _____ telephone in my apartment yet. I just moved in

   yesterday.

10. A: Could you answer _____ telephone? Thanks.

    B: Hello?

7-7 USING Ø (NO ARTICLE) TO MAKE GENERALIZATIONS

(a) *Ø Apples* are good for you. (b) *Ø Students* use *Ø pens* and *Ø pencils*. (c) I like to listen to *Ø music*. (d) *Ø Rice* is good for you.	No article (symbolized by Ø) is used to make generalizations with • plural count nouns, as in (a) and (b), and • noncount nouns, as in (c) and (d).
(e) Tom and Ann ate some fruit. ***The*** *apples* were very good, but ***the*** *bananas* were too ripe. (f) We went to a concert last night. ***The*** *music* was very good.	COMPARE: In (a), the word *apples* is general. It refers to all apples, any apples. No article (Ø) is used. In (e), the word *apples* is specific, so *the* is used in front of it. It refers to the specific apples that Tom and Ann ate. COMPARE: In (c), *music* is general. In (f), *the music* is specific.

□ EXERCISE 30. Sentence practice.
   Directions: Complete the sentences with ***the*** or **Ø** (no article).

   1. _____Ø_____ sugar is sweet.

   2. Could you please pass me _____*the*_____ sugar?

   3. Oranges are orange, and _____ bananas are yellow.

4. There was some fruit on the table. I didn't eat _____ bananas because they were soft and brown.

5. Everybody needs _____ food to live.

6. We ate at a good restaurant last night. _____ food was excellent.

7. _____ salt tastes salty, and _____ pepper tastes hot.

8. Could you please pass me _____ salt? Thanks. And could I have

   _____ pepper too?

9. _____ coffee is brown.

10. Steven made some coffee and some tea. _____ coffee was very good.

    I didn't taste _____ tea.

11. _____ pages in this book are full of grammar exercises.

12. _____ books consist of _____ pages.

13. There was some food on the table. The children ate _____ fruit, but they

    didn't want _____ vegetables.

14. I like _____ fruit. I also

    like _____ vegetables.

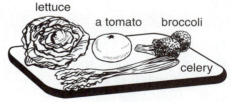
lettuce
a tomato   broccoli
celery

□ EXERCISE 31. Listening.

Directions: Listen to each sentence. Decide if the given noun has a general or a specific use.

1. vegetables   (general)   specific

2. cats   general   specific

3. teacher   general   specific

4. bananas   general   specific

5. cars   general   specific

6. keys   general   specific

7. computers   general   specific

8. ducks   general   specific

□ **EXERCISE 32. Listening: article review.**

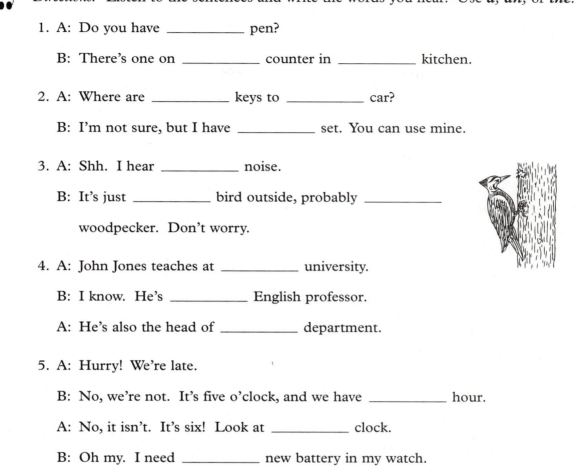

Directions: Listen to the sentences and write the words you hear. Use *a, an*, or *the*.

1. A: Do you have _____ pen?

   B: There's one on _____ counter in _____ kitchen.

2. A: Where are _____ keys to _____ car?

   B: I'm not sure, but I have _____ set. You can use mine.

3. A: Shh. I hear _____ noise.

   B: It's just _____ bird outside, probably _____

   woodpecker. Don't worry.

4. A: John Jones teaches at _____ university.

   B: I know. He's _____ English professor.

   A: He's also the head of _____ department.

5. A: Hurry! We're late.

   B: No, we're not. It's five o'clock, and we have _____ hour.

   A: No, it isn't. It's six! Look at _____ clock.

   B: Oh my. I need _____ new battery in my watch.

7-8	**USING *SOME* AND *ANY***	
STATEMENT	(a) Alice has ***some money***.	Use *some* in affirmative statements.
NEGATIVE	(b) Alice doesn't have ***any money***.	Use *any* in negative statements.
QUESTION	(c) Does Alice have ***any money?*** (d) Does Alice have ***some money?***	Use either *some* or *any* in a question.
(e) I don't have ***any money***. (noncount noun) (f) I don't have ***any matches***. (plural count noun)		*Any* is used with noncount nouns and plural count nouns.

☐ EXERCISE 33. Sentence practice.

    Directions: Use **some** or **any** to complete the sentences.

1. Sue has _____*some*_____ money.

2. I don't have _____*any*_____ money.

3. Do you have _*some/any*_ money?

4. Do you need _____ help?

5. No, thank you. I don't need _____ help.

6. Ken needs _____ help.

7. Anita usually doesn't get _____ mail.

8. We don't have _____ fruit in the apartment. We don't have

    _____ apples, _____ bananas, or _____ oranges.

9. The house is empty. There aren't _____ people in the house.

10. I need _____ paper. Do you have _____ paper?

11. Heidi can't write a letter because she doesn't have _____ paper.

12. Steve is getting along fine. He doesn't have _____ problems.

13. I need to go to the grocery store. I need to buy _____ food. Do you

    need to buy _____ groceries?

14. I'm not busy tonight. I don't have _____ homework to do.

15. I don't have _____ money in my purse.

16. There are _____ beautiful flowers in my garden this year.

☐ EXERCISE 34. Let's talk: class activity.

    Directions: Ask a classmate a question about what he or she sees in this room. Use **any** in the question.

    Examples: desks, monkeys
    SPEAKER A: *(Speaker B),* do you see any desks in this room?
    SPEAKER B: Yes, I do. I see some desks / a lot of desks / twenty desks.
    SPEAKER B: *(Speaker C),* do you see any monkeys in this room?
    SPEAKER C: No, I don't. I don't see any monkeys.
    Etc.

1. books	8. paper	15. pillows
2. flowers	9. backpacks	16. red sweaters
3. dictionaries	10. children	17. dogs or cats
4. birds	11. hats	18. bookshelves
5. furniture	12. signs on the wall	19. women
6. food	13. bicycles	20. light bulbs
7. curtains	14. erasers	

□ **EXERCISE 35. Sentence practice.**

Directions: Use ***any*** or ***a***. Use ***any*** with noncount nouns and plural count nouns. Use ***a*** with singular count nouns.

1. I don't have _____*any*_____ money.

2. I don't have _____*a*_____ pen.

3. I don't have _____*any*_____ brothers or sisters.

4. We don't need to buy _____ new furniture.

5. Mr. and Mrs. Kelly don't have _____ children.

6. I can't make _____ coffee. There isn't _____ coffee in the house.

7. Ann doesn't want _____ cup of coffee.

8. I don't like this room because there aren't _____ windows.

9. Amanda is very unhappy because she doesn't have _____ friends.

10. I don't need _____ help. I can finish my homework by myself.

11. I don't have _____ comfortable chair in my dormitory room.

12. I'm getting along fine. I don't have _____ problems.

13. Joe doesn't have _____ car, so he has to take the bus to school.

14. I don't have _____ homework to do tonight.

15. I don't need _____ new clothes.★

16. I don't need _____ new suit.

_____
★*Clothes* is always plural. The word *clothes* does not have a singular form.

Directions: Correct the errors.

```
        some
```

1. I need ~~an~~ advice from you.

2. I don't like hot weathers.

3. I usually have a egg for breakfast.

4. Sun rises every morning.

5. The students in this class do a lot of homeworks every day.

6. How many language do you know?

7. I don't have many money.

8. John and Susan don't have some children.

9. A pictures are beautiful. You're a good photographer.

10. There isn't a traffic early in the morning.

11. I can't find any bowl for my soup.

☐ EXERCISE 37.   Review: pairwork.

Directions: Work in pairs. Ask and answer questions about the things and people in the picture on p. 209.

Example:
PARTNER A: How many boys are there in the picture?
PARTNER B: There are three boys in the picture.
PARTNER A: Are there any flowers?
PARTNER B: No, there aren't any flowers in the picture.
PARTNER A: Are you sure?
PARTNER B: Well, hmmm. I don't see any flowers.
PARTNER A: Oh?
Etc.

Directions: Make the nouns plural where necessary.

                                  cities

1. Toronto and Bangkok are big ~~city.~~

2. I need some information. *(no change)*

3. Horse are large animals.

4. I like to listen to music when I study.

5. I have two small child.

6. I like to tell them story.

7. There are sixty minute in an hour.

8. Children like to play with toy.

9. My bookcase has three shelf.

10. There are five woman and seven man in this class.

11. Taiwan and Cuba are island.

12. I drink eight glass of water every day.

13. Tomato are red when they are ripe.

14. Before dinner, I put dish, spoon, fork, knife, and napkin on the table.

15. I have many friend. I don't have many enemy.

□ EXERCISE 39.   Let's talk: review.

Directions: Imagine that a new shopping center is coming to your neighborhood. A drugstore and a grocery store are already in place. Decide what other stores you want to add. Your teacher will help you with vocabulary you don't know.

PART I. Work alone.

Choose any six businesses from the list and write their names in any of the six available spaces on Blueprint #1 on p. 211.

✓ *a bank*	✓ *a grocery store*	*a post office*
a bookstore	*an ice-cream shop*	*a shoe store*
a camera shop	*an Internet café*	*a sports equipment store*
✓ *a drugstore*	*a laundromat*	*a vegetarian food store*
a drycleaner's	*a movie theater*	*a video rental store*
an exercise gym	*a music store*	
a fast-food restaurant	*a pet supply store*	

BLUEPRINT #1
(your business locations)

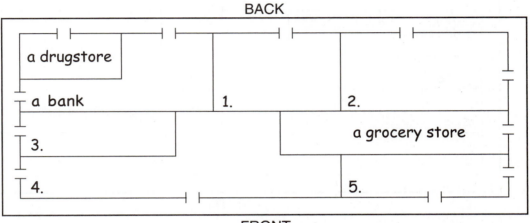

PART II. Work with a partner, but do not look at each other's blueprints.

Partner A: Ask your partner about the location of his/her new businesses.
Write your partner's answers on your copy of Blueprint #2.

Partner B: Ask your partner about the location of his/her new businesses.
Write your partner's answers on your copy of Blueprint #2.

When you are finished, compare your answers. Does your Blueprint #1 match your partner's Blueprint #2?

Question and answer pattern.

PARTNER A: Is there **a/an** _____?
PARTNER B: Yes, there is. / No, there isn't.
PARTNER A: Where is **the** _____?
PARTNER B: It's next to / beside / in back of / in front of **the** _____.

Example:

PARTNER A: Is there **an** exercise gym?

PARTNER B: No, there isn't.

PARTNER A: Is there **a** bank?

PARTNER B: Yes, there is.

PARTNER A: Where is **the** bank?

PARTNER B: It's in front of **the** drugstore.

BLUEPRINT #2
(your partner's business locations)

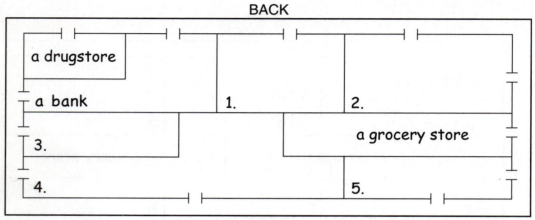

CHAPTER 8
Expressing Past Time, Part 1

8-1 USING *BE:* PAST TIME

PRESENT TIME	PAST TIME
(a) I *am* in class *today*.	(b) I *was* in class *yesterday*.
(c) Alice *is* at the library *today*.	(d) Alice *was* at the library *yesterday*.
(e) My friends *are* at home *today*.	(f) My friends *were* at home *yesterday*.

SIMPLE PAST TENSE OF *BE*

Singular	Plural
I was	*we were*
you were (one person)	*you were* (more than one person)
she was	*they were*
he was	
it was	

$$\left.\begin{array}{l} I \\ she \\ he \\ it \end{array}\right\} + \ was$$

$$\left.\begin{array}{l} we \\ you \\ they \end{array}\right\} + \ were$$

□ EXERCISE 1. Sentence practice.

Directions: Change the sentences to past time.

1. Bob is in class today. → *He was in class yesterday too.*

2. I'm in class today. → *I was in class yesterday too.*

3. Mary is at the library today.

4. We're in class today.

5. You're busy today.

6. I'm happy today.

7. The classroom is hot today.

8. Ann is in her office today.

9. Tom is in his office today.

10. Ann and Tom are in their offices today.

□ **EXERCISE 2. Let's talk: class activity.**

Directions: Talk about today and yesterday. Close your book for this activity.

Example:
TEACHER: I'm in class.
SPEAKER A: I'm in class **today**. I was in class **yesterday too**.
TEACHER: *(to Speaker B) (Speaker A)* is in class.
SPEAKER B: *(Speaker A)* is in class **today**. She/He was in class **yesterday too**.

1. We're in class.
2. I'm in class.
3. (. . .) is in class.
4. (. . .) and (. . .) are in class.
5. (. . .) is here.

6. (. . .) is absent.
7. I'm tired.
8. (. . .) and (. . .) are *(in the first row)*.
9. The door is open/closed.
10. It's hot/cold.

8-2 PAST OF *BE*: NEGATIVE

(a) I **was not** in class yesterday. (b) I **wasn't** in class yesterday.	NEGATIVE CONTRACTIONS **was** + **not** = **wasn't** **were** + **not** = **weren't**
(c) They **were not** at home last night. (d) They **weren't** at home last night.	$\left.\begin{array}{c} I \\ she \\ he \\ it \end{array}\right\}$ + *wasn't* $\left.\begin{array}{c} we \\ you \\ they \end{array}\right\}$ + *weren't*

□ **EXERCISE 3. Sentence practice.**

Directions: Study the time expressions. Then complete the sentences. Use **wasn't** or **weren't**. Use a past time expression.

PRESENT		PAST
today	→	*yesterday*
this morning	→	*yesterday morning*
this afternoon	→	*yesterday afternoon*
tonight	→	*last night*
this week	→	*last week*

1. Ken is here today, but _____ *he wasn't here yesterday.* _____

2. I'm at home tonight, but _____ *I wasn't at home last night.* _____

3. Olga is busy today, but _____

4. Tom is at the library tonight, but _____

5. Alex and Rita are at work this afternoon, but _____

6. You're here today, but _____

7. Dr. Ruckman is in her office this morning, but _____

8. It's cold this week, but _____

□ **EXERCISE 4. Let's talk: class activity.**

Directions: Think about your first day in this class. Check (✓) the words that describe how you felt. Then answer your teacher's questions.

Example: happy
  TEACHER: Were you happy the first day of class?
SPEAKER A: Yes, I was happy.
SPEAKER B: No, I wasn't happy.
  TEACHER: *(to Speaker C)* Tell me about *(Speaker A)* and *(Speaker B)*.
SPEAKER C: *(Speaker A)* was happy. *(Speaker B)* wasn't happy.

1. _____ excited   4. _____ relaxed (not nervous)

2. _____ scared/afraid   5. _____ quiet

3. _____ nervous   6. _____ talkative

□ **EXERCISE 5. Listening.**

Directions: Listen to the sentences. Circle the verbs you hear.

1. was	(wasn't)	6. were	weren't
2. was	wasn't	7. was	wasn't
3. was	wasn't	8. was	wasn't
4. was	wasn't	9. were	weren't
5. were	weren't	10. were	weren't

□ **EXERCISE 6. Let's talk: find someone who . . . .**

Directions: Interview your classmates about their days in elementary school. Find people who can answer *yes* to your questions. Write down their names.
Speaker A: Make a complete question with the given words. Use the past tense. Ask *(Speaker B)* the question.
Speaker B: Answer the question.

Example: you \ shy

SPEAKER A: Were you shy?
SPEAKER B: No, I wasn't.
SPEAKER A: *(to Speaker C)* Were you shy?
SPEAKER C: Yes, I was.

	First name
1. you \ shy	
2. you \ outgoing (not shy)	
3. you \ talkative	
4. you \ happy	
5. you \ hardworking	
6. you \ quiet	

	First name
7. you \ noisy	
8. you \ athletic	
9. you \ active	
10. you \ well-behaved	
11. you \ a serious student	
12. you \ artistic	

8-3 PAST OF *BE:* QUESTIONS

YES/NO QUESTIONS		SHORT ANSWER + (LONG ANSWER)	
(a) **Were** **you** in class yesterday? *(be)* + (subject)	→ →	**Yes, I was.** **No, I wasn't.**	(I was in class yesterday.) (I wasn't in class yesterday.)
(b) **Was** **Carlos** at home last night? *(be)* + (subject)	→	**Yes, he was.** **No, he wasn't.**	(He was at home last night.) (He wasn't at home last night.)
INFORMATION QUESTIONS		SHORT ANSWER + (LONG ANSWER)	
(c) **Where** **were** **you** yesterday? *Where* + *(be)* + (subject)	→	**In class.**	(I was in class yesterday.)
(d) **Where** **was** **Jennifer** last night? *Where* + *(be)* + (subject)	→	**At home.**	(She was at home last night.)

Directions: Make questions and give short answers.

1. *(you \ at home \ last night)*

   A: _____*Were you at home last night?*_____

   B: No, _____*I wasn't.*_____

2. *(Mr. Yamamoto \ absent from class \ yesterday)*

   A: _____

   B: Yes, _____

3. *(Oscar and Anya \ at home \ last night)*

   A: _____

   B: Yes, _____

4. *(you \ nervous \ the first day of class)*

   A: _____

   B: No, _____

5. *(Ahmed \ at the library \ last night)*

   A: _____

   B: Yes, _____

6. *(Mr. Shin \ in class \ yesterday)*

   A: _____

   B: No, _____

   A: Where _____

   B: At home.

7. *(you and your family \ in Canada \ last year)*

A: _____

B: No, _____

A: Where _____

B: In Ireland.

8. *(you \ be \ at the library \ right now)*

A: _____

B: No, _____

A: Where _____

B: In class.

□ EXERCISE 8. Let's talk: pairwork.

Directions: Work with a partner. Ask and answer questions. If your partner answers *yes,* the exercise item is finished. If your partner answers *no,* ask a *where*-question.

Example: in class \ now
PARTNER A *(book open):* *(Partner B),* are you in class now?
PARTNER B *(book closed):* Yes, I am.

Example: at the library \ last night
PARTNER A *(book open):* *(Partner B),* were you at the library last night?
PARTNER B *(book closed):* No, I wasn't.
PARTNER A *(book open):* Where were you?
PARTNER B *(book closed):* I was (at home \ in my room \ at a party, etc.).

1. at home \ now
2. at home \ yesterday morning
3. at home \ last night
4. in class \ six hours ago

5. in *(a place in this city)* \ now
6. in *(this city)* \ last year
7. *(your teacher)* \ in class \ yesterday
8. *(two classmates)* \ here \ yesterday

Switch roles.
Partner A: Close your book.
Partner B: Open your book. Your turn now.

9. in *(this country)* \ two weeks ago
10. in *(this country)* \ two years ago
11. in *(a city)* \ now
12. at *(a park in this city)* \ yesterday afternoon

13. at *(a famous place in this city)* \ this morning★
14. at *(a popular place for students)* \ last night
15. at home \ this morning
16. *(two students)* \ *(this building)* \ yesterday afternoon

☐ **EXERCISE 9. Question practice.**

Directions: Make questions and give short answers.

1. *(you \ in class \ yesterday)*

   A: _____ *Were you in class yesterday?* _____

   B: Yes, _____ *I was.* _____

2. *(Anita \ in class \ today)*

   A: _____ *Is Anita in class today?* _____

   B: No, _____ *she isn't.* _____ She's absent.

3. *(you \ tired \ last night)*

   A: _____

   B: Yes, _____. I went to bed early.

4. *(you \ hungry \ right now)*

   A: _____

   B: No, _____, but I'm thirsty.

5. *(the weather \ hot in New York City \ last summer)*

   A: _____

   B: Yes, _____. It was very hot.

6. *(the weather \ cold in Alaska \ in the winter)*

   A: _____

   B: Yes, _____. It's very cold.

_____

★If you are asking this question in the morning, use a present verb. If it is now afternoon or evening, use a past verb.

7. (*Yoko and Mohammed \ here \ yesterday afternoon*)

A: _____

B: Yes, _____

8. (*the students \ in this class \ intelligent*)

A: _____

B: Of course _____! They are very intelligent!

9. (*Mr. Tok \ absent \ today*)

A: _____

B: Yes, _____

A: Where _____

B: _____

10. (*Tony and Benito \ at the party \ last night*)

A: _____

B: No, _____

A: Where _____

B: _____

11. (*Amy \ out of town \ last week*)

A: _____

B: Yes, _____

A: Where _____

B: _____

_____

12. *(Mr. and Mrs. Rice \ in town \ this week)*

A: _____

B: No, _____. They're out of town.

A: Oh? Where _____

B: _____

8-4 THE SIMPLE PAST TENSE: USING *-ED*

SIMPLE PRESENT SIMPLE PAST	(a) I **walk** to school *every day*. (b) I **walked** to school *yesterday*.	verb + *-ed* = the simple past tense
SIMPLE PRESENT SIMPLE PAST	(c) Ann **walks** to school *every day*. (d) Ann **walked** to school *yesterday*.	*I* *you* *she* *he* } + *walked (verb + **-ed**)* *it* *we* *they* }

☐ EXERCISE 10. Sentence practice.

Directions: Complete the sentences orally in the simple past. Then write the answers.

1. Every day I walk. Yesterday I _____.

2. Every day I work. Yesterday I _____.

3. Every day Omar shaves. Yesterday Omar _____.

4. Every night Paula watches TV. Last night she _____ TV.

5. Every day Mrs. Wu cooks. Last night she _____.

6. Every day people smile. Yesterday they _____.

7. Every week it rains. Last week it _____.

8. Every day we ask questions. Yesterday we _____ questions.

9. Every day I talk on the phone. Yesterday I _____ on the phone.

10. Every day Tomo listens to music. Yesterday he _____ to music.

☐ **EXERCISE 11. Sentence practice.**

Directions: Complete the sentences. Use the words in the list. Use the simple present or the simple past.

ask	erase	smile	walk
cook	✓rain	stay	watch
dream	shave	wait	work

1. It often _____*rains*_____ in the morning. It _____*rained*_____ yesterday.

2. I _____ to school every morning. I _____ to school yesterday morning.

3. Sue often _____ questions. She _____ a question in class yesterday.

4. I _____ a movie on television last night. I usually _____ TV in the evening because I want to improve my English.

5. Mike _____ his own dinner yesterday evening. He _____ his own dinner every evening.

6. I usually _____ home at night because I have to study. I _____ home last night.

7. I have a job at the library. I _____ at the library every evening. I _____ there yesterday evening.

8. When I am asleep, I often _____. I _____ about my family last night.★

9. Linda usually _____ for the bus at a bus stop in front of her apartment building. She _____ for the bus there yesterday morning.

10. The teacher _____ some words from the board a couple of minutes ago. He used his hand instead of an eraser.

_____

★The past of *dream* can be *dreamed* or *dreamt*.

11. Our teacher is a warm, friendly person. She often _____ when she is talking to us.

12. Rick doesn't have a beard anymore. He _____ it five days ago.

Now he _____ every morning.

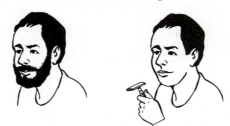

☐ EXERCISE 12. Let's talk: pairwork.

Directions: Work with a partner. Check (✓) all the activities you did yesterday. Tell your partner. Begin with **Yesterday I** . . . . Share a few of your partner's answers with the class.

1. ____ ask the teacher a question
2. ____ cook dinner
3. ____ wash some clothes
4. ____ listen to music on the radio
5. ____ use a computer
6. ____ stay home in the evening
7. ____ walk in a park

8. ____ watch TV
9. ____ work at my desk
10. ____ wait for a bus
11. ____ smile at several people
12. ____ talk on a cell phone
13. ____ dream in English
14. ____ dream in my language

☐ EXERCISE 13. Pronunciation practice.

Directions: Pronounce the words in each group.

GROUP A: Final **-ed** is pronounced /t/ if the verb ends in a voiceless sound.*

1. walked	3. laughed	5. missed	7. stretched
2. washed	4. helped	6. sniffed	8. watched

GROUP B: Final **-ed** is pronounced /d/ if the verb ends in a voiced sound.

1. closed	3. rubbed	5. filled	7. loved	9. stirred
2. waited	4. turned	6. seemed	8. stayed	10. hugged

GROUP C: Final **-ed** is pronounced /əd/ if the verb ends in the letter "d" or "t."

1. rent   2. need   3. visit   4. add

_____

*See Chart 3-8, p. 66, for information about voiceless and voiced sounds.

☐ **EXERCISE 14. Listening.**

Directions: Listen to each sentence and circle the verb you hear.

1. play	plays	(played)
2. play	plays	played
3. watch	watches	watched
4. enjoy	enjoys	enjoyed
5. watch	watches	watched
6. ask	asks	asked
7. answer	answers	answered
8. listen	listens	listened
9. like	likes	liked
10. work	works	worked

☐ **EXERCISE 15. Let's talk: class activity.**

Directions: Answer the questions your teacher asks you. Practice pronouncing *-ed*. Close your book for this activity.

Example: walk to the front of the room
 TEACHER: *(Speaker A)*, walk to the front of the room.
SPEAKER A: *(walks to the front of the room)*
 TEACHER: *(to Speaker B)* What did *(Speaker A)* do?
SPEAKER B: She/He walked to the front of the room.
 TEACHER: *(to Speaker A)* What did you do?
SPEAKER A: I walked to the front of the room.

1. smile	11. wash your hands *(pantomime)*
2. laugh	12. touch the floor
3. cough	13. point at the door
4. sneeze	14. fold a piece of paper
5. shave *(pantomime)*	15. count your fingers
6. erase the board	16. push *(something in the room)*
7. sign your name	17. pull *(something in the room)*
8. open the door	18. yawn
9. close the door	19. pick up your pen
10. ask a question	20. add two and two on the board

PAST TIME WORDS: *YESTERDAY, LAST,* AND *AGO*

YESTERDAY	LAST	AGO

(a) Bob was here . . .
    yesterday.
    yesterday morning.
    yesterday afternoon.
    yesterday evening.
	(b) Sue was here . . .
	    last night.
	    last week.
	    last month.
	    last year.
	
	    last spring.
	    last summer.
	    last fall.
	    last winter.
	
	    last Monday.
	    last Tuesday.
	    last Wednesday.
	    etc.
		(c) Tom was here . . .
		    five minutes ago.
		    two hours ago.
		    three days ago.
		    a (one) week ago.
		    six months ago.
		    a (one) year ago.

NOTICE

In (a): *yesterday* is used with *morning, afternoon,* and *evening.*

In (b): *last* is used with *night,* with long periods of time *(week, month, year),* with seasons *(spring, summer, etc.),* and with days of the week.

In (c): *ago* means "in the past." It follows specific lengths of time (e.g., *two minutes + ago, five years + ago*).

☐ **EXERCISE 16. Sentence practice.**

Directions: Complete the sentences. Use ***yesterday*** or ***last***.

1. I dreamed about you _____*last*_____ night.

2. I was downtown _____ morning.

3. Two students were absent _____ Friday.

4. Ann wasn't at home _____ night.

5. Ann wasn't at home _____ evening.

6. Carmen was out of town _____ week.

7. I visited my aunt and uncle _____ fall.

8. Roberto walked home _____ afternoon.

9. My sister arrived in Miami _____ Sunday.

10. We watched TV _____ night.

11. Ali played with his children _____ evening.

12. Yoko arrived in Los Angeles _____ summer.

13. I visited my relatives in San Francisco _____ month.

14. My wife and I moved into a new house _____ year.

15. Mrs. Porter washed the kitchen floor _____ morning.

☐ EXERCISE 17. Sentence practice.

Directions: Complete the sentences with your own words. Use **ago**.

1. I'm in class now, but I was at home _____ *ten minutes ago / two hours ago / etc.*

2. I'm in class today, but I was absent from class _____

3. I'm in this country now, but I was in my country _____

4. I was in *(name of a city)* _____

5. I was in elementary school _____

6. I arrived in this city _____

7. There is a nice park in this city. I was at the park _____

8. We finished Exercise 16 _____

9. I was home in bed _____

10. It rained in this city _____

☐ EXERCISE 18. Listening.

Directions: Listen to the sentences and answer the questions.

PART I. Write today's date.

Today's date is _____.

Listen to the sentences and write the dates.

1. _____.

2. _____.

3. _____.

4. _____.

5. _____.

6. _____.

7. _____.

PART II. Write the correct time.

Right now, the time is _____.

Listen to the sentences and write the times you hear.

8. _____.

9. _____.

10. _____.

8-6 THE SIMPLE PAST: IRREGULAR VERBS (GROUP 1)

Some verbs do not have **-ed** forms. Their past forms are irregular.

PRESENT PAST	
come – came *do – did* *eat – ate* *get – got* *go – went* *have – had* *put – put* *see – saw* *sit – sat* *sleep – slept* *stand – stood* *write – wrote*	(a) I ***come*** to class ***every day***. (b) I ***came*** to class ***yesterday***. (c) I ***do*** my homework ***every day***. (d) I ***did*** my homework ***yesterday***. (e) Ann ***eats*** breakfast ***every morning***. (f) Ann ***ate*** breakfast ***yesterday morning***.

☐ **EXERCISE 19. Let's talk: class activity.**

Directions: Practice using irregular verbs. Close your book for this activity.

Example: **come–came**
TEACHER: come–came. I come to class every day. I came to class yesterday.
      What did I do yesterday?
STUDENTS: *(repeat)* come–came. You came to class yesterday.

1. ***do–did***   We do exercises in class every day. We did exercises yesterday. What did we do yesterday?

2. ***eat–ate***   I eat lunch at 12:00 every day. Yesterday I ate lunch at 12:00. What did I do at 12:00 yesterday?

3. ***get–got***   I get up early every day. I got up early yesterday. What did I do yesterday? Did you get up early yesterday? What time did you get up?

4. ***go–went*** I go downtown every day. I went downtown yesterday. What did I do yesterday? Did you go downtown? Where did you go?

5. ***have–had*** I have breakfast every morning. I had breakfast yesterday morning. What did I do yesterday morning? I had toast and fruit for breakfast. What did you have?

6. ***put–put*** I like hats. I put on a hat every day. What did I do yesterday?

7. ***see–saw*** I see my best friend every day. Yesterday I saw my best friend. What did I do yesterday? Did you see your best friend? Who did you see?

8. ***sit–sat*** I usually sit at my desk in the mornings. I sat at my desk yesterday morning. What did I do yesterday morning?

9. ***sleep–slept*** Sometimes I sleep for a long time at night. I slept for 10 hours last night. What did I do last night? Did you sleep for 10 hours last night? How long did you sleep last night?

10. ***stand–stood*** I stand at the bus stop every day. I stood at the bus stop yesterday. What did I do yesterday?

11. ***write–wrote*** I usually write in my journal every day. Yesterday I wrote in my journal. What did I do yesterday? Did you write in your journal? What did you write about?

□ EXERCISE 20. Let's talk: pairwork.

Directions: Work with a partner. Take turns changing the sentences from the present to the past.

Example: I have class every day.
PARTNER A: I have class every day. I had class yesterday. Your turn now.

Example: Roberto gets mail from home every week.
PARTNER B: Roberto gets mail from home every week. Roberto got mail from home last week. Your turn now.

Partner A
1. Rita gets some mail every day.
2. They go downtown every day.
3. The students stand in line at the cafeteria every day.
4. I see my friends every day.
5. Hamid sits in the front row every day.
6. I sleep for eight hours every night.

Partner B
1. We have lunch every day.
2. I write e-mails to my parents every week.
3. Wai-Leng comes to class late every day.
4. I do my homework every day.
5. I eat breakfast every morning.
6. Roberto puts his books in his briefcase every day.

□ **EXERCISE 21. Verb review.**

Directions: Complete the sentences. Use the words in parentheses. Use the simple present, the present progressive, or the simple past. Pay attention to spelling.

1. I (get) _____*got*_____ up at eight o'clock yesterday morning.

2. Mary (talk) _____ to John on the phone last night.

3. Mary (talk) _____ to John on the phone right now.

4. Mary (talk) _____ to John on the phone every day.

5. Jim and I (eat) _____ lunch at the cafeteria two hours ago.

6. We (eat) _____ lunch at the cafeteria every day.

7. I (go) _____ to bed early last night.

8. My roommate (study) _____ Spanish last year.

9. Sue (write) _____ an e-mail to her parents yesterday.

10. Sue (write) _____ an e-mail to her parents every week.

11. Sue is in her room right now. She (sit) _____ at her desk.

12. Maria (do) _____ her homework last night.

13. Yesterday I (see) _____ Fumiko at the library.

14. I (have) _____ a dream last night. I (dream)

    _____ about my friends. I (sleep) _____

    for eight hours.

15. A strange thing (happen) _____ to me yesterday. I

    couldn't remember my own telephone number.

16. My wife (come) _____ home around five every day.

17. Yesterday she (come) _____ home at 5:15.

18. Our teacher (stand) _____ in the middle of the room

    right now.

19. Our teacher (stand) _____ in the front of the room

    yesterday.

20. Tom *(put)* _____ the butter in the refrigerator yesterday.

21. He *(put)* _____ the milk in the refrigerator every day.

22. Pablo usually *(sit)* _____ in the back of the room, but

yesterday he *(sit)* _____ in the front row. Today he *(be)*

_____ absent. He *(be)* _____

absent two days ago too.

☐ **EXERCISE 22. Listening.**

Directions: Listen to the beginning of each sentence. Circle the correct
completion(s). There may be more than one correct answer.

Example: He did . . . . (his homework) (a good job) absent

1. a chair	some rice	some numbers
2. on the floor	a man	together
3. late	yesterday	car
4. an answer	pretty	a book
5. a good grade	last month	a new truck
6. a watch	next to my parents	at the bus stop

☐ **EXERCISE 23. Let's talk: small groups.**

Directions: Work in small groups. Use numbers to put the sentences in correct story
order. Then finish the story. Share it with the class.

__2__ He looked up at the stars.

_____ He put the postcard down and went to sleep.

_____ The bear stood next to his tent.

_____ The next morning, John sat up and rubbed his eyes.

__1__ One night, John went camping.

_____ They were beautiful.

_____ He wrote a postcard to his girlfriend.

_____ The bear had his postcard.

_____ He saw a bear.

8-7 THE SIMPLE PAST: NEGATIVE

	SUBJECT	+ *DID*	+ *NOT*	+ MAIN VERB	
(a)	I	*did*	*not*	*walk*	to school yesterday.
(b)	You	*did*	*not*	*walk*	to school yesterday.
(c)	Tom	*did*	*not*	*eat*	lunch yesterday.
(d)	They	*did*	*not*	*come*	to class yesterday.

INCORRECT: *I did not walked to school yesterday.*
INCORRECT: *Tom did not ate lunch yesterday.*

$\left. \begin{array}{l} I \\ you \\ she \\ he \\ it \\ we \\ they \end{array} \right\}$ + ***did not*** + main verb★

Notice: The simple form of the main verb is used with ***did not***.

(e) I ***didn't walk*** to school yesterday.
(f) Tom ***didn't eat*** lunch yesterday.

NEGATIVE CONTRACTION
did + ***not*** = ***didn't***

★EXCEPTION: ***did*** is NOT used when the main verb is ***be***. See Charts 8-2, p. 214, and 8-3, p. 216.
    CORRECT: Joe *wasn't* here yesterday.
    INCORRECT: Joe *didn't be* here yesterday.

☐ **EXERCISE 24. Sentence practice.**

Directions: Complete the sentences. Use ***not***.

1. I don't go to the park every day. I went to the park last week, but I
    _____*didn't go*_____ there yesterday.

2. We don't have rain every day. We had rain two days ago, but we
    _____ rain yesterday.

3. Linda doesn't sit in the front row every day. She sat there yesterday, but she
    _____ there two days ago.

4. Mrs. Romano and her son don't talk on the phone every day. They talked to each
    other last weekend, but they _____ on the phone last night.

☐ **EXERCISE 25. Let's talk: pairwork.**

Directions: Work with a partner. Take turns using ***I don't . . . every day*** and ***I didn't
. . . yesterday***.

Example: walk to school
PARTNER A: I don't walk to school every day. I didn't walk to school yesterday. Your
    turn now.

Example: listen to the radio
PARTNER B: I don't listen to the radio every day. I didn't listen to the radio yesterday.
    Your turn now.

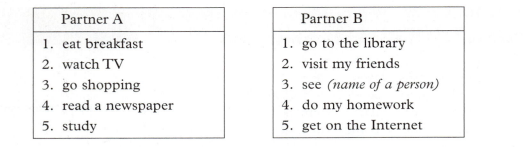

Partner A	Partner B
1. eat breakfast	1. go to the library
2. watch TV	2. visit my friends
3. go shopping	3. see *(name of a person)*
4. read a newspaper	4. do my homework
5. study	5. get on the Internet

☐ **EXERCISE 26. Let's talk: class activity.**

Directions: Practice present and past negatives. Close your books for this activity.

Speaker A: Use **I don't** and **I didn't**. Use an appropriate past time expression with **didn't**.

Speaker B: Report what Speaker A said. Use **She/He doesn't** and then **She/He didn't** with an appropriate past time expression.

Example: walk to school every morning

TEACHER: walk to school every morning

SPEAKER A: I don't walk to school every morning. I didn't walk to school yesterday morning.

TEACHER: *(to Speaker B)* Tell me about *(Speaker A)*.

SPEAKER B: She/He doesn't walk to school every morning. She/He didn't walk to school yesterday morning.

1. eat breakfast every morning
2. watch TV every night
3. talk to *(someone)* every day
4. play soccer every afternoon
5. study grammar every evening
6. dream in English every night
7. visit my aunt and uncle every year
8. write to my parents every week
9. read the newspaper every morning
10. pay all of my bills every month

☐ **EXERCISE 27. Sentence practice.**

Directions: Complete the sentences. Use the words in parentheses. Use simple present, simple past, or present progressive.

1. Jasmin *(come, not)* _____*didn't come*_____ to the meeting yesterday. She

   (stay) _____ in her office.

2. I *(go)* _____ to a movie last night, but I *(enjoy, not)*

   _____ it. It *(be, not)* _____ very good.

3. Sue (read) _____ a magazine right now. She (watch, not)

_____ TV. She (like, not) _____ to

watch TV during the day.

4. Toshi is a busy student. Sometimes he (eat, not) _____

lunch because he (have, not) _____ enough time between

classes. Yesterday he (have, not) _____ time for lunch. He

(get) _____ hungry during his afternoon class.

☐ **EXERCISE 28. Let's talk: small groups.**

Directions: Work in groups of six to eight students. Tell your group things you ***didn't
do yesterday***. Repeat the information from the other students in your group.

Example:
SPEAKER A: I didn't go to the zoo yesterday.
SPEAKER B: *(Speaker A)* didn't go to the zoo yesterday. I didn't have lunch in Beijing
yesterday.
SPEAKER C: *(Speaker A)* didn't go to the zoo yesterday. *(Speaker B)* didn't have lunch
in Beijing yesterday. I didn't swim in the Pacific Ocean yesterday.
Etc.

Suggestions:

go *(someplace)*	drive to *(a place)*
walk to *(a place)*	fly to *(a place)*
have *(a meal)*	study *(a subject)*
eat *(something)*	buy *(something)*
swim *(in a place)*	sleep in *(a place)*
sing *(in the shower)*	wear *(something)*
visit *(a person)*	see *(someone)*
talk to *(a person)*	wake up *(at a time)*
use *(something)*	

8-8 THE SIMPLE PAST: YES/NO QUESTIONS

DID + SUBJECT + MAIN VERB	SHORT ANSWER + (LONG ANSWER)
(a) **Did** **Mary** **walk** to school? → **Yes, she did.** (She walked to school.) → **No, she didn't.** (She didn't walk to school.) (b) **Did** **you** **come** to class? → **Yes, I did.** (I came to class.) → **No, I didn't.** (I didn't come to class.)	

☐ EXERCISE 29. Question practice.

Directions: Make questions. Give short answers.

1. A: _____*Did you walk downtown yesterday?*_____

   B: _____*Yes, I did.*_____ (I walked downtown yesterday.)

2. A: _____*Did it rain last week?*_____

   B: _____*No, it didn't.*_____ (It didn't rain last week.)

3. A: _____

   B: _____ (I ate lunch at the cafeteria.)

4. A: _____

   B: _____ (Mr. Kwan didn't go out of town last week.)

5. A: _____

   B: _____ (I had a cup of tea this morning.)

6. A: _____

   B: _____ (Benito and I went to a party last night.)

7. A: _____

   B: _____ (Olga studied English in high school.)

8. A: _____

   B: _____ (Yoko and Ali didn't do their homework last night.)

9. A: _____

   B: _____ (I saw Gina at dinner last night.)

10. A: _____

    B: _____ (I didn't dream in English last night.)

□ EXERCISE 30.   Listening.

Directions: Listen to the questions and write the words you hear.

Example:
You will hear: Did you eat breakfast this morning?
You will write: _____*Did you*_____ eat breakfast this morning?

1. _____ do well on the test?

2. _____ finish the assignment?

3. _____ make sense?

4. _____ answer your question?

5. _____ need more help?

6. _____ understand the homework?

7. _____ explain the project?

8. _____ complete the project?

9. _____ do well?

10. _____ pass the class?

□ EXERCISE 31.   Let's talk: pairwork.

Directions: Work with a partner. Ask questions about her/his activities this morning.

Example: walk to school
PARTNER A *(book open):*   Did you walk to school this morning?
PARTNER B *(book closed):* Yes, I did. OR No, I didn't.

1. get up at seven
2. eat breakfast
3. study English
4. walk to class
5. talk to *(name of a person)*
6. see *(name of a person)*

Switch roles.

Partner A: Close your book.

Partner B: Open your book. Your turn to talk now.

7. make your bed

8. go shopping

9. have a cup of tea

10. watch TV

11. listen to the radio

12. read a newspaper

□ **EXERCISE 32. Let's talk: find someone who . . . .**

Directions: Interview your classmates. Find people who can answer *yes* to your questions. Write down their names.

Speaker A: Make a complete question with the given verb. Use the past tense. Ask *(Speaker B)* the question.

Speaker B: Answer the question. Give both a short answer and a long answer.

Example: eat ice cream \ yesterday?

SPEAKER A: Did you eat ice cream yesterday?

SPEAKER B: No, I didn't.

SPEAKER A: *(Ask another student.)* Did you eat ice cream yesterday?

SPEAKER C: Yes, I did. I ate ice cream yesterday.

	First name
1. eat rice \ yesterday	
2. do homework \ last night	
3. get an e-mail \ yesterday	
4. go shopping \ yesterday	
5. sleep well \ last night	
6. a. have coffee for breakfast \ this morning b. put sugar in your coffee \ this morning	
7. see a good movie \ last week	
8. write in English \ today	
9. sit on the floor \ yesterday	
10. stand in line for something \ last week	

Directions: Listen to the reductions in spoken English. In spoken questions, ***did*** and the pronoun that follows are often reduced.

PART I. Listen to the examples.

1. **Did you** ("dih-juh") read the paper this morning?

2. A: Tom called.

   B: **Did he** ("dih-de") leave a message?

3. A: Sara called.

   B: **Did she** ("dih-she") leave a message?

4. **Did it** ("dih-dit") rain yesterday?

5. A: The children are watching TV.

   B: **Did they** ("dih-they") finish their homework?

6. I can't find my notebook. **Did I** ("dih-di") leave it on your desk?

PART II. Listen to the sentences. You will hear reduced speech ***did*** + *pronoun.* Write the non-reduced forms.

Examples:
You will hear: "Dih-dit" rain yesterday?
You will write: _____*Did it*_____ rain yesterday?

You will hear: "Dih-juh" come to class yesterday?
You will write: _____*Did you*_____ come to class yesterday?

1. _____ finish the homework assignment?

2. _____ take a long time?

3. _____ hear my question?

4. _____ hear my question?

5. _____ speak loud enough?

6. _____ understand the information?

7. _____ understand the information?

8. _____ want more help?

9. _____ explain it okay?

10. _____ do a good job?

8-9 IRREGULAR VERBS (GROUP 2)

bring – brought	*drive – drove*	*run – ran*
buy – bought	*read – read* ⋆	*teach – taught*
catch – caught	*ride – rode*	*think – thought*
drink – drank		

⋆The past form of *read* is pronounced the same as the color *red*.

☐ **EXERCISE 34. Let's talk: class activity.**

Directions: Practice using irregular verbs. Close your book for this activity.

Example: **teach–taught**
TEACHER: teach–taught. I teach class every day. I taught class yesterday. What did I do yesterday?
STUDENTS: *(repeat)* teach–taught. You taught class.

1. **bring–brought**   I bring my book to class every day. I brought my book to class yesterday. What did I do yesterday?

2. **buy–bought**   I buy books at the bookstore. I bought a book yesterday. What did I do yesterday?

3. **catch–caught**   I catch the bus every day. I caught the bus yesterday. What did I do yesterday? Sometimes I catch a cold. Yesterday I caught a bad cold. What did I do yesterday?

4. **think–thought**   I often think about my family. I thought about my family yesterday. What did I do yesterday?

5. **REVIEW:**   What did I bring to class yesterday? What did you bring yesterday? What did I buy yesterday? What did you buy yesterday? Did you teach class yesterday? Who did? Did I walk to class yesterday, or did I catch the bus? What did I think about yesterday? What did you think about yesterday?

6. **run–ran**   Sometimes I'm late for class, so I run. Yesterday I was late, so I ran. What did I do yesterday?

7. **read–read**   I like to read books. I read every day. Yesterday I read a book. What did I do yesterday? What did you read yesterday?

8. **drink–drank**   I usually drink a cup of coffee in the morning. I drank a cup of coffee this morning. What did I do this morning? Did you drink a cup of coffee this morning? What do you usually drink in the morning? Do you drink the same thing every morning?

9. **drive–drove**   I usually drive my car to school. I drove my car to school this morning. What did I do this morning? Who has a car? Did you drive to school this morning?

10. **ride–rode**   Sometimes I ride the bus to school. I rode the bus yesterday morning. What did I do yesterday morning? Who rode the bus to school this morning?

11. **REVIEW:** I was late for class yesterday morning, so what did I do? What did I read yesterday? What did you read yesterday? Did you read a newspaper this morning? What did I drink this morning? What did you drink this morning? I have a car. Did I drive to school this morning? Did you? Did you ride the bus?

☐ **EXERCISE 35. Sentence practice.**

Directions: Complete the sentences. Use the words in parentheses.

1. A: Why are you out of breath?

   B: I *(run)* _____ to class because I was late.

2. A: I *(ride)* _____ the bus to school yesterday. How did you get to

   school?

   B: I *(drive)* _____ my car.

3. A: Did you decide to change schools?

   B: I *(think)* _____ about it, but then I decided to stay here.

4. A: *(you, go)* _____ shopping yesterday?

   B: Yes. I *(buy)* _____ a new pair of shoes.

5. A: *(you, study)* _____ last night?

   B: No, I didn't. I was tired. I *(read)* _____ a magazine and then

   (go) _____ to bed early.

6. A: Do you like milk?

   B: No. I *(drink)* _____ milk when I *(be)* _____

   a child, but I don't like milk now.

7. A: Did you leave your dictionary at home?

   B: No. I *(bring)* _____ it to class with me.

8. Yesterday Yoko *(teach)* _____ us how to say "thank you" in

   Japanese. Kim *(teach)* _____ us how to say "I love you" in

   Korean.

8-10 IRREGULAR VERBS (GROUP 3)

break – broke	*meet – met*	*sing – sang*
fly – flew	*pay – paid*	*speak – spoke*
hear – heard	*ring – rang*	*take – took*
leave – left	*send – sent*	*wake up – woke up*

9. A: Did you enjoy your fishing trip?

   B: I had a wonderful time! I *(catch)* _____ a lot of fish.

☐ EXERCISE 49. Let's talk: game.
   Directions: Your teacher will say the simple form of a verb. Your team will give the past tense. Close your book for this activity.

   Example:
   TEACHER: Team A: come
     TEAM A: *(all together)* came
   TEACHER: That's one point.

   TEACHER: Team B: eat
     TEAM B: *(all together)* ate
   TEACHER: That's one point.

   1. fly
   2. bring
   3. read
   4. tell
   5. stand
   6. teach
   7. drink
   8. wear
   9. buy
   10. speak

   11. pay
   12. hear
   13. catch
   14. find
   15. sleep
   16. think
   17. ride
   18. break
   19. say
   20. get

   21. leave
   22. have
   23. pay
   24. meet
   25. sit
   26. take
   27. ring
   28. write
   29. sing
   30. wake up

☐ EXERCISE 50. Chapter review: error analysis.
   Directions: Correct the errors.

   1. Someone stealed my bicycle two day ago.

   2. Did you went to the party yesterday weekend?

   3. I hear a really interesting story yesterday.

   4. The teacher not ready for class yesterday.

   5. Did came Joe to work last week?

   6. Yesterday night I staied home and working on my science project.

   7. Several students wasn't on time for the final exam yesterday.

   8. Your fax came before ten minutes. Did you got it?

9. Did you all your friends to your graduation party invite?

10. I sleeped too late this morning and was missed the bus.

11. The market no have any bananas yesterday. I get there too late.

12. Was you nervous about your test the last week?

13. I didn't saw you at the party. Did you be there?

☐ EXERCISE 51. Review.

Directions: Think about the years your grandparents grew up in. What kinds of things did they do? What kinds of things didn't they do? Write sentences. Work with a partner or in small groups.

Example: My grandparents didn't use computers.
My grandfather walked to work.

CHAPTER 9
Expressing Past Time, Part 2

THE SIMPLE PAST: USING *WHERE, WHEN, WHAT TIME,* AND *WHY*

QUESTION					SHORT ANSWER
(a)		*Did* you *go*	downtown?	→	Yes, I did. / No, I didn't.
(b) *Where*		*did* you *go?*		→	*Downtown.*
(c)		Were you	downtown?	→	Yes, I was. / No, I wasn't.
(d) *Where*		were you?		→	*Downtown.*
(e)		*Did* you *run*	because you were late?	→	Yes, I did. / No, I didn't.
(f) *Why*		*did* you *run?*		→	*Because I was late.*
(g)		*Did* Ann *come*	at six?	→	Yes, she did. / No, she didn't.
(h) *When* / *What time*		*did* Ann *come?*		→	*At six.*

COMPARE		
(i) *What time* did Ann come?	→ *At six.* → *Seven o'clock.* → *Around 9:30.*	*What time* usually asks for a specific time on a clock.
(j) *When* did Ann come?	→ *At six.* → *Friday.* → *June 15th.* → *Last week.* → *Three days ago.*	The answer to *when* can be various expressions of time.

☐ EXERCISE 1. Question practice.
Directions: Make questions. Use *where, when, what time,* or *why.*

1. A: _____Where did you go yesterday?_____

   B: To the zoo. (I went to the zoo yesterday.)

2. A: _____

   B: Last month. (Mr. Chu arrived in Canada last month.)

3. A: _____

   B: At 7:05. (My plane arrived at 7:05.)

4. A: _____

   B: Because I was tired. (I stayed home last night because I was tired.)

5. A: _____

   B: Because I stayed up the night before. (I was tired because I stayed up the night before.)

6. A: _____

   B: To Greece. (Sara went to Greece for her vacation.)

7. A: _____

   B: Around midnight. (I finished my homework around midnight.)

8. A: _____

   B: Five weeks ago. (I came to this city five weeks ago.)

9. A: _____

   B: Because Tony made a funny face. (I laughed because Tony made a funny face.)

10. A: _____

    B: Upstairs. (Kate is upstairs.)

11. A: _____

    B: In ten minutes. (The movie starts in ten minutes.)

12. A: _____

    B: Because she wanted to surprise Joe. (Tina was behind the door because she wanted to surprise Joe.)

13. A: _____

    B: Because he wants big muscles. (Jim lifts weights because he wants big muscles.)

□ **EXERCISE 2. Let's talk: class activity.**

    Directions: Make questions. Use question words. Close your book for this activity.

    Example:
    TEACHER: I got up at 7:30.
    STUDENT: When/What time did you get up?

    1. I went to the zoo.
    2. I went to the zoo yesterday.
    3. I went to the zoo yesterday because I wanted to see the animals.
    4. (. . .) went to the park.
    5. (. . .) went to the park yesterday.
    6. (. . .) went to the park yesterday because the weather was nice.
    7. (. . .) was at the park yesterday.
    8. I am in class.
    9. I came to class (ten minutes) ago.
    10. I was late because traffic was heavy.
    11. (. . .) was at home last night.
    12. He/She finished his/her homework around midnight.
    13. (. . .) went to bed at 7:30 last night.
    14. He/She went to bed early because he/she was tired.
    15. (. . .) was at the airport yesterday.
    16. He/She went to the airport because a friend came to visit.
    17. The plane arrived at 4:30.
    18. (. . .) and (. . .) went to *(name of a restaurant)* last night.
    19. They went to a restaurant because it was (. . .)'s birthday.
    20. They got home around ten-thirty.

□ **EXERCISE 3. Let's talk: pairwork.**

    Directions: Work with a partner. Ask and answer questions using the simple past.
    Partner A: Make up any question that includes the given verb. Use the simple past.
              Ask your partner the question. Your book is open.
    Partner B: Answer the question. Give a short answer and a long answer. Your book
              is closed.

    Example: speak
    PARTNER A *(book open):* Did you speak to Mr. Lee yesterday?
    PARTNER B *(book closed):* Yes, I did. I spoke to him yesterday. OR
                             No, I didn't. I didn't speak to him yesterday.

    Example: finish
    PARTNER A *(book open):* What time did you finish your homework last night?
    PARTNER B *(book closed):* Around nine o'clock. I finished my homework around nine
                             o'clock.

1. drink	3. study	5. fly	7. wake up
2. eat	4. take	6. talk	8. come

Switch roles.

Partner A: Close your book.

Partner B: Open your book. Your turn now.

9. see	11. work	13. buy	15. watch
10. sleep	12. have	14. send	16. read

☐ **EXERCISE 4. Listening.**

Directions: Look at the information on the datebook pages. Write answers to the questions you hear.

Tom's Day

Mon.	April 4
7:00 AM School meeting with teacher	

Susan's Day

Mon.	April 4
12:00 Noon City Café business meeting	

Bill's Day

Mon.	April 4
10:00 AM Dr. Clark dental checkup	

Nancy's Day

Mon.	April 4
1:00 P.M. Gym workout	

Example:

You will hear: Where did Nancy go?

You will write: _____ *(To the) gym* _____ .

1. _____ .

2. _____ .

3. _____ .

4. _____ .

5. _____ .

6. _____ .

7. _____ .

8. _____ .

9. _____ .

10. _____ .

11. _____ .

12. _____ .

☐ EXERCISE 5. Question practice.

    Directions: Complete the questions.

    1. A: I didn't go to class yesterday.

       B: Why didn't   *you go to class*   ?

       A: Because I was sick.

    2. A: I didn't finish my homework.

       B: Why didn't _____?

       A: Because I didn't have enough time.

    3. A: I didn't eat breakfast this morning.

       B: Why didn't _____?

       A: Because I wasn't hungry.

    4. A: I didn't clean my apartment last week.

       B: Why didn't _____?

       A: Because I was too tired.

    5. A: I didn't answer the phone all day.

       B: Why didn't _____?

       A: Because I wanted to finish my work.

☐ EXERCISE 6. Question practice: pairwork.

    Directions: Work with a partner. Take turns completing the conversations with questions that begin with ***why, when, what time,*** and ***where.***

    1. PARTNER A: _____*Where do you want to go for your vacation?*_____
       PARTNER B: Hawaii.

    2. PARTNER B: _____
       PARTNER A: Ten o'clock.

    3. PARTNER A: _____
       PARTNER B: Because I was tired.

    4. PARTNER B: _____
       PARTNER A: South America.

5. PARTNER A: _____
   PARTNER B: Last week.

6. PARTNER B: _____
   PARTNER A: Because I forgot.

7. PARTNER A: _____
   PARTNER B: Downtown.

8. PARTNER B: _____
   PARTNER A: Several months ago.

9. PARTNER A: _____
   PARTNER B: At a Chinese restaurant.

9-2 QUESTIONS WITH *WHAT*

What is used in a question when you want to find out about a thing. *Who* is used when you want to find out about a person. (See Chart 9-3, p. 260, for questions with *who*.)

(QUESTION + WORD)	HELPING + VERB	SUBJECT +	MAIN VERB	ANSWER
(a)	*Did*	Carol	*buy* a car?	→ **Yes, she did.** *(She bought a car.)*
(b) *What*	*did*	Carol	*buy?*	→ **A car.** *(She bought a car.)*
(c)	*Is*	Fred	*holding* a book? →	**Yes, he is.** *(He's holding a book.)*
(d) *What*	*is*	Fred	*holding?*	→ **A book.** *(He's holding a book.)*

S V O (e) Carol bought *a car.*	In (e): *a car* is the object of the verb.
O V S V (f) *What* did Carol buy?	In (f): *What* is the object of the verb.

☐ EXERCISE 7. Question practice.
   Directions: Make questions.

   1. A: _____Did you buy a new tape recorder?_____
      B: Yes, I did. (I bought a new tape recorder.)

   2. A: _____What did you buy?_____
      B: A new tape recorder. (I bought a new tape recorder.)

3. A: _____

   B: Yes, she is. (Mary is carrying a suitcase.)

4. A: _____

   B: A suitcase.   (Mary is carrying a suitcase.)

5. A: _____

   B: Yes, I do.   (I see an airplane.)

6. A: _____

   B: An airplane. (I see an airplane.)

7. A: _____

   B: Some soup. (Bob ate some soup for lunch.)

8. A: _____

   B: Yes, he did. (Bob ate some soup for lunch.)

9. A: _____

   B: A sandwich. (Bob usually eats a sandwich for lunch.)

10. A: _____

    B: No, he doesn't. (Bob doesn't like salads.)

11. A: _____

    B: No, I'm not. (I'm not afraid of snakes.) Are you?

12. A: _____

    _____

    B: The map on the wall. (The teacher is pointing to
       the map on the wall.)

□ **EXERCISE 8. Question practice: pairwork.**

   Directions: Work in pairs. Ask a classmate a question. Use ***what*** and either a past or
   a present verb. Remember, you can look at your book. When you speak, look at your
   partner.

   Example: eat
   PARTNER A: What did you eat for breakfast this morning? / What do you usually eat for
                   dinner? / Etc.
   PARTNER B: (*free response*)
   PARTNER A: Your turn now.

Partner A	Partner B
1. eat	1. be interested in
2. wear	2. be afraid of
3. look at	3. dream about
4. study	4. have
5. think about	5. need to buy

☐ EXERCISE 9. Question practice.

Directions: Ask your teacher for the meaning of the given words. Begin your question with **What**.

Example: century
STUDENT: What does "century" mean? OR What is the meaning of "century"?
TEACHER: "Century" means "100 years."

1. muggy
2. awful
3. quiet
4. century
5. murder

6. grocery store
7. empty
8. ill
9. attic
10. simple

11. invitation
12. enjoy
13. forest
14. pretty difficult
15. old-fashioned

☐ EXERCISE 10. Listening.

Directions: Listen to the questions. Write the words you hear.

Example:
You will hear: Where did they go?
You will write: _____*Where did they*_____ go?

1. _____ arrive?

2. _____ leave?

3. _____ live?

4. _____ want?

5. _____ mean?

6. _____ study?

7. _____ go?

8. _____ end?

9-3 QUESTIONS WITH *WHO*

QUESTION	ANSWER	
(a) **What** did they see? →	**A boat.** *(They saw a boat.)*	**What** is used to ask questions about *things.*
(b) **Who** did they see? →	**Jim.** *(They saw Jim.)*	**Who** is used to ask questions about *people.*
(c) **Who** did they see? →	**Jim.** *(They saw Jim.)*	(c) and (d) have the same meaning. **Whom** is used in formal English as the object of a verb or a preposition. In (c): **Who,** not **whom,** is usually used in everyday English. In (d): **Whom** is used in very formal English. **Whom** is rarely used in everyday spoken English.
(d) **Whom** did they see? →	**Jim.** *(They saw Jim.)*	
(e) **Who(m)** did they see? →	**Jim.** *(They saw **Jim**.)*	In (e): **Who(m)** is the object of the verb. Usual question word order *(question word + helping verb + subject + main verb)* is used.
(f) **Who** came? →	**Mary.** *(**Mary** came.)*	In (f), (g), and (h): **Who** is the subject of the question. Usual question word order is NOT used. When **who** is the subject of a question, do NOT use **does, do,** or **did**. Do NOT change the verb in any way: the verb form in the question is the same as the verb form in the answer.
(g) **Who** lives there? →	**Ed.** *(**Ed** lives there.)*	
(h) **Who** saw Jim? →	**Ann.** *(**Ann** saw Jim.)*	
INCORRECT: *Who did come?*		

☐ EXERCISE 11. Question practice.

Directions: Make questions for the given answers.

Example: The teacher saw John. The teacher talked to John. The teacher helped John.

→ _____Who saw John_____? The teacher.

→ _____Who talked to John_____? The teacher.

→ _____Who helped John_____? The teacher.

→ _____Who did the teacher see_____? John.

→ _____Who did the teacher talk to_____? John.

→ _____Who did the teacher help_____? John.

1. John called Yuko. John visited Yuko. John studied with Yuko.

   _____? John.

   _____? John.

   _____? John.

   _____? Yuko.

   _____? Yuko.

   _____? Yuko.

2. Mary carried the baby. Mary helped the baby. Mary sang to the baby.

   _____? The baby.

   _____? The baby.

   _____? The baby.

   _____? Mary.

   _____? Mary.

   _____? Mary.

3. Ron talked to the children. Ron watched the children. Ron played with the children.

   _____? Ron.

   _____? The children.

   _____? Ron.

   _____? The children.

   _____? Ron.

   _____? The children.

□ EXERCISE 12. Question practice.
   Directions: Make questions.

   1. A: _____
      B: Mary. (I saw Mary at the party.)

2. A: _____

   B: Mary. (Mary came to the party.)

3. A: _____

   B: John. (John lives in that house.)

4. A: _____

   B: John. (Janet called John.)

5. A: _____

   B: My aunt and uncle. (I visited my aunt and uncle.)

6. A: _____

   B: My cousin. (My cousin visited me.)

7. A: _____

   B: Ken. (I talked to Ken.)

8. A: _____

   B: Bob. (Bob helped Ann.)

9. A: _____

   B: Ann. (Bob helped Ann.)

10. A: _____

    B: Yes, he did. (Bob helped Ann.)

11. A: _____

    B: Bob and Ann. (I'm thinking about Bob and Ann.)

12. A: _____

    B: No, I'm not. (I'm not confused.)

☐ EXERCISE 13. Let's talk: pairwork.

Directions: Work with a partner and make questions. Then change roles and make new questions. When you have finished speaking, write answers.

1. A: _____

   B: Yesterday.

2. B: _____

   A: My brother.

3. A: _____
   B: A new pair of sandals.

4. B: _____
   A: At 7:30.

5. A: _____
   B: At Rossini's Restaurant.

6. B: _____
   A: Tomorrow afternoon.

7. A: _____
   B: In an apartment.

8. B: _____
   A: My roommate.

9. A: _____
   B: Because I wanted to.

10. B: _____
    A: Ann.

11. A: _____
    B: A bird.

12. B: _____
    A: The zoo.

☐ **EXERCISE 14. Listening.**

Directions: Listen to each question and circle the best answer.

Example: Why was John late?   Yesterday.   At the park.   ⟨Because he slept too long.⟩

1. Next month.	In a small town.	Ten minutes ago.
2. Tomorrow morning.	Because it was late.	At midnight.
3. In a minute.	Some help.	John and Sarah.
4. To the store.	At 10:00.	I am.
5. On the bus.	Because her car didn't start.	Mary did.
6. An apartment downtown.	Next week.	Because we like the city.
7. It's down the street.	Two hours ago.	At the theater.
8. Because I didn't have time.	My friends.	It was fun.

9-4 IRREGULAR VERBS (GROUP 5)

cost – cost	*hit – hit*	*shut – shut*
cut – cut	*hurt – hurt*	*spend – spent*
forget – forgot	*lend – lent*	*understand – understood*
give – gave	*make – made*	

*NOTE: Irregular verb groups 1 to 4 can be found in Charts 8-6, p. 227, 8-9, p. 238, 8-10, p. 241, and 8-11, p. 244.

□ EXERCISE 15. Let's talk: class activity.

Directions: Practice using irregular verbs. Close your book for this activity.

Example: teach–taught
TEACHER: teach–taught. I teach class every day. I taught class yesterday. What did I do yesterday?
STUDENTS: *(repeat)* teach–taught. You taught class.

1. ***cost–cost***   I bought a hat yesterday. I paid twenty dollars for it. It cost twenty dollars. What did I buy yesterday? How much did it cost?

2. ***cut–cut***   (. . .) cuts vegetables when he/she makes a salad. Two nights ago, while he/she was making a salad, he/she cut his/her finger with the knife. What happened two nights ago?

3. ***forget–forgot***   Sometimes I forget my wallet. Last night, I forgot it at a restaurant. What did I do last night?

4. ***give–gave***   People give gifts when someone has a birthday. Last week, (. . .) had a birthday. I gave him/her *(something)*. What did I do?

5. ***hit–hit***   (. . .) lives in an apartment. The neighbors are very noisy. When they make too much noise, (. . .) hits the wall with his/her hand. Last night he/she couldn't get to sleep because of the noise, so he/she hit the wall with his/her hand. What did (. . .) do last night? What does he/she usually do when the neighbors make too much noise?

6. ***hurt–hurt***   When I have a headache, my head hurts. Yesterday I had a headache. My head hurt. How did my head feel yesterday? How does your head feel when you have a headache?

7. ***lend–lent***   I lend money to my friends if they need it. Yesterday I lent *(an amount of money)* to (. . .). What did I do?

8. ***make–made***   I make good chocolate cake. Last week I made a cake for (. . .)'s birthday. What did I do last week?

9. ***shut–shut***   I shut the garage door every night at 10:00 P.M. I shut it early last night. What did I do last night?

10. ***spend–spent***   I usually spend Saturdays with my parents. Last Saturday, I spent the day with my friends instead. What did I do last Saturday?

11. ***understand–understood***   I always understand (. . .) when he/she speaks. He/She just said something, and I understood it. What just happened?

Directions: Complete the sentences. Use the words in parentheses.

1. A: How much (*a new car, cost*) _____?

   B: It (*cost*) _____ a lot! New cars are expensive.

2. A: Did you get a ticket for the rock concert?

   B: Yes, and it was really expensive! It (*cost*) _____ fifty dollars.

3. A: Where's your history book?

   B: I (*give*) _____ it to Robert.

4. A: I had a car accident yesterday morning.

   B: What happened?

   A: I (*hit*) _____ a telephone pole.

5. A: May I have your homework, please?

   B: I'm sorry, but I don't have it. I (*forget*) _____ it.

   A: You (*forget*) _____ it!?

6. A: Did you eat breakfast?

   B: Yeah. I (*make*) _____ some scrambled eggs and toast for myself.

7. Jack (*put*) _____ on his clothes every morning.

8. Jack (*put*) _____ on his clothes this morning after he got up.

9. A: Did you enjoy going into the city to see a show?

   B: Yes, but I (*spend*) _____ a lot of money. I can't afford to do that

   very often.

10. A: May I see your dictionary?

    B: I don't have it. I (*lend*) _____ it to George.

11. A: Is that knife sharp?

   B: It's very sharp. It (cut) _____ anything easily.

12. A: Why are you wearing a bag over your head?

   B: I went to a barber this morning. He (cut) _____ my hair too

   short.

   A: Let me see. Oh, it looks fine.

☐ EXERCISE 17. Listening.

Directions: Listen to the beginning of each sentence. Circle the correct
completion(s). There may be more than one correct answer.

Example: John made . . . .   (his lunch)   (furniture)   in the morning

   1. the answer   the conversation   the teacher

   2. money   to her house   some furniture

   3. your hair   some paper   between

   4. tomorrow   a tree   an animal

   5. remember   his appointment   the question

9-5 IRREGULAR VERBS (GROUP 6)

blow – blew	*grow – grew*	*swim – swam*
draw – drew	*keep – kept*	*throw – threw*
fall – fell	*know – knew*	*win – won*
feel – felt		

☐ EXERCISE 18. Let's talk: class activity.

Directions: Practice using irregular verbs. Close your book for this activity.

Example: fall–fell
TEACHER: fall–fell.   Rain falls. Leaves fall. Sometimes people fall. Yesterday I fell
           down. I hurt my knee. How did I hurt my knee yesterday?
STUDENTS: *(repeat)* fall–fell.   You fell (down).

1. **blow–blew**   The sun shines. Rain falls. Wind blows. Last week we had a storm.
It rained hard, and the wind blew hard. Tell me about the storm last week.

2. ***draw–drew*** I draw once a week in art class. Last week I drew a portrait of myself. What did I do in art class last week?

3. ***fall–fell*** Sometimes I fall down. Yesterday I fell down. I felt bad when I fell down. What happened to me yesterday?

4. ***feel–felt*** You can feel an object. You can also feel an emotion or sensation. Sometimes I feel sleepy in class. I felt tired all day yesterday. How did I feel yesterday? How did you feel yesterday?

5. ***grow–grew*** Trees grow. Flowers grow. Vegetables grow. Usually I grow vegetables in my garden, but last year I grew only flowers. What did I grow in my garden last year?

6. ***keep–kept*** Now I keep my money in *(name of a local bank)*. Last year I kept my money in *(name of another local bank)*. Where did I keep my money last year?

7. ***know–knew*** (. . .) knows a lot about English grammar. On the grammar test last week, she/he knew all the answers. What did (. . .) know last week?

8. ***swim–swam*** I swim in *(name of a lake, sea, ocean, or local swimming pool)* every summer. I swam in *(name of a lake, sea, ocean, or local swimming pool)* last summer. What did I do last summer?

9. ***throw–threw*** I can hand you this (piece of chalk), or I can throw it to you. I just threw this (piece of chalk) to (. . .). What did I just do?

10. ***win–won*** You can win a game or lose a game. Last weekend *(name of a local sports team)* won a game/match against *(name of another team)*. How did *(name of the local sports team)* do last weekend? Did they win or lose?

□ **EXERCISE 19. Sentence practice.**

Directions: Complete the sentences. Use the past form of the verbs in the list.

blow	grow	swim
draw	keep	throw
fall	know	win
feel		

1. A: Did you enjoy your tennis game with Jackie?

   B: Yes, but I lost. Jackie _____.

2. A: How did you break your leg?

   B: I _____ down on the ice on the sidewalk.

3. A: Did you give the box of candy to your girlfriend?

   B: No, I didn't. I _____ it and ate it myself.

4. A: That's a nice picture.

   B: I agree. Anna _____ it. She's a good artist.

5. A: Did you have a garden when you lived at home?

   B: Yes. I _____ vegetables and flowers.

6. A: I burned my finger.
   B: Did you put ice on it?

   A: No. I _____ on it.

7. A: Did you finish the test?

   B: No. I _____ all of the answers,
      but I ran out of time.

8. A: Did you have fun at the beach?

   B: Lots of fun. We sunbathed and _____ in the ocean.

9. A: What's the matter? You sound like you have a frog in your throat.

   B: I think I'm catching a cold. I _____ okay yesterday, but I don't
      feel very good today.

10. A: How did you break the window, Tommy?

    B: Well, I _____ a ball to Annie, but I missed Annie and hit the
       window instead.

□ EXERCISE 20. Listening.

Directions: Listen to the beginning of each sentence. Circle the correct
completion(s). There may be more than one correct answer.

Example: Tim knew . . . .   (the answer)   a ball   (my father)

   1. tomorrow   on a car   in the park

   2. the game   a prize   lost

   3. on the paper   a picture   with some chalk

   4. happy   in the morning   excited

   5. a ball   not   a pillow

9-6 IRREGULAR VERBS (GROUP 7)

become – became	*build – built*	*hide – hid*
bend – bent	*feed – fed*	*hold – held*
bite – bit	*fight – fought*	*shake – shook*

☐ **EXERCISE 21. Let's talk: class activity.**

Directions: Practice using irregular verbs. Close your book for this activity.

Example: hold–held
TEACHER: hold–held.   I often hold my book open when I teach. Yesterday I held my book open when we practiced grammar. What did I do with my book?
STUDENTS: *(repeat)* hold–held. You held your book open.

1. ***become–became***   When strangers meet, they can become friends. I met (. . .) *(a length of time)* ago. We became friends. What happened between (. . .) and me?

2. ***bend–bent***   When I drop something, I bend over to pick it up. I just dropped my pen, and then I bent over to pick it up. What did I do?

3. ***bite–bit***   Sometimes dogs bite people. Yesterday my friend's dog bit my hand while we were playing. What happened to my hand?

4. ***build–built***   I have some friends who know how to build houses. They built their own house next to the river. What did my friends do?

5. ***feed–fed***   I have a (dog, cat, parrot, etc.). I have to feed it every day. Yesterday I fed it once in the morning and once in the evening. What did I do yesterday?

6. ***fight–fought***   People fight in wars. People fight diseases. They fight for freedom and equality. My country fought a war against *(name of another country)* in *(a time period)*. What happened in *(that time period)*?

7. ***hide–hid***   I have a coin in my hand. Close your eyes while I hide it. Okay, open your eyes. I hid the coin. Where's the coin? Why don't you know?

8. ***hold–held***   When it rains, I hold my umbrella. Yesterday it rained. I held my umbrella. What did I do yesterday?

9. ***shake–shook***   People sometimes shake their finger or their head. Sometimes they shake when they're cold. Right now I'm shaking my (finger/head). What did I just do?

□ **EXERCISE 22. Sentence practice.**

   Directions: Complete the sentences. Use the past form of the verbs in the list.

become	*build*	*hide*
bend	*feed*	*hold*
bite	*fight*	✓ *shake*

1. When my dog got out of the lake, it _____*shook*_____ itself. Dogs always do

   that when they're wet.

2. I _____ my husband's birthday present in the closet yesterday. I

   didn't want him to find it.

3. Nancy and Tom saved money. They didn't buy a bookcase for their new

   apartment. They _____ one.

4. The baby is sleeping peacefully. She's not hungry. Her mother _____

   her before she put her in bed.

5. David is a Canadian citizen. Maria was born in Puerto Rico, but when she

   married David, she _____ a Canadian citizen too.

6. Doug is a new father. He felt very happy when he _____ his baby

   in his arms for the first time.

7. Many countries in the world _____ in World War II.

8. A: Ow!

   B: What's the matter?

   A: I _____ my tongue.

9. We saw a strong man at the circus. He _____

   an iron bar with his bare hands.

EXERCISE 23. Listening.

Directions: Listen to the beginning of each sentence. Circle the correct completion(s). There may be more than one correct answer.

Example: I bent . . . .   (my arm)   a building   the road

1. the dog   happy   her baby
2. next week   usually   a new house
3. a stick   my hand   sad
4. in the bedroom   behind a tree   their money
5. some chalk   the classroom   some papers

□ EXERCISE 24. Class activity.

Directions: Answer the questions the teacher asks you. Use a short response and a long response. Close your book for this activity.

Example:
TEACHER: Did you write a letter yesterday?
STUDENT: Yes, I did. I wrote a letter yesterday.

1. Did you fly to *(this city)?*
2. Did you drink a cup of tea this morning?
3. Did you come to class yesterday?
4. Did you go downtown yesterday?
5. Did you eat breakfast this morning?
6. Did you lend some money to (. . .)?
7. Did you lose your pen yesterday? Did you find it?
8. Did you give your dictionary to (. . .)?
9. Did you throw your eraser to (. . .)? (. . .), did you catch it?
10. Did someone steal your wallet? Did you get it back?
11. Did you wake up at seven this morning?
12. Did you get up at seven this morning?
13. Did the wind blow yesterday?
14. Did you shut the door?
15. Did class begin at (. . .)?
16. Did you say hello to (. . .)?
17. Did you tell (. . .) to sit down? (. . .), did you sit down?
18. Did you hear my last question?
19. Did you teach your daughter/son to count to ten?
20. Did you bring your books to class today?
21. Did you forget your books?
22. Did you see (. . .) yesterday?

23. Did you meet (. . .)'s wife?

24. Did you leave your sunglasses at the restaurant?

25. Did you read the newspaper this morning?

26. Did you go shopping yesterday?

27. Did you drive your car to school today?

28. Did you ride a horse to school today?

29. Did a barber cut your hair?

30. Did you run to class this morning?

31. Did your pen cost *(an amount of money)*?

32. Did you understand my question?

33. Did you come to class yesterday?

34. Did you make a mistake?

35. Did you take the bus to school today?

36. Did you write a letter yesterday? Did you send it?

37. Did the telephone ring?

38. Did you break your arm?

39. Did you shake your head?

40. Did you draw a picture?

41. Did you bend your elbow?

42. Did you win a million dollars?

43. Did you feel good yesterday?

44. Did you feed the birds at the park?

45. Did you bite your finger?

46. Did you hurt your finger?

47. Did you hold (. . .)'s hand?

48. Did you build a bookcase?

49. Did you stand at the bus stop?

50. Did you sing in the shower this morning?

51. Did you grow up in *(name of a country)*?

52. Did you become an adult?

53. Did *(name of a sports team)* win yesterday?

54. Did you fall down yesterday?

55. Did you think about me yesterday?

56. Did you fight yesterday?

57. Which pen do you want? Did you choose this one?

58. Did you hide your money under your mattress?

59. Did your car hit a telephone pole yesterday?

60. Did you put your books under your desk?

9-7 *BEFORE* AND *AFTER* IN TIME CLAUSES

(a) $\overset{S \quad V}{I\ ate\ breakfast.}$ = a main clause	A clause is a group of words that has a subject and a verb.
(b) **before** $\overset{S \quad V}{I\ went\ to\ class}$ = a time clause	A main clause is a complete sentence. Example (a) is a complete sentence. Example (b) is an incomplete sentence. It must be connected to a main clause, as in (c) and (d).
(c) $\underset{\text{main clause}}{\underline{I\ ate\ breakfast}}$ $\underset{\text{time clause}}{\underline{\textbf{\textit{before}}\ \textit{I\ went\ to\ class.}}}$	
(d) $\underset{\text{time clause}}{\underline{\textbf{\textit{Before}}\ \textit{I\ went\ to\ class,}}}$ $\underset{\text{main clause}}{\underline{I\ ate\ breakfast.}}$	A time clause can begin with **before** or **after**: **before** + S + V = a time clause **after** + S + V = a time clause
(e) $\underset{\text{main clause}}{\underline{We\ took\ a\ walk}}$ $\underset{\text{time clause}}{\underline{\textbf{\textit{after}}\ \textit{we\ finished\ our\ work.}}}$	A time clause can follow a main clause, as in (c) and (e). A time clause can come in front of a main clause, as in (d) and (f).* There is no difference in meaning between (c) and (d) or (e) and (f).
(f) $\underset{\text{time clause}}{\underline{\textbf{\textit{After}}\ \textit{we\ finished\ our\ work,}}}$ $\underset{\text{main clause}}{\underline{we\ took\ a\ walk.}}$	
(g) We took a walk $\underset{\text{prep. phrase}}{\underline{\textit{after\ the\ movie.}}}$	**Before** and **after** don't always introduce a time clause. They are also used as prepositions followed by a noun object, as in (g) and (h). See Charts 1-7, p. 18, and 6-1, p. 158, for information about prepositional phrases.
(h) I had a cup of coffee $\underset{\text{prep. phrase}}{\underline{\textit{before\ class.}}}$	

*NOTE: When a time clause comes before the main clause, a comma is used between the two clauses. A comma is not used when the time clause comes after the main clause.

☐ **EXERCISE 25. Sentence practice.**

Directions: Find the main clauses and the time clauses.

1. Before I ate the banana, I peeled it.
   → *main clause = I peeled it*
   → *time clause = before I ate the banana*

2. We arrived at the airport before the plane landed.

3. I went to a movie after I finished my homework.

4. After the children got home from school, they watched TV.

5. Before I moved to this city, I lived at home with my parents.

Directions: Add a capital letter and period to the complete sentences. Write "Inc." to mean "Incomplete" if the group of words is a time clause and not a complete sentence.

1. we went home → ***W***~~e~~*e went home* .

2. after we left my uncle's house → *Inc.*

3. we went home after we left my uncle's house

   → ***W***~~e~~*e went home after we left my uncle's house* .

4. before we ate our picnic lunch

5. we went to the zoo

6. we went to the zoo before we ate our picnic lunch

7. the children played games after they did their work

8. the children played games

9. after they did their work

10. the lions killed a zebra

11. after the lions killed a zebra

12. they ate it

13. after the lions killed a zebra, they ate it

□ EXERCISE 27. Let's talk: small groups.

Directions: Work in small groups. Combine the two ideas into one sentence by using ***before*** and ***after*** to introduce time clauses. Make four sentences for each item.

Example: I put on my coat. I went outside.
SPEAKER A: Before I went outside, I put on my coat.
SPEAKER B: I put on my coat before I went outside.
SPEAKER C: After I put on my coat, I went outside.
SPEAKER D: I went outside after I put on my coat.

1. She ate breakfast.

She went to work.

2. He did his homework.

He went to bed.

3. We bought tickets.

We entered the movie theater.

Directions: Use the given words to write sentences of your own. Use the simple past.

Example: after I
→ I went to college after I graduated from high school.
→ After I finished dinner, I watched TV.
Etc.

1. before I came here
2. after I got home last night
3. I went _____ before I
4. after we
5. before they
6. Mr. _____ after he

9-8 *WHEN* IN TIME CLAUSES

(a) ***When*** *the rain stopped,* we took a walk. OR We took a ***walk*** *when the rain stopped.*	***When*** can introduce a time clause. ***when*** + s + v = a time clause In (a): ***When*** *the rain stopped* is a time clause.
(b) *When* ***Tom*** *was a child,* ***he*** *lived with his aunt.* OR ***Tom*** *lived with his aunt when* ***he*** *was a child.*	In (b): Notice that the noun *(Tom)* comes before the pronoun *(he)*.
COMPARE (c) *When did the rain stop?* = a question (d) *when the rain stopped* = a time clause	***When*** is also used to introduce questions.★ A question is a complete sentence, as in (c). A time clause is not a complete sentence, as in (d).

★See Charts 3–12, p. 80, and 9–1, p. 252, for information about using *when* in questions.

☐ EXERCISE 29. Sentence practice.

Directions: Make sentences by combining the ideas in Column A with those in Column B. Then change the position of the time clause.

Example: When the phone rang,
→ When the phone rang, I answered it.★
→ I answered the phone when it rang.

★ NOTE: If a sentence with a *when*-clause talks about two actions, the action in the *when*-clause happens first. (See Chart 9-12, p. 284.) In the sentence *When the phone rang, I answered it:* first the phone rang, and then I answered it. Not logically possible: *When I answered the phone, it rang.*

Column A	Column B
1. When the phone rang,	A. when I dropped it.
2. When I was in Japan,	B. I closed my umbrella.
3. Maria bought some new shoes	C. when he was in high school.
4. I took a lot of photographs	✓D. I answered it.
5. Jim was a soccer player	E. when she went shopping yesterday.
6. When the rain stopped,	F. I stayed in a hotel in Tokyo.
7. The antique vase broke	G. when I was in Hawaii.

☐ **EXERCISE 30. Sentence practice.**

Directions: Add a capital letter and a question mark to complete the sentences. Write "Inc." to mean "Incomplete" if the group of words is a time clause and not a question.

1. when did Jim arrive → *When did Jim arrive?*

2. when Jim arrived → *Inc.*

3. when you were a child

4. when were you in Iran

5. when did the movie end

6. when the movie ended

7. when Mr. Wang arrived at the airport

8. when Khalid and Bakir went to a restaurant on First Street yesterday

9. when I was a high school student

10. when does the museum open

☐ **EXERCISE 31. Sentence practice.**

Directions: Complete the sentences with your own words. Don't change the order of the given words.

1. When did _____

2. When I _____

3. I _____ when _____

4. When were _____

5. When the _____

6. The _____ when _____

9-9 THE PRESENT PROGRESSIVE AND THE PAST PROGRESSIVE

PRESENT PROGRESSIVE (in progress right now) (a) It's 10:00 now. Boris *is sitting* in class.	The present progressive describes an activity in progress right now, at the moment of speaking. See Chart 4-1, p. 92. In (a): Right now it is 10:00. Boris began to sit before 10:00. Sitting is in progress at 10:00.
PAST PROGRESSIVE (in progress yesterday) (b) It was 10:00. Boris *was sitting* in class.	The past progressive describes an activity in progress at a particular time in the past. In (b): Boris began to sit in class before 10:00 yesterday. At 10:00 yesterday, sitting in class was in progress.

PRESENT PROGRESSIVE FORM: *AM, IS, ARE* + *-ING*
(c) It's 10:00. I *am sitting* in class.
           Boris *is sitting* in class.
           We *are sitting* in class.
	The forms of the present progressive and the past progressive consist of *be* + *-ing*. The present progressive uses the present forms of *be: am, is,* and *are* + *-ing*.

PAST PROGRESSIVE FORM: *WAS, WERE* + *-ING* (d) It was 10:00. Boris *was sitting* in class. We *were sitting* in class.	The past progressive uses the past forms of *be: was* and *were* + *-ing*.

Boris *is sitting* in class right now at ten o'clock.

Boris *was sitting* in class yesterday at ten o'clock.

☐ **EXERCISE 32. Sentence practice.**

Directions: Use the words in parentheses to complete the sentences. Discuss the meaning of the phrase "in progress."

1. Paul started to eat dinner at 7:00. At 7:05, Mary came. Paul *(eat)*

_____ when Mary *(come)* _____ at 7:05.

2. Bobby was at home yesterday evening. His favorite program was on television last night. It started at 8:00. It ended at 9:00. At 8:30, his friend Kristin called.

When Kristin *(call)* _____ at 8:30, Bobby *(watch)* _____

_____ TV.

3. Rosa played her guitar for an hour yesterday morning. She started to play her guitar at 9:30. She stopped at 10:30. Mike arrived at her apartment at 10:00. At

10:00, Rosa *(play)* _____ her guitar.

□ **EXERCISE 33. Let's talk: class activity.**

Directions: Look at the picture. Use the past progressive to describe the activities that were in progress.

Mr. and Mrs. Gold invited some friends to their house for the weekend. A thief stole Mrs. Gold's jewelry at midnight on Saturday. What were the guests doing at midnight?

9-10 USING *WHILE* WITH THE PAST PROGRESSIVE

(a) The phone rang *while I was sleeping.* OR (b) *While I was sleeping,* the phone rang.*	*while* + subject + verb = a time clause *While I was sleeping* is a time clause. A *while*-clause describes an activity that was in progress at the time another activity happened. The verb in a *while*-clause is often past progressive *(e.g., was sleeping).*

*NOTE: When a time clause comes before the main clause, a comma is used between the two clauses. A comma is not used when the time clause comes after the main clause.

☐ **EXERCISE 34. Let's talk: class activity.**

Directions: Combine the sentences. Use *while*.

1. I was studying last night.
   Rita called.
   → *While I was studying last night, Rita called.*
   → *Rita called while I was studying last night.*

2. Someone knocked on my apartment door.
   I was eating breakfast yesterday morning.

3. I was cooking dinner yesterday evening.
   I burned my hand.

4. Yoko raised her hand.
   The teacher was talking.

5. A tree fell on my car.
   I was driving home yesterday.

6. I was studying last night.
   A mouse suddenly appeared on my desk.

9-11 *WHILE* VS. *WHEN* IN PAST TIME CLAUSES

(a) The mouse appeared *while **I was studying***. OR	The verb in a *while*-clause is often past progressive, as in (a) and (b).
(b) *While **I was studying***, the mouse appeared.	
(c) *When the mouse **appeared***, I was studying. OR	The verb in a *when*-clause is often simple past, as in (c) and (d).
(d) I was studying *when the mouse **appeared***.	

☐ **EXERCISE 35. Sentence practice.**

Directions: Complete the sentences. Use the past progressive in the *while*-clauses. Use the simple past in the *when*-clauses.

1. While I (wash) __was washing__ dishes last night, I (get) _____got_____

   a phone call from my best friend.

2. When my best friend (call) _____ last night, I (wash) _____

   _____ dishes.

3. My friend Jessica (come) _____ while I (eat) _____

   _____ dinner last night.

4. I (eat) _____ dinner when my friend Jessica (come)

   _____ last night.

5. My friend Ricardo (come) _____ while I (watch) _____

   _____ a rented movie on my VCR last night. I (invite)

   _____ him to join me.

6. I (watch) _____ a rented movie on my VCR last night

   when my friend Ricardo (come) _____.

7. Jason (wear) _____ a suit and tie when I (see)

   _____ him yesterday.

8. While I *(watch)* _____ TV last night and *(relax)*

_____ after a long day, my new puppy *(take)* _____

my wallet from my bedside table.

☐ **EXERCISE 36. Let's talk: class activity.**

Directions: Perform and describe actions using *while*-clauses or *when*-clauses. Close your book for this activity.

Student A: Perform the action your teacher gives you. Then use the present progressive to describe what you are doing. Continue to perform the action.

Student B: Perform your action, then stop.

Student A: After Student B stops, you stop too.

Example: A: Erase the board.

 B: Open the door.

 TEACHER: *(Student A),* please erase the board. What are you doing?

 STUDENT A: I'm erasing the board right now.

 TEACHER: *(Student B),* would you please open the door?

 STUDENT B: *(opens the door)*

 TEACHER: Thank you. You may both sit down. *(Student C),* will you please describe the two actions we saw?

 STUDENT C: While *(Student A)* was erasing the board, *(Student B)* opened the door. OR *(Student A)* was erasing the board when *(Student B)* opened the door.

1. A: Write on the board.
   B: Drop a book on the floor.
2. A: Walk around the room.
   B: Say hello to *(Student A).*
3. A: Look out the window.
   B: Take *(Student A)*'s grammar book.
4. A: Draw a picture on the board.
   B: Ask *(Student A)* a question.

9-12 SIMPLE PAST vs. PAST PROGRESSIVE

(a) Jane *called* me yesterday. (b) I *talked* to Jane for an hour last night. (c) We *went* to Jack's house last Friday. (d) What time *did* you *get up* this morning?	The *simple past* describes activities or situations that began and ended at a particular time in the past (e.g., *yesterday, last night*).
(e) I *was studying* when Jane called me yesterday. (f) While I *was studying* last night, Jane called.	The *past progressive* describes an activity that was in progress (was happening) at the time another action happened. In (e) and (f): The studying was in progress when Jane called.
(g) I *opened* my umbrella when it *began* to rain.	If both the *when*-clause and the main clause in a sentence are simple past, it means that the action in the *when*-clause happened first, and the action in the main clause happened second. In (g): First, it began to rain; second, I opened my umbrella.
COMPARE (h) When the phone *rang*, I *answered* it. (i) When the phone *rang*, I *was studying*.	In (h): First, the phone rang; second, I answered it. In (i): First, the studying was in progress; second, the phone rang.

□ EXERCISE 37. Sentence practice.

Directions: Complete the sentences. Use the simple past or the past progressive.

1. While my cousin and I *(have)* _____ dinner at the

   restaurant last night, we *(see)* _____ a friend of mine. I *(introduce)*

   _____ her to my cousin.

2. When I *(hear)* _____ a knock at the door last night, I *(walk)*

   _____ to the door and *(open)* _____ it. When I *(open)*

   _____ the door, I *(see)* _____ my brother. I *(greet)*

   _____ him and *(ask)* _____ him to come in.

3. My cousin and I (watch) _____ a movie on TV last night

when my brother (come) _____. He (watch) _____

the end of the movie with us.

4. While I (walk) _____ to class yesterday morning, I (see)

_____ Abdullah. We (say) _____ hello and (walk)

_____ the rest of the way to school together.

□ **EXERCISE 38. Sentence practice.**

Directions: Complete the sentences. Use the simple past or the past progressive.

1. Mrs. Reed (turn) _____ on the radio in her car while she (drive)

_____ home yesterday. She (listen) _____

_____ to some music when she suddenly (hear)

_____ a siren. When she (look) _____ in her rear-view

mirror, she (see) _____ an ambulance behind her. She immediately

(pull) _____ her car to the side of the road and (wait)

_____ for the ambulance to pass.

2. A: I *(be)* _____ at my friends' house last night. While we *(eat)*

_____ dinner, their cat *(jump)* _____ on

the table. My friends *(seem, not)* _____ to care, but I

lost my appetite.

B: What *(you, say)* _____?

A: Nothing.

B: Why *(you, ask, not)* _____ your friends to get their

cat off the table?

A: I *(want, not)* _____ to be impolite.

B: I think your friends were impolite to let their cat sit on the table during dinner.

□ **EXERCISE 39. Sentence practice.**

Directions: Use the information in the timeline to make sentences with the simple
past and past progressive. Use **while**, **when**, **before**, and **after**.

Example: 1967: entered Lakeside School
→ *In 1967, Bill Gates entered Lakeside School.*
→ *While he was studying at Lakeside, he began to work with computers.*

Bill Gates: a brief history

1955: was born

1967: entered Lakeside School

1967–1973: studied at Lakeside School

1968: wrote his first computer program

1970: started his first software company

1973: graduated from Lakeside

1973–1977: studied at Harvard University

1975:   began to design programs for personal computers

1975:   started Microsoft

1975–2000: worked as Chief Executive Officer for Microsoft

1977:   left Harvard

1994:   got married

1996:   his first child was born

☐ EXERCISE 40. Listening.

Directions: Listen to the story. Complete the sentences with the verbs you hear.

I _____ a strange experience yesterday. I _____

my book on the bus when a man _____ down next to me and

_____ me if I wanted some money. I _____ his

money. I _____ very confused. I _____ up and

_____ toward the door of the bus.

While I _____ for the door to open, the man

_____ to give me the money. When the door _____, I

_____ off the bus quickly. I still _____ why he

_____ to give me money.

☐ EXERCISE 41. Verb review.

Directions: Choose the best completions.

1. I was watching TV. I heard a knock on the door. When I heard the knock on the
   door, I _____ it.
   A. open
   B. am opening
   C. opened
   D. was opening

2. "When _____ you talk to Jane?"
   "Yesterday."
   A. do   B. are   C. did   D. were

3. I _____ TV when Gina called last night. We talked for an hour.
   A. watch
   B. watched
   C. was watching
   D. am watching

4. Mike is in his bedroom right now. He _____, so we need to be quiet.
   A. is sleeping   C. slept
   B. sleeps   D. was sleeping

5. Kate _____ tell us the truth yesterday. She lied to us.
   A. don't   B. doesn't   C. didn't   D. wasn't

6. I saw a fish while I _____ in the ocean yesterday.
   A. swim   C. were swimming
   B. was swimming   D. swimming

7. When I heard the phone ring, I _____ it.
   A. answer   C. answered
   B. am answering   D. was answering

8. "_____ you go to concerts often?"
   "Yes. I go at least once a month."
   A. Do   B. Did   C. Was   D. Were

9. While I _____ dinner last night, I burned my finger.
   A. cooking   B. cook   C. was cooking   D. was cook

10. Where _____ after work yesterday?
   A. you went   B. you did go   C. did you went   D. did you go

☐ EXERCISE 42. Let's talk: interview.
   Directions: Interview someone you know about his/her activities yesterday morning,
   yesterday afternoon, and last night. Then use this information to write a paragraph.
   Use time expressions (***first, next, then, at . . . o'clock, later, after, before, when,***
   etc.) to show the order of the activities.

☐ EXERCISE 43. Chapter review: error analysis.
   Directions: Correct the errors.

   1. Did you went downtown yesterday?

   2. Yesterday I speak to Ken before he leaves his office and goes home.

   3. I heared a good joke last night.

   4. When Pablo finished his work.

   5. I visitted my relatives in New York City last month.

6. Where you did go yesterday afternoon?

7. Ms. Wah was flew from Singapore to Tokyo last week.

8. When I see my friend yesterday, he didn't spoke to me.

9. Why Mustafa didn't came to class last week?

10. Where were you bought those shoes? I like them.

11. Mr. Adams teached our class last week.

12. I writed a letter last night.

13. Who you wrote a letter to?

14. Who did open the door? Jack openned it.

☐ **EXERCISE 44. Verb review.**

Directions: Complete the sentences with the words in parentheses.

PART I.

Yesterday Fish (be) _____ *in the river. He* (see) _____ *Bear on*
$\qquad\quad$ 1 $\qquad\qquad\qquad\qquad\qquad\qquad$ 2

the bank of the river. Here is their conversation.

BEAR: Good morning, Fish.

FISH: Good morning, Bear. How (you, be) _____ today?
$\qquad\qquad\qquad\qquad\qquad\qquad\qquad\qquad\qquad\qquad\qquad\quad$ 3

BEAR: I (do) _____ fine, thank you. And you?
$\qquad\qquad\qquad\qquad$ 4

FISH: Fine, thanks.

BEAR: *(you, would like)* _____ to get out of the river and
      <u>5</u>

      (sit) _____ with me? I *(need)* _____ someone to talk to.
            <u>6</u>   <u>7</u>

FISH: I *(need, not)* _____ to get out of the river for us to
                        <u>8</u>

      talk. We can talk just the way we are now.

BEAR: Hmmm.

FISH: Wait! What *(you, do)* _____?
                              <u>9</u>

BEAR: I *(get)* _____ in the river to join you.
              <u>10</u>

FISH: Stop! This *(be)* _____ my river! I *(trust, not)* _____
                        <u>11</u>   <u>12</u>

      you. What *(you, want)* _____?
                              <u>13</u>

BEAR: Nothing. Just a little conversation. I *(want)* _____ to tell you
                                                    <u>14</u>

      about my problems. I *(have)* _____ a bad day yesterday.
                                    <u>15</u>

FISH: Oh? What happened?

PART II.

BEAR: While I was walking through the woods, I *(see)* _____ a beehive. I
                                                      <u>16</u>

      (love) _____ honey. So I *(stop)* _____. When I
              <u>17</u>   <u>18</u>

      (reach) _____ inside the beehive to get some honey, a great big
                <u>19</u>

      bee *(come)* _____ up behind me and stung* my ear. The sting *(be)*
                    <u>20</u>

      _____ very painful.
      <u>21</u>

_____

Stung is the past form of the verb *sting*, which means "to cause sharp pain."

FISH: I *(believe, not)* _____ you. Bees can't hurt bears. I
22

(believe, not) _____ your story about a great big bee.
23

All bees *(be)* _____ the same size, and they *(be, not)*
24

_____ big.
25

BEAR: But it is true! Here. Come a little closer and look at my ear. I'll show you

where the big bee stung it.

FISH: Okay. Where *(it, be)* _____? Where *(the bee, sting)*
26

_____ you?
27

BEAR: Right here. See?

FISH: Stop! What *(you, do)* _____? Let go of me! Why
28

(you, hold) _____ me?
29

BEAR: I *(hold)* _____ you because I'm going to eat you for
30

dinner.

FISH: Oh no! You *(trick)* _____ me! Your story about the great big
31

bee never *(happen)* _____!
32

PART III.

BEAR: That's right. I *(get)* _____ in the river because I *(want)*
33

_____ *(catch)* _____ you for dinner. And I
34   35

did! I *(catch)* _____ you for dinner.
36

FISH: Watch out! Behind you! Oh no! Oh no! It's a very, very big bee. It's huge!

It *(look)* _____ really angry!
37

BEAR: I *(believe, not)* _____ you!
38

FISH: But it *(be)* _____ true! A great big bee *(come)* _____
39   40

toward you. It's going to attack you and sting you!

BEAR: What? Where? I *(see, not)* _____ a bee! Oh no, Fish, you
41

are getting away from me. Oh no! I *(drop)* _____ you!
42

Come back! Come back!

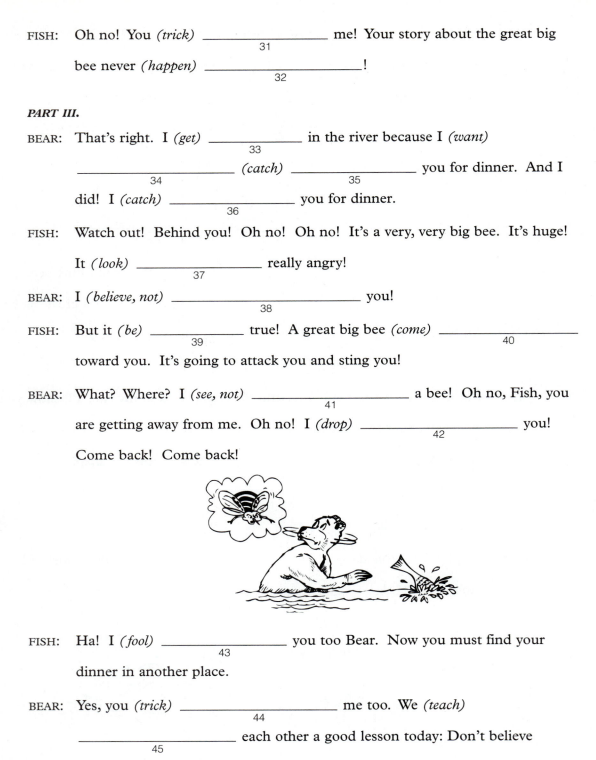

FISH: Ha! I *(fool)* _____ you too Bear. Now you must find your
43

dinner in another place.

BEAR: Yes, you *(trick)* _____ me too. We *(teach)*
44

_____ each other a good lesson today: Don't believe
45

everything you hear.

FISH: Thank you for teaching me that lesson. Now I will live a long and happy life.

BEAR: Yes, we *(learn)* _____ a valuable lesson today, and that's
46

good. But I *(be)* _____ still hungry. Hmmm. I *(have)*
47

_____ a gold tooth in my mouth. *(you, would like)*
48

_____ to come closer and look at it?
49

CHAPTER 10
Expressing Future Time, Part 1

☐ **EXERCISE 1. Preview: let's talk.**

Directions: Answer your teacher's questions. Give a short answer and a long answer. Close your book for this activity.

Example:
TEACHER: Are you going to eat dinner at home tonight?
STUDENT: Yes, I am. I'm going to eat dinner at home tonight. OR
No, I'm not. I'm not going to eat dinner at home tonight.

1. Are you going to come to class tomorrow?
2. Is *(name of a student)* going to be here tomorrow? Please ask her/him.
3. Are *(names of two students)* going to be here tomorrow? Please ask them.
4. When are you going to go to bed tonight?
5. What time are you going to get up tomorrow morning?
6. Where is *(name of a student)* going to go tomorrow after class? Please ask her/him.

10-1 FUTURE TIME: USING *BE GOING TO*

(a) I **am going to go** downtown tomorrow.	**Be going to** expresses (talks about) the future.
(b) Sue **is going to be** here tomorrow afternoon.	FORM: **am** ⎫
(c) We **are going to come** to class tomorrow morning.	**is** ⎬ + **going** + infinitive⋆
	are ⎭
(d) I**'m not going to go** downtown tomorrow.	NEGATIVE: **be** + **not** + **going to**
(e) Ann **isn't going to study** tonight.	
(f) "**Are** you **going to come** to class tomorrow?" "No, I'm not."	QUESTION: **be** + *subject* + **going to** A form of **be** is used in the short answer to a yes/no question with **be going to,** as in (f) and (g). (See Chart 2-2, p. 25, for information about short answers with **be.**)
(g) "**Is** Jim **going to be** at the meeting tomorrow?" "Yes, he is."	
(h) "What time **are** you **going to eat** dinner tonight?" "Around six."	

⋆Infinitive = **to** + the simple form of a verb *(to come, to go, to see, to study, etc.).*

□ **EXERCISE 2. Let's talk: pairwork.**

Directions: Work with a partner. Which of the given activities are you going to do tomorrow? Which ones are you not going to do tomorrow?

Partner A: Your book is open. Ask a question. Use ***Are you going to . . . tomorrow?***

Partner B: Your book is closed. Answer the question. Give both a short answer and a long answer. Use ***I'm going to . . . tomorrow*** OR ***I'm not going to . . . tomorrow*** in the long answer.

Example: go downtown
PARTNER A *(book open):*   Are you going to go downtown tomorrow?
PARTNER B *(book closed):* Yes, I am. I'm going to go downtown tomorrow. OR
                            No, I'm not. I'm not going to go downtown tomorrow.

1. get up before eight o'clock
2. come to class
3. stay home all day
4. eat lunch
5. get a ride with *(someone)*

6. get a haircut
7. watch TV in the evening
8. do something interesting in the evening
9. go to bed early
10. go to bed late

Switch roles.
Partner A: Close your book.
Partner B: Open your book. Your turn now.

11. get up early
12. get up late
13. walk to school
14. study grammar
15. get some exercise

16. eat dinner
17. eat dinner alone
18. listen to music after dinner
19. go shopping
20. do something interesting and unusual

□ **EXERCISE 3. Let's talk: class interview.**

Directions: Walk around the room. Ask your classmates questions. Write down their names and their answers. Share some of their answers with the class.

Example: tomorrow
SPEAKER A: What are you going to do tomorrow?
SPEAKER B: I'm going to go shopping / get a haircut / walk to school.

Question	First name	Answer
1. tomorrow		
2. tomorrow morning		

Question	First name	Answer
3. tomorrow afternoon		
4. tomorrow night		
5. at 7:00 tomorrow morning		
6. at 9:00 tomorrow morning		
7. at noon tomorrow		
8. at 5:00 tomorrow afternoon		
9. around 6:30 tomorrow evening		
10. after 8:00 tomorrow night		

☐ **EXERCISE 4. Sentence practice.**

Directions: Complete the sentences. Use ***be going to*** and the given expressions (or your own words).

call the manager	✓ go to the bookstore	see a dentist
call the police	go to an Italian restaurant	stay in bed today
get something to eat	lie down and rest for a while	take a long walk in the park
go to the beach	look it up in my dictionary	take it to the post office
go to bed	major in psychology	take them to the laundromat

1. I need to buy a book. I _____ *am going to go to the bookstore.* _____

2. It's midnight now. I'm sleepy. I _____

3. Sue is hungry. She _____

4. My clothes are dirty. I _____

5. I have a toothache. I _____

6. I'm writing a composition. I don't know how to spell a word. I _____

_____

7. George has to mail a package. He _____

8. It's a nice day today. Mary and I _____

9. Sue and I want to go swimming. We _____

10. I have a headache. I _____

11. It's late at night. I hear a burglar! I _____

12. I want to be a psychologist. When I go to the university, I _____

_____

13. I feel terrible. I think I'm getting the flu. I _____

14. Ivan and Natasha want to go out to eat. They _____

15. Rosa lives in an apartment. There's a problem with the plumbing. She _____

_____

☐ **EXERCISE 5. Let's talk: class activity.**

Directions: Listen to the teacher describe common activities. Picture these activities in your mind. Use ***be going to*** to tell what you think your classmates are going to do. Close your book for this activity.

Example:
TEACHER: (. . .) is carrying his/her textbooks and notebooks. He/She is walking toward the library. What is (. . .) going to do?
STUDENT: (. . .) is going to study at the library.

1. (. . .) is standing next to the chalkboard. He/She is picking up a piece of chalk. What is (. . .) going to do?

2. (. . .) has some letters in his/her hand. He/She is walking toward the post office. What is (. . .) going to do?

3. (. . .) is holding a phone book. He/She is looking for (. . .)'s name. What is (. . .) going to do?

4. (. . .) put some water on the stove to boil. She got a cup and saucer and some tea out of the cupboard. What is (. . .) going to do?

5. (. . .) is putting on his/her coat. He/She is walking toward the door. What is (. . .) going to do?

6. (. . .) has a basket full of dirty clothes. He/She is walking toward a laundromat. What is (. . .) going to do?

7. (. . .) bought some meat and vegetables at the store. He/She is holding a bag of rice. He/She just turned on the stove. What is (. . .) going to do?

8. (. . .) and (. . .) are walking into *(name of a local restaurant)*. It's seven o'clock in the evening. What are (. . .) and (. . .) going to do?

9. (. . .) gave (. . .) a diamond engagement ring. What are (. . .) and (. . .) going to do?

10. (. . .) and (. . .) have airplane tickets. They're putting clothes in their suitcases. Their clothes include swimming suits and sandals. What are (. . .) and (. . .) going to do?

□ EXERCISE 6. Let's talk: interview.

Directions: Walk around the room. Ask your classmates questions using **be going to**. Write down their names and their answers. Share some of their answers with the class.

Example: when \ go downtown
SPEAKER A: When are you going to go downtown?
SPEAKER B: Tomorrow afternoon. / In a couple of days. / Around noon. / Etc.

Question	First name	Answer
1. where \ go after class today		
2. what time \ get home tonight		
3. when \ eat dinner		
4. where \ eat dinner		
5. what time \ go to bed tonight		
6. what time \ get up tomorrow morning		
7. where \ be tomorrow morning		
8. when \ see your family again		
9. where \ live next year		
10. when \ take a trip and where \ go		

□ EXERCISE 7. Let's talk: class activity.

Directions: Your teacher will ask you questions. Use **be going to** in your answers. Close your book for this activity.

Example: You want to buy some tea. What are you going to do? What is (. . .) going to do and why?

TEACHER: You want to buy some tea. What are you going to do?
SPEAKER A: I'm going to go to the grocery store.
TEACHER: *(to Speaker B)* What is *(Speaker A)* going to do and why?
SPEAKER B: *(Speaker A)* is going to go to the grocery store because he/she wants to buy some tea.

1. You have a toothache. What are you going to do? What is (. . .) going to do and why?
2. You need to mail a package. Where are you going to go? Where is (. . .) going to go and why?
3. Your clothes are dirty.
4. It's midnight. You're sleepy.
5. It's late at night. You hear a burglar.
6. You need to buy some groceries.
7. You want to go swimming.
8. You want to go fishing.
9. You want to buy a new coat.
10. You're hungry.
11. You have a headache.
12. It's a nice day today.
13. You need to cash a check.
14. You want some (pizza) for dinner.
15. You're reading a book. You don't know the meaning of a word.

10-2 USING THE PRESENT PROGRESSIVE TO EXPRESS FUTURE TIME

(a) Sue *is going to leave*	at 8:00 tomorrow.	Sometimes the present progressive is used to express future time.
(b) Sue *is leaving*	at 8:00 tomorrow.	(a) and (b) mean the same thing.
(c) We *are going to drive*	to Toronto next week.	(c) and (d) mean the same thing.
(d) We *are driving*	to Toronto next week.	The present progressive is used for future meaning when the speaker is talking about plans that have already been made.

COMMON VERBS

come	drive	go	meet	spend	stay
do	fly	leave	return	start	take

☐ EXERCISE 8. Sentence practice.

Directions: Rewrite the sentences using the present progressive.

1. My mother and I are going to leave for our trip at 10:00 tomorrow.
   → *My mother and I are leaving for our trip at 10:00 tomorrow.*

2. We are going to fly to Athens.

3. We are going to spend a week there.

4. My brother is going to meet us there.

5. He is going to take the train.

6. We are going to go sightseeing together.

7. I am going to come back by boat, and they are going to return by train.

☐ EXERCISE 9. Listening.

Directions: Listen to each sentence. Decide if the meaning is present or future time. Circle the correct answer.

1. (present)	future		5. present	future
2. present	future		6. present	future
3. present	future		7. present	future
4. present	future		8. present	future

☐ EXERCISE 10. Let's talk: interview.

Directions: Walk around the room. Ask your classmates questions using the present progressive. Write down their names and their answers. Share some of their answers with the class.

Example: what \ do \ tonight
SPEAKER A: What are you doing tonight?
SPEAKER B: I'm staying home and watching a DVD.

Question	First name	Answer
1. where \ go \ after school		
2. what time \ have dinner		
3. when \ go \ to bed tonight		
4. what time \ get up \ tomorrow		
5. what \ do \ tomorrow		
6. what \ do \ this weekend		

Directions: Listen to each sentence. Circle the verb you hear.

1. (is going to rain)   is raining   rains
2. am going to leave   am leaving   leave
3. is going to start   is starting   starts
4. is going to come   is coming   comes
5. is going to call   is calling   calls
6. Are you going to study   Are you studying   Do you study
7. are going to have   are having   have
8. aren't going to go   aren't going   don't go
9. is going to ride   is riding   rides
10. is going to help   is helping   helps

10-3 WORDS USED FOR PAST TIME AND FUTURE TIME

PAST	FUTURE	
yesterday	tomorrow	PAST: It *rained* **yesterday**. FUTURE: It's *going to rain* **tomorrow**.
yesterday morning yesterday afternoon yesterday evening last night	tomorrow morning tomorrow afternoon tomorrow evening tomorrow night	PAST: I *was* in class **yesterday morning**. FUTURE: I'm *going to be* in class **tomorrow morning**.
last week last month last year last weekend last spring last summer last fall last winter last Monday, etc.	next week next month next year next weekend next spring next summer next fall next winter next Monday, etc.	PAST: Mary *went* downtown **last week**. FUTURE: Mary *is going to go* downtown **next week**. PAST: Bob *graduated* from high school **last spring**. FUTURE: Ann *is going to graduate* from high school **next spring**.
. . . minutes ago . . . hours ago . . . days ago . . . weeks ago . . . months ago . . . years ago	in . . . minutes (from now) in . . . hours (from now) in . . . days (from now) in . . . weeks (from now) in . . . months (from now) in . . . years (from now)	PAST: I *finished* my homework **five minutes ago**. FUTURE: Pablo *is going to finish* his homework **in five minutes**.

□ **EXERCISE 12. Sentence practice.**

Directions: Complete the sentences. Use *yesterday, last, tomorrow,* or *next.*

1. I went swimming _____*yesterday*_____ morning.

2. Ken is going to go to the beach _____*tomorrow*_____ morning.

3. I'm going to take a trip _____ week.

4. Maria went to Miami _____ week for a short vacation.

5. We had a test in class _____ afternoon.

6. _____ afternoon we're going to go on a picnic.

7. My sister is going to arrive _____ Tuesday.

8. Mr. Koh bought a used car _____ Friday.

9. My brother is going to enter the university _____ fall.

10. _____ spring I took a trip to San Francisco.

11. Mia is going to fly to London _____ month.

12. Rick lived in Tokyo _____ year.

13. I'm going to study at the library _____ night.

14. _____ night I watched TV.

15. _____ evening I'm going to go to a baseball game.

16. Mrs. Chang went to the opera _____ evening.

☐ **EXERCISE 13. Sentence practice.**

Directions: Complete the sentences. Use the given time expression with **ago** or **in**.

1. *ten minutes*   Class is going to end _____ *in ten minutes.* _____

2. *ten minutes*   Ann's class ended _____ *ten minutes ago.* _____

3. *an hour*   The post office isn't open. It closed _____

4. *an hour*   Jack is going to call us _____

5. *two more*   I'm studying abroad now, but I'm going to be back home
   months
                     _____

6. *two months*   My wife and I took a trip to Morocco _____

7. *a minute*   Karen left _____

8. *half an hour*   I'm going to meet David at the coffee shop _____

9. *one more week*   The new highway is going to open _____

10. *a year*   I was living in Korea _____

☐ **EXERCISE 14. Sentence practice.**

Directions: Change the sentences using **ago** or **in**. Use the calendar to calculate length of time. "Today" is September 9.

1. Beth and Tom are going to get married on September 14.

   → *Beth and Tom are going to get married in five days.*

2. They are going to leave for their honeymoon on Sept. 15.

3. Beth and Tom got engaged on June 9.

4. They are going to return from their honeymoon on Sept. 23.

5. Beth and Tom met in 2002.

6. They began dating a year later.

7. Tom is going to quit his job September 30.

8. Beth and Tom are going to open a restaurant together on December 9.

SEPTEMBER						
Sun.	Mon.	Tues.	Wed.	Thurs.	Fri.	Sat.
1	2	3	4	5	6	7
8	9	10	11	12	13	14
15	16	17	18	19	20	21
22	23	24	25	26	27	28
29	30					

☐ **EXERCISE 15. Listening.**

Directions: Listen to the beginning of each sentence. Circle the correct completion.

1.	five minutes ago	(in five minutes)
2.	one hour ago	in one hour
3.	two weeks ago	in two weeks
4.	one year ago	in one year
5.	ten minutes ago	in ten minutes
6.	a few minutes ago	in a few minutes
7.	last spring	next spring
8.	last summer	next summer
9.	last weekend	next weekend
10.	yesterday evening	tomorrow evening

☐ **EXERCISE 16. Let's talk: interview.**

Directions: Walk around the room. Ask a different student each pair of questions. Write down their names and their answers. Share some of their answers with the class.

Question	First name	Answer
1. where \ go \ yesterday where \ go\ tomorrow		
2. who \ call \ last week who \ call \ next week		
3. who \ call \ yesterday who \ call \ tomorrow		
4. what \ watch on TV \ last week what \ watch on TV \ next week		
5. where \ live \ five years ago where \ live \ in five years		

☐ **EXERCISE 17. Sentence practice.**

Directions: Complete the sentences. Use *yesterday, last, tomorrow, next, in,* or *ago*.

1. I went to the zoo _____*last*_____ week.

2. Yolanda went to the zoo a week _____.

3. Peter Nelson is going to go to the zoo _____ Saturday.

4. We're going to go to the zoo _____ two more days.

5. My children went to the zoo _____ morning.

6. My cousin is going to go to the zoo _____ afternoon.

7. Kim Yang-Don graduated from Sogang University _____ spring.

8. We're going to have company for dinner _____ night.

9. We had company for dinner three days _____.

10. We're going to have dinner at our friends' house _____ two days.

11. _____ evening we're going to go to a concert.

12. _____ Friday I went to a party.

13. _____ morning the students took a test.

14. My little sister arrived here _____ month.

15. She is going to leave _____ two weeks.

16. _____ year Yuko is going to be a freshman in college.

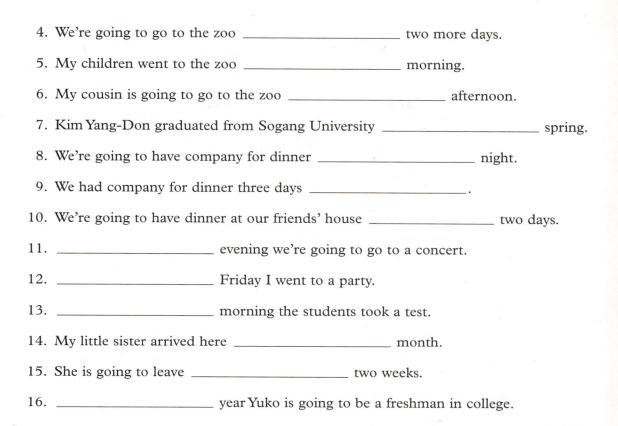

10-4 USING *A COUPLE OF* OR *A FEW* WITH *AGO* (PAST) AND *IN* (FUTURE)

(a) Sam arrived here **one** (OR **a**) year ago. (b) Jack is going to be here *in **two** minutes.* (c) I talked to Ann ***three*** days ago.	Numbers are often used in time expressions with ***ago*** and ***in***.
(d) I saw Carlos ***a couple*** of months ago. (e) He's going to return to Mexico *in **a couple of** months.* (f) I got a letter from Gina ***a few*** weeks ago. (g) I'm going to see Gina *in **a few** weeks.*	***A couple of*** and ***a few*** are also commonly used. ***A couple of*** means "two." *A couple of months ago = two months ago.* ***A few*** means "a small number, not a large number." *A few weeks ago = three, four, or five weeks ago.*
(h) I began college last year. I'm going to graduate *in **two more** years.* My sister is almost finished with her education. She's going to graduate *in **a few more** months.*	Frequently, the word ***more*** is used in future time expressions that begin with ***in***.

☐ EXERCISE 18. Let's talk: small groups.

Directions: Work in small groups. Take turns completing the sentences. Use information from your own life. Use the words in *italics* with **ago** or **in**. Use numbers *(one, two, three, ten, sixteen, etc.)* or the expressions **a couple of** or **a few**.

1. *days*   We studied Chapter 9 _____*a couple of days ago/three days ago/etc.*_____

2. *days*   We're going to finish this chapter _____*in a few more days / in*_____

               _____*three or four days / etc.*_____

3. *hours*   I ate breakfast _____

4. *hours*   I'm going to eat lunch/dinner _____

5. *minutes* We finished Exercise 17 _____

6. *minutes* This class is going to end _____

7. *years*   I was born _____

8. *years*   My parents got married _____

9. *weeks* ⎫ I arrived in this city _____ , and
    months⎬
    years ⎭ I'm going to leave this city _____

☐ EXERCISE 19. Sentence practice.

Directions: Complete the sentences with your own words. Write about your life. For example, what did you do a few days ago? What are you going to do in a few days? Share some of your sentences with the class.

1. _____ a few days ago.

2. _____ in a few days (from now).

3. _____ in a few more minutes.

4. _____ three hours ago.

5. _____ in four more hours.

6. _____ a couple of days ago.

7. _____ in a couple of months (from now).

8. _____ many years ago.

9. _____ in a couple of minutes (from now).

Directions: Listen to the sentences. Circle *same* if the sentence in the book has the same meaning. Circle *different* if the meaning is different.

1. Jean is going to leave in two days.   (same)   different

2. Tom is going to leave in three weeks.   same   different

3. The doctor is going to call in one hour.   same   different

4. Tim graduated from high school two years ago.   same   different

5. We sold our house five years ago.   same   different

6. The mail came ten minutes ago.   same   different

7. The phone rang five minutes ago.   same   different

8. John is going to be here in forty minutes.   same   different

---

10-5 USING *TODAY, TONIGHT,* AND *THIS* + *MORNING, AFTERNOON, EVENING, WEEK, MONTH, YEAR*

PRESENT	(a) Right now it's 10 A.M. We are in our English class. We **are studying** English **this morning**.	*today* *tonight* *this morning* *this afternoon* *this evening* *this week* *this weekend* *this month* *this year*	These words can express present, past, or future time.
PAST	(b) Right now it's 10 A.M. Nancy left home at 9 A.M. to go downtown. She isn't at home right now. Nancy **went** downtown **this morning**.		
FUTURE	(c) Right now it's 10 A.M. Class ends at 11 A.M. After class today, I'm going to go to the post office. I**'m going to go** to the post office **this morning**.		

☐ EXERCISE 21. Sentence practice.

Directions: Answer the questions with your own words.

1. What is something you did earlier this year?

   → I _____*came to this city*_____ this year.

2. What is something you are doing this year?

   → I _____*am studying English*_____ this year.

3. What is something you are going to do this year?

   → I _____*am going to visit my relatives in Cairo*_____ this year.

4. What is something you did earlier today?

→ I _____ today.

5. What is something you are doing today, right now?

→ I _____ today.

6. What is something you are going to do later today?

→ I _____ today.

7. What is something you did earlier this morning / afternoon / evening?

→ I _____ this _____ .

8. What is something you are going to do later this morning / afternoon / evening?

→ I _____ this _____ .

□ EXERCISE 22. Sentence practice.

Directions: Complete the sentences with your own words. Discuss the different verb tenses that are possible.

1. _____ today.

2. _____ this morning.

3. _____ this afternoon.

4. _____ this evening.

5. _____ tonight.

6. _____ this week.

7. _____ this month.

8. _____ this year.

□ EXERCISE 23. Let's talk: small groups.

Directions: Work in small groups. Take turns being Speaker A and asking your classmates questions about future activities.

Speaker A: Begin your question with ***When are you going to . . . ?***
Speaker B: Answer Speaker A's question.
Speaker A: Ask Speaker C a question that begins with ***When is (B) going to . . . ?***
Speaker C: Answer in a complete sentence.

Example: go downtown

SPEAKER A: When are you going to go downtown?
SPEAKER B: This weekend. / Tomorrow morning. / In a couple of days. / Etc.
SPEAKER A: When is (. . .) going to go downtown?
SPEAKER C: He/She is going to go downtown this weekend.

1. have dinner
2. do your grammar homework
3. go shopping
4. go to *(name of a class)*
5. visit *(name of a place in this city)*
6. call *(name of a student)* on the phone
7. go to *(name of a restaurant)* for dinner
8. see your family again
9. buy a car
10. see *(name of a new movie)*
11. go to *(name of an event)*
12. take a vacation

☐ EXERCISE 24. Let's talk: pairwork.

Directions: Work with a partner. Ask questions using the given verbs or your own words.

Example: tomorrow morning
PARTNER A: Are you going to come to class tomorrow morning?
PARTNER B: Yes, I am. OR No, I'm not.

Example: yesterday morning
PARTNER A: Did you eat breakfast yesterday morning?
PARTNER B: Yes, I did. OR No, I didn't.

Remember: You can use the given verbs or your own words.

buy	*drive*	*shop*
call	*eat*	*sleep*
come	*get up*	*visit*
do	*go*	*wake up*
drink	*send*	*wash*

1. last night
2. tomorrow night
3. tonight
4. tomorrow afternoon
5. yesterday afternoon
6. this afternoon
7. last Friday
8. next Friday
9. next week

Switch roles.
10. last week
11. this week
12. yesterday morning
13. tomorrow morning
14. this morning
15. later today
16. a couple of hours ago
17. in a couple of hours (from now)
18. this evening

11. A: _____

   B: In Chicago. (Mike will be in Chicago next week.)

12. A: _____

   B: No, _____ (I won't be home early tonight.)

13. A: _____

   B: In a few minutes. (Dr. Smith will be back in a few minutes.)

14. A: _____

   B: Yes, _____ (I'll be ready to leave at 8:15.)

□ **EXERCISE 30. Let's talk: pairwork.**

   Directions: Work with a partner.

   PART I. Imagine you are visiting Paris. Check (✓) the fun things you will do on your trip.

   Paris activities:

   _____ visit the Eiffel Tower

   _____ ride the elevator to the top

   _____ drink coffee in a French café

   _____ buy a painting from a street artist

   _____ ride a boat on the Seine River

   _____ see the Mona Lisa at the Louvre museum

   _____ speak French

   _____ buy some clothes at a French shop

   _____ eat dinner in an expensive French restaurant

   _____ visit Notre Dame cathedral

   _____ take a bus tour of Paris

   _____ buy some French perfume

PART II. Take turns asking and answering questions about your activities.

Example: visit the Eiffel Tower
PARTNER A: Will you visit the Eiffel Tower?
PARTNER B: Yes, I will. OR No, I won't.
PARTNER A: Your turn now.

Partner A	Partner B
1. visit the Eiffel Tower	1. ride the elevator to the top
2. drink coffee in a French café	2. buy a painting from a street artist
3. ride a boat on the Seine River	3. see the Mona Lisa at the Louvre museum
4. speak French	4. buy some clothes at a French shop
5. eat dinner in an expensive French restaurant	5. visit Notre Dame cathedral
6. take a bus tour of Paris	6. buy some French perfume

☐ EXERCISE 31. Listening.

Directions: Read the story. Then listen to the questions and circle the correct answers. NOTE: Jane is a high school student. She is thinking about next year. New Year's is in one week. She wants to change some of her habits. She is going to make some New Year's resolutions.

Jane is a good student. She studies a lot, but she likes to go to parties on weekends. She wants to attend a good university, so next year she will study on weekends too. She has a healthy lifestyle, but sometimes she forgets to exercise. She will exercise four times a week. Now, she only exercises two times a week. She doesn't smoke, but she wants to lose a little weight. She will start a new diet next year. Jane loves her grandmother, but she doesn't see her very much. Jane misses her. Next year, she will visit her once a week. Jane is planning a lot of changes, and she thinks she will be happier.

1. (Yes, she will.)   No, she won't.

2. Yes, she will.   No, she won't.

3. Yes, she will.   No, she won't.

4. Yes, she will.   No, she won't.

5. Yes, she will.   No, she won't.

6. Yes, she will.   No, she won't.

7. Yes, she will.   No, she won't.

8. Yes, she will.   No, she won't.

□ **EXERCISE 32. Listening.**

 Directions: ***Won't*** and ***want*** sound similar. Listen carefully to the sentences and circle the verbs you hear.

1. won't   (want)

2. won't   want

3. won't   want

4. won't   want

5. won't   want

6. won't   want

7. won't   want

8. won't   want

10-8 VERB SUMMARY: PRESENT, PAST, AND FUTURE

	STATEMENT	NEGATIVE	QUESTION
SIMPLE PRESENT	I *eat* lunch every day. He *eats* lunch every day.	I *don't eat* breakfast. She *doesn't eat* breakfast.	*Do* you *eat* breakfast? *Does* she *eat* lunch?
PRESENT PROGRESSIVE	I *am eating* an apple right now. She *is eating* an apple. They *are eating* apples.	I'*m not eating* a pear. She *isn't eating* a pear. They *aren't eating* pears.	*Am* I *eating* a banana? *Is* he *eating* a banana? *Are* they *eating* bananas?
SIMPLE PAST	He *ate* lunch yesterday.	He *didn't eat* breakfast.	*Did* you *eat* breakfast?
BE GOING TO	I *am going to eat* lunch at noon. She *is going to eat* lunch at noon. They *are going to eat* lunch at noon.	I'*m not going to eat* breakfast tomorrow. She *isn't going to eat* breakfast tomorrow. They *aren't going to eat* breakfast tomorrow.	*Am* I *going to see* you tomorrow? *Is* she *going to eat* lunch tomorrow? *Are* they *going to eat* lunch tomorrow?
WILL	He *will eat* lunch tomorrow.	He *won't eat* breakfast tomorrow.	*Will* he *eat* lunch tomorrow?

Directions: Complete the sentences with the verbs in parentheses.

1. Right now, Anita *(sit)* _____*is sitting*_____ at her desk.

2. She *(do, not)* _____ homework. She *(write)*

   _____ an e-mail to her parents.

3. She *(write)* _____ an e-mail to

   her parents every week.

4. She *(write, not)* _____

   an e-mail every day.

5. Her parents *(expect, not)* _____

   _____ to get an e-mail every day.

6. Last night Anita *(write)* _____ an e-mail to her brother. Then

   she *(start)* _____ to write an e-mail to her sister.

7. While Anita was writing an e-mail to her sister last night, her phone *(ring)*

   _____. It *(be)* _____ her sister!

8. Anita *(finish, not)* _____ the e-mail to her sister last night.

   After she *(talk)* _____ to her sister, she *(go)*

   _____ to bed.

9. Tomorrow she *(write)* _____ an e-mail to her cousin in

   Brazil.

10. Anita *(write, not)* _____ an e-mail to her parents

    tomorrow.

11. *(you, write)* _____ an e-mail to someone every day?

12. *(you, write)* _____ an e-mail to someone yesterday?

13. *(you, write)* _____ an e-mail to someone tomorrow?

Directions: Listen to the sentences. Write the verbs you hear.

1. Bill _____ meat, eggs, or fish.

2. He _____ a vegetarian. He _____ meat from animals. He _____ it as a child either.

3. His wife Beth _____ meat, but she _____ a vegetarian.

4. She _____ the taste of meat.

5. They _____ a new restaurant tomorrow.

6. John _____ probably _____ a dish with lots of vegetables.

7. Beth _____ vegetables for a main dish. She _____ probably _____ for some type of fish.

8. _____ themselves?

9. _____ back to this restaurant?

10-9 VERB SUMMARY: FORMS OF *BE*

	STATEMENT	NEGATIVE	QUESTION
SIMPLE PRESENT	I *am* from Korea. He *is* from Egypt. They *are* from Venezuela.	I *am not* from Jordan. She *isn't* from China. They *aren't* from Italy.	*Am* I in the right room? *Is* she from Greece? *Are* they from Kenya?
SIMPLE PAST	Ann *was* late yesterday. They *were* late yesterday.	She *wasn't* on time. They *weren't* on time.	*Was* she in class? *Were* they in class?
BE GOING TO	I *am going to be* late. She *is going to be* late. They *are going to be* late.	I'*m not going to be* on time. She *isn't going to be* on time. They *aren't going to be* on time.	*Am* I *going to be* late? *Is* she *going to be* late? *Are* they *going to be* late tomorrow?
WILL	He *will* be at home tomorrow.	He *won't* be at home tomorrow.	*Will* he be at home tomorrow?

☐ **EXERCISE 35.** Sentence practice: review of *be.*

Directions: Complete the sentences with the verbs in parentheses.

1. I *(be)* _____ in class right now. I *(be, not)* _____ here
   yesterday. I *(be)* _____ absent yesterday. *(you, be)* _____
   in class yesterday? *(Carmen, be)* _____ here yesterday?

2. Carmen and I *(be)* _____ absent from class yesterday. We *(be, not)*
   _____ here.

3. My friends *(be)* _____ at Fatima's apartment tomorrow evening. I
   (be) _____ there too. *(you, be)* _____ there?
   (Yuko, be) _____ there?

4. A whale *(be, not)* _____ a fish. It *(be)* _____ a mammal.
   Dolphins *(be, not)* _____ fish either.
   They *(be)* _____ mammals.

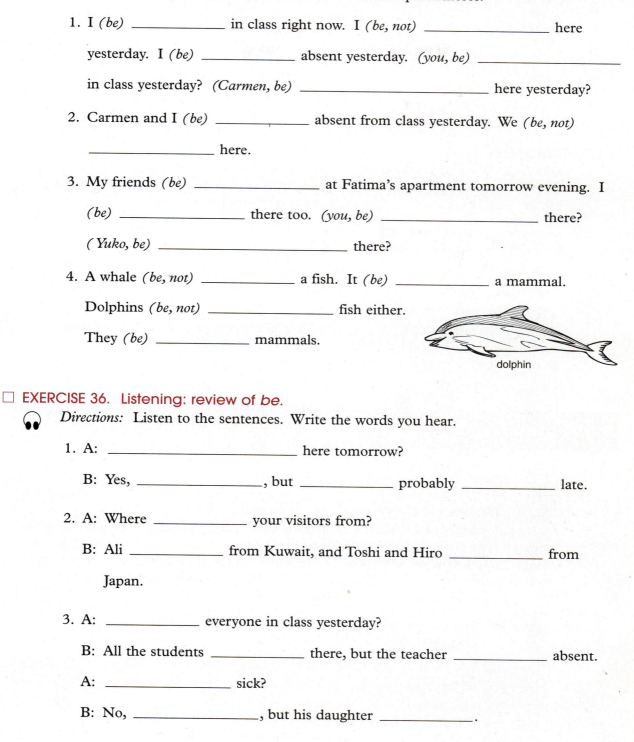
dolphin

☐ **EXERCISE 36.** Listening: review of *be.*

Directions: Listen to the sentences. Write the words you hear.

1. A: _____ here tomorrow?

   B: Yes, _____, but _____ probably _____ late.

2. A: Where _____ your visitors from?

   B: Ali _____ from Kuwait, and Toshi and Hiro _____ from
   Japan.

3. A: _____ everyone in class yesterday?

   B: All the students _____ there, but the teacher _____ absent.

   A: _____ sick?

   B: No, _____, but his daughter _____.

4. A: Let's hurry! _____ really late.

   B: _____ late. I think your watch

   _____ fast.

   A: My watch _____ fast. Maybe your watch _____ slow!

   B: Let's not argue. _____ there any sooner if we argue.

☐ EXERCISE 37. Review.

Directions: Pretend you are going to start a self-improvement plan for this coming year. What are some things you are going to do/will do to improve yourself and your life this year? Make a list, then share some of your ideas with the class.

Example: I will stop smoking.
I am going to get more exercise.
Etc.

☐ EXERCISE 38. Review: small groups.

Directions: Work in small groups. What is going to happen in the lives of your classmates in the next 50 years? Make predictions about your classmates' futures. Share some of your predictions with the class.

Example:
SPEAKER A: Heidi is going to become a famous research scientist.
SPEAKER B: Ali will have a happy marriage and lots of children.
SPEAKER C: Carlos will live in a quiet place and write poetry.
Etc.

☐ EXERCISE 39. Review: small groups.

Directions: In the mail is a letter from your bank. In the envelope is a gift of a lot of money. (As a class, decide on the amount of money in the gift.) You can keep the money if you follow the directions in the letter. There are six different versions of the letter. Choose one (or more) of the letters and describe what you are going to do. Then break into small groups and share your answers.

LETTER #1: You have to spend the money on a wonderful vacation. What are you going to do?

LETTER #2: You have to spend the money to help other people. What are you going to do?

LETTER #3: You have to spend the money to improve your school or place of work. What are you going to do?

LETTER #4: You have to spend the money on your family. What are you going to do?

LETTER #5: You have to spend the money to make the world a better place. What are you going to do?

LETTER #6: You have to spend the money to improve your country. What are you going to do?

☐ EXERCISE 40. Review: Chapters 8 → 10.
Directions: Correct the errors.

1. Is Ivan will go to work tomorrow?

2. When you will call me?

3. Will Tom to meet us for dinner tomorrow?

4. We went to a movie yesterday night.

5. Did you found your keys?

6. What time you are going to come tomorrow?

7. My sister is going to meet me at the airport. My brother won't to be there.

8. Mr. Wong will sells his business and retires next year.

9. Do you will be in Venezuela next year?

10. I'm going to return home in a couple of month.

11. I saw Jim three day ago.

12. A thief stoled my bicycle.

☐ EXERCISE 41. Review: verb forms.
Directions: Complete the sentences with the verbs in parentheses. Give short answers to questions where necessary.

1. A: *(you, have)* _____Do you have_____ a bicycle?

   B: Yes, I _____do_____. I *(ride)* _____ride_____ it to work every day.

2. A: *(you, walk)* _____ to work yesterday?

   B: No, I _____. I *(ride)* _____ my bicycle.

3. A: Where *(you, study, usually)* _____?

   B: In my room.

   A: *(you, go)* _____ to the library to study sometimes?

   B: No. I *(like, not)* _____ to study at the library.

4. A: *(you, be)* _____ in class tomorrow?

   B: Yes, I _____. But I *(be, not)* _____ in class the day

   after tomorrow.

5. A: *(whales, breathe)* _____ air?

   B: Yes, they _____.

   A: *(a whale, have)* _____ lungs?

   B: Yes, it _____.

   A: *(a whale, be)* _____ a fish?

   B: No, it _____. It *(be)* _____ a mammal.

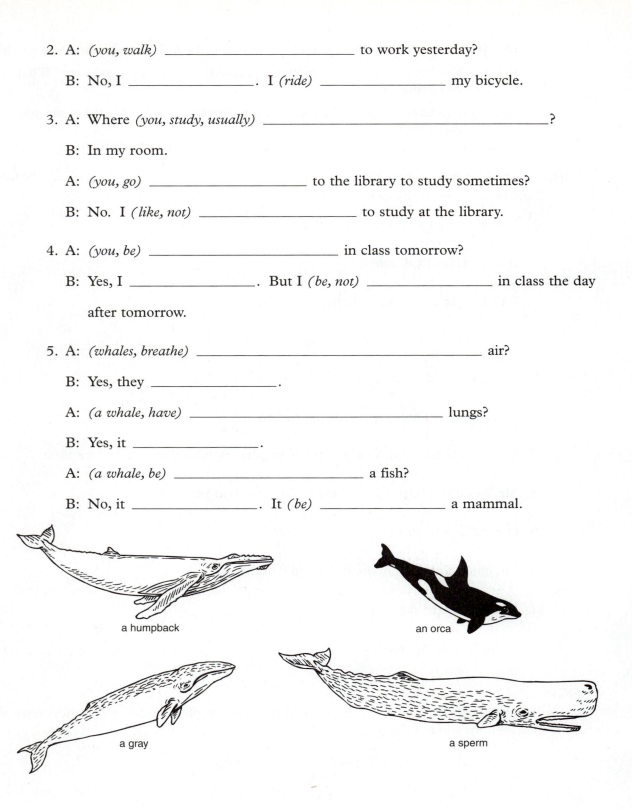

a humpback

an orca

a gray

a sperm

6. A: *(Yuko, call)* _____ you last night?

B: Yes, she _____. We *(talk)* _____ for a few

minutes.

A: *(she, tell)* _____ you about her brother, Tom?

B: No, she _____. She *(say, not)* _____ anything

about him. Why?

A: Tom *(be)* _____ in an accident.

B: That's too bad. What happened?

A: A dog *(run)* _____ in front of his bicycle. He *(want, not)*

_____ to hit the dog. When he *(try)* _____ to

avoid the dog, his bike *(run)* _____ into the path of a truck. The

truck hit Tom. It was an unfortunate accident.

B: *(he, be)* _____ in the hospital now?

A: No, he _____. He *(be)* _____ at home.

Directions: Work in groups of three. The name of the man in the pictures is Alex. What is he doing? Why? Make up probable reasons. Each student in your group will give a different description of Alex's activities. Follow the directions below. Later, share your group's ideas about Alex's activities with the rest of the class.

SPEAKER A: Assume each picture shows things that Alex is doing right now and/or does every day. Use the pictures to describe some of Alex's activities. Use present tenses.

SPEAKER B: Assume the pictures show things that Alex is going to do tomorrow. Describe these activities.

SPEAKER C: Assume the pictures show things that Alex did yesterday. Describe these activities.

CHAPTER 11
Expressing Future Time, Part 2

11-1 MAY/MIGHT vs. WILL

(a) It **may rain** tomorrow. (b) Anita **may be** at home *now*.	**May** + verb (simple form) expresses a possibility in the future, as in (a), or a present possibility, as in (b).
(c) It **might rain** tomorrow. (d) Anita **might be** at home *now*.	**Might** has the same meaning as **may**. (a) and (c) have the same meaning.
(e) Tom **will be** at the meeting tomorrow. (f) Ms. Lee **may/might be** at the meeting tomorrow.	In (e): The speaker uses **will** because he feels sure about Tom's presence at the meeting tomorrow. In (f): The speaker uses **may/might** to say, "I don't know if Ms. Lee will be at the meeting, but it is possible."
(g) Ms. Lee **may/might not be** at the meeting tomorrow.	Negative form: **may/might** + **not** NOTE: (f) and (g) have essentially the same meaning: Ms. Lee may or may not be at the meeting.
INCORRECT: *Ms. Lee may will be at the meeting tomorrow.* *INCORRECT:* *Ms. Lee might will be at the meeting tomorrow.*	**May** and **might** are not used with **will**.

☐ **EXERCISE 1. Sentence practice.**

Directions: Complete the sentences. Use **will** or **won't** if you're sure. Use **may/might** if you're not sure.

1. I _____ be in class next Monday.

→ *I **will be** in class next Monday.* = You're sure.

→ *I **will not (won't) be** in class next Monday.* = You're sure.

→ *I **may/might be** in class next Monday.* OR

→ *I **may/might not be** in class next Monday.* = It's possible, but you're not sure.

2. I _____ eat breakfast tomorrow morning.

3. I _____ be in class tomorrow.

4. I _____ get an e-mail from a friend of mine tomorrow.

5. I _____ watch TV for a little while after dinner tonight.

6. We _____ have a grammar test in class tomorrow.

7. I _____ eat dinner at a restaurant tonight.

8. It _____ be cloudy tomorrow.

9. The sun _____ rise tomorrow morning.

10. I _____ choose a career in music after I finish school.

11. The population of the earth _____ continue to grow.

12. Cities _____ become more and more crowded.

13. Some people think we _____ communicate with beings

from outer space soon.

□ EXERCISE 2. Let's write and talk.
Directions: Write two paragraphs. Use the given words. Use your own paper.
Paragraph 1: Write about your activities *yesterday.*
Paragraph 2: Write about your activities *tomorrow.*
Then show your paragraphs to a partner. Your partner will share some of your activities with the class.

PARAGRAPH 1.

I got up at _____ yesterday morning. After that, _____. Around _____
o'clock, _____. Later _____. At _____ o'clock, _____. Then _____.
_____ a little later. Then at _____ o'clock _____.

PARAGRAPH 2.

I'm going to get up at _____ tomorrow morning. Then _____. After that, _____. Around _____ o'clock, _____. Later _____. At _____ o'clock, _____. Next _____. _____ a little later. Then at _____ o'clock, _____.

☐ **EXERCISE 3. Let's talk: pairwork.**

Directions: Work with a partner. Take turns completing the sentences about yourself and other people in the list.

yourself ("I")	a friend
your partner ("you")	the leader of your country
a classmate	a world leader
your teacher	a movie star
a member of your family	a famous athlete

Partner A	Partner B
1. In five years, _____ will _____.	1. _____ might not _____ tomorrow.
2. Next year, _____ may not _____.	2. Next year, _____ won't _____.
3. _____ might _____ tomorrow.	3. In 20 years, _____ may _____.
4. _____ might or might not _____ next week.	4. Next week, _____ may or may not _____.
5. _____ won't _____ in 2020.	5. _____ will _____ in a few years.

11-2 *MAYBE* (ONE WORD) vs. *MAY BE* (TWO WORDS)

(a) "Will Abdullah be in class tomorrow?" "I don't know. *Maybe. Maybe Abdullah will be* in class tomorrow, and *maybe he won't.*"	The adverb *maybe* (one word) means "possibly."
(b) | *Maybe* | | Abdullah | | will be | here. adverb subject verb	*Maybe* comes in front of a subject and verb.
(c) | Abdullah | | *may be* | here tomorrow. subject verb	*May be* (two words) is used as the verb of a sentence.

☐ EXERCISE 4.   Sentence practice.

Directions: Find the sentences where **maybe** is used as an adverb and where **may** is used as part of the verb.

1. Maybe it will rain tomorrow. → **Maybe** = *an adverb*

2. It may rain tomorrow. → **may rain** = *a verb;* **may** *is part of the verb*

3. We may go to the art museum tomorrow.

4. Maybe Ann would like to go to the museum with us.

5. She may like to go to art museums.

6. It's cold and cloudy today. It may be cold and cloudy tomorrow. Maybe the weather will be warm and sunny this weekend.

☐ EXERCISE 5.   Sentence practice.

Directions: Complete the sentences with **maybe** or **may be**.

1. A: I _____*may be*_____ a little late tonight.

   B: That's okay. I won't worry about you.

2. A: Will you be here by seven o'clock?

   B: It's hard to say. _____*Maybe*_____ I'll be a little late.

3. A: It _____ cold tomorrow.

   B: That's okay. Let's go to the beach anyway.

4. A: Will the plane be on time?

   B: I think so, but it _____ a few minutes late.

5. A: Do you want to go to the park tomorrow?

   B: Sure. That sounds like fun.

   A: Let's talk to Carlos too. _____ he would like to go with us.

6. A: Where's Mr. Chu?

   B: Look in Room 506 down the hall. I think he _____ there.

   A: No, he's not there. I just looked in Room 506.

   B: _____ he's in Room 508.

□ EXERCISE 6. Listening.

Directions: Listen to the sentences. Circle the use of *may* that you hear.

Examples: _____ I'll see you tomorrow.   (Maybe) May + verb

I _____ you later today.   maybe (may + verb)

1. *maybe*	*may* + verb		5. *Maybe*	*May* + verb
2. *maybe*	*may* + verb		6. *Maybe*	*May* + verb
3. *maybe*	*may* + verb		7. *maybe*	*may* + verb
4. *maybe*	*may* + verb		8. *Maybe*	*May* + verb

□ EXERCISE 7. Sentence practice.

Directions: Rewrite the sentences. Use the words in parentheses.

1. Maybe I will study.

    a. *(might)* _____ I might study. _____

    b. *(may)* _____ I may study. _____

2. The teacher might give a test.

    a. *(maybe)* _____

    b. *(may)* _____

3. Maybe Janet will be home early.

    a *(may)* _____

    b. *(might)* _____

4. She might be late.

    a. *(may)* _____

    b. *(maybe)* _____

5. It may rain tomorrow.

    a. *(maybe)* _____

    b. *(might)* _____

□ **EXERCISE 8. Sentence practice.**

Directions: Answer the questions. Use **maybe** or **may/might**.

1. A: Is David going to come to the party?

   B: I don't know. _____*Maybe*_____ .

2. A: What are you going to do tomorrow?

   B: I don't know. I _____*may/might*_____ go swimming.

3. A: What are you going to do tomorrow?

   B: I don't have any plans. _____ I'll go swimming.

4. A: Where is Robert?

   B: I don't know. He _____ be at his office.

5. A: Where is Robert?

   B: I don't know. _____ he's at his office.

6. A: Are Kate and Steve going to get married?

   B: _____ . Who knows?

7. A: Are you going to move to Portland or to Seattle?

   B: I don't know. I _____ move to San Francisco.

8. A: Where are you planning to go on your vacation?

   B: _____ we'll go to Mexico. We haven't decided yet.

   We _____ go to Florida.

9. A: I'd like to have a pet.
   B: Oh? What kind of pet would you like to get?

   A: Oh, I don't know. I haven't decided yet. _____ I'll get a

   canary. Or _____ I'll get a snake. I'm not sure. I

   _____ get a frog. Or I _____ get a turtle.
   B: What's wrong with a cat or dog?

□ **EXERCISE 9. Let's talk.**

Directions: Work in groups or as a class. The group leader or your teacher will ask you questions. Answer them by using *I don't know* + *maybe* or *may/might*. If you work in groups, choose a new leader where indicated.

Example:
TEACHER/LEADER: What are you going to do tonight?
STUDENT: I don't know. Maybe I'll watch TV. / I may watch TV. / I might watch TV.

1. What are you going to do tonight?
2. What are you going to do tomorrow?
3. What are you going to do after class today?
4. What are you going to do this weekend?
5. What are you going to do this evening?

Choose a new leader.

6. Who is going to go shopping tomorrow? What are you going to buy?
7. Who is going to go out to eat tonight? Where are you going to go?
8. Who is going to get married? When?
9. Who is going to watch TV tonight? What are you going to watch?

Choose a new leader.

10. Who is absent today? Where is he/she?
11. Is it going to rain tomorrow? What is the weather going to be like tomorrow?
12. Who is planning to go on a vacation? Where are you going to go?
13. Who wants to have a pet? What kind of pet are you going to get?

□ **EXERCISE 10. Let's talk: pairwork.**

Directions: Work with a partner. Use the phrases below to tell your partner about your activities tomorrow. Use *will/won't, going to/not going to, maybe, may,* and *might*.

Example: go to a movie \ go shopping
PARTNER A: I'm not going to go to a movie tomorrow. I might go shopping.
PARTNER B: I might go to a movie. Maybe I'll go shopping.

1. wake up early \ sleep in
2. eat a big breakfast \ eat a small breakfast
3. stay home \ go to school
4. get some exercise in the afternoon \ take a nap in the afternoon
5. do my homework in the evening \ watch TV in the evening
6. eat ice cream \ eat vegetables

7. cook dinner \ eat out

8. clean my house (apartment, bedroom, car, kitchen) \ read a book

9. shop on the Internet \ shop at a store

10. visit a friend \ visit a chat room on the Internet

☐ EXERCISE 11. Listening.

Directions: Listen to each sentence. Circle the letter of the sentence that has the same meaning as the sentence you hear.

1. (a.) Maybe I will be absent.

  b. I'm going to be absent.

2. a. Our plans will change.

  b. Our plans might change.

3. a. It is going to rain.

  b. Maybe it will rain.

4. a. We may finish this grammar book soon.

  b. We will finish this grammar book soon.

5. a. Maybe John will get good news tomorrow.

  b. John is going to get good news tomorrow.

6. a. The class may start on time.

  b. The class is going to start on time.

☐ EXERCISE 12. Let's talk: class activity.

Directions: Your teacher will ask you questions. Use the given information to make guesses. Include **may/might** and **maybe** in some of your guesses. Close your book for this activity.

Example:

TEACHER: (. . .) is absent today. Why? Do you have any possible explanations?
STUDENT A: He/She **may be** sick.
STUDENT B: He/She **might be** out of town today.
STUDENT C: **Maybe** he/she is late today and will come soon.

1. What is (. . .) going to do after class today?

2. (. . .) said, "I have very exciting plans for this weekend." What is he/she going to do this weekend?

3. (. . .) has an airplane ticket in his pocket. I saw it. Do you know where he/she is going to go?

4. (. . .) said, "I don't like it here in this city." Why doesn't (. . .) like it here? Do you have any idea?

5. (. . .) doesn't like it here. What is he/she going to do?

6. (. . .) has something very special in his/her pocket, but he/she won't show anyone what it is. What do you suppose is in his/her pocket?

7. Can you think of some good things that may happen to you this year?

8. What are some good things that might happen to (. . .) this year or next year?

9. Can you think of some bad things that might happen in the world this year or next?

10. What are some good things that may happen in the world this year?

11. What new inventions do you think we may have in the future to make our lives easier?

☐ EXERCISE 13. Let's talk: pairwork.

Directions: Work with a partner. Check the boxes that describe your activities tomorrow. Show your answers to your partner. She/He will make sentences about you and share some of them with the class.

Example: You may/might get up at 7:00. OR Maybe you'll get up at 7:00. You'll come to class. OR You're going to come to class. You won't sing in the shower. OR You're not going to sing in the shower.

Activity	Yes	No	Maybe
1. eat lunch			
2. go shopping			
3. send some e-mails			
4. watch TV			
5. talk on the phone			
6. play soccer			
7. read an English language newspaper			
8. look up information on the Internet			
9. have dinner with friends			
10. listen to the radio			

11-3 FUTURE TIME CLAUSES WITH *BEFORE, AFTER,* AND *WHEN*

(a) *Before Ann **goes** to work tomorrow,* she will eat breakfast. INCORRECT: *Before Ann will go to work tomorrow, she will eat breakfast.* INCORRECT: *Before Ann is going to go to work tomorrow, she will eat breakfast.*	In (a): *Before Ann goes to work tomorrow* is a future time clause.* A future time clause uses the SIMPLE PRESENT TENSE, not *will* or *be going to.*
(b) I'm going to finish my homework *after I **eat** dinner tonight.* (c) *When I **go** to New York next week,* I'm going to stay at the Hilton Hotel.	In (b): *after I eat dinner tonight* = a future time clause. In (c): *When I go to New York next week* = a future time clause. Notice: A comma follows an adverb clause when it comes at the beginning of a sentence.

*See Chart 9-7, p. 273, for more information about time clauses.

□ EXERCISE 14. Sentence practice.
   Directions: <u>Underline</u> the time clauses.

   1. <u>When we go to the park tomorrow</u>, we're going to go to the zoo.

   2. After I get home tonight, I'm going to make an overseas call to my parents.

   3. Mr. Kim will finish his report before he leaves the office today.

   4. I'll get some fresh fruit when I go to the grocery store tomorrow.

   5. Before I go to bed tonight, I'm going to write a letter to my brother.

   6. I'm going to look for a job at a computer company after I graduate next year.

□ EXERCISE 15. Sentence practice.
   Directions: Complete the sentences with the words in parentheses.

   1. Before I (go) _____*go*_____ to bed tonight, I (watch) _____*am going to*_____

      _____*watch/will watch*_____ my favorite show on TV.

   2. I (buy) _____ a new coat when I (go) _____

      shopping tomorrow.

   3. After I (finish) _____ my homework this evening, I (take)

      _____ a walk.

4. When I *(see)* _____ Eduardo tomorrow, I *(ask)*

_____ him to join us for dinner this weekend.

5. When I *(go)* _____ to Australia next month, I *(meet)*

_____ my Aunt Emily for the first time.

6. Mrs. Polanski *(change)* _____ her clothes before she *(work)*

_____ in her garden this afternoon.

☐ **EXERCISE 16. Let's talk: class activity.**

Directions: Your teacher will ask you questions. Give complete answers using time clauses. Close your book for this activity.

Example: Who's going to go shopping later today? What are you going to do after you go shopping?

TEACHER: Who's going to go shopping later today?
SPEAKER A: *(raises his/her hand)*
TEACHER: What are you going to do after you go shopping?
SPEAKER A: After I go shopping, I'm going to go home. OR I'm going to go home after I go shopping.
TEACHER: *(to Speaker B)* What is *(Speaker A)* going to do after he/she goes shopping?
SPEAKER B: After *(Speaker A)* goes shopping, he/she is going to go home. OR *(Speaker A)* is going to go home after he/she goes shopping.

1. Who's going to study tonight? What are you going to do after you study tonight?
2. Who else is going to study tonight? What are you going to do before you study tonight?
3. Who's going to watch TV tonight? What are you going to do before you watch TV?
4. Who's going to watch TV tonight? What are you going to do after you watch TV?
5. Who's going to go shopping tomorrow? What are you going to buy when you go shopping tomorrow?

6. (. . .), what are you going to do tonight? What are you going to do before you . . . ? What are you going to do after you . . . tonight?

7. (. . .), what are you going to do tomorrow? What are you going to do before you . . . tomorrow? What are you going to do after you . . . tomorrow?

8. Who's going out of town soon? Where are you going? What are you going to do when you go to *(name of place)*?

9. Who's going to eat dinner tonight? What are you going to do before you eat dinner? What are you going to do after you eat dinner? What are you going to have when you eat dinner?

10. (. . .), what time are you going to get home today? What are you going to do before you get home? What are you going to do when you get home? What are you going to do after you get home?

11-4 CLAUSES WITH *IF*

(a)	<u>**If it rains tomorrow,**</u> <u>we will stay home.</u> *if*-clause main clause	An *if*-clause begins with *if* and has a subject and a verb. An *if*-clause can come before or after a main clause. Notice: A comma follows an *if*-clause when it comes at the beginning of a sentence.
(b)	<u>We will stay home</u> <u>**if it rains tomorrow.**</u> main clause *if*-clause	
(c)	**If it rains** tomorrow, we won't go on a picnic.	The SIMPLE PRESENT (not *will* or *be going to*) is used in an *if*-clause to express future time.
(d)	I'm going to buy a new car next year **if I have** enough money. **If I don't have** enough money next year for a new car, I'm going to buy a used car.	

☐ EXERCISE 17. Sentence practice.

Directions: Complete the sentences with the words in parentheses.

1. If Ali *(be)* _____*is*_____ in class tomorrow, I *(ask)* _____*am going to/will ask*_____

   him to join us for coffee after class.

2. If the weather *(be)* _____ nice tomorrow, I *(go)* _____

   _____ to Central Park with my friends.

3. I *(stay, not)* _____ home tomorrow if the weather *(be)* _____

   _____ nice.

4. If I *(feel, not)* _____ well tomorrow, I *(go, not)* _____

   _____ to work.

5. Masako *(stay)* _____ in bed tomorrow if she

   (feel, not) _____ well.

6. I *(stay)* _____ with my aunt and uncle if I *(go)* _____

   to Miami next week.

7. If my friends *(be)* _____ busy tomorrow, I *(go)* _____

   to a movie by myself.

8. If we *(continue)* _____ to pollute the land and oceans with

   poisons and waste, future generations *(suffer)* _____ .

□ **EXERCISE 18. Let's talk: pairwork.**

    Directions: Work with a partner. Ask and answer questions.
    Partner A: Ask a question that begins with ***What are you going to do . . . ?*** Your
                  book is open.
    Partner B: Answer the question. Include the *if*-clause in your answer. Your book is
                  closed.

    Example: . . . if the weather is nice tomorrow?
    PARTNER A *(book open):* What are you going to do if the weather is nice tomorrow?
    PARTNER B *(book closed):* If the weather is nice tomorrow, I'm going to sit outside in
                         the sun. OR I'm going to sit outside in the sun if the
                         weather is nice tomorrow.

1. . . . if the weather is cold tomorrow?
2. . . . if the weather is hot tomorrow?
3. . . . if you don't understand a question that I ask you?
4. . . . if class is canceled tomorrow?
5. . . . if you don't feel well tomorrow?
6. . . . if you go to *(name of a place in this city)* tomorrow?

Switch roles.

Partner A: Close your book.

Partner B: Open your book. Your turn now.

7. . . . if it rains tonight?

8. . . . if you're hungry after class today?

9. . . . if you go to *(name of a place in this city)* tomorrow?

10. . . . if you don't study tonight?

11. . . . if you lose your grammar book?

12. . . . if someone steals your *(name of a thing: bicycle, wallet, etc.)?*

☐ EXERCISE 19. Listening.

Directions: Listen to the questions. Write your answers in complete sentences.

1. _____ .

2. _____ .

3. _____ .

4. _____ .

☐ EXERCISE 20. Let's talk: pairwork.

Directions: Work with a partner.

Step 1: Write your activities for next week in the blank datebook on the next page. If you don't have many planned activities, make up some interesting ones. Then, give your datebook to your partner.

Step 2: In writing, describe your partner's activities next week. Try to include some time clauses beginning with **when**, **after**, and **before**. Ask your partner questions about the activities on his/her datebook to get more information.

Example:

STEP 1: (Ali)

Sunday	
7:00	Tennis with Talal
9:00	breakfast
1:00	lunch with Ivan
2:00	soccer game
6:00	study

STEP 2: One partner interviews the other (Ali) about his calendar and then writes:

On Sunday, Ali is going to play tennis with Talal early in the morning. They're going to play on the tennis courts here at school. After they play tennis, they're going to have breakfast.

In the afternoon, Ali is going to meet Ivan for lunch at Cozy's Café. They're going to have a sandwich before they go to the soccer game at Memorial Stadium.

When Ali gets home in the evening, he will study before he watches TV and goes to bed.

PARTNER A'S DATEBOOK: Fill in the calendar with your activities for next week.

Sunday	Monday	Tuesday	Wednesday	Thursday	Friday	Saturday

11-5 EXPRESSING HABITUAL PRESENT WITH TIME CLAUSES AND *IF*-CLAUSES

(a) FUTURE	After Ann *gets* to work today, she *is going to have/will have* a cup of coffee.	(a) expresses a specific activity in the future. The SIMPLE PRESENT is used in the time clause. *Be going to* or *will* is used in the main clause.
(b) HABITUAL PRESENT	After Ann *gets* to work (every day), she always *has* a cup of coffee.	(b) expresses habitual activities, so the SIMPLE PRESENT is used in both the time clause and the main clause.
(c) FUTURE	If it *rains* tomorrow, I *am going to/will* wear my raincoat to school.	(c) expresses a specific activity in the future. The SIMPLE PRESENT is used in the *if*-clause. *Be going to* or *will* is used in the main clause.
(d) HABITUAL PRESENT	If it *rains*, I *wear* my raincoat.	(d) expresses habitual activities, so the SIMPLE PRESENT is used in both the *if*-clause and the main clause.

☐ EXERCISE 21. Sentence practice.

Directions: Complete the sentences with the words in parentheses.

1. When I *(go)* _____ to Miami, I *(stay, usually)* _____

   _____ with my aunt and uncle.

2. When I *(go)* _____ to Miami next week, I *(stay)* _____

   _____ with my aunt and uncle.

3. Before I *(go)* _____ to class today, I *(have)* _____

   a cup of tea.

4. Before I *(go)* _____ to class, I *(have, usually)* _____

   _____ a cup of tea.

5. I'm often tired in the evening after a long day at work. If I *(be)* _____

   tired in the evening, I *(stay, usually)* _____ home and

   (go) _____ to bed early.

6. If I *(be)* _____ tired this evening, I *(stay)* _____

   home and *(go)* _____ to bed early.

7. After I *(get)* _____ home in the evening, I *(sit, usually)* _____

   _____ in my favorite chair and *(read)* _____ the

   newspaper.

8. After I *(get)* _____ home tonight, I *(sit)* _____ in

   my favorite chair and *(read)* _____ the newspaper.

9. People *(yawn, often)* _____ and *(stretch)* _____

   when they *(wake)* _____ up.

10. Before the teacher *(walk)* _____ into the room every day, there *(be)*

    _____ a lot of noise in the classroom.

11. When I (go) _____ to Taiwan next month, I (stay) _____

_____ with my friend Mr. Chu. After I (leave) _____

Taiwan, I (go) _____ to Hong Kong.

12. Ms. Wah (go) _____ to Hong Kong often. When she (be) _____

there, she (like) _____ to take the ferry across the bay, but she (take)

_____ the subway under the bay if she (be) _____ in a hurry.

☐ EXERCISE 22. Let's talk: class activity.

Directions: Your teacher will ask you questions. Answer them in complete sentences. Close your book for this activity.

Example:
TEACHER: What do you do when you get up in the morning?
SPEAKER A: When I get up in the morning, I eat breakfast.
SPEAKER B: I listen to music when I get up in the morning.

1. What do you do when you get up in the morning?
2. What are you going to do when you get up tomorrow morning?
3. What do you usually do before you eat breakfast?
4. What are you going to do after class today?
5. What are you going to do when you get home?
6. What do you usually do after you get home?
7. What do you like to do if the weather is nice?
8. What are you going to do if the weather is nice tomorrow?

☐ EXERCISE 23. Sentence practice.

Directions: Complete the sentences with your own words.

1. Before I go to bed tonight, _____.

2. Before I go to bed, I usually _____.

3. I'm going to _____ tomorrow after I _____.

4. When I go to _____, I'm going to _____.

5. When I go to _____, I always _____.

6. If the weather _____ tomorrow, I _____.

7. I will visit _____ when I _____.

8. I'll _____ if I _____ .

9. If the weather _____ tomorrow, _____ you

    going to _____ ?

10. Are you going to _____ before you _____ ?

11. Do you _____ before you _____ ?

12. After I _____ tonight, I _____ .

□ EXERCISE 24. Listening.

Directions: Listen to each sentence and circle the correct completion.

1. (I watch TV.)   I'm going to watch TV.

2. I get a good night's sleep.   I'll get a good night's sleep.

3. I do my homework.   I'll do my homework.

4. I go shopping.   I'll go shopping.

5. I exercise.   I'll exercise.

6. I call my parents.   I'll call my parents.

7. I'm happy.   I'll be happy.

8. I know a lot of grammar.   I'll know a lot of grammar.

11-6 USING *WHAT* + A FORM OF *DO*

		In (a) and (b), ***What*** + *a form of **do*** is used to ask about activities.
PRESENT (a) *What **do** you **do** every day?* (b) *What **are** you **doing** right now?* (c) *What **do** you **do**?*	→ *I work every day.* → *I'm studying English.* → *I'm a teacher.*	
PAST (d) *What **did** you **do** yesterday?*	→ *I went to school yesterday.*	In (c): *What do you do?* means *What kind of work do you do?* OR *What is your job?*
FUTURE (e) *What **are** you **going to do** tomorrow?* (f) *What **will** we **do** if it rains tomorrow?*	→ *I'm going to go downtown tomorrow.* → *We'll stay home if it rains tomorrow.*	

□ **EXERCISE 25. Question practice.**

Directions: Complete the sentences with the words in parentheses.

1. A: What *(you, do)* ___do you do___ every Friday?

   B: I *(come)* ___come___ to class.

2. A: What *(you, do)* _____ last Friday?

   B: I *(come)* _____ to class.

3. A: What *(you, do)* _____ next Friday?

   B: I *(come)* _____ to class.

4. A: What *(you, do)* _____ yesterday evening?

   B: I *(watch)* _____ TV.

5. A: What *(you, do)* _____ every evening?

   B: I *(watch)* _____ TV.

6. A: What *(you, do)* _____ tomorrow evening?

   B: I *(watch)* _____ TV.

7. A: What *(you, do)* _____ right now?

   B: I *(do)* _____ a grammar exercise.

8. A: What *(Maria, do)* _____ every morning?

   B: She *(go)* _____ to work.

9. A: What *(the students)* _____ right now?

   B: They *(work)* _____ on this exercise.

10. A: What *(they, do)* _____ in class tomorrow?

    B: They *(take)* _____ a test.

11. A: What *(Boris, do)* _____ last night?

    B: He *(go)* _____ to a movie.

12. A: What *(the teacher, do)* _____ every day at the

    beginning of class?

    B: She *(put)* _____ her books on her desk, *(look)* _____ at the

    class, and *(say)* _____ "Good morning."

□ EXERCISE 26. Let's talk: pairwork.

Directions: Work with a partner. Ask your partner questions. Use **What** + a form of
do with the given time expression.

Example: yesterday
PARTNER A *(book open):*   What did you do yesterday?
PARTNER B *(book closed):* I read a newspaper yesterday.

1. last night   5. yesterday afternoon

2. every day   6. tomorrow morning

3. right now   7. every morning

4. tomorrow

Switch roles.
Partner A: Close your book.
Partner B: Open your book. Your turn to ask questions.

8. right now   12. this afternoon

9. last Saturday   13. tonight

10. next Saturday   14. next week

11. this morning

□ EXERCISE 27. Review: verb forms.

Directions: Complete the sentences with the words in parentheses. Use any
appropriate verb form.

1. A: I *(skip)* _____ class tomorrow.

   B: Why?

   A: Why not?

   B: That's not a very good reason.

2. A: How did you get here?

   B: I *(take)* _____ a plane. I *(fly)* _____ here from Bangkok.

3. A: How do you usually get to class?

   B: I *(walk, usually)* _____, but sometimes I *(take)*

   _____ the bus.

4. A: Where's my book! Someone *(steal)* _____ it!

   B: Take it easy. Your book *(be)* _____ right here.

   A: Oh.

5. A: Where *(you, meet)* _____ your wife?

   B: I *(meet)* _____ her at a party ten years ago.

6. A: What time *(the movie, begin)* _____ last night?

   B: 7:30.

   A: *(you, be)* _____ late?

   B: No. We *(make)* _____ it in time.

7. A: Where's your homework?

   B: I *(lose)* _____ it.

   A: Oh?

   B: I *(forget)* _____ it.

   A: Oh?

   B: I *(give)* _____ it to Roberto to give to you, but he *(lose)*

   _____ it.

   A: Oh?

   B: Someone *(steal)* _____ it.

   A: Oh?

   B: Well, actually I *(have, not)* _____ enough time to finish it

   last night.

   A: I see.

8. A: *(you, stay)* _____

   here during vacation next week?

   B: No. I *(take)* _____ a trip to

   Miami. I *(visit)* _____

   my aunt and uncle.

   A: How long *(you, be)* _____ away?

   B: About five days.

9. A: Why *(you, wear)* _____ a cast on your foot?

   B: I *(break)* _____ my ankle.

   A: How?

   B: I *(step)* _____ in a hole while I was running in the park.

10. A: *(you, see)* _____ Randy yesterday?

    B: No, but I *(speak)* _____ to him on the phone. He *(call)*

    _____ me yesterday evening.

    A: Is he okay?

    B: Yes. He still has a cold, but he's feeling much better.

    A: That's good.

11. A: Is Carol here?

    B: No, she *(be, not)* _____. She *(leave)* _____ a few minutes

    ago.

    A: *(she, be)* _____ back soon?

    B: I think so.

    A: Where *(she, go)* _____?

    B: She *(go)* _____ to the drugstore.

Directions: Complete the conversations with the words you hear.

1. A: _____ that?

   B: What?

   A: The man in the red shirt _____ the man in the blue shirt.

   B: _____ sure?

   A: Yes, _____ the whole thing.

2. A: _____ late for the movie?

   B: No. The movie _____ at 7:30, and _____ to the theater at 7:26.

3. A: _____ that noise?

   B: What noise?

   A: Listen again.

   B: Now _____ it. _____ someone _____?

4. A: _____ to the zoo this afternoon?

   B: _____ to go, but I can't because _____ study.

   A: That's too bad.

   B: _____ to the zoo?

   A: Yes. The weather _____ perfect, and _____

   outside and _____.

□ EXERCISE 29. Review.

Directions: Circle the correct completions.

1. "Are you going to go to the baseball game tomorrow afternoon?"
"I don't know. I _____."
    A. will   B. am going to   C. maybe   (D.) might

2. "Are Jane and Eric going to be at the meeting?"
"No, they're too busy. They _____ be there."
    A. don't   B. won't   C. will   D. may

3. "Are you going to go to the market today?"
   "No. I went there _____ Friday."
      A. yesterday   B. next   C. last   D. ago

4. "When are you going to go to the bank?"
   "I'll go there before I _____ to the post office tomorrow morning."
      A. will go   B. go   C. went   D. am going

5. "Why is the teacher late today?"
   "I don't know. _____ he slept late."
      A. Maybe   B. Did   C. May   D. Was

6. "Do you like to go to New York City?"
   "Yes. When I'm in New York, I always _____ new things to do and places to go."
      A. found   B. find   C. will find   D. finds

7. "Is Ken going to talk to us this afternoon about our plans for tomorrow?"
   "No. He'll _____ us this evening."
      A. calls   B. calling   C. call   D. called

8. "_____ are you going to do after class today?"
   "I'm going to go home."
      A. When   B. Where   C. What   D. What time

9. "Where _____ Ivonne live before she moved into her new apartment?"
   "She lived in a dormitory at the university."
      A. did   B. does   C. is   D. was

10. "What time _____ Olga and Boris going to arrive?"
    "Six."
      A. is   B. do   C. will   D. are

☐ **EXERCISE 30. Chapter review: error analysis.**
   Directions: Correct the errors.

   1. If it will be cold tomorrow morning, my car won't start.

   2. We maybe late for the concert tonight.

   3. What time you are going to come tomorrow?

   4. Fatima will call us tonight when she will arrive home safely.

   5. Emily may will be at the party.

6. When I'll see you tomorrow, I'll return your book to you.

7. I may to don't be in class tomorrow.

8. Ahmed puts his books on his desk when he walked into his apartment.

9. I'll see my parents when I will return home for a visit next July.

10. What do you doing all day at work?

□ EXERCISE 31. Review.

Directions: Complete the sentences. Use the words in parentheses. Use any appropriate verb form.

PART I.

Peter and Rachel are brother and sister. Right now their parents (be) _____
                                                                        1
abroad on a trip, so they (stay) _____ with their grandmother. They
                                          2
(like) _____ to stay with her. She (make, always) _____
            3   4
wonderful food for them. And she (tell) _____ them stories every night before they
                                                 5
(go) _____ to bed.
          6

Before Peter and Rachel (go) _____ to bed last night, they (ask)
                                          7
_____ Grandma to tell them a story. She (agree) _____. The
          8   9
children (put) _____ on their pajamas, (brush) _____ their teeth,
                      10   11
and (sit) _____ with their grandmother in her big chair to listen to a story.
                12

PART II.

GRANDMA: That's good. Sit here beside me and get comfortable.

CHILDREN: What *(you, tell)* _____ us about tonight,

                  13

Grandma?

GRANDMA: Before I *(begin)* _____ the story, I *(give)* _____

                14   15

each of you a kiss on the forehead because I love you very much.

CHILDREN: We *(love)* _____ you too, Grandma.

               16

GRANDMA: Tonight I *(tell)* _____ you a story about Rabbit and

                  17

Eagle. Ready?

CHILDREN: Yes!

GRANDMA: Rabbit had light gray fur and a white tail. He lived with his family in a

hole in a big, grassy field. Rabbit *(be)* _____ afraid of many things, but

                              18

he *(be)* _____ especially afraid of Eagle. Eagle liked to eat rabbits for

        19

dinner. One day while Rabbit was eating grass in the field, he *(see)*

_____ Eagle in the sky above him. Rabbit *(be)* _____ very

    20   21

afraid and *(run)* _____ home to his hole as fast as he could.

                22

    Rabbit *(stay)* _____ in his hole day after day because he *(be)*

                      23

_____ afraid to go outside. He *(get)* _____ very hungry, but

    24   25

still he *(stay)* _____ in his hole. Finally, he *(find)* _____

                26   27

the courage to go outside because he *(need)* _____ *(eat)*

                                    28

_____.

    29

    Carefully and slowly, he *(put)* _____ his little pink nose outside

                                    30

the hole. He *(smell, not)* _____ any dangerous animals.

                                  31

And he *(see, not)* _____ Eagle anywhere, so he *(hop)*

                    32

_____ out and *(find)* _____ some delicious new

    33   34

grass to eat. While he was eating the grass, he *(see)* _____ a shadow on
⎯⎯35

the field and *(look)* _____ up. It was Eagle! Rabbit said, "Please
⎯⎯36

don't eat me, Eagle! Please don't eat me!"

PART III.

GRANDMA: On this sunny afternoon, Eagle was on her way home to her nest when she

(hear) _____ a faint sound below her. "What is that sound?" Eagle said
⎯⎯37

to herself. She looked around, but she *(see, not)* _____
⎯⎯38

anything. She *(decide)* _____ to ignore the sound and go home. She
⎯⎯39

was tired and *(want)* _____ *(rest)* _____ in her nest.
⎯⎯40   ⎯⎯41

Then below her, Rabbit *(say)* _____ again in a very loud voice,
⎯⎯42

"Please don't eat me, Eagle! Please don't eat me!"

This time Eagle *(hear)* _____ Rabbit clearly. Eagle *(spot)*
⎯⎯43

_____ Rabbit in the field, *(fly)* _____ down, and *(pick)*
⎯⎯44   ⎯⎯45

_____ Rabbit up in her talons.
⎯⎯46

"Thank you, Rabbit," said Eagle. "I was hungry and *(know, not)*

_____ where I could find my dinner. It's a good thing you
   47

called to me." Then Eagle *(eat)* _____ Rabbit for dinner.
                                        48

PART IV.

GRANDMA: There's a lesson to learn from this story, children. If you *(be)* _____
                                                                             49

afraid and expect bad things to happen, bad things will happen. The opposite is

also true. If you *(expect)* _____ good things to happen, good
                                    50

things will happen. *(you, understand)* _____?
                                                        51

Now it's time for bed.

CHILDREN: Please tell us another story!

GRANDMA: Not tonight. I'm tired. After I *(have)* _____ a warm drink, I *(go)*
                                                          52

_____ to bed. All of us need *(get)* _____ a good
        53   54

night's sleep. Tomorrow *(be)* _____ a busy day.
                                        55

CHILDREN: What *(we, do)* _____ tomorrow?
                                        56

GRANDMA: After we *(have)* _____ breakfast, we *(go)* _____
                                57   58

to the zoo at Woodland Park. When we *(be)* _____ at the zoo, we
                                                    59

(see) _____ lots of wonderful animals. Then in the afternoon we
                60

(see) _____ a play at the Children's Theater. But before we *(see)*
                61

_____ the play, we *(have)* _____ a picnic lunch in
        62   63

the park.

CHILDREN: Wow! We *(have)* _____ a wonderful day tomorrow!
                                    64

GRANDMA: Now off to bed! Goodnight, Rachel and Peter. Sleep tight.*

CHILDREN: Goodnight, Grandma. Thank you for the story!

_____

* *Sleep tight* means "Sleep well. Have a good night's sleep."

□ EXERCISE 32. Let's talk: small groups.

Directions: Work in small groups. Choose a leader. Answer your leader's questions. Look at the story in Exercise 31, p. 349, if you need to.

1. What did Rabbit look like?
2. Where did he live?
3. Who was he afraid of?
4. Why did he hide in his hole?
5. Why did he come out of his hole?
6. What did he do when he saw Eagle?
7. Did Eagle see Rabbit before Rabbit spoke in a loud voice?
8. What happened to Rabbit?
9. What's the moral of the story?

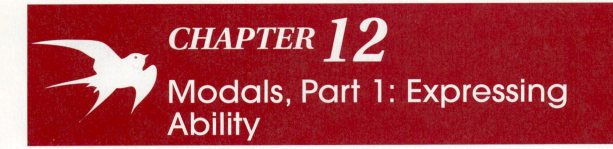

CHAPTER 12
Modals, Part 1: Expressing Ability

☐ **EXERCISE 1. Let's talk: class activity.**

Directions: Answer your teacher's questions. Close your book for this activity.

Example:
TEACHER: Can you sing?
SPEAKER: Yes, I can sing. OR No, I can't sing.

1. Can you speak *(a language)*?
2. Can you play *(a musical instrument)*?
3. Can you lift your desk?
4. Can you touch the ceiling?
5. Can you count to five in *(a language)*?
6. Can you walk to the back of the room with your eyes closed? Who would like to try?

12-1 USING *CAN*	
(a) I have some money. I ***can buy*** a book. (b) We have time and money. We ***can go*** to a movie. (c) Tom is strong. He ***can lift*** the heavy box.	***Can*** expresses *ability* and *possibility*.
(d) CORRECT: Yuko *can **speak*** English.	The simple form of the main verb follows ***can***. In (d): *speak* is the main verb.
(e) *INCORRECT: Yuko can to speak English.*	An infinitive with ***to*** does NOT follow ***can***. In (e): *to speak* is incorrect.
(f) *INCORRECT: Yuko can speaks English.*	A main verb following ***can*** does not have a final ***-s***. In (f): *speaks* is incorrect.

(g) Alice ***can not*** come.
 Alice ***cannot*** come.
 Alice ***can't*** come.
	NEGATIVE
	     can + ***not*** = ***can not*** OR ***cannot***
	 CONTRACTION
	     can + ***not*** = ***can't***

□ **EXERCISE 2. Sentence practice.**

Directions: Make sentences from the given words. Use **can** or **can't**.

Examples: A bird \ sing
→ A bird can sing.

A horse \ sing
→ A horse can't sing.

1. A bird \ fly
2. A cow \ fly
3. A child \ drive a car
4. An adult \ drive a car
5. A newborn baby \ walk
6. A fish \ breathe air
7. A fish \ swim

8. A deaf person \ hear
9. A blind person \ see
10. An elephant \ swim
11. An elephant \ climb trees
12. A cat \ climb trees
13. A boat \ float on water
14. A rock \ float on water

□ **EXERCISE 3. Let's talk: class activity.**

Directions: Make sentences about yourself. Use *I can* or *I can't*.

Example: speak Chinese
Response: I can speak Chinese. OR I can't speak Chinese.

1. whistle
2. ride a bicycle
3. touch my ear with my elbow
4. play the piano*
5. play the guitar
6. lift a piano
7. drive a stick-shift car
8. fix a flat tire

9. swim
10. float on water
11. ski
12. do arithmetic
13. make a paper airplane
14. sew a button on a shirt
15. wiggle my ears
16. eat with chopsticks

———————

*In expressions with *play,* the* is usually used with musical instruments: *play the piano, play the guitar, play the violin, etc.*

☐ **EXERCISE 4. Game: small group activity.**

> *Directions:* Work in small groups. Discuss each statement. Then circle *yes* or *no.*
> When you are finished, check your answers with your teacher. The group with the
> most correct answers wins.

an octopus

1. Some birds can't fly.   yes   no
2. Elephants can jump.   yes   no
3. Tigers can't swim.   yes   no
4. An octopus can change colors.   yes   no
5. Kangaroos can walk.   yes   no
6. A baby kangaroo lives in its mother's
    pouch for a short time.   yes   no
7. Some fish can climb trees.   yes   no
8. Horses can't sleep when they stand up.   yes   no
9. Turtles can't live more than 100 years.   yes   no
10. Whales can hold their breath underwater.   yes   no

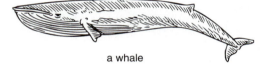

a whale

12-2 PRONUNCIATION OF *CAN* AND *CAN'T*

(a) Rick **can come** to the meeting. (b) Mike **can't come** to the meeting.	*Can* is usually pronounced "kun"—/kən/. *Can't* is usually pronounced with the same vowel sound as "ant"—/kænt/.* Native speakers usually drop the /t/.

*Sometimes native speakers also have trouble hearing the difference between *can* and *can't.*

☐ **EXERCISE 5. Listening.**

Directions: Listen to each sentence. Circle the word you hear.

1. (can)   can't   6. can   can't
2. can   can't   7. can   can't
3. can   can't   8. can   can't
4. can   can't   9. can   can't
5. can   can't   10. can   can't

☐ **EXERCISE 6. Listening.**

Directions: Read the want ad. Then listen to John talk about his job skills. Last, circle the answer to the question.

> **Job opening at small, international hotel.** Need person with the following: good typing and word-processing skills, excellent knowledge of English, friendly manner on the phone. Also needs to help guests with their suitcases and be available weekends.

QUESTION:
Is John a good person for this job?   yes   no

12-3 USING *CAN:* QUESTIONS

(QUESTION + **CAN** + SUBJECT + MAIN VERB WORD)						ANSWER
(a)		*Can*	*you*	*speak*	Arabic?	→ *Yes, I can.*
						→ *No, I can't.*
(b)		*Can*	*Rosa*	*come*	to the party?	→ *Yes, she can.*
						→ *No, she can't.*
(c)	*Where*	*can*	*I*	*buy*	a hammer?	→ *At a hardware store.*
(d)	*When*	*can*	*you*	*help*	me?	→ *Tomorrow afternoon.*

☐ **EXERCISE 7. Question practice.**

Directions: Make yes/no questions. Give short answers.

1. A: _____ *Can Jean speak English?* _____

   B: _____ *Yes, she can.* _____ (Jean can speak English.)

2. A: _____ *Can you speak French?* _____

   B: _____ *No, I can't.* _____ (I can't speak French.)

3. A: _____

   B: _____ (Jim can't play the piano.)

4. A: _____

   B: _____ (I can whistle.)

5. A: _____

   B: _____ (I can go shopping with you this afternoon.)

6. A: _____

   B: _____ (Carmen can't ride a bicycle.)

7. A: _____

   B: _____ (Elephants can swim.)

8. A: _____

   B: _____ (The students can finish this exercise quickly.)

9. A: _____

   B: _____ (The doctor can see you tomorrow.)

10. A: _____

   B: _____ (I can stand on my head.)

11. A: _____

   B: _____ (We can't have pets in the

dormitory.)

☐ EXERCISE 8. Let's talk: pairwork.

> *Directions:* Work with a partner.
> Partner A: Ask a question. Use ***Can you . . . ?***
> Partner B: Answer the question. Then ask ***How about you?*** and repeat the
> question.

> *Example:* speak Arabic
> PARTNER A: Can you speak Arabic?
> PARTNER B: Yes, I can. OR No, I can't. How about you? Can you speak Arabic?
> PARTNER A: Yes, I can. OR No, I can't. Your turn now.

Partner A	Partner B
1. ride a bicycle	1. ride a horse
2. play the piano	2. play the guitar
3. sing	3. whistle
4. touch your knee with your nose	4. touch your ear with your elbow
5. drive a stick-shift car	5. fix a flat tire
6. spell Mississippi	6. spell the teacher's last name
7. swim	7. float on water

☐ **EXERCISE 9. Let's talk: pairwork.**

Directions: Work with a partner.
Partner A: Ask a question. Use ***Where can I . . . ?*** Your book is open.
Partner B: Answer the question. Your book is closed.

Example: buy a notebook
PARTNER A *(book open):* Where can I buy a notebook?
PARTNER B *(book closed):* At the bookstore. / At *(a local store)*. / Etc.

1. buy a camera
2. get a dozen eggs
3. buy a fan
4. get a good dinner
5. go swimming
6. play tennis
7. catch a bus
8. find a vegetarian restaurant
9. buy a diamond ring

a fan

Switch roles.
Partner A: Close your book.
Partner B: Open your book. Your turn to ask questions.

10. buy a hammer
11. see a tiger
12. get a newspaper
13. buy a notebook
14. get a taxi
15. get a sandwich
16. cash a check
17. rent a DVD
18. buy cold medicine

cold medicine

☐ **EXERCISE 10. Listening.**

🎧 *Directions:* Listen to the conversations. Write the words you hear.

    1. A: Hello?

       B: _____ speak to Mr. Jones, please?

       A: I'm sorry. _____ to the phone right now.

             _____ take a message? _____ return your call in about a half-hour.

       B: Yes. Please tell him Bob Anderson called.

    2. A: _____ me lift this box?

       B: It looks very heavy. _____ to help you, but I think we need a third person.

       A: No, I'm very strong. I think _____ it together.

    3. A: _____ the TV. _____ turn it up?

       B: _____ turn it up. I'm doing my homework. If I turn it up, I

             _____ concentrate.

       A: _____ your homework in another room?

       B: Oh, all right.

12-4 USING *KNOW HOW TO*

(a) I can swim.	(a) and (b) have basically the same meaning.
(b) I ***know how to swim***.	***Know how to*** expresses ability.
(c) Can you cook?	(c) and (d) have basically the same meaning.
(d) ***Do*** you ***know how to cook?***	

☐ **EXERCISE 11. Let's talk: pairwork.**

    Directions: Work with a partner.
    Partner A: Ask a question. Use ***know how to*** in your question. Your book is open.
    Partner B: Answer the question. Your book is closed.

Example: swim
PARTNER A *(book open):* Do you know how to swim?
PARTNER B *(book closed):* Yes, I do. OR No, I don't.

1. cook
2. dance
3. play the piano
4. get to the post office from here

5. fix a flat tire
6. drive a stick-shift car
7. wiggle your nose
8. sew

Switch roles.
Partner A: Close your book.
Partner B: Open your book. Your turn to ask questions.

9. play the guitar
10. get to the airport from here
11. use a digital camera
12. use a screwdriver

13. get to *(a store)* from here
14. count to five in *(a language)*
15. add, subtract, multiply, and divide
16. find the square root of nine

a screwdriver

□ EXERCISE 12. Let's talk: find someone who . . . .

Directions: Walk around the room. Ask your classmates questions. Find someone who can answer *yes* to each question. Write down his/her name. Use **Do you know how to . . . ?** Share a few of their answers with the class.

Ability	First name
1. play a musical instrument	
2. play a sport	
3. speak three or four languages	
4. eat with chopsticks	
5. take care of a snake	
6. sew	
7. fix a car	
8. draw	
9. swim	
10. create movies on a computer	

□ **EXERCISE 13. Let's write: small groups.**

Directions: Work in small groups. Complete the sentences as a group. Use a separate sheet of paper. Share some of your completions with the class.

1. Babies know how to . . . .
2. Babies don't know how to . . . .
3. Birds know how to . . . .
4. Birds don't know how to . . . .
5. I know how to . . . .
6. I don't know how to . . . .
7. *(name of a classmate)* knows how to . . . .
8. Our teacher doesn't know how to . . . .
9. Do you know how to . . . ?

12-5 USING *COULD:* PAST OF *CAN*

(a) I am in Hawaii. I *can go* to the beach every day. (b) I was in Hawaii *last month*. I *could go* to the beach every day when I was there.	*could* = the past form of *can*
(c) I *can't go* to the movie today. I have to study. (d) I $\begin{Bmatrix} \textbf{\textit{couldn't go}} \\ \textbf{\textit{could not go}} \end{Bmatrix}$ to the movie *last night*. I had to study.	NEGATIVE *could* + *not* = *couldn't*
(e) *Could you speak* English before you came here?	QUESTION *could* + *subject* + *main verb*

□ **EXERCISE 14. Let's talk: pairwork.**

Directions: Work with a partner. Circle the answers that describe your childhood. Then tell your partner what you could and couldn't do when you were a child.

When I was a child, ...

1. I could stand on my head.   yes   no
2. I could ride a bike with no hands.   yes   no
3. I could sing in another language.   yes   no
4. I could tell time before the age of five.   yes   no
5. I could do cartwheels.   yes   no
6. I could read before the age of five.   yes   no
7. I could hold my breath underwater for one minute.   yes   no
8. I could *(complete the sentence with your own words)*.   yes   no

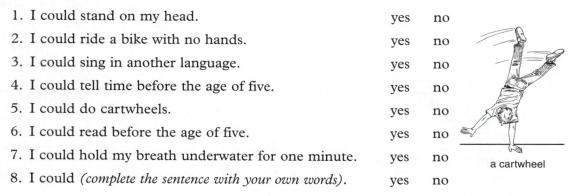

a cartwheel

☐ EXERCISE 15. Sentence practice.

Directions: Complete the sentences by using ***couldn't***. Use the expressions in the list or your own words.

call you	go to the movie
come to class	light the candles
✓ do my homework	listen to music
get into my car	wash his clothes
go swimming	watch TV

1. I _____*couldn't do my homework*_____ last night because I was too tired.

2. I _____ yesterday because I lost your telephone number.

3. I _____ last night because my TV set is broken.

4. Tom _____ because he didn't have any matches.

5. The teacher _____ yesterday because he was sick.

6. I _____ last night because my radio doesn't work.

7. Ken _____ because he didn't have any laundry soap.

8. We _____ yesterday because the water was too cold.

9. I _____ yesterday because I locked all the doors and left the keys inside.

10. I _____ last night because I had to study.

☐ EXERCISE 16. Sentence practice.

Directions: Mr. Chang had a bad day yesterday. There are many things he wanted to do, but couldn't. Tell what he couldn't do yesterday and give a reason. Use ***because***.

Example: eat breakfast \ get up late
→ Mr. Chang couldn't eat breakfast because he got up late.

Example: go downtown during the day \ have to work

→ Mr. Chang couldn't go downtown during the day because he had to work.

1. eat lunch \ leave his wallet at home
2. finish his report \ have to go to a meeting
3. leave work at five \ have to finish his report
4. play tennis after work \ it \ be raining
5. enjoy his dinner \ his wife \ be angry at him
6. watch his favorite TV program after dinner \ his TV set \ not work
7. read quietly \ his children \ be very noisy
8. go to bed early \ his neighbors \ come to visit

☐ **EXERCISE 17. Let's talk: class activity.**

Directions: Your teacher will make a statement. Give some of the negative results for the situations. Use **can't** or **couldn't**. Close your book for this activity.

Examples:

TEACHER: There's no chalk in the classroom.
STUDENT: We can't write on the board.

TEACHER: There was no chalk in the classroom yesterday.
STUDENT: We couldn't write on the board.

1. I have only *(a small amount of money)* in my pocket / in my purse today.
2. Some people don't know how to use a computer.
3. Your parents had rules for you when you were a child.
4. This school has rules for students.
5. All of you are adults. You are not children.
6. You didn't know much English last year.
7. You don't speak fluent English yet.
8. Millions of people in the world live in poverty.

☐ **EXERCISE 18. Review: error analysis.**

Directions: Correct the errors.

1. Could you to drive a car when you were thirteen years old?

2. If your brother goes to the graduation party, he can meets my sister.

3. I couldn't opened the door because I didn't have a key.

4. Please turn up the radio. I can't to hear it.

5. When Ernesto arrived at the airport last Tuesday, he can't find the right gate.

6. Mr. Lo was born in Hong Kong, but now he lives in Canada. He cannot understand spoken English before he moved to Canada, but now he speak and understand English very well.

12-6 USING *BE ABLE TO*

PRESENT	(a) I *am able to touch* my toes. (b) I *can touch* my toes.	(a) and (b) have basically the same meaning.
FUTURE	(c) I *will be able to go* shopping tomorrow. (d) I *can go* shopping tomorrow.	(c) and (d) have basically the same meaning.
PAST	(e) I *wasn't able to finish* my homework last night. (f) I *couldn't finish* my homework last night.	(e) and (f) have basically the same meaning.

☐ **EXERCISE 19. Sentence practice.**
Directions: On a separate sheet of paper, make sentences with the same meaning. Use *be able to*.

1. I can be here tomorrow at ten o'clock.
   → *I'll (I will) be able to be here tomorrow at ten o'clock.*

2. Two students couldn't finish the test.
   → *Two students weren't able to finish the test.*

3. Mark is bilingual. He can speak two languages.

4. Sue can get her own apartment next year.

5. Animals can't speak.

6. Can you touch your toes without bending your knees?

7. Jack couldn't describe the thief.

8. Could you do the homework?

9. I couldn't sleep last night because my apartment was too hot.

10. My roommate can speak four languages. He's multilingual.

11. I'm sorry that I couldn't call you last night.

12. I'm sorry, but I can't come to your party next week.

13. Can we take vacations on the moon in the 22nd century?

☐ EXERCISE 20. Sentence practice.
   Directions: Complete the sentences with your own words.

1. I wasn't able to _____ last night because

   _____ .

2. We'll be able to _____ in the 22nd century.

3. I'm sorry, but I won't be able to _____ .

4. Birds are able to _____ .

5. My friend is multilingual. She's able to _____ .

6. I'm bilingual. I'm able to _____ .

7. The students weren't able to _____ in class

   yesterday because _____ .

8. Will you be able to _____ tomorrow?

9. _____ wasn't able to _____

   because _____ .

10. _____ isn't able to _____

    because _____ .

11. _____ won't be able to _____

    because _____ .

□ EXERCISE 21. Listening review: *can / be able to / know how to.*

🎧 *Directions:* Listen to the conversations. Complete the sentences with the words you hear.

1. A: _____ to John last night?

   B: _____ reach him. I _____ again later today.

2. A: _____ bread?

   B: Yes, I _____ bread. What about you?

   A: No. _____ me?

   B: Sure, _____.

3. A: _____ the teacher?

   B: I _____ her in the beginning, but now I

   _____ most of her lectures.

   A: I still _____ her very well.

4. A: Professor Jones, when _____ correct our

   tests?

   B: I began last night, but I _____ finish. I _____

   _____ again tonight. I hope _____

   _____ hand them back to you tomorrow.

5. A: Hello?

   B: Hi. This is Jan Smith. I'm wondering if _____ get in to see Dr.

   Brown today or tomorrow.

   A: Well, she _____ you tomorrow morning at

   11:00. _____ in then?

   B: Yes, _____. Please tell me where you are. I _____

   _____ the way to your office.

(a) The box is **very** *heavy,* but Tom **can** *lift* it.	**Very** and **too** come in front of adjectives; *heavy* and *hot* are adjectives.
(b) The box is **too** *heavy.* Bob **can't** *lift* it.	**Very** and **too** do NOT have the same meaning.
(c) The coffee is **very** *hot,* but I **can** *drink* it.	In (a): *very heavy* = It is difficult but possible for Tom to lift the box.
(d) The coffee is **too** *hot.* I **can't** *drink* it.	In (b): *too heavy* = It is impossible for Bob to lift the box.

Tom

Bob

(e) The coffee is **too** hot. NEGATIVE RESULT: I can't drink it.	In the speaker's mind, the use of **too** implies a negative result.
(f) The weather is **too** cold. NEGATIVE RESULT: We can't go to the beach.	

☐ EXERCISE 22. Class activity.

> *Directions:* Make sentences for each picture. Use **very** or **too** and **can** or **can't** to describe the pictures.

> *Example:* suitcase \ heavy \ lift
> → The suitcase is very heavy, but Mark can lift it.
> → The suitcase is too heavy. James can't lift it.

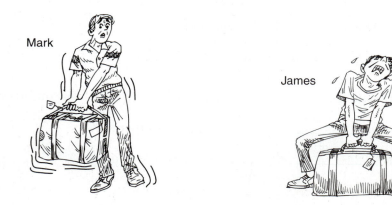

Mark

James

1. soup \ hot \ eat

Jack

Ricardo

2. coat \ small \ wear

Tom

Susan

3. shoes \ tight \ wear

Marika

Mai

4. problem \ hard

Robert   Talal

☐ **EXERCISE 23. Sentence practice.**

Directions: Complete the sentences. Use the expressions in the list or your own words.

buy it	*lift it*
do his homework	*reach the cookie jar*
eat it	*sleep*
go swimming	*take a break*

1. The soup is too hot. I can't _____

2. The diamond ring is too expensive. I can't _____

3. The weather is too cold. We can't _____

4. I am too busy.

   I can't _____

5. Ali is too tired.

   He can't _____

6. Peggy is too short.

   She can't _____

7. It's too noisy in the dorm at night.

   I can't _____

8. The piano is too heavy.

   I can't _____

□ EXERCISE 24. Sentence practice.

Directions: Complete the sentences. Use *too*. Use adjectives in the list or your own words.

cold	*small*
expensive	*tall*
heavy	*tired*
noisy	*young*

1. You can't lift a car. A car is _____

2. Jimmy is ten. He can't drive a car. He's _____

3. I can't study in the dorm at night. It's _____,

4. I don't want to go to the zoo. The weather is _____

5. Ann doesn't want to play tennis this afternoon. She's _____

6. I can't buy a new car. A new car is _____

7. John has gained weight. He can't wear his old shirt. It's _____

8. The basketball player can't stand up straight in the subway. He's _____

□ EXERCISE 25. Sentence practice.

Directions: Complete the sentences. Use *too* or *very*.

1. The tea is _____*very*_____ hot, but I can drink it.

2. The tea is _____*too*_____ hot. I can't drink it.

3. I can't put my dictionary in my pocket. My dictionary is _____ big.

4. An elephant is _____ big. A mouse is _____ small.

5. I can't buy a boat because it's _____ expensive.

6. A sports car is _____ expensive, but Anita can buy one if she wants to.

7. We went to the Rocky Mountains for our vacation. The mountains are

_____ beautiful.

8. I can't eat this food because it's _____ salty.

9. Amanda doesn't like her room in the dorm. She thinks it's _____ small.

10. I lost your dictionary. I'm _____ sorry. I'll buy you a new one.

11. A: Do you like your math course?

B: Yes. It's _____ difficult, but I enjoy it.

12. A: Do you like your math course?

B: No. It's _____ difficult. I don't like it because I can't understand the math.

13. A: It's seven-thirty. Do you want to go to the movie?

B: We can't. It's _____ late. The movie started at seven.

14. A: Did you enjoy your dinner last night?

B: Yes. The food was _____ good!

15. A: Are you going to buy that dress?

B: No. It doesn't fit. It's _____ big.

16. A: Do you think Carol is smart?

B: Yes, I do. I think she's _____ intelligent.

17. A: My daughter wants to get married.

B: What? But she can't! She's _____ young.

18. A: Can you read that sign across the street?

B: No, I can't. It's _____ far away.

12-8 USING *TWO, TOO,* AND *TO*

TWO	(a) I have *two* children.	*Two, too,* and *to* have the same pronunciation. In (a): *two* = a number.
TOO	(b) Timmy is *too* young. He can't read. (c) Ann saw the movie. I saw the movie *too*.	In (b): *too young = impossible to do because of his youth.* In (c): *too = **also***.
TO	(d) I talked *to* Jim. (e) I want *to* watch television.	In (d): *to* = a preposition. In (e): *to* = part of an infinitive.

☐ **EXERCISE 26. Sentence practice.**

Directions: Complete the sentences. Use *two, too,* or *to.*

1. I'd like a cup of coffee. Bob would like a cup _____*too*_____.

2. I had _____ cups of coffee yesterday.

3. I can't drink my coffee. It's _____ hot. The coffee is _____ hot

   for me _____ drink.

4. I talked _____ Jim. Jane wants _____ talk _____ Jim

   _____.

5. I walked _____ school today. Alex walked _____ school today

   _____.

6. I'm going _____ take the bus _____ school tomorrow.

7. Shh. I want _____ listen _____ the news broadcast.

8. I can't study. The music is _____ loud.

9. The weather is _____ cold for us _____ go _____ the

   beach.

10. I have _____ apples. Ken wants _____ have _____

    apples _____.

(a) Olga is *at* home. Ivan is *at* work. Yoko is *at* school.	In (a): *at* is used with *home, work,* and *school.*★
(b) Sue is *in* bed. Tom is *in* class. Paul is *in* jail/prison.	In (b): *in* is used with *bed, class,* and *jail/prison.*★
(c) Mr. Lee is *in* the hospital.	In (c): *in* is used with *the hospital.* Note: American English = *in the hospital.* British English = *in hospital.*
(d) Ahmed is *in* the kitchen. (e) David is *in* Mexico City.	In (d): *in* is used with rooms: *in the kitchen, in the classroom, in the hall, in my bedroom, etc.* In (e): *in* is used with cities, states/provinces, countries, and continents: *in Mexico City, in Florida, in Italy, in Asia, etc.*
(f) A: Where's Ivan? B: He isn't here. He's *at* the bank.	In (f): *at* is usually used with locations in a city: *at the post office, at the bank, at the library, at the bookstore, at the park, at the theater, at the restaurant, at the football stadium, etc.*
COMPARE (g) In Picture 2, Ivan is *in* the bank. He is not outside the bank.	In (g): A speaker uses *in* with a building only when it is important to say that someone is inside, not outside, the building. Usually a speaker uses *at* with a building. *in the bank* = inside the bank building.

① ENTRANCE
BANK
Ivan is *at* the bank.

② 6%
Ivan is *at* the bank.
Ivan is *in* (inside) the bank.

★Notice: In these common expressions of place, *the* is not used in front of *home, work, school, bed, class, jail/prison.*

□ EXERCISE 27. Sentence practice.

Directions: Complete the sentences with **at** or **in**. In some sentences, both prepositions are correct.

1. A: Is Jennifer here?

   B: No, she's _____*at*_____ the bookstore.*

2. A: Where's Jack?

   B: He's _____*in*_____ his room.

3. When I was _____ work yesterday, I had an interesting telephone call.

4. Poor Anita. She's _____ the hospital again for more surgery.

5. Mr. Gow wasn't _____ class yesterday. He was _____ home.

   He wasn't feeling well.

6. Last year at this time, Eric was _____ Korea. This year he's _____

   Spain.

7. A: Where's Donna?

   B: She's _____ New York. She's attending a conference.

8. There's a fire extinguisher _____ the hall.

9. The children are _____ home this morning. They aren't _____

   school.

10. A: Where's Olga? I was supposed to meet her here at five.

    B: She's _____ the library. She's studying for a test.

    A: Oh. Maybe she forgot that she was supposed to meet me here.

11. A: Where's Robert?

    B: He's _____ the computer room.

12. There are thirty-seven desks _____ our classroom.

13. We ate _____ a good restaurant last night. The food was delicious.

_____

*ALSO CORRECT: *She's *in* the bookstore,* but only if the speaker wants to say that she is inside, not outside, the bookstore. Usually a speaker uses *at* with a building to identify someone's location. See Chart 12–9, p. 374.

14. A thief broke the window of a jewelry store and stole some valuable jewelry. The police caught him. Now he's _____ jail. He's going to be _____ prison for a long time.

15. Singapore is _____ Asia.

16. We had a good time _____ the zoo yesterday.

17. A: Where's Fatima?

    B: She's _____ the supermarket.

18. A: Where can I get some fresh tomatoes?

    B: _____ the market on Waterfront Street.

19. A: Here's your hotel key, Ms. Fox. You're _____ Room 609.

    B: Thank you. Where are the elevators?

20. A: Is Mike up?

    B: No, he's _____ bed.

    A: Well, it's time to get up. I'm going to wake him up. Hey, Mike! You can't sleep all day! Get up!

    C: Go away!

□ EXERCISE 28. Let's talk: class activity.

Directions: Complete the sentence *I was ... yesterday* by using the words your teacher gives you and the correct preposition, *at* or *in*. Close your book for this activity.

Example:
TEACHER: work
STUDENT: I was at work yesterday.

1. class	7. work
2. the library	8. Room 206
3. *(a city)*	9. a hotel
4. home	10. *(a continent)*
5. this room	11. (. . .)'s living room
6. the bookstore	12. *(a building)*

☐ **EXERCISE 29. Let's talk: pairwork.**

Directions: Work with a partner. Ask questions about place. Use **at** or **in** in your answers.

Partner A: Begin the question with **Where were you.**

Partner B: Use **at** or **in** in the answer. Then ask **How about you?** and repeat the question.

Example: yesterday afternoon

PARTNER A: Where were you yesterday afternoon?

PARTNER B: I was in class. How about you? Where were you yesterday afternoon?

PARTNER A: I was in class too. / I was at home. / Etc. Your turn now.

Partner A	Partner B
1. at nine o'clock last night	1. at two o'clock yesterday afternoon
2. after class yesterday	2. this morning at six o'clock
3. six weeks ago	3. five years ago
4. on your last vacation	4. when you were ten years old

☐ **EXERCISE 30. Review: let's talk.**

Directions: Work in small groups. What **can** or **can't** the following people/animals/things do? Why or why not? Discuss the topics and report to the rest of the class. You can also use **be able to** or **know how to** in your sentences.

Example: a tiger

SPEAKER A: A tiger can kill a water buffalo because a tiger is very strong and powerful.

SPEAKER B: A tiger can sleep in the shade of a tree all day if it wants to. It doesn't have a job, and it doesn't go to school.

SPEAKER C: A tiger can't speak *(a human language)*. It's an animal.

SPEAKER D: A tiger can communicate with other tigers. Animals can talk to each other in their own languages.

1. the students in this class
2. young children
3. a monkey
4. *(a classmate)*
5. international students who live in *(this country)*
6. teenagers
7. people who live in *(this city)*
8. people who are illiterate
9. money
10. computers
11. our teacher
12. *(the leader of this country or your country)*

□ EXERCISE 31. Chapter review: error analysis.

Directions: Correct the errors.

1. We will can go to the museum tomorrow afternoon.

2 We can't count all of the stars in the universe. There are to many.

3. Can you to stand on your head?

4. I saw a beautiful vase at a store yesterday, but I couldn't bought it.

5. The shirt is too small. I can wear it.

6. Sam know how to count to 1000 in English.

7. When I was on vacation, I can swim every day.

8. When we lived at Tokyo, we took the subway every day.

9. Honeybees not able to live in very cold climates.

10. Where we can go in the city for an inexpensive meal?

11. James can reads newspapers in five languages.

12. Sorry. I didn't be able to get tickets for the concert.

13. I can't finish my homework because I'm to tired.

CHAPTER 13
Modals, Part 2: Advice, Necessity, Requests, Suggestions

13-1 USING *SHOULD*

(a) My clothes are dirty. I **should wash** them. (b) Tom is sleepy. He **should go** to bed. (c) You're sick. You **should see** a doctor.	**Should** means "This is a good idea. This is good advice."
(d) I You She He } **should go**. It We They	**Should** is followed by the simple form of a verb. INCORRECT: *He should goes.* INCORRECT: *He should to go.*
(e) You **should not leave** your grammar book at home. You need it in class. (f) You **shouldn't leave** your grammar book at home.	NEGATIVE: *should not* CONTRACTION: *should + not = shouldn't*

☐ EXERCISE 1. Sentence practice.

> *Directions:* Complete the conversations. Begin the sentences with **You should**. Use the expressions in the list or your own words.

buy a new pair of shoes	✓*go to the post office*
call the manager	*go to bed and take a nap*
go to the bank	*see a dentist*
go to the immigration office	*study harder*

1. A: I want to mail a package.

   B: ___*You should go to the post office.*_____

2. A: I'm sleepy.

    B: _____

3. A: I need to cash a check.

    B: _____

4. A: I have a toothache.

    B: _____

5. A: I'm getting poor grades in all of my classes at school.

    B: _____

6. A: The toilet in my apartment doesn't work.

    B: _____

7. A: I need to get a new visa.

    B: _____

8. A: My shoes have holes in the bottom.

    B: _____

□ EXERCISE 2. Let's talk: small groups.

Directions: Work in small groups. Make sentences with **should** and **shouldn't**.
Share some of your answers with the class.

1. Sue has a headache from working at her computer too long.
   Sue . . .
   a. see a doctor.
   b. take some headache medicine.
   c. lie down.
   d. go to the hospital emergency room.
   e. take a 15-minute break from the computer.

2. John stayed late after school to help his teacher. He missed the last bus and needs a
   ride home. It takes two hours to walk to his home, and it is a 20-minute ride by car.
   John . . .
   a. call a taxi.
   b. hitchhike.
   c. ask his teacher for a ride.
   d. call a friend for a ride.
   e. walk.

3. Mary's baby doesn't want to take a nap. He is crying.
   Mary . . .
   a. hold him.
   b. rock him.
   c. let him cry until he falls asleep.
   d. feed him.
   e. let him play.

4. The teacher is giving a final exam. One student keeps looking at a paper under his exam paper. It has the answers on it.
   The teacher . . .
   a. take the paper away and give the student another chance.
   b. give the student a failing grade for the test.
   c. give the student a failing grade for the class.
   d. send the student to see the director of the school.

5. Susan is 16 years old. A boy in her class wants her to go to dinner and a movie with him. This will be her first date.
   Her parents . . .
   a. let her go if her older brother goes too.
   b. make her wait until she is older.
   c. go with her.
   d. let her go by herself.
   e. let her go to dinner only.

☐ EXERCISE 3. Sentence practice.

Directions: Complete the sentences. Use ***should*** or ***shouldn't***.

1. Students _____*should*_____ come to class every day.

2. Students _____*shouldn't*_____ skip class.

3. We _____ waste our money on things we don't need.

4. It's raining. You _____ take your umbrella when you leave.

5. Jimmy, you _____ pull the cat's tail!

6. People _____ be cruel to animals.

7. Your plane leaves at 8:00. You _____ get to the airport by 6:00.

8. Life is short. We _____ waste it.

9. You _____ smoke in a public place because the smoke bothers other people.

10. We _____ cross a street at an intersection. We

_____ jaywalk.

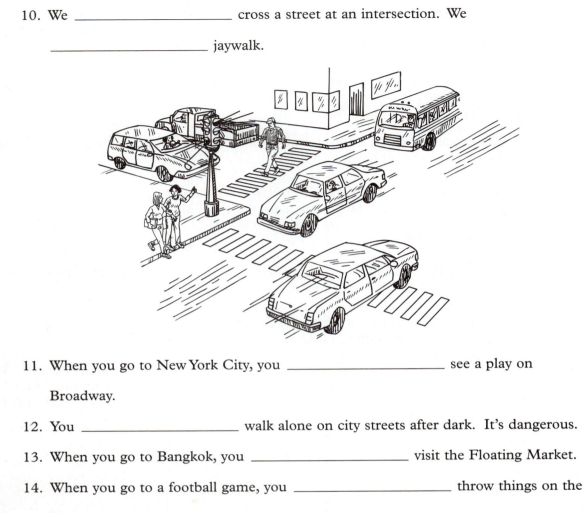

11. When you go to New York City, you _____ see a play on

Broadway.

12. You _____ walk alone on city streets after dark. It's dangerous.

13. When you go to Bangkok, you _____ visit the Floating Market.

14. When you go to a football game, you _____ throw things on the

field.

☐ EXERCISE 4. Let's talk: small groups.

Directions: Work in small groups. For each situation, give advice by making a list of sentences using ***should*** and ***shouldn't***. Speaker A should request advice first, then Speaker B, etc.

1. SPEAKER A: English is not my native language. What advice can you give me about good ways to learn English?

2. SPEAKER B: I am a teenager. What advice can you give me about being a good person and living a happy life?

3. SPEAKER C: I am a newcomer. What advice can you give me about going to this school and living in this city?

4. SPEAKER D: I have a job interview tomorrow. What advice can you give me about going to a job interview?

EXERCISE 5. Listening.

Directions: Listen to each sentence and circle the verb you hear. After you check your answers, listen again. If you agree, circle *yes*. If you don't, circle *no*.

DO YOU AGREE?

1.	should	shouldn't	yes	no
2.	should	shouldn't	yes	no
3.	should	shouldn't	yes	no
4.	should	shouldn't	yes	no
5.	should	shouldn't	yes	no
6.	should	shouldn't	yes	no
7.	should	shouldn't	yes	no
8.	should	shouldn't	yes	no

EXERCISE 6. Writing.

Directions: Write a paragraph about your hometown on a separate piece of paper. Include answers to the tourist's questions.

I'm a tourist. I'm going to visit your hometown. Is your hometown a good place for a tourist to visit? Why? What should I do when I'm there? Where should I go? What should I see? What shouldn't I do? Are there places I shouldn't visit? Will I enjoy my visit?

13-2 USING *HAVE* + INFINITIVE *(HAVE TO / HAS TO)*

(a) People ***need to eat*** food. (b) People ***have to eat*** food.	(a) and (b) have basically the same meaning.
(c) Jack ***needs to study*** for his test. (d) Jack ***has to study*** for his test.	(c) and (d) have basically the same meaning. ***Have*** + *infinitive* has a special meaning: it expresses the same idea as ***need***.
(e) I ***had to study*** last night.	PAST FORM: ***had*** + *infinitive*.
(f) ***Do*** you ***have to*** *leave* now? (g) What time ***does*** Jim ***have to*** *leave*? (h) Why ***did*** they ***have to*** *leave* yesterday?	QUESTION FORM: ***do, does***, or ***did*** is used in questions with ***have to***.
(i) I ***don't have to*** *study* tonight. (j) The concert was free. We ***didn't have to*** *buy* tickets.	NEGATIVE FORM: ***don't, doesn't***, or ***didn't*** is used with ***have to***.

☐ EXERCISE 7. Let's talk: class activity.

Directions: Answer the questions your teacher asks you. Close your book for this activity.

1. What do you want to do today?
2. What do you have to do today?
3. What do you want to do tomorrow?
4. What do you have to do tomorrow?
5. What does a student need to do or have to do?
6. Who has to go shopping? Why?
7. Who has to go to the post office? Why?
8. Who has to go to the bank? Why?
9. Where do you have to go today? Why?
10. Where do you want to go tomorrow? Why?
11. What did you have to do yesterday? Why?
12. Did you have responsibilities at home when you were a child? What did you have to do?
13. If you're driving a car and the traffic light turns red, what do you have to do?
14. What do you have to do before you cross a busy street?
15. Do you have to learn English? Why?
16. Who has a job? What are some of the things you have to do when you're at work?
17. What kind of job did you have in the past? What did you have to do when you had that job?

☐ EXERCISE 8. Let's talk: class activity.

Directions: Make sentences using **have to/has to** and **because**.

Example: go downtown \ buy some new shoes
SPEAKER A: I have to go downtown because I have to buy some new shoes.
 TEACHER: *(to Speaker B)* Why does *(Speaker A)* have to go downtown?
SPEAKER B: *(Speaker A)* has to go downtown because he/she has to buy some new shoes.

1. go to the drugstore \ buy some toothpaste
2. go to the grocery store \ get some bread
3. go shopping \ get a new coat
4. go to the post office \ mail a package
5. stay home tonight \ study grammar
6. go to the hospital \ visit a friend
7. go to the bank \ cash a check
8. go downtown \ go to the immigration office
9. go to the bookstore \ buy a notebook
10. go to *(name of a store in the city)* \ buy *(a particular thing at that store)*

Directions: Complete the sentences with the words in parentheses. Use a form of
have/has + *infinitive.*

1. A: Jack can't join us for dinner tonight.

   B: Why not?

   A: *(he, work)* _____He has to work._____

   B: *(he, work)* _____Does he have to work_____ tomorrow night too? If he

      doesn't, maybe we should postpone the dinner until then.

2. A: Why *(you, go)* _____ to the library later tonight?

   B: *(I, find)* _____ some information for my research paper.

3. A: It's almost four-thirty. What time *(Sue, leave)* _____

      _____ for the airport?

   B: Around five. *(she, be)* _____ at the airport at

      six-fifteen.

4. A: Why did you go to the bookstore after class yesterday?

   B: *(I, buy)* _____ some colored pencils.

   A: Oh? Why *(you, buy)* _____ colored pencils?

   B: I need them for some drawings I plan to do for my art class.

5. A: *(I, go)* _____ to the store.

   B: Why?

   A: Because *(I, get)* _____ some rice and fresh fruit.

6. A: Kate didn't come to the movie with us last night.

   B: Why?

   A: Because *(she, study)* _____ for a test.

7. A: What time *(you, be)* _____ at the dentist's office?

    B: Three. I have a three o'clock appointment.

8. A: *(Tom, find)* _____ a new apartment?

    B: Yes, he does. His old apartment is too small.

9. A: *(Yoko, take, not)* _____ another English

    course. Her English is very good.

    B: *(you, take)* _____ another English course?

    A: Yes, I do. I need to study more English.

10. A: Was Steve at home yesterday evening?

    B: No. *(he, stay)* _____ late at the office.

    A: Why?

    B: *(he, finish)* _____ a report for his boss.

☐ EXERCISE 10. Listening.

Directions: In spoken English, **have to** is often pronounced "hafta." **Has to** is often pronounced "hasta." Listen to each sentence and circle the correct verb.

1. (have to)   has to
2. have to   has to
3. have to   has to
4. have to   has to
5. have to   has to
6. have to   has to
7. have to   has to
8. have to   has to
9. have to   has to
10. have to   has to

13-3 USING *MUST*

(a) People need food. People **have to eat** food. (b) People need food. People **must eat** food.	(a) and (b) have the same meaning: *must eat = have to eat.*
(c) $\left.\begin{array}{l} I \\ You \\ She \\ He \\ It \\ We \\ They \end{array}\right\}$ **must work**.	***Must*** is followed by the simple form of a verb. INCORRECT: *He must works.* INCORRECT: *He must to work.*
(d) You **must not be** late for work if you want to keep your job.	***must not*** = Don't do this! You don't have a choice.
(e) You **don't have to go** to the movie with us if you don't want to.	***don't have to*** = It's not necessary; you have a choice.

Compare the following examples. Notice the difference between **must** and **should**.

MUST	*SHOULD*
SOMETHING IS VERY IMPORTANT. SOMETHING IS NECESSARY. YOU DO NOT HAVE A CHOICE.	SOMETHING IS A GOOD IDEA, BUT YOU HAVE A CHOICE.
(f) I **must study** tonight. I'm going to take a very important test tomorrow.	(g) I **should study** tonight. I have some homework to do, but I'm tired. I'll study tomorrow morning. I'm going to go to bed now.
(h) You **must take** an English course. You cannot graduate without it.	(i) You **should take** an English course. It will help you.
(j) Johnny, this is your mother speaking. You **must eat** your vegetables. You can't leave the table until you eat your vegetables.	(k) Johnny, you **should eat** your vegetables. They're good for you. You'll grow up to be strong and healthy.

□ EXERCISE 11. Sentence practice.

Directions: Complete the sentences. Use ***must*** and expressions in the list. There are more expressions than you will need.

close the door behind you	*pay an income tax*
go to medical school	*read English newspapers and magazines*
✓*have a driver's license*	*speak English outside of class every day*
have a library card	*stop*
have a passport	*study harder*
listen to English on the radio and TV	*talk to myself in English*
make new friends who speak English	*take one tablet every six hours*

1. According to the law,* a driver _____ *must have a driver's license.* _____

2. If a traffic light is red, a car _____

3. If you want to check a book out of the library, you _____

   _____

4. Nancy has a job in Chicago. She earns a good salary. According to the law, she

   _____

5. I failed the last two tests in my biology class. According to my professor, I

   _____

6. I want to improve my English. According to my teacher, I _____

   _____

7. I want to travel abroad. According to the law, I _____

8. If you want to become a doctor, you _____

9. Jimmy! It's cold outside. When you come inside, you _____

   _____

10. John's doctor gave him a prescription. According to the directions on

    the bottle, John _____

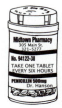

_____

* *According to the law = the law says.*

☐ **EXERCISE 12. Sentence practice.**

Directions: Answer the questions.

1. When must you have a passport?
2. If you live in an apartment, what is one thing you must do and one thing you must not do?
3. Name one thing a driver must do and one thing a driver must not do.
4. If you are on an airplane, what is one thing you must do and one thing you must not do?
5. Name something you must have a ticket for. Name something you don't have to have a ticket for.

☐ **EXERCISE 13. Sentence practice.**

Directions: Circle the correct completions.

1. If you want to keep your job, you _____ be late for work.
   (A.) must not   B. don't have to   C. doesn't have to

2. My office is close enough to my apartment for me to walk to work. I _____ take a bus. I take a bus only in bad weather.
   A. must not   B. don't have to   C. doesn't have to

3. Some schools require schoolchildren to wear uniforms to school, but my children's school doesn't require uniforms. My children _____ wear uniforms to school.
   A. must not   B. don't have to   C. doesn't have to

4. Jimmy, it is very important to be careful with matches.
   You _____ play with matches.
   A. must not
   B. don't have to
   C. doesn't have to

5. Jack is twenty-four, but he still lives with his parents. That saves him a lot of money. For example, he _____ pay rent or buy his own food.
   A. must not   B. don't have to   C. doesn't have to

6. The water in that river is badly polluted. You _____ drink it.
   A. must not   B. don't have to   C. doesn't have to

7. If you have a credit card, you _____ pay for something in cash. You can charge it.
   A. must not   B. don't have to   C. doesn't have to

8. When an airplane is taking off, you have to be in your seat with your seat belt on.
   You _____ stand up and walk around when an airplane is taking off.
   A. must not   B. don't have to   C. doesn't have to

☐ **EXERCISE 14. Let's talk: small groups.**

Directions: Work in small groups. Make sentences about your English class. Use **should / have to / don't have to** with the given phrases. Share a few of your answers with the class.

Example: Students . . . study.
Response: Students have to study.

Students . . .
1. come to class.

2. sit quietly.

3. take attendance.

4. bring pencil and paper to class.

5. listen carefully.

6. speak English in class.

7. stand up when the teacher enters the room.

8. knock on the door before entering the room.

9. raise their hands when they want to talk.

10. do their homework.

11. memorize vocabulary.

12. bring an English–English dictionary to class.

13. write homework answers in their books.

☐ **EXERCISE 15. Listening.**

Directions: Listen to each pair of sentences. One sentence uses **should,** and the other uses **must.** Decide which sentence you agree with. Write **a** or **b** in the blank. Discuss your answers as a class.

Example:
You will hear: a. People must obey traffic laws.
               b. People should obey traffic laws.
You will write: ___a___

1. _____   4. _____   7. _____

2. _____   5. _____   8. _____

3. _____   6. _____   9. _____

(a) ***May I borrow*** your pen? (b) ***Could I borrow*** your pen? (c) ***Can I borrow*** your pen?	(a), (b), and (c) have the same meaning: I want to borrow your pen. I am asking politely to borrow your pen.
(d) *May I **please** borrow* your pen? (e) *Could I **please** borrow* your pen? (f) *Can I **please** borrow* your pen?	***Please*** is often used in polite questions.

TYPICAL RESPONSES
(g) ***Yes, of course.***
(h) ***Of course.***
(i) ***Certainly.***
(j) ***Sure.*** (informal)★
(k) ***No problem.*** (informal)★
	TYPICAL CONVERSATION
	  A: *May I please borrow your pen?*
	  B: ***Yes, of course.*** *Here it is.*
	  A: *Thank you. / Thanks.*

★Informal English is typically used between friends and family members.

☐ **EXERCISE 16. Let's talk: pairwork.**

> *Directions:* Work with a partner. Look at the pictures. Make conversations. Use ***May I, Can I,*** or ***Could I*** and typical responses.

☐ **EXERCISE 17. Let's talk: pairwork.**

Directions: Work with a partner. Ask and answer polite questions using ***May I, Can I***, or ***Could I***.

Example: Your partner has a pencil. You want to borrow it.
PARTNER A: (. . .), may I (please) borrow your pencil?
PARTNER B: Certainly. Here it is.
PARTNER A: Thank you. Your turn now.

Partner A	Partner B
1. You partner has a dictionary. You want to borrow it.	1. Your partner has a pen. You want to use it for a minute.
2. Your partner has an eraser. You want to use it for a minute.	2. Your partner has a pencil sharpener. You want to borrow it.
3. Your partner has a book. You want to see it.	3. Your partner has a dictionary. You want to see it.
4. You are at your partner's home. You want to use the phone.	4. You are at your partner's home. You want a glass of water.
5. You are at a restaurant. Your partner is a waiter/waitress. You want to have a cup of coffee.	5. You are at a restaurant. Your partner is a waiter/waitress. You want to have the check.

(a) ***Could you (please) open*** the door? (b) ***Would you (please) open*** the door?	(a) and (b) have the same meaning: I want you to open the door. I am asking you politely to open the door.
TYPICAL RESPONSES (c) ***Yes, of course.*** (d) ***Certainly.*** (e) ***I'd be glad to.*** (f) ***I'd be happy to.*** (g) ***Sure.*** (informal) (h) ***No problem.*** (informal)	A TYPICAL CONVERSATION A: *Could you please open the door?* B: ***I'd be glad to.*** A: *Thank you. / Thanks.*

☐ EXERCISE 18. Let's talk: pairwork.

Directions: Work with a partner to complete the conversations. Use ***Could you*** or ***Would you*** and give typical responses. Then write them down and discuss them with the rest of the class.

1. A: Excuse me, sir. _____

    B: _____

    A: _____

2. A: _____

    B: Excuse me? I didn't understand what you said.

    A: _____

    B: _____

□ **EXERCISE 19. Let's talk: pairwork.**

Directions: Work with a partner. Make and answer requests. Use **Could you** or **Would you**.

Example: You want your partner to open the window.
PARTNER A: (. . .), could you (please) open the window?
PARTNER B: Certainly.
PARTNER A: Thank you. Your turn.

1. You want your partner to close the door.
2. You want your partner to turn on the light.
3. You want your partner to turn off the light.
4. You want your partner to pass you the salt and pepper.
5. You want your partner to hand you that book.
6. You want your partner to translate a word for you.
7. You want your partner to tell you the time.
8. You want your partner to open the window.
9. You want your partner to hold your books for a minute.
10. You want your partner to lend you *(an amount of money)*.

□ **EXERCISE 20. Let's talk: pairwork.**

Directions: Work with a partner. Ask and answer polite questions that might fit each situation. Share your conversations with the rest of the class.

Example: A professor's office: Partner A is a student. Partner B is the professor.
PARTNER A: *(knock, knock)* May I come in?
PARTNER B: Certainly. Come in. How are you today?
PARTNER A: Fine, thanks.

OR

PARTNER A: Hello, Professor Alvarez. Could I talk to you for a few minutes? I have some questions about the last assignment.
PARTNER B: Of course. Have a seat.
PARTNER A: Thank you.

1. A restaurant: Partner A is a customer. Partner B is a waitress/waiter.
2. A classroom: Partner A is a teacher. Partner B is a student.
3. A kitchen: Partner A is a visitor. Partner B is at home.
4. A clothing store: Partner A is a customer. Partner B is a salesperson.
5. An apartment: Partner A and B are roommates.
6. A car: Partner A is a passenger. Partner B is the driver.
7. An office: Partner A is a boss. Partner B is an employee.
8. A house: Partner B answers the phone. Partner A wants to talk to *(someone)*.

13-6 IMPERATIVE SENTENCES

(a) *"**Close the door,** Jimmy. It's cold outside."* *"Okay, Mom."*	In (a): ***Close the door*** is an *imperative sentence.* The sentence means "Jimmy, I want you to close the door. I am telling you to close the door."
(b) ***Sit*** down. (c) ***Be*** careful!	An imperative sentence uses the simple form of a verb *(close, sit, be, etc.).*
(d) ***Don't open*** *the window.* (e) ***Don't be*** *late.*	NEGATIVE ***don't*** + *the simple form of a verb*
(f) ORDERS: ***Stop,*** thief! (g) DIRECTIONS: ***Open*** your books to page 24. (h) ADVICE: ***Don't worry.*** (i) REQUESTS: ***Please close*** the door.	Imperative sentences give orders, directions, and advice. With the addition of ***please,*** as in (i), imperative sentences are used to make polite requests.

☐ EXERCISE 21. Sentence practice.

Directions: <u>Underline</u> the imperative verbs in the conversations.

1. CINDY: We're leaving.

   BETH: <u>Wait</u> for me!

   CINDY: <u>Hurry</u> up! We'll be late.

   BETH: Okay. Okay. I'm ready. Let's go.

2. TOM: What's the matter?

   JIM: I have the hiccups.

   TOM: Hold your breath.

   BOB: Drink some water.

   JOE: Breathe into a paper bag.

   KEN: Eat a piece of bread.

   JIM: It's okay. The hiccups are gone.

3. MARY: We need to leave soon.

   IVAN: I'm ready.

   MARY: Don't forget your house key.

   IVAN: I have it.

   MARY: Okay.

4. YUKO: How do I get to the post office from here?

   ERIC: Walk two blocks to 16th Avenue. Then turn right on Forest Street. Go two more blocks to Market Street and turn left. The post office is halfway down the street on the right-hand side.

   YUKO: Thanks.

5. ANDY: Bye, Mom. I'm going over to Billy's house.

   MOM: Wait a minute. Did you clean up your room?

   ANDY: I'll do it later.

   MOM: No. Do it now, before you leave.

   ANDY: Do I have to?

   MOM: Yes.

   ANDY: What do I have to do?

   MOM: Hang up your clothes. Make your bed. Put your books back on the shelf. Empty the wastepaper basket. Okay?

   ANDY: Okay.

□ EXERCISE 22. Sentence practice.
   Directions: Write an imperative sentence in each conversation balloon.

□ **EXERCISE 23. Let's talk: class activity.**

Directions: Listen to your teacher's questions. Make some typical imperative sentences for these situations. Close your book for this activity.

Example:
TEACHER: Your friend (. . .) has a headache. What are some typical sentences for this situation?
SPEAKER A: Take an aspirin.
SPEAKER B: Lie down and close your eyes for a little while.
SPEAKER C: Put a cold cloth across your forehead.
SPEAKER D: Take a hot bath and relax.
Etc.

1. You are the teacher of this class. You are assigning homework for tomorrow. What are some typical imperative sentences for this situation?
2. Your friend (. . .) has the hiccups. What are some typical imperative sentences for this situation?
3. Your eight-year-old son/daughter is walking out the door to go to school. What are some typical imperative sentences for this situation?
4. (. . .) wants to improve his/her general health. Tell him/her what to do and what not to do.

5. (. . .) is going to cook rice for the first time this evening. Tell him/her how to cook rice.

6. (. . .) is going to visit your country for the first time next month. Tell him/her what to do and what to see as a tourist in your country.

13-7 MODAL AUXILIARIES

(a) Anita	can could may might go to class. must should will	An auxiliary is a helping verb. It comes in front of the simple form of a main verb. The following helping verbs are called "modal auxiliaries": *can, could, may, might, must, should, will, would.*
(b) Anita	is able to is going to go to class. has to	Expressions that are similar to modal auxiliaries are *be able to, be going to, have to.*

☐ **EXERCISE 24. Review: verb forms.**

Directions: Add *to* where necessary. If *to* is not necessary, write "X."

1. My sister can ___X___ play the guitar very well.

2. We have ___to___ pay our rent on the first of the month.

3. Could you please _____ open the window? Thanks.

4. I wasn't able _____ visit my friends yesterday because I was busy.

5. You shouldn't _____ drink twenty cups of coffee a day.

6. Will you _____ be at the meeting tomorrow?

7. Does everyone have _____ be at the meeting?

8. You must not _____ miss the meeting. It's important.

9. Jennifer might not _____ be there tomorrow.

10. May I _____ use your telephone?

11. We couldn't _____ go to the concert last night because we didn't have tickets.

12. Can you _____ play a musical instrument?

13. What time are you going _____ arrive?

14. It may _____ be too cold for us to go swimming tomorrow.

13-8 SUMMARY CHART: MODAL AUXILIARIES AND SIMILAR EXPRESSIONS

AUXILIARY*	MEANING	EXAMPLE
(a) *can*	ability	I *can* sing.
	polite question	*Can* you please help me?
(b) *could*	past ability	I *couldn't* go to class yesterday.
	polite question	*Could* you please help me?
(c) *may*	possibility	It *may* rain tomorrow.
	polite question	*May* I help you?
(d) *might*	possibility	It *might* rain tomorrow.
(e) *must*	necessity	You *must* have a passport.
(f) *should*	advisability	You *should* see a doctor.
(g) *will*	future happening	My sister *will* meet us at the airport.
(h) *would*	polite question	*Would* you please open the door?
(i) *be able to*	ability	I *wasn't able to* attend the meeting.
(j) *be going to*	future happening	Tina *is going to* meet us at the airport.
(k) *have to/has to*	necessity	I *have to* study tonight.
(l) *had to*	past necessity	I *had to* study last night too.

*See the following charts for more information: *can*, Chart 12-1, p. 354, and Chart 12-3, p. 357; *could*, Chart 12-5, p. 362; *may* and *might*, Chart 11-1, p. 325; *must*, Chart 13-3, p. 387; *should*, Chart 13-1, p. 379; *will*, Chart 10-6, p. 310, Chart 10-7, p. 312, and Chart 11-1, p. 325; *would*, Chart 13-5, p. 393; *be able to*, Chart 12-6, p. 365; *be going to*, Chart 10-1, p. 294; *have/has/had to*, Chart 13-2, p. 383.

☐ EXERCISE 25. Let's talk: small groups.

Directions: Work in small groups. Each person in the group should give a different response. Share a few of your answers with the class.

Example: Name something you *had to* do yesterday.
SPEAKER A: I had to go to class.
SPEAKER B: I had to go to the post office to buy some stamps.
SPEAKER C: I had to study for a test.

1. Name something you *can* do.
2. Name something you *couldn't* do yesterday.
3. Name something you *may* do tomorrow,
4. Name something you *might* do tomorrow.
5. Name something you *must* do this week.
6. Name something you *have to* do today.
7. Name something you *don't have to* do today.
8. Name something you *should* do this evening.
9. Name something you *will* do this evening.
10. Name something you *are going to* do this week.
11. Name something you *weren't able to* do when you were a child.
12. Name something you *had to* do when you were a child.
13. You want to borrow something from a classmate. Ask a polite question with *could*.
14. You want a classmate to do something for you. Ask a polite question with *would*.
15. A classmate has something that you want. Ask a polite question with *may*.
16. Name something that *may* happen in the world in the next ten years.
17. Name something that (probably) *won't* happen in the world in the next ten years.
18. Name some things that this school *should* do or *shouldn't* do to make the school a better place for students.

☐ EXERCISE 26. Sentence practice.

Directions: Circle the correct completions.

1. Tom _____ every day.
   (A.) shaves   B. is shaving   C. has to shaves

2. _____ go to class every day?
   A. Are you   B. Do you have   C. Do you

3. Yoko _____ to be here tomorrow.
   A. will   B. may   C. is going

4. Jack _____ be in class yesterday.
   A. didn't   B. can't   C. couldn't

5. Fatima _____ to her sister on the phone yesterday.
   A. spoke   B. can speak   C. speaks

6. I _____ my rent last month.
   A. might pay   B. will pay   C. paid

7. Shh. Ken _____ on the phone right now.
   A. talks   B. can talk   C. is talking

8. I want to go to a movie tonight, but I _____ home and study.
   A. should stay   B. stayed   C. stay

9. We _____ to the zoo tomorrow.
   A. will going   B. might go   C. will can go

10. I _____ in class right now.
    A. sit   B. am sitting   C. sitting

☐ EXERCISE 27. Listening.

Directions: Listen to each sentence. Circle the letter of the sentence that is closest in meaning.

1. a. It will snow.
   b. It may snow.
   c. It must snow.

2. a. He should work.
   b. He must work.
   c. He might work.

3. a. She can swim.
   b. She may swim.
   c. She will swim.

4. a. The teacher should correct papers.
   b. The teacher had to correct papers.
   c. The teacher wanted to correct papers.

5. a. You may study for the test.
   b. You must study for the test.
   c. You should study for the test.

6. a. We should go to a movie.
   b. It's possible we will go to a movie.
   c. We have to go to a movie.

7. a. We couldn't help.

    b. We didn't need to help.

    c. We weren't able to help.

8. a. I didn't want to go to school.

    b. I didn't have to go to school.

    c. I wasn't able to go to school.

13-9 USING *LET'S*

(a) Bob: What should we do tonight?
     Ann: **Let's go to a movie.**
     Bob: Okay.
(b) Sue: I'm tired.
     Ted: I'm tired too. **Let's take a break.**
     Sue: That's a good idea!
	Let's (do something) = I have a suggestion for you and me. (let's = let us)
	In (a): *Let's go to a movie. = I think we should go to a movie. Do you want to go to a movie?*

☐ **EXERCISE 28. Sentence practice.**

Directions: Complete the conversations with **let's**. Use the words in the list or your own words.

eat	*go to a seafood restaurant*
get a cup of coffee	*go to the zoo*
go dancing	✓*leave at six-thirty*
go to Florida	*walk*
go to a movie	

1. A: What time should we leave for the airport?

    B: *Let's leave at six-thirty.*
    A: Okay.

2. A: Where should we go for our vacation?

    B: _____
    A: That's a good idea.

3. A: Where do you want to go for dinner tonight?

    B: _____

4. A: The weather is beautiful today. _____

   B: Okay. Great!

5. A: I'm bored. _____

   B: I can't. I have to study.

6. A: Should we take the bus downtown or walk downtown?

   B: It's a nice day. _____

7. A: Dinner's ready! The food's on the table!

   B: Great! _____. I'm starving!

8. A: Where should we go Saturday night?

   B: _____

   A: Wonderful idea!

9. A: We have an hour between classes. _____

   B: Okay. That sounds good.

☐ EXERCISE 29. Let's talk: pairwork.
    Directions: Work with a partner. Practice using *let's*.
    Partner A: Read your sentence aloud. You can look at your book before you speak.
                When you speak, look at your partner. Your book is open.
    Partner B: Use *let's* in your response. Your book is closed.
    Partner A: Respond to Partner B's suggestion.

    Example: It's a beautiful day today. What should we do?
    PARTNER A *(book open):* It's a beautiful day today. What should we do?
    PARTNER B *(book closed):* Let's go to Woodland Park Zoo.
    PARTNER A *(book open):* Great! What a good idea! Let's go!

    1. What time should we go out to dinner tonight?
    2. When should we go to *(name of a place)*?
    3. What should we do this evening?
    4. I want to do something fun tomorrow.

    Switch roles.
    Partner A: Close your book.
    Partner B: Open your book. Your turn now.

    5. What should we do tomorrow? It's a holiday, and we don't have to go to class.
    6. I'm bored. Think of something we can do.

7. My plane leaves at six. What time should we leave for the airport?

8. It's *(name of a classmate)*'s birthday tomorrow. Should we do something special for him/her?

□ **EXERCISE 30. Review: Chapters 12 and 13.**
  Directions: Correct the errors.

1. Would you please to help me?

2. I will can go to the meeting tomorrow.

3. My brother wasn't able calling me last night.

4. Ken should writes us a letter.

5. I have to went to the store yesterday.

6. Susie! You must not to play with matches!

7. May you please hand me that book?

8. Ann couldn't answered my question.

9. Shelley can't goes to the concert tomorrow.

10. Let's going to a movie tonight.

11. Don't to interrupt. It's not polite.

12. Can you to stand on your head?

13. I saw a beautiful dress at a store yesterday, but I couldn't bought it.

14. Closing the door please. Thank you.

15. May I please to borrow your dictionary? Thank you.

CHAPTER 14
Nouns and Modifiers

☐ **EXERCISE 1. Noun and adjective practice.**

Directions: How are the given words usually used? Circle NOUN or ADJ (adjective). Then use each word in a sentence.

1. busy   NOUN   (ADJ)   →   *I'm very busy right now.*
2. computer   (NOUN)   ADJ   →   *Computers are machines.*
3. tall   NOUN   ADJ   8. monkey   NOUN   ADJ
4. apartment   NOUN   ADJ   9. young   NOUN   ADJ
5. Tom   NOUN   ADJ   10. music   NOUN   ADJ
6. hand   NOUN   ADJ   11. expensive   NOUN   ADJ
7. good   NOUN   ADJ   12. grammar   NOUN   ADJ

14-1 MODIFYING NOUNS WITH ADJECTIVES AND NOUNS

ADJECTIVE + NOUN (a) I bought an ***expensive*** book.	Adjectives can modify nouns, as in (a). See Chart 6-2, p. 161, for a list of common adjectives.
NOUN + NOUN (b) I bought a ***grammar*** book.	Nouns can modify other nouns. In (b): *grammar* is a noun that is used as an adjective to modify another noun *(book)*.
NOUN + NOUN (c) He works at a ***shoe*** store. INCORRECT: *He works at a shoes store.*	A noun that is used as an adjective is always in its singular form. In (c): the store sells shoes, but it is called a *shoe* (singular form) *store*.
ADJECTIVE + NOUN + NOUN (d) I bought an ***expensive*** ***grammar*** book. INCORRECT: *I bought a grammar expensive book.*	Both an adjective and a noun can modify a noun; the adjective comes first, the noun second.

☐ **EXERCISE 2. Sentence practice.**

Directions: <u>Underline</u> the adjectives and identify the nouns they modify.

1. I drank some <u>hot</u> tea.

2. My grandmother is a wise woman.

3. English is not my native language.

4. The busy waitress poured coffee into the empty cup.

5. A young man carried the heavy suitcase for Fumiko.

6. I sat in an uncomfortable chair at the restaurant.

7. There is international news on the front page of the newspaper.

8. My uncle is a wonderful man.

☐ **EXERCISE 3. Sentence practice.**

Directions: <u>Underline</u> the nouns used as adjectives and identify the nouns they modify.

1. We sat at the <u>kitchen</u> table.

2. I bought some new CDs at the music store.

3. We met Jack at the train station.

4. Vegetable soup is nutritious.

5. The movie theater is next to the furniture store.

6. The waiter handed us a lunch menu.

7. The traffic light was red, so we stopped.

8. Ms. Bell gave me her business card.

☐ **EXERCISE 4. Listening.**

Directions: Listen to the sentences. Decide if the given word is used as a noun or adjective. Circle your choice.

1. kitchen	NOUN	ADJ	6. car	NOUN	ADJ
2. kitchen	NOUN	ADJ	7. car	NOUN	ADJ
3. apartment	NOUN	ADJ	8. chicken	NOUN	ADJ
4. apartment	NOUN	ADJ	9. chicken	NOUN	ADJ
5. music	NOUN	ADJ	10. grammar	NOUN	ADJ

□ **EXERCISE 5. Sentence practice.**

Directions: Complete the sentences. Use the information in the first part of the sentence. Use a noun that modifies another noun in the completion.

1. Vases that are used for flowers are called ____*flower vases.*____

2. A cup that is used for coffee is called ____*a coffee cup.*____

3. A story that appears in a newspaper is called _____

4. Rooms in hotels are called _____

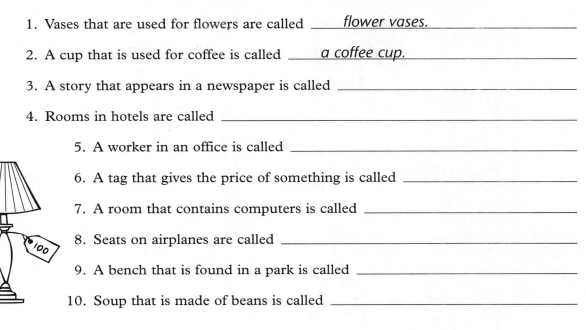

5. A worker in an office is called _____

6. A tag that gives the price of something is called _____

7. A room that contains computers is called _____

8. Seats on airplanes are called _____

9. A bench that is found in a park is called _____

10. Soup that is made of beans is called _____

□ **EXERCISE 6. Let's talk: small groups.**

Directions: Work in small groups. Which noun in the list can be used with all three of the nouns used as modifiers? For example, in the first sentence below, the completion can be *a university education, a high school education,* and *a college education.*

class	official	soup
✓education	program	store
keys	race	tickets
number	room	trip

1. Jane has a $\left\{\begin{array}{l}\text{university}\\\text{high school}\\\text{college}\end{array}\right\}$ ____*education.*____

2. We went to a $\left\{\begin{array}{l}\text{furniture}\\\text{shoe}\\\text{clothing}\end{array}\right\}$ _____

3. I took a $\left\{\begin{array}{l}\text{history}\\\text{math}\\\text{science}\end{array}\right\}$ _____

4. We watched a
$$\begin{cases} \text{horse} \\ \text{car} \\ \text{foot} \end{cases}$$
_____

5. I talked to a
$$\begin{cases} \text{government} \\ \text{city} \\ \text{school} \end{cases}$$
_____

6. Mom made some
$$\begin{cases} \text{vegetable} \\ \text{bean} \\ \text{chicken} \end{cases}$$
_____

7. He told me about a
$$\begin{cases} \text{radio} \\ \text{television} \\ \text{computer} \end{cases}$$
_____

8. We took a/an
$$\begin{cases} \text{boat} \\ \text{bus} \\ \text{airplane} \end{cases}$$
_____

9. I couldn't find my
$$\begin{cases} \text{car} \\ \text{house} \\ \text{door} \end{cases}$$
_____

10. We bought some
$$\begin{cases} \text{theater} \\ \text{concert} \\ \text{airplane} \end{cases}$$
_____

11. We visited Sue in her
$$\begin{cases} \text{hospital} \\ \text{hotel} \\ \text{dormitory} \end{cases}$$
_____

12. What is your
$$\begin{cases} \text{telephone} \\ \text{apartment} \\ \text{license plate} \end{cases}$$
_____

Directions: Each item lists two nouns and one adjective. Write them in the correct order.

1. *homework*   The teacher gave us a _____ *long homework assignment.* _____
   long
   assignment

2. *program*   I watched a _____
   good
   television

3. *road*   We drove on a _____
   mountain
   dangerous

4. *automobile*   Janet was in a _____
   bad
   accident

5. *article*   I read an _____
   magazine
   interesting

6. *delicious*   Mrs. Green made some _____
   vegetable
   soup

7. *card*   My sister gave me a _____
   funny
   birthday

8. *narrow*   People don't like to sit in _____
   seats
   airplane

(a) a **large red** car INCORRECT: *a red large car*	In (a): two adjectives *(large* and *red)* modify a noun *(car).* Adjectives follow a particular order. In (a): an adjective describing **size** *(large)* comes before **color** *(red).*
(b) a **beautiful young** woman (c) a **beautiful red** car (d) a **beautiful Greek** island	The adjective *beautiful* expresses an opinion. Opinion adjectives usually come before all other adjectives. In (b): opinion precedes age. In (c): opinion precedes color. In (d): opinion precedes nationality.
(e) OPINION ADJECTIVES *dangerous favorite important* *difficult good interesting* *dirty happy strong* *expensive honest wonderful*	There are many opinion adjectives. The words in (e) are examples of common opinion adjectives.

USUAL WORD ORDER OF ADJECTIVES

(1) **OPINION**	(2) **SIZE**	(3) **AGE**	(4) **COLOR**	(5) **NATIONALITY***	(6) **MATERIAL**
beautiful	*large*	*young*	*red*	*Greek*	*metal*
delicious	*tall*	*old*	*blue*	*Chinese*	*glass*
kind	*little*	*middle-aged*	*black*	*Mexican*	*plastic*

(f) some **delicious Mexican** food (g) a **small glass** vase (h) a **kind old Chinese** man	A noun is usually modified by only one or two adjectives, although sometimes there are three.
(i) RARE *a beautiful small old brown Greek metal coin*	It is very rare to find a long list of adjectives in front of a noun.

*NOTE: Adjectives that describe nationality are capitalized: **K**orean, **V**enezuelan, **S**audi **A**rabian, etc.

☐ EXERCISE 8. Adjective practice.

    Directions: Put the *italicized* words in the correct order.

    1. *glass*   a _____*tall glass*_____ vase
       tall

    2. *delicious*   some _____ food
       Thai

    3. *red*   some _____ tomatoes
       small

4. *old*
   big
   brown

   some _____ cows

5. *narrow*
   dirt

   a _____ road

6. *young*
   serious

   a _____ woman

7. *long*
   black
   beautiful

   _____ hair

8. *Chinese*
   famous
   old

   a/an _____ work of art

9. *leather*
   brown
   thin

   a _____ belt

10. *wonderful*
    old
    Native American

    a/an _____ story

☐ EXERCISE 9. Sentence practice.

Directions: Complete the sentences with words from the list.

Asian	✓*cotton*	*polite*
brick	*important*	*soft*
Canadian	*leather*	*unhappy*
coffee		

1. Jack is wearing a white _____*cotton*_____ shirt.

2. Hong Kong is an important _____ city.

3. I'm wearing some comfortable old _____ shoes.

4. Tommy was a/an _____ little boy when he broke his favorite toy.

5. Ann has a/an _____ wool blanket on her bed.

6. Our dorm is a tall red _____ building.

7. The computer is a/an _____ modern invention.

8. My nephew has good manners. He is always a/an _____ young

man, especially to his elders.

9. Jack always carries a large blue _____ cup with him.

10. Ice hockey is a popular _____ sport.

□ **EXERCISE 10. Sentence practice.**

Directions: Add adjectives or nouns used as adjectives to complete the sentences. Share some of your answers with the class.

1. We had some hot _____ food.

2. My dog, Rover, is a/an _____ old dog.

3. We bought a blue _____ blanket.

4. Alice has _____ gold earrings.

5. Tom has short _____ hair.

6. Mr. Lee is a/an _____ young man.

7. Jack lives in a large _____ brick house.

8. I bought a big _____ suitcase.

9. Sally picked a/an _____ red flower.

10. Ali wore an old _____ shirt to the picnic.

Directions: Many, but not all, of the sentences contain mistakes in the word order of modifiers. Correct the mistakes. Make changes in the use of **a** and **an** as necessary.

                              an old wood

1. Ms. Lane has ~~a wood old~~ desk in her office.

2. She put the flowers in a blue glass vase. *(no change)*

3. The Great Wall is a Chinese landmark famous.

4. Ken is a man young honest.

5. I read a newspaper article interesting this morning.

6. Spiro gave me a wonderful small black Greek box as a birthday present.

7. Alice reached down and put her hand in the mountain cold stream.

8. Pizza is my favorite food Italian.

9. There was a beautiful flower arrangement on the kitchen table.

10. Jack usually wears brown old comfortable shoes leather.

11. Gnats are black tiny insects.

12. I used a box brown cardboard to mail a gift to my sister.

13. Tony has a noisy electric fan in his bedroom window.

14. James is a middle-aged handsome man with brown short hair.

15. When Jane was on her last business trip, she had a cheap rental car, but she stayed in a room expensive hotel.

☐ **EXERCISE 12. Let's talk: pairwork.**

    Directions: Work with a partner. Practice modifying nouns.

    Partner A: Say the words in each item. Don't let your intonation drop because Student B is going to finish the phrase. Your book is open.

    Partner B: Complete Student A's phrase with a noun. Your book is closed. Respond as quickly as you can with the first noun that comes to mind.

    Share a few of your answers with the class.

Example: a dark . . .
PARTNER A *(book open):* a dark
PARTNER B *(book closed):* night (room, building, day, cloud, etc.)

Example: some ripe . . .
PARTNER A *(book open):* some ripe
PARTNER B *(book closed):* soup
PARTNER A *(book open):* Some ripe soup? I don't think we use "ripe" with "soup."
PARTNER B *(book closed):* Okay. How about "some ripe fruit" OR "some ripe bananas"?
PARTNER A *(book open):* That's good. Some ripe fruit or some ripe bananas.

1. a kitchen . . .
2. a busy . . .
3. a public . . .
4. a true . . .
5. some expensive . . .
6. an interesting old . . .
7. an airplane . . .
8. a dangerous . . .
9. a beautiful Korean . . .
10. some delicious Mexican . . .

11. a birthday . . .
12. a computer . . .
13. a baby . . .
14. a soft . . .
15. an easy . . .
16. a government . . .
17. some hot . . .
18. a flower . . .
19. a bright . . .
20. some small round . . .

Switch roles.
Partner A: Close your book.
Partner B: Open your book. Your turn now.

21. a telephone . . .
22. a fast . . .
23. some comfortable . . .
24. a foreign . . .
25. a famous Italian . . .
26. a bus . . .
27. a history . . .
28. a rubber bicycle . . .
29. a hospital . . .
30. a movie . . .

31. some great old . . .
32. a television . . .
33. a very deep . . .
34. an office . . .
35. a gray wool . . .
36. an afternoon . . .
37. an empty . . .
38. a wonderful South American . . .
39. a bedroom . . .
40. a science . . .

☐ **EXERCISE 13. Listening.**

👂 *Directions:* Listen to each sentence. Circle the best completion(s). There may be more than one answer.

Example: We watched an interesting TV . . . . store (movie) (show)

1. card   cake   party

2. friend   bus   keys

3. jeans   shoes   flowers

4. test   classroom   eraser

5. room   games   desk

6. mail   article   story

14-3 EXPRESSIONS OF QUANTITY: *ALL OF, MOST OF, SOME OF, ALMOST ALL OF*

(a) Rita ate **all of** *the food* on her plate. (b) Mike ate **most of** *his food.* (c) Susie ate **some of** *her food.*	**All of, most of,** and **some of** express quantities. *all of* = 100% *most of* = a large part, but not all *some of* = a small or medium part
(d) Matt ate **almost all of** *his food.* *INCORRECT:* Matt ate almost of his food.	*all of* = 100% *almost all of* = 95%–99% **Almost** is used with **all; all** cannot be omitted.

□ EXERCISE 14. **Sentence practice.**

Directions: Complete the sentences with *(almost)* **all of**, **most of**, or **some of**.

1. 2, 4, 6, 8: _____*All of*_____ these numbers are even.

2. 1, 3, 5, 7: _____ these numbers are odd.

3. 1, 3, 4, 6, 7, 9: _____ these numbers are odd.

4. 1, 3, 4, 6, 7, 8: _____ these numbers are odd.

5. 1, 3, 4, 5, 7, 9: _____ these numbers are odd.

6. _____ the birds in Picture A are flying.

7. _____ the birds in Picture B are flying.

8. _____ the birds in Picture C are flying.

9. _____ the birds in Picture D are flying.

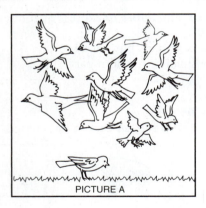

PICTURE A

PICTURE B

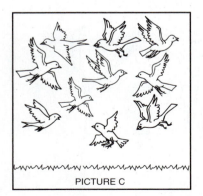

PICTURE C

PICTURE D

10. _____ the students in this class have dark hair.

11. _____ the students in this class are using pens rather than

pencils to do this exercise.

12. _____ the students in this class wear glasses.

13. _____ the students in this class can speak English.

14-4 EXPRESSIONS OF QUANTITY: SUBJECT–VERB AGREEMENT

(a) *All of my **work is** finished.*	In (a): *all of* + **singular** noun + **singular** verb.
(b) *All of my **friends are** kind.*	In (b): *all of* + **plural** noun + **plural** verb.
(c) *Some of my **homework is** finished.*	In (c): *some of* + **singular** noun + **singular** verb.
(d) *Some of my **friends are** coming to my* *birthday party.*	In (d): *some of* + **plural** noun + **plural** verb.
	When a subject includes an expression of quantity, the verb agrees with the noun that immediately follows *of*.

COMMON EXPRESSIONS OF QUANTITY		
all of	*a lot of*	*most of*
almost all of	*half of*	*some of*

□ EXERCISE 15. Sentence practice.

Directions: Choose the correct completions.

1. All of that money _____*is*_____ mine.

(is / are)

2. All of the windows _____ open.

(is / are)

3. We saw one movie. Some of the movie _____ interesting.

(was / were)

4. We saw five movies. Some of the movies _____ interesting.

(was / were)

5. A lot of those words _____ new to me.

(is / are)

6. A lot of that vocabulary _____ new to me.

(is / are)

7. Half of the glasses _____ empty, and half of the glasses _____ full.
   <u>(is / are)</u>   <u>(is / are)</u>

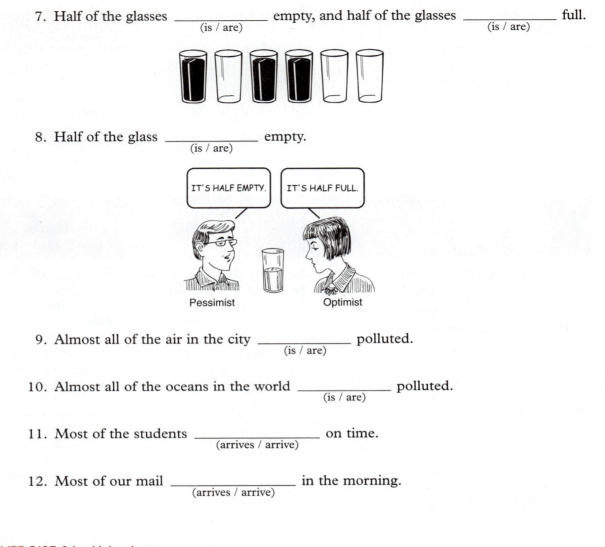

8. Half of the glass _____ empty.
   <u>(is / are)</u>

IT'S HALF EMPTY.   IT'S HALF FULL.

Pessimist   Optimist

9. Almost all of the air in the city _____ polluted.
   <u>(is / are)</u>

10. Almost all of the oceans in the world _____ polluted.
    <u>(is / are)</u>

11. Most of the students _____ on time.
    <u>(arrives / arrive)</u>

12. Most of our mail _____ in the morning.
    <u>(arrives / arrive)</u>

□ EXERCISE 16. Listening.

Directions: Listen to each sentence. Circle the percentage that means the same as the quantity you hear.

Example: Half of the class was late.   100% (50%) 10%

1.	100%	80%	10%
2.	100%	30%	0%
3.	80%	50%	25%
4.	90%	100%	10%
5.	10%	20%	70%
6.	25%	50%	85%

14-5 EXPRESSIONS OF QUANTITY: *ONE OF, NONE OF*

ONE OF + PLURAL NOUN (a) Sam is **one of** my **friends**. INCORRECT: Sam is one of my friend.	**One of** is followed by a specific **plural noun**, as in (a). It is INCORRECT to follow **one of** with a singular noun.
ONE OF + PL. NOUN + SING. VERB (b) **One of** my **friends** **is** here. INCORRECT: One of my friends are here.	When **one of** + *a plural noun* is the subject of a sentence, it is followed by a **singular verb**, as in (b): ONE OF + PLURAL NOUN + SINGULAR VERB.
(c) **None of** the students **was** late. (d) **None of** the students **were** late.	In (d): Not one of the students was late. **none of** = **not one of** The verb following **none of** + *a plural noun* can be singular, as in (c), or plural, as in (d). Both are correct.*

* In very formal English, a singular verb is used after **none of** + *a plural noun: None of the students*
was late. In everyday English, both singular and plural verbs are used.

☐ **EXERCISE 17. Sentence practice.**
    Directions: Make sentences from the given words and phrases.

1. one of my \ teacher \ be \ *(name of a teacher)*

      One of my teachers is Ms. Lopez.

2. *(name of a student)* \ be \ one of my \ classmate

    _____

3. one of my \ book \ be \ red

    _____

4. one of my \ book \ have \ a green cover

    _____

5. *(name of a place)* \ be \ one of my favorite \ place \ in the world

    _____

6. one of the \ student \ in my class \ always come \ late

    _____

7. *(name of a person)* \ be \ one of my best \ friend

    _____

8. one of my \ friend \ live \ in *(name of a place)*

_____

9. *(title of a TV program)* \ be \ one of the best \ program \ on TV

_____

10. *(name of a person)* \ be \ one of the most famous \ people* \ in the world

_____

11. one of my biggest \ problem \ be \ my inability to understand spoken English

_____

12. *(name of a newspaper)* \ be \ one of the \ leading newspaper \ in *(name of a city)*

_____

13. none of the \ student \ in my class \ speak \ *(name of a language)*

_____

14. none of the \ furniture \ in this room \ be \ soft and comfortable

_____

☐ EXERCISE 18. Let's talk.

Directions: Work alone to complete the sentences with your own words. Then take turns sharing your sentences with a small group or with the class.

1. One of my favorite _____ is _____ .

2. _____ is one of the most interesting _____ in the world.

3. One of the _____ in my _____ is _____ .

4. _____ is one of my best _____ .

5. One of _____ .

6. None of _____ .

_____

* *People* is a plural noun even though it does not have a final **-s**.

□ EXERCISE 19. Sentence practice.

Directions: Choose the correct verbs.

1. My grammar book _____*is*_____ red.
   (is / are)

2. Some of my books _____ on my desk.
   (is / are)

3. One of my books _____ blue and green.
   (is / are)

4. My favorite colors _____ red and yellow.
   (is / are)

5. Sue's favorite color _____ green.
   (is / are)

6. One of my favorite colors _____ red.
   (is / are)

7. Some of the students in my class _____ lap-top computers.
   (has / have)

8. One of the students in Pablo's class _____ a mustache.
   (has / have)

9. My best friends _____ in Brazil.
   (lives / live)

10. One of my best friends _____ in Australia.
    (lives / live)

11. None of these letters _____ for you.
    (is / are)

12. None of this mail _____ for you.
    (is / are)

BRAZIL

□ EXERCISE 20. Sentence practice.

Directions: Complete the sentences with **is** or **are**.

1. Some of the children's toys _____*are*_____ broken.

2. Most of my classmates _____ always on time for class.

3. One of my classmates _____ always late.

4. All of my friends _____ kind people.

5. One of my friends _____ Sam Brown.

6. Most of the rivers in the world _____ polluted.

7. Some of the Pacific Ocean _____ badly polluted.

8. Most of this page _____ white.

9. Most of the pages in this book _____ full of grammar exercises.

10. One of the pages in this book _____ the title page.

☐ EXERCISE 21. Listening.

Directions: Complete the sentences with the words you hear.

1. _____ is hard.

2. _____ is missing.

3. _____ are here yet.

4. _____ were late.

5. _____ is absent.

6. _____ was vegetarian.

7. _____ were helpful.

8. _____ was scary.

☐ EXERCISE 22. Listening review.

Directions: Look at the pictures as you listen to each sentence. Circle the correct answer.

Example: None of the people are mad.   yes   (no)

1. yes   no   3. yes   no   5. yes   no   7. yes   no

2. yes   no   4. yes   no   6. yes   no   8. yes   no

□ EXERCISE 23. Let's talk: class activity.

Directions: Your teacher will ask you questions. Answer them using complete sentences. Use any expression of quantity (*all of, most of, some of, a lot of, one of, three of,* etc.). Close your book for this activity.

Examples:
TEACHER: How many of the people in this room are wearing shoes?
STUDENT: All of the people in this room are wearing shoes.

TEACHER: How many of us are wearing blue jeans?
STUDENT: Some of us are wearing blue jeans.

1. How many people in this room have (short) hair?
2. How many of the students in this class have red grammar books?
3. How many of us are sitting down?
4. How many of your classmates are from *(name of a country)*?
5. How many of the people in this room can speak (English)?
6. How many of the women in this room are wearing earrings? How many of the men?
7. What is one of your favorite TV programs?
8. How many of the people in this city are friendly?
9. Who is one of the most famous people in the world?
10. How many of the married women in your country work outside the home?

14-6 INDEFINITE PRONOUNS: *NOTHING* AND *NO ONE*

(a) I ***didn't say anything.*** (b) I ***said nothing.*** INCORRECT: *I didn't say nothing.*	(a) and (b) have the same meaning. *Anything* is used when the verb is negative. *Nothing* is used when the verb is affirmative.
(c) Bob ***didn't see anyone*** at the park. (d) Bob ***saw no one*** at the park. INCORRECT: *Bob didn't see no one at the park.*	(c) and (d) have the same meaning. *Anyone* is used when the verb is negative. *No one* is used when the verb is affirmative.

□ EXERCISE 24. Sentence practice.

Directions: Complete the sentences. Use ***anything, nothing, anyone,*** or ***no one.***

1. Jim doesn't know _____ about butterflies.

2. Jim knows _____ about butterflies.

3. Jean didn't tell _____ about her problem.

4. Jean told _____ about her problem.

5. There's _____ in my pocket. It's empty.

6. There isn't _____ in my pocket.

7. Liz went to a shoe store, but she didn't buy _____.

8. Liz bought _____ at the shoe store.

9. I got _____ in the mail today. My mailbox was empty.

10. George sat quietly in the corner. He didn't speak to _____.

11. The office is closed from 12:00 to 1:00. _____ is there during the lunch hour.

12. I know _____ about nuclear physics.

13. _____ was at home last night. Both my roommate and I were out.

14. Joan has a new apartment. She doesn't know _____ in her apartment building yet.

15. A: Do you know _____ about Iowa?

    B: Iowa? I know _____ about Iowa.

    A: It's an agricultural state that is located between the Mississippi and Missouri rivers.

14-7 INDEFINITE PRONOUNS: *SOMETHING, SOMEONE, ANYTHING, ANYONE*

STATEMENT	(a) Mary bought *something* at the store. (b) Jim talked to *someone* after class.	In a statement, use *something* or *someone*.
NEGATIVE	(c) Mary didn't buy *anything* at the store. (d) Jim didn't talk to *anyone* after class.	In a negative sentence, use *anything* or *anyone*.
QUESTION	(e) Did Mary buy *something* at the store? Did Mary buy *anything* at the store? (f) Did Jim talk to *someone* after class? Did Jim talk to *anyone* after class?	In a question, use either *something/someone* or *anything/anyone*.

☐ EXERCISE 25. Sentence practice.

Directions: Complete the sentences. Use ***something***, ***someone***, ***anything***, or ***anyone***.★

1. I have _____*something*_____ in my pocket.

2. Do you have _____ in your pocket?

3. Ken doesn't have _____ in his pocket.

4. I bought _____ when I went shopping yesterday.

5. Rosa didn't buy _____ when she went shopping.

6. Did you buy _____ when you went shopping?

7. My roommate is speaking to _____ on the phone.

8. Yuko didn't tell _____ her secret.

9. I talked to _____ at the phone company about my bill.

10. Did you talk to _____ about your problem?

11. Kim gave me _____ for my birthday.

12. Paul didn't give me _____ for my birthday.

13. Did Paul give you _____ for your birthday?

14. My brother is sitting at his desk. He's writing an e-mail to _____.

15. The hall is empty. I don't see _____.

16. A: Listen. Do you hear a noise?

    B: No, I don't. I don't hear _____.

17. A: Did you talk to Jim on the phone last night?

    B: No. I didn't talk to _____.

18. A: Where's your bicycle?

    B: _____ stole it.

_____

★ *Someone* and *somebody* have the same meaning. *Anyone* and *anybody* have the same meaning.

19. A: Does _____ have some change? I need to use the pay

      phone.

   B: Here.

   A: Thanks. I'll pay you back later.

20. A: What did you do last weekend?

   B: I didn't do _____. I stayed home.

14-8 USING *EVERY*

(a) ***Every student*** has a book. (b) *All of the students* have books.	(a) and (b) have essentially the same meaning. In (a): *every* + **singular** noun + **singular** verb.
INCORRECT: *Every of the students has a book.* INCORRECT: *Every students have books.*	***Every*** is not immediately followed by *of*. ***Every*** is immediately followed by a **singular** noun, NOT a plural noun.
(c) ***Everyone*** **has** a book. (d) ***Everybody*** **has** a book.	(c) and (d) have the same meaning. ***Everyone*** and ***everybody*** are followed by a **singular** verb.
(e) I looked at ***everything*** in the museum. (f) ***Everything*** **is** okay.	In (e): ***everything*** = each thing In (f): ***Everything*** is followed by a **singular** verb.

☐ EXERCISE 26. Sentence practice.

   Directions: Choose the correct completions.

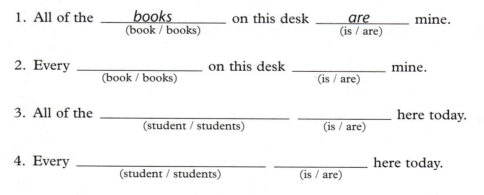

   1. All of the _____*books*_____ on this desk _____*are*_____ mine.
                    (book / books)   (is / are)

   2. Every _____ on this desk _____ mine.
             (book / books)   (is / are)

   3. All of the _____ _____ here today.
                  (student / students)   (is / are)

   4. Every _____ _____ here today.
             (student / students)   (is / are)

5. Every _____ at my college _____ tests regularly.
             (teacher / teachers)   (gives / give)

6. All of the _____ at my college _____ a lot of tests.
              (teacher / teachers)   (gives / give)

7. Every _____ in my country _____ bedtime stories.
            (child / children)   (likes / like)

8. All of the _____ in my country _____ that story.
            (child / children)   (knows / know)

9. All of the _____ in this class _____ studying English.
            (person / people)   (is / are)

10. Everyone in this class _____ to learn English.
                      (wants / want)

11. _____ all of the _____ in this class speak English well?
    (Does / Do)   (student / students)

12. _____ every _____ in the world like to listen to music?
    (Does / Do)   (person / people)

13. _____ all of the _____ in the world enjoy dancing?
    (Does / Do)   (person / people)

14. _____ everybody in the world have enough to eat?
    (Does / Do)

15. Every _____ in Sweden _____ a good transportation system.
           (city / cities)   (has / have)

16. One of the _____ in my class _____ from Iceland.
          (student / students)   (is / are)

☐ EXERCISE 27. Review: error analysis.
   Directions: Correct the errors.

  1. I work hard every days.

  2. I live in an apartment with one of my friend.

  3. We saw a pretty flowers garden in the park.

  4. Almost of the students are in class today.

5. Every people in my class are studying English.

6. All of the cities big in North America has traffic problems.

7. One of my cars are dark green.

8. Nadia drives a blue small car.

9. Istanbul is one of my favorite city in the world.

10. Every of students in the class have a grammar book.

11. The work will take a long time. We can't finish every things today.

12. Everybody in the world want peace.

14-9 LINKING VERBS + ADJECTIVES

BE + ADJECTIVE (a) The flowers ***were beautiful.***	Adjectives can follow ***be,*** as in (a). The adjective describes the subject of the sentence. See Chart 1-6, p. 12.
LINKING VERB + ADJECTIVE (b) The flowers ***looked beautiful.*** (c) The flowers ***smelled good.*** (d) I ***feel good.*** (e) Candy ***tastes sweet.*** (f) That book ***sounds interesting.***	Adjectives can follow a few other verbs. These verbs are called "linking verbs." The adjective describes the subject of the sentence. Common linking verbs are *look, smell, feel, taste,* and *sound.*

☐ EXERCISE 28. Let's talk: pairwork.

Directions: Work with a partner to practice using linking verbs. Take turns completing the sentences.

PART I. Describe how you feel today. Begin your sentence with ***I feel*** . . . .

1. good		7. lazy
2. fine		8. nervous
3. terrible		9. happy
4. terrific		10. calm
5. sleepy		11. sick
6. tired		12. old

PART II. Name things that . . . .

13. taste good   17. taste sour

14. taste terrible   18. smell good

15. taste delicious   19. smell bad

16. taste sweet   20. smell wonderful

PART III. Name something in this room that looks . . . .

21. clean   25. expensive

22. dirty   26. comfortable

23. new   27. messy

24. old   28. familiar

☐ **EXERCISE 29. Let's talk.**

Directions: Work in groups or as a class. Take turns showing and describing emotions.

Speaker A: Choose one of the emotions listed below. Show that emotion through the expression on your face and through your actions. Don't tell anyone which emotion you're trying to show.

Speaker B: Describe how Speaker A looks. Use the linking verb *look* and an adjective.

1. angry   5. busy

2. sad/unhappy   6. comfortable

3. happy   7. surprised

4. tired/sleepy   8. nervous

☐ **EXERCISE 30. Sentence practice.**

Directions: Use any possible completions for these sentences. Use the words in the list or your own words.

easy	*good / terrific / wonderful / great*	*interesting*
hard / difficult	*terrible / awful*	*tired /sleepy*

1. Rosa told me about a new book. I want to read it. It sounds

        interesting / good / terrific   .

2. Karen learned how to make paper flowers. She told me how to do it. It sounds

   _____.

3. There's a new play at the community theater. I read a review of it in the

   newspaper. I'd like to see it. It sounds _____.

4. Professor Wilson is going to lecture on the problems of overpopulation tomorrow evening. I think I'll go. It sounds _____.

5. Chris explained how to fix a flat tire. I think I can do it. It sounds

_____.

6. Shelley didn't finish her dinner because it didn't taste _____.

7. What's for dinner? Something smells _____. Ummm! What is it?

8. Amy didn't get any sleep last night because she studied all night for a test. Today she looks _____.

9. Ymmmm! This dessert tastes _____. What is it?

10. A: What's the matter? Do you feel okay?

   B: No. I feel _____. I think I'm getting a cold.

11. A: Do you like my new dress, darling?

   B: You look _____, honey.

12. A: Pyew!* Something smells _____! Do you smell it too?

   B: I sure do. It's the garbage in the alley.

□ EXERCISE 31. Let's talk.

Directions: Work in pairs or small groups. In a given time limit (e.g., fifteen seconds, thirty seconds, a minute), think of as many adjectives or nouns used as adjectives as you can that describe the given nouns. Make a list.

Example: car
Response: big, little, fast, slow, comfortable, small, large, old, new, used, noisy, quiet, foreign, electric, antique, police, etc.

1. weather   5. country
2. animal   6. person
3. food   7. river
4. movie   8. student

_____

* *Pyew* is sometimes said "p.u." Both *Pyew* and *p.u.* mean that something smells very bad.

14-10 ADJECTIVES AND ADVERBS

		ADJECTIVE	ADVERB	
(a)	Ann is a *careful* driver. (adjective) (b) Ann drives *carefully*. (adverb)	*careful* *slow* *quick* *easy*	*carefully* *slowly* *quickly* *easily*	An *adjective* describes a noun. In (a): *careful* describes *driver*. An *adverb* describes the action of a verb. In (b): *carefully* describes *drives*. Most adverbs are formed by adding *-ly* to an adjective.
(c)	John is a *fast* driver. (adjective) (d) John drives *fast*. (adverb)	*fast* *hard* *early* *late*	*fast* *hard* *early* *late*	The adjective form and the adverb form are the same for *fast, hard, early, late*.
(e)	Linda is a *good* writer. (adjective) (f) Linda writes *well*. (adverb)	*good*	*well*	*Well* is the adverb form of *good*.★

★ *Well* can also be used as an adjective to mean "not sick." *Paul was sick last week, but now he's well.*

☐ EXERCISE 32. Sentence practice.

Directions: Complete the sentences with the adjective or adverb in *italics*.

1. *quiet, quietly*   My hometown is small and _____quiet_____ .

2. *quiet, quietly*   Mr. Wilson whispered. He spoke _____quietly_____ .

3. *clear, clearly*   Anna pronounces every word _____ .

4. *clear, clearly*   We like to go boating in _____ weather.

5. *careless, carelessly*   Boris makes a lot of mistakes when he writes. He's a

   _____ writer.

6. *careless, carelessly*   Boris writes _____ .

7. *easy, easily*   The teacher asked an _____ question.

8. *easy, easily*   I answered the teacher's question _____ .

9. *good, well*   David is kind, generous, and thoughtful. He is a

_____ person.

10. *good, well*   Jake has poor eyesight. He can't see _____
without his glasses.

☐ EXERCISE 33. Sentence practice.

Directions: Complete the sentences with the correct form (adjective or adverb) of the
words in *italics*.

1. *careful*   Do you drive _____?

2. *correct*   Carmen gave the _____ answer to the question.

3. *correct*   She answered the question _____.

4. *fast*   Mike is a _____ reader.

5. *quick*   Mike reads _____.

6. *fast*   Mike reads _____.

7. *neat*   Barbara has _____ handwriting. It is easy to read what

she writes.

8. *neat*   Barbara writes _____.

9. *hard*   I study _____.

10. *hard*   The students took a _____ test.

11. *honest*   Roberto answered the question _____.

12. *slow*   Karen and Fumiko walked through the park _____.

13. *quick*   We were in a hurry, so we ate lunch _____.

14. *careless*   I made some _____ mistakes in my last

    composition.

15. *early*   Last night we had dinner _____ because we had to

    leave for the theater at 6:00.

16. *early*   We had an _____ dinner last night.

17. *loud*   I speak _____ when I talk to my grandfather

    because he has trouble hearing.

18. *slow, clear*   Kim speaks English _____ and

    _____.

☐ EXERCISE 34. Sentence practice.

Directions: Complete the sentences with the correct form (adjective or adverb) of the
words in *italics*.

1. *good*   Did you sleep _____ last night?

2. *fast*   Anita is a _____ learner.

3. *quick*   She learns everything _____.

4. *fast*   Ahmed walks too _____. I can't keep up with him.

5. *soft*   Please speak _____. The children are asleep.

6. *hard*   It rained _____ yesterday.

7. *late*   I paid my telephone bill _____.

8. *easy*   Ron lifted the heavy box _____. He's very strong.

9. *quiet*   Olga entered the classroom _____ because she was
    late for class.

10. *beautiful*   The flowers look _____.

11. *good*   We had a _____ time at the party last night.

12. *good*   Your science project looks _____.

13. *fluent*   Nadia speaks French _____.

□ EXERCISE 35. Review.

Directions: Choose the correct completions.

1. The teacher gave a test paper to every _____ in the class.
   A. student (circled)   B. students   C. of student   D. of students

2. Rosa is a _____ woman.
   A. beautiful Mexican young   C. Mexican beautiful young
   B. beautiful young Mexican   D. young beautiful Mexican

3. _____ the students in our class have dark hair.
   A. All most of   C. Almost
   B. Almost of   D. Almost all of

4. I had some _____ soup for lunch.
   A. vegetable good   C. vegetables good
   B. good vegetables   D. good vegetable

5. Jack introduced me to one _____.
   A. friends   B. of his friend   C. of his friends   D. his friends

6. The flowers _____.
   A. looked beautiful   C. beautiful look
   B. looked beautifully   D. beautifully look

7. _____ have jobs after school.
   A. A lot of students   C. A lots of students
   B. A lot students   D. A lot student

8. I didn't talk to _____.
   A. something   B. anyone   C. nothing   D. no one

□ EXERCISE 36. Chapter review: error analysis.

Directions: Correct the errors.

1. Everybody want to be happily.

2. One of the building on Main Street is the post office.

3. I didn't see nobody at the mall.

4. At the library, you need to do your work quiet.

5. I walk in the park every days.

6. Mr. Jones teaches English very good.

7. The answer looks clearly. Thank you for explaining it.

8. Every grammar test have a lot of difficult questions.

□ EXERCISE 37. Review: small groups.

Directions: Play this game in small groups. Think of a noun. Describe this noun to your group by giving clues, but don't mention the noun. The group will guess the noun you're thinking of.

Example:
SPEAKER A: I'm thinking of a kind of plant. It's small and colorful. It smells good.
  GROUP 1: A flower!
SPEAKER B: I'm thinking of a person. She has short black hair. She's wearing a blue sweater and a black skirt today.
  GROUP 1: That's too easy! Yoko!
SPEAKER C: I'm thinking of a very big cat. It's a wild animal.
  GROUP 1: A lion!
SPEAKER C: No. It's orange and black. It lives in Asia. It has stripes.
  GROUP 1: A tiger!

□ EXERCISE 38. Review.

Directions: Bring to class an object from your country. In a small group, describe your object and tell your classmates about it. What is it? How is it used? Why is it special? Answer questions from the group.

When all of the groups finish discussing the objects, all of the objects should be placed in the center of the room.

Speaker A: Choose one of the objects. Ask questions about it. Find out who it belongs to and what it is. (The owner of the object should NOT speak. People from the owner's group will give Student A the necessary information.)
Speaker B: Choose another one of the objects and ask questions.
Etc.

After all of the objects have been discussed and placed in the middle of the room, choose five of them to write about. Write a short paragraph on each object. What is it? What does it look like? Whose is it? What's it for? Why is it special? Why is it interesting to you? Etc.

CHAPTER 15
Possessives

15-1 POSSESSIVE NOUNS

		SINGULAR NOUN	POSSESSIVE FORM	To show that a person possesses something, add an apostrophe (') and *-s* to a singular noun.
(a)	My *friend* has a car. My ***friend's*** *car* is blue.	*friend*	*friend's*	POSSESSIVE NOUN, SINGULAR: *noun + apostrophe (') + -s*
(b)	The *student* has a book. The ***student's*** *book* is red.	*student*	*student's*	

		PLURAL NOUN	POSSESSIVE FORM	Add an apostrophe (') at the end of a plural noun (after the *-s*).
(c)	The *students* have books. The ***students'*** *books* are red.	*students*	*students'*	POSSESSIVE NOUN, PLURAL: *noun + -s + apostrophe (')*
(d)	My *friends* have a car. My ***friends'*** *car* is blue.	*friends*	*friends'*	

☐ EXERCISE 1. Punctuation practice.

Directions: Add apostrophes to the possessive nouns.

Jim's
1. ~~Jims~~ last name is Smith.

2. Bobs cat likes to sleep on the sofa.

3. My teachers names are Ms. Rice and Mr. Molina.

4. My mothers first name is Marika.

5. My parents telephone number is 555-9876.

6. My Uncle George is my fathers brother.

7. Nicole is a girls name.

8. Erica and Heidi are girls names.

9. Do you like Toms shirt?

10. Do you know Anitas brother?

11. Alexs friends visited him last night.

12. The teacher collected the students test papers at the end of the class.

13. How long is an elephants trunk?

14. A monkeys hand looks like a human hand.

15. Monkeys hands have thumbs.

☐ EXERCISE 2. Sentence practice.

    Directions: Complete the sentences. Use your classmates' names.

1. _____ hair is short and straight.

2. _____ grammar book is on her desk.

3. _____ last name is _____.

4. I don't know _____ address.

5. _____ eyes are brown.

6. _____ shirt is blue.

7. _____ briefcase is on the floor.

8. I need to borrow _____ dictionary.

□ EXERCISE 3. Let's talk: small groups.

Directions: Work in small groups. Take turns making sentences about things that belong to students in your group. Write down five of them.

Example:
SPEAKER A: Kim's dictionary is on his desk.
SPEAKER B: Anna's purse is brown.
SPEAKER C: Pablo's shirt is green.
Etc.

□ EXERCISE 4. Listening.

Directions: Listen to each sentence and circle the word you hear.

1. Bob   Bob's
2. Bob   Bob's
3. teacher   teacher's
4. teacher   teacher's
5. friend   friend's
6. friend   friend's
7. manager   manager's
8. cousin   cousin's

□ EXERCISE 5. Sentence practice.

Directions: Complete the sentences.

1. My husband's _____*brother*_____ is my brother-in-law.

2. My father's _____ is my uncle.

3. My mother's _____ is my grandmother.

4. My sister's _____ are my nieces and nephews.

5. My aunt's _____ is my mother.

6. My wife's _____ is my mother-in-law.

7. My brother's _____ is my sister-in-law.

8. My father's _____ and _____ are my grandparents.

9. My niece is my brother's _____.

10. My nephew is my sister's _____.

☐ EXERCISE 6. Sentence practice.

Directions: Choose the correct completions.

1. The _____ work hard.
   - (A.) students
   - B. student's
   - C. students'

2. My _____ name is Honey.
   - A. cats
   - B. cat's
   - C. cats'

3. My _____ are traveling in Spain.
   - A. cousins
   - B. cousin's
   - C. cousins'

4. My _____ meeting them in two weeks.
   - A. uncle
   - B. uncle's
   - C. uncles'

5. Two of my _____ live near me.
   - A. friends
   - B. friend's
   - C. friends'

6. My _____ names are Mark and Kevin.
   - A. friend
   - B. friend's
   - C. friends'

7. My best _____ name is Rob.
   - A. friends
   - B. friend's
   - C. friends'

8. The three _____ coats are in the closet.
   - A. boys
   - B. boy's
   - C. boys'

9. The _____ riding his bike.
   - A. boys
   - B. boy's
   - C. boys'

10. We have three _____ and one girl in my family.
    - A. boys
    - B. boy's
    - C. boys'

15-2 POSSESSIVE: IRREGULAR PLURAL NOUNS

(a) The ***children's*** *toys* are on the floor.	Irregular plural nouns *(children, men, women, people)* have an irregular plural possessive form. The apostrophe (') comes <u>before</u> the final **-s**.
(b) That store sells ***men's*** *clothing.*	
(c) That store sells ***women's*** *clothing.*	REGULAR PLURAL POSSESSIVE NOUN: the ***students'*** *books*
(d) I like to know about other ***people's*** *lives.*	IRREGULAR PLURAL POSSESSIVE NOUN: the ***women's*** *books*

☐ **EXERCISE 7. Sentence practice.**

Directions: Complete the sentences with the possessive form of the nouns in *italics*.
These books belong to . . .

   1. *Mary*   They're _____*Mary's*_____ books.

   2. *my friend*   They're _____ books.

   3. *my friends*   They're _____ books.

   4. *the child*   They're _____ books.

   5. *the children* They're _____ books.

   6. *the woman*   They're _____ books.

   7. *the women*   They're _____ books.

☐ **EXERCISE 8. Sentence practice.**

Directions: Complete the sentences with the possessive form of the nouns in *italics*.

   1. *children*   That store sells _____*children's*_____ books.

   2. *girl*   Rita is a _____ name.

   3. *girls*   Rita and Sue are _____ names.

   4. *women*   Rita and Sue are _____ names.

   5. *uncle*   Roberto is living at his _____ house.

   6. *person*   A biography is the story of a _____ life.

   7. *people*   Biographies are the stories of _____ lives.

   8. *students* _____ lives are busy.

   9. *brother*   Do you know my _____ wife?

  10. *brothers* Do you know my _____ wives?

  11. *wife*   Ron fixed his _____

             old sewing machine.

12. *dog*   My _____ name is Fido.

13. *dogs*   My _____ names are Fido and Rover.

14. *men*   Are Jim and Tom _____ names?

15. *man, woman* Chris can be a _____ nickname or a

                  _____ nickname.

16. *children*   Our _____ school is near our house.

☐ EXERCISE 9. Punctuation practice.

Directions: Add apostrophes and final **-s** as necessary to make possessive nouns.

                   Paul's
1. Someone stole ~~Paul~~ bicycle.

2. Do you know Yuko roommate?

3. I can't remember all of my classmate names.

4. My roommate desk is always a mess.

5. What is your parent new address?

6. It's important to respect other people opinions.

7. My husband sister is visiting us this week.

8. Excuse me. Where is the men room?

9. That store sells children toys.

10. I have my father nose.*

11. Where is Rosa apartment?

12. Does that store sell women clothes?

Tina's Boutique

---

* *I have my father's nose = My nose looks like my father's nose; I inherited the shape of my nose from my father.*

15-3 POSSESSIVE PRONOUNS: *MINE, YOURS, HIS, HERS, OURS, THEIRS*

	POSSESSIVE ADJECTIVE	POSSESSIVE PRONOUN	
(a) This book belongs to me. It is **my** book. It is **mine**.			A *possessive adjective* is used in front of a noun: **my** book.
	my **your** **her** **his** **our** **their**	**mine** **yours** **hers** **his** **ours** **theirs**	
(b) That book belongs to you. It is **your** book. It is **yours**. (c) That book is **mine**. INCORRECT: *That is mine book.*			A *possessive pronoun* is used alone, without a noun following it, as in (c).

☐ EXERCISE 10. Sentence practice.

Directions: Complete the sentences. Use object pronouns, possessive adjectives, and possessive pronouns.

1. *I* own this book.

    This book belongs to _____me_____.

    This is _____my_____ book.

    This book is _____mine_____.

2. *They* own these books.

    These books belong to _____.

    These are _____ books.

    These books are _____.

3. *You* own that book.

    That book belongs to _____.

    That is _____ book.

    That book is _____.

4. *She* owns this pen.

    This pen belongs to _____.

    This is _____ pen.

    This pen is _____.

5. *He* owns that pen.

    That pen belongs to _____.

    That is _____ pen.

    That pen is _____.

6. *We* own those books.

    Those books belong to _____.

    Those are _____ books.

    Those books are _____.

□ EXERCISE 11. Sentence practice.

Directions: Complete the sentences. Use the correct possessive form of the words in *italics*.

1. *I*   a. This bookbag is _____*mine*_____.

    Sue   b. That bookbag is _____*Sue's*_____.

    I   c. _____*My*_____ bookbag is red.

    she   d. _____*Hers*_____ is green.

2. *we*   a. These books are _____.

    they   b. Those books are _____.

    we   c. _____ books are on the table.

    they   d. _____ are on the desk.

3. *Tom*   a. This raincoat is _____.

    Mary   b. That raincoat is _____.

    he   c. _____ is light brown.

    she   d. _____ is light blue.

4. *I*   a. This notebook is _____.

    you   b. That one is _____.

    I   c. _____ has _____ name on it.

    you   d. _____ has _____ name on it.

5. *Jim*   a. _____ apartment is on Pine Street.

    we   b. _____ is on Main Street.

    he   c. _____ apartment has three rooms.

    we   d. _____ has four rooms.

6. *I*   a. This is _____ pen.

   you   b. That one is _____ .

   I   c. _____ is in _____ pocket.

   you   d. _____ is on _____ desk.

7. *we*   a. _____ car is a Chevrolet.

   they   b. _____ is a Volkswagen.

   we   c. _____ gets 17 miles to the gallon.

   they   d. _____ car gets 30 miles to the gallon.

8. *Ann*   a. These books are _____ .

   Paul   b. Those are _____ .

   she   c. _____ are on _____ desk.

   he   d. _____ are on _____ desk.

☐ EXERCISE 12. Sentence practice.

Directions: Choose the correct completions.

1. Is this _____*your*_____ pen?

(your / yours)

2. Please give this dictionary to Olga. It's _____ .

(her / hers)

3. A: Don't forget _____ hat. Here.

(your / yours)

   B: No, that's not _____ hat. _____ is green.

(my / mine)   (My / Mine)

4. A: Please take this wood carving as a gift from me. Here. It's _____ .

(your / yours)

   B: Thank you. You're very thoughtful.

5. A: Isn't that the Smiths' car? That one over there. The blue one.

   B: No, that's not _____ . _____ car is dark blue.

(their / theirs)   (Their / Theirs)

6. A: Abdul and I really like _____ new apartment. It has lots of space.
      (our / ours)

   How do you like _____?
                  (your / yours)

   B: _____ is small, but it's comfortable.
      (Our / Ours)

7. A: Excuse me. Is this _____ umbrella?
                        (your / yours)

   B: I don't have an umbrella. Ask Ken. Perhaps it's _____.
                                                        (him / his)

8. A: When do _____ classes begin?
               (your / yours)

   B: September second. How about _____? When do _____
                                   (your / yours)   (your / yours)
      begin?

   A: _____ begin August twenty-ninth.
      (My / Mine)

9. A: Maria, _____ spaghetti sauce is delicious!
            (your / yours)

   B: Thank you, but it's not as good as _____.
                                         (your / yours)

   A: Oh, no. _____ is much better! It tastes just as good as Anna's.
              (Your /Yours)

   B: Do you like Anna's spaghetti sauce? I think _____ is too salty.
                                                   (her / hers)

   A: Maybe. _____ husband makes good spaghetti sauce too.
             (My / Mine)

      _____ is thick and rich.
      (His / He)

   B: Making spaghetti sauce is easy,
      but everyone's sauce is just a little
      different.

Your spaghetti sauce is delicious, Maria.

Thank you.

15-4 QUESTIONS WITH *WHOSE*

(a) **Whose book** is this?	→ Mine. → It's mine. → It's my book.	**Whose** asks about possession. **Whose** is often used with a noun (e.g., *whose book*), as in (a) and (b).
(b) **Whose books** are these?	→ Rita's. → They're Rita's. → They're Rita's books.	
(c) **Whose** is this? *(The speaker is pointing to a book.)* (d) **Whose** are these? *(The speaker is pointing to some books.)*		**Whose** can be used without a noun if the meaning is clear, as in (c) and (d).
(e) **Who's** your teacher?		In (e): **Who's** = **who is**. **Whose** and **who's** have the same pronunciation.

> Whose is this? There's no name on it. Who's the artist?

☐ **EXERCISE 13. Sentence practice.**

Directions: Choose the correct completions.

1. Whose watch ___*is*___ ___*this*___?
   (is / are) (this / these)

2. Whose glasses _____ _____?
   (is / are) (that / those)

3. Whose teddy bear _____ _____?
   (is / are) (this / these)

4. Whose hat _____ _____?
   (is / are) (that / those)

5. Whose shoes _____ _____?
   (is / are) (that / those)

6. Whose keys _____ _____?
   (is / are) (this / these)

☐ **EXERCISE 14. Let's talk: pairwork.**

Directions: Work with a partner. Touch or point to something in the classroom that belongs to someone and ask a question with **Whose**.

Example:
SPEAKER A: *(points to a book)* Whose book is this?
SPEAKER B: It's mine. / Mine. / It's my book.
SPEAKER A: Your turn to ask.
SPEAKER B: Whose book is that?
SPEAKER A: It's Po's. / Po's. / It's Po's book.

☐ **EXERCISE 15. Sentence practice.**

Directions: Circle the correct completions.

1. (Who's) Whose _____ your roommate this year?

2. Who's Whose _____ pen is this?

3. Who's Whose _____ on the phone?

4. Who's Whose _____ that?

5. Who's Whose _____ is that?

6. Who's Whose _____ making so much noise?

☐ **EXERCISE 16. Listening.**

Directions: Listen to each sentence. Circle **Whose** or **Who's**.

1. Whose Who's   6. Whose Who's

2. Whose Who's   7. Whose Who's

3. Whose Who's   8. Whose Who's

4. Whose Who's   9. Whose Who's

5. Whose Who's   10. Whose Who's

☐ **EXERCISE 17. Chapter review: error analysis.**

Directions: Correct the errors.

1. Whose that woman?

2. What are those peoples names?

3. Mr. and Mrs. Swan like their's apartment.

4. The two student's study together in the library every afternoon.

5. Who's book is this?

6. Those shoes in the bag are their, not our.

7. My fathers' sister has M.D. and Ph.D. degrees.

8. Did you meet your childrens teacher?

9. This is mine pillow and that one is your.

☐ **EXERCISE 18. Let's talk: review of Chapters 14 and 15.**

Directions: Work in pairs or small groups. Read the facts about eight friends.

Facts:
- Jack, Jim, Jake, John, Jill, Julie, Joan, and Jan are all friends.
- Two of them are secretly engaged.
- They met five months ago.
- They are going to get married next year.

Who is engaged? Read the clues to find out. (Be careful! Some of the clues are only additional information. They will not help you find the answer.)

Fill in the chart as you work through the clues to solve the puzzle.

Engaged	Jack	Jim	Jake	John	Jill	Julie	Joan	Jan
yes								
no						X		

Clues:
1. For Julie's wedding next month, she is planning to wear her mother's long, white wedding dress. Her mother wore it 30 years ago.
   → *Julie's wedding is next month. The engaged couple is getting married next year, so it's not Julie.*
2. Joan's husband is working in another city right now. They hope to see each other soon.
3. Jill and Jack love each other. They met at Jill's sister's wedding.
4. Jill's sister got married a year ago.
5. Of all the friends, Jim is the only computer-science student.
6. Joan is a computer-science teacher. She began teaching two years ago.
7. Jan's boyfriend is a medical student.
8. All of the friends think Julie is very funny.
9. John loves Jan, but she doesn't love him. He's a friend to her, not a boyfriend.

CHAPTER *16*
Making Comparisons

16-1 COMPARISONS: USING *THE SAME (AS)*, *SIMILAR (TO)*, AND *DIFFERENT (FROM)*

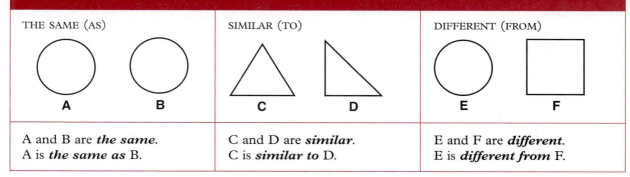

THE SAME (AS)	SIMILAR (TO)	DIFFERENT (FROM)
A and B are *the same*. A is *the same as* B.	C and D are *similar*. C is *similar to* D.	E and F are *different*. E is *different from* F.

☐ EXERCISE 1. Let's talk: class activity.

Directions: Which of the pictures are the same, similar, or different?

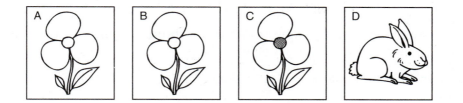

1. Are Pictures A and B the same?

2. Are Pictures A and C the same?

3. Are Pictures A and C similar?

4. Are Pictures A and C different?

5. Are Pictures C and D similar?

6. Are Pictures C and D different?

☐ EXERCISE 2. Sentence practice.

Directions: Complete the sentences. Use *the same (as)*, *similar (to)*, and *different (from)* in your completions.

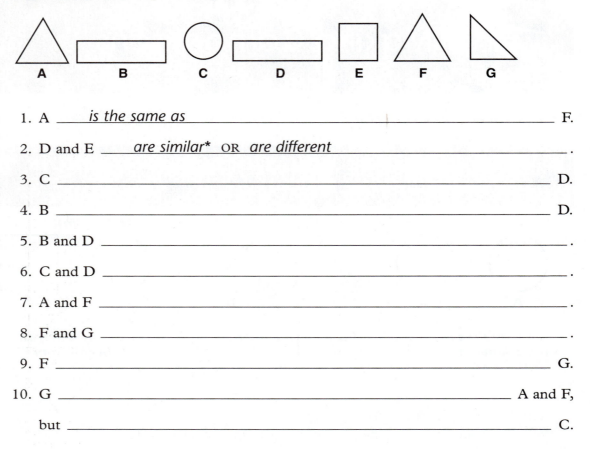

1. A ___*is the same as*___ F.

2. D and E ___*are similar** OR *are different*___ .

3. C _____ D.

4. B _____ D.

5. B and D _____ .

6. C and D _____ .

7. A and F _____ .

8. F and G _____ .

9. F _____ G.

10. G _____ A and F,

but _____ C.

☐ EXERCISE 3. Listening.

Directions: Listen to the comparisons of Pictures A through G in Exercise 2. Are these comparisons correct? Circle *yes* or *no*.

Example: A and F are the same.   (yes)   no

1. yes   no   5. yes   no
2. yes   no   6. yes   no
3. yes   no   7. yes   no
4. yes   no

---

* *Similar* gives the idea that two things are the same in some ways (e.g., both D and E have four edges) but different in other ways (e.g., D is a rectangle and E is a square).

☐ EXERCISE 4. Error analysis.

Directions: Correct the errors.

1. A rectangle is similar a square.

2. Pablo and Rita come from same country.

3. Girls and boys are differents. Girls are different to boys.

4. My cousin is the same age with my brother.

5. Dogs are similar with wolves.

6. Jim and I started to speak at a same time.

☐ EXERCISE 5. Let's talk: class activity.

Directions: Answer the questions.

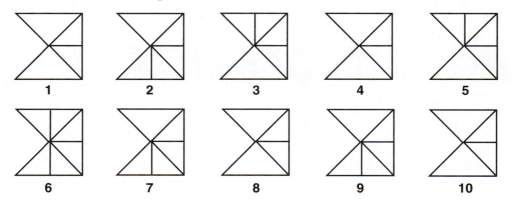

1. Which of the figures are the same?
2. Is there at least one figure that is different from all the rest?

Just for fun:
3. How many triangles are there in figure 1? *(answer: Seven.)*
4. How many triangles are there in figure 2?
5. How many triangles are there in figure 6?

☐ EXERCISE 6. Let's talk: class activity.

Directions: Your teacher will ask you questions. Practice using **the same (as)**, **similar (to)**, and **different (from)**. Close your book for this activity.

Example: Look at (. . .)'s clothes and (. . .)'s clothes. What is different about them?
Response: Their shoes are different. (. . .) is wearing running shoes, and (. . .) is wearing sandals.

1. Look around the room. Name things that are the same.

2. Look around the room. Name things that are similar but not the same.

3. Find two pens that are the same length. Find two pieces of paper that are the same size. Find two notebooks that are different sizes.

4. Find two people in the class who are wearing (earrings). Are their (earrings) the same, similar, or different?

5. Who in the class has a (notebook, briefcase, backpack) that is similar to yours? Does anyone have a (notebook, briefcase, backpack) that is the same as yours?

6. Do any of the people in this room have the same hairstyle? Name two people who have similar hairstyles.

7. Whose shirt is the same color as yours today? Name some things in this room that are the same color. Name things that are similar colors.

8. Do any of the people in this room come from the same country? Who? Name two people who come from different countries.

9. Name an animal that is similar to a tiger. Name a bird that is similar to a duck.

10. Are Egypt and Italy on the same continent? Egypt and Algeria? Thailand and Korea? Mexico and Brazil?

16-2 COMPARISONS: USING *LIKE* AND *ALIKE*

You have a ballpoint pen with blue ink. I have a ballpoint pen with blue ink.
 	
 (a) Your pen *is like* my pen.
 (b) Your pen and my pen *are alike*.
 (c) Our pens *are alike*.
	like = similar to
	 alike = similar
	 Like and *alike* have the same meaning, but the sentence patterns are different.
	  This + *be* + *like* + that.
	  This and that + *be* + *alike*.

☐ EXERCISE 7. Sentence practice.
   Directions: Complete the sentences with *like* and *alike*.

1. You and I have similar books. In other words, your book is _____*like*_____ mine. Our books are _____*alike*_____ .

2. Mr. Chang and I have similar coats. In other words, Mr. Chang's coat is _____ mine. Our coats are _____ .

3. Ken and Sue have similar cars. In other words, their cars are _____ .

4. You and I have similar hats. In other words, your hat is _____ mine.

5. A town is _____ a city in some ways.

6. A foot and a hand are _____ in some ways, but different in other

ways.

7. A dormitory and an apartment building are _____ in many ways.

8. A motorcycle is _____ a bicycle in some ways.

☐ **EXERCISE 8. Let's talk: pairwork.**

Directions: Work with a partner. Take turns making sentences with *like*. Check off
(✓) the things in Column B that compare with the items in Column A. Discuss the
ways in which the two things you are comparing are similar.

Example: a pencil, a bus

Column A	Column B
1. a pencil 2. a bus	a glass a human hand ✓a pen a lemon ✓a taxi

PARTNER A: A pencil is like a pen in some ways. They are both used for writing.
Your turn now.

PARTNER B: A bus is like a taxi. You can ride in both of them. Your turn now.

Etc.

Column A	Column B
1. a bush	a glass
2. a cup	a human hand
3. a hill	a lemon
4. honey	a chair
5. a monkey's hand	a mountain
6. an orange	an ocean
7. an alley	a street
8. a sea	sugar
9. a sofa	a bird
10. a sports jacket	a suit coat
11. a butterfly	a tree

Mary is 25 years old.
John is 20 years old.

(a) Mary is **older than** John.
(b) Health is **more important than** money.

INCORRECT: *Mary is more old than John.*
INCORRECT: *Health is importanter than money.*

When we use adjectives (e.g., *old, important*) to compare two people or two things, the adjectives have special forms.
In (a): We add -*er* to an adjective, OR
In (b): We use **more** in front of an adjective.
The use of -*er* or **more** is called the COMPARATIVE FORM.

Notice in the examples: **than** follows the comparative form: *older **than**, more important **than***.

	ADJECTIVE	COMPARATIVE	
ADJECTIVES WITH ONE SYLLABLE	**big** **cheap** **old**	**bigger** **cheaper** **older**	Add -*er* to one-syllable adjectives.
			Spelling note: If an adjective ends in one vowel and one consonant, double the consonant: *big–bigger, fat–fatter, hot–hotter, thin–thinner.*
ADJECTIVES THAT END IN -*Y*	**funny** **pretty**	**funnier** **prettier**	If an adjective ends in -*y*, change the -*y* to -*i* and add -*er*.
ADJECTIVES WITH TWO OR MORE SYLLABLES	**famous** **important** **interesting**	**more famous** **more important** **more interesting**	Use **more** in front of adjectives that have two or more syllables (except adjectives that end in -*y*).
IRREGULAR COMPARATIVE FORMS	**good** **bad** **far**	**better** **worse** **farther/further**	The comparative forms of **good**, **bad**, and **far** are irregular.

☐ EXERCISE 9. Comparative practice.

Directions: Write the comparative form for these adjectives.

1. old _____*older than*_____

2. small _____

3. big _____

4. important _____

5. easy _____

6. difficult _____

7. long _____

8. heavy _____

9. expensive _____

10. sweet _____

11. hot _____

12. good _____

13. bad _____

14. far _____

□ EXERCISE 10. Sentence practice.

Directions: Complete the sentences. Use the comparative form of the words in *italics*.

1. *comfortable*   This chair is _____*more comfortable than*_____ that chair.

2. *deep*   The Pacific Ocean is _____ the

Mediterranean Sea.

3. *important*   Love is _____ money.

4. *lazy*   I'm _____ my roommate.

5. *tall*   My brother is _____ I am.*

6. *heavy*   Iron is _____ wood.

7. *difficult*   My physics course is _____

my math course.

8. *hot*   Thailand is _____ Korea.

9. *thin*   A giraffe's neck is _____ an elephant's neck.

10. *warm*   It's _____ today _____ yesterday.

11. *good*   Nadia's English is _____ her husband's.

12. *long*   The Nile River is _____ the Mississippi.

_____

*Formal written English: *My brother is taller than I (am)*.
Informal spoken English: *My brother is taller than me*.

13. *intelligent* A dog is _____ a chicken.

14. *short* My little finger is _____ my middle finger.

15. *bad* The weather yesterday was _____ it is today.

16. *far* Your apartment is _____ from school

_____ mine.

17. *strong* A horse is _____ a person.

18. *curly* Ken's hair is _____ mine.

19. *nervous* The groom was _____

at the wedding

_____

the bride.

☐ EXERCISE 11. Let's talk: pairwork.

Directions: Work with a partner. Use the adjective in parentheses to compare each pair of items. Use **more** or **-er**.

Example: a mouse, an elephant (small)
Response: A mouse is smaller than an elephant.

Partner A	Partner B
1. a bus, car (big)	1. this book, that one (good)
2. my old shoes, my new shoes (comfortable)	2. my hair, her hair (curly)
3. your hair, my hair (dark)	3. her hair, his hair (straight)
4. my arm, your arm (long)	4. the weather here the weather in my hometown (bad)
5. biology, chemistry (interesting)	5. this chapter, Chapter 10 (easy)
6. I, my brother (thin)	6. Japanese grammar, English grammar (difficult)

☐ EXERCISE 12. Let's talk: class activity.

Directions: Practice comparative forms.

PART I. Your teacher will put several different books in a central place. Compare one to another, using the given adjectives.

Example: big
Response: This book is bigger than that book/that one.

1. large	5. difficult	9. expensive
2. interesting	6. easy	10. cheap
3. small	7. good	11. thick
4. heavy	8. bad	12. important

PART II. The given adjectives describe a man named Bob. A man named Jack does not have the same qualities. Draw pictures of Bob and Jack on the board. Compare Bob to Jack.

Example: tall
Response: Bob is taller than Jack.

Bob is . . . .

1. tall	5. young	9. friendly★
2. strong	6. happy	10. responsible
3. lazy	7. kind	11. famous
4. intelligent	8. generous	12. busy

☐ EXERCISE 13. Listening.

Directions: Listen to each sentence. Circle the adjective you hear.

Example: Sky Airlines is _____ than World Airlines.   cheap   (cheaper)

1. cold	colder	7. safe	safer
2. cold	colder	8. safe	safer
3. cold	colder	9. safe	safer
4. happy	happier	10. fresh	fresher
5. happy	happier	11. funny	funnier
6. happy	happier	12. funny	funnier

★The comparative of *friendly* has two possible forms: *friendlier than* or *more friendly than.*

□ EXERCISE 14. Sentence practice.

Directions: Complete the sentences. Use the comparative form of the words in the list (or your own words).

big	*easy*	*important*
bright	*expensive*	*intelligent*
cheap	*fast*	*large*
cold	*high*	*warm*
comfortable	*hot*	*sweet*

1. An elephant is ____*bigger than / larger than*____ a mouse.

2. A lemon is sour. An orange is _____ a lemon.

3. The weather today is _____ it was yesterday.

4. Sometimes Mrs. Gay's feet hurt when she wears high heels.

   Bedroom slippers are _____

   _____ shoes with high heels.

5. I can afford a radio, but not a TV set. A radio is _____

   a TV set.

6. An airplane moves quickly. An airplane is _____ an

   automobile.

7. A person can think logically. A person is _____

   _____ an animal.

8. Hills are low. Mountains are _____ hills.

9. The sun gives off a lot of light. The sun is _____ the moon.

10. A motorcycle costs a lot of money. A motorcycle is _____

    _____ a bicycle.

11. Arithmetic isn't difficult. Arithmetic is _____ algebra.

12. Good health is _____ money.

☐ **EXERCISE 15. Let's talk.**

Directions: Work in pairs, in groups, or as a class. Make comparisons.

Example: an elephant to a mouse
Response: An elephant is bigger than a mouse / more intelligent than a mouse. Etc.

1. an orange to a lemon
2. a lake to an ocean
3. good health to money
4. a radio to a TV set
5. an airplane to an automobile
6. a person to an animal
7. the sun to the moon
8. a mountain to a hill
9. arithmetic to algebra
10. bedroom slippers to high heels
11. a horse to a person
12. your little finger to your ring finger
13. love to money
14. your hair to (. . .)'s hair
15. food in *(your country)* to food in *(another country)*
16. the weather today to the weather yesterday

☐ **EXERCISE 16. Let's talk: small groups.**

Directions: Work in small groups. Take turns making sentences using **-er**/**more** with the given adjectives. Share a few of your sentences with the class.

Example: large
Response: Canada is larger than Mexico. / My feet are larger than yours. / Etc.

1. tall	11. small
2. important	12. intelligent
3. cold	13. big
4. curly	14. heavy
5. expensive	15. cheap
6. long	16. sweet
7. easy	17. high
8. comfortable	18. interesting
9. old	19. good
10. strong	20. bad

□ **EXERCISE 17. Let's talk: pairwork.**

Directions: Work with a partner. Write a sentence using *-er/more* with an adjective from the list in Exercise 16. Tear the sentence into pieces, with only <u>one</u> word or phrase on each piece. Give the pieces to a classmate, who will reassemble your sentence. Repeat this exercise several times, using a different adjective for each new sentence you write.

□ **EXERCISE 18. Let's talk: pairwork.**

Directions: Work in pairs. Make comparisons.
Partner A: Ask your partner a question. Your book is open.
Partner B: Answer in a complete sentence. Your book is closed.

Example: Name something that is sweeter than an apple.
PARTNER A: What's sweeter than an apple? / Can you name something that is sweeter than an apple? / Name something that is sweeter than an apple.
PARTNER B: Candy is sweeter than an apple.

1. Name a country that is larger than Mexico.

2. Name a planet that is closer to or farther away from the sun than the earth.

3. Name someone in the class who is younger than (I am, you are).

4. Name an animal that is more dangerous than a wild dog.

5. Name a bird that is larger than a chicken.

6. Name something that is more expensive than (an object in this room)

7. Name a sport that is more popular internationally than baseball.

8. Name someone who is more famous than *(name of a famous person)*.

Switch roles.
Partner A: Close your book.
Partner B: Open your book. Your turn now.

9. Name someone who is taller than you.

10. Name something that is more interesting than *(name of a field of study)*.

11. Name an ocean that is smaller than the Pacific Ocean.

12. Name a place that is farther away from here than *(name of a place)*.

13. Name an animal that is stronger than a horse.

14. Name a game that is, in your opinion, more exciting than *(name of a sport)*.

15. Name a place that is colder than this city.

16. Name a place that is more beautiful than this city.

16-4 THE SUPERLATIVE: USING -EST AND MOST

(a) COMPARATIVE My thumb is **shorter than** my index finger.	The comparative (**-er**/**more**) compares two things or people.	
(b) SUPERLATIVE My hand has five fingers. My thumb is **the shortest** (finger) of all.	The superlative (**-est**/**most**) compares three or more things or people.	

	ADJECTIVE	COMPARATIVE	SUPERLATIVE
ADJECTIVES WITH ONE SYLLABLE	**old** **big**	**older** (than) **bigger** (than)	**the oldest** (of all) **the biggest** (of all)
ADJECTIVES THAT END IN -Y	**pretty** **easy**	**prettier** (than) **easier** (than)	**the prettiest** (of all) **the easiest** (of all)
ADJECTIVES WITH TWO OR MORE SYLLABLES	**expensive** **important**	**more expensive** (than) **more important** (than)	**the most expensive** (of all) **the most important** (of all)
IRREGULAR FORMS	**good** **bad** **far**	**better** (than) **worse** (than) **farther/further** (than)	**the best** (of all) **the worst** (of all) **the farthest/furthest** (of all)

□ **EXERCISE 19. Comparative and superlative practice.**

Directions: Write the comparative and superlative forms of the given adjectives.

		COMPARATIVE	SUPERLATIVE
1.	long	*longer (than)*	*the longest (of all)*
2.	small	_____	_____
3.	heavy	_____	_____
4.	comfortable	_____	_____
5.	hard	_____	_____
6.	difficult	_____	_____
7	hot*	_____	_____

*Spelling note: If an adjective ends in one vowel and one consonant, double the consonant to form the superlative: *big–biggest, fat–fattest, hot–hottest, thin–thinnest.*

	COMPARATIVE	SUPERLATIVE
8. easy	_____	_____
9. cheap	_____	_____
10. interesting	_____	_____
11. pretty	_____	_____
12. strong	_____	_____
13. good	_____	_____
14. bad	_____	_____
15. far	_____	_____

☐ EXERCISE 20. Sentence practice.

Directions: Complete the sentences. Use the superlative form of the adjectives in *italics*.

1. *large*   *The largest* _____ city in Canada is Toronto.

2. *long*   The Nile is _____ river in the world.

3. *interesting* I'm taking four classes. My history class is _____

   _____ of all.

4. *high*   Mt. McKinley in Alaska is _____ mountain in

   North America.

5. *tall*   The Sears Tower is _____ building in Chicago.

6. *big*   Lake Superior is _____ lake in North America.

7. *short*   February is _____ month of the year.

8. *far*   Pluto is _____ planet from the sun.

9. *beautiful*   In my opinion, Seattle is _____

   city in the United States.

10. *bad*   In my opinion, Harry's Steak House is _____

                  restaurant in the city.

11. *good*   In my opinion, the Doghouse Cafe has _____ food

                  in the city.

12. *comfortable* Ken is sitting in _____ chair in

                  the room.

13. *fast*   The _____ way to travel is by airplane.

14. *good*   When you feel depressed, laughter is _____ medicine.

15. *large*   Asia is _____ continent in the world.

16. *small*   Australia is _____ continent in the world.

17. *expensive*   Sally ordered _____ food on

                  the menu for dinner last night.

18. *easy*   Taking a taxi is _____ way to get to the

                  airport.

19. *important*   I think good health is _____

                  thing in life.

20. *famous*   The Gateway Arch is _____

                  landmark in St. Louis, Missouri.

□ EXERCISE 21. Listening.

Directions: Look at the people in the picture and listen to each sentence. Circle the correct answer.

Example: Pam is the youngest.   yes   (no)

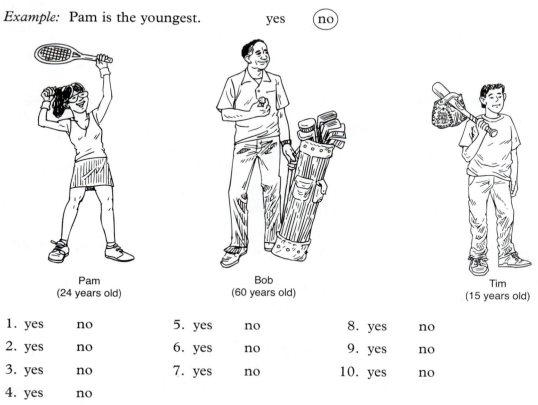

Pam
(24 years old)

Bob
(60 years old)

Tim
(15 years old)

1. yes   no   5. yes   no   8. yes   no
2. yes   no   6. yes   no   9. yes   no
3. yes   no   7. yes   no   10. yes   no
4. yes   no

□ EXERCISE 22. Sentence practice.

Directions: Work in small groups or as a class. Make comparisons about each group of pictures.

A. COMPARE THE SIZES OF THE THREE BALLS.

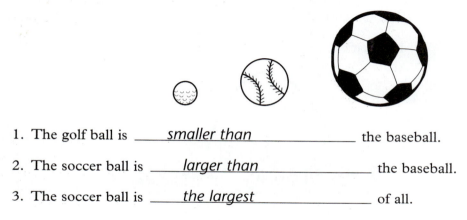

1. The golf ball is _____ *smaller than* _____ the baseball.

2. The soccer ball is _____ *larger than* _____ the baseball.

3. The soccer ball is _____ *the largest* _____ of all.

B. COMPARE THE AGES OF THE CHILDREN.

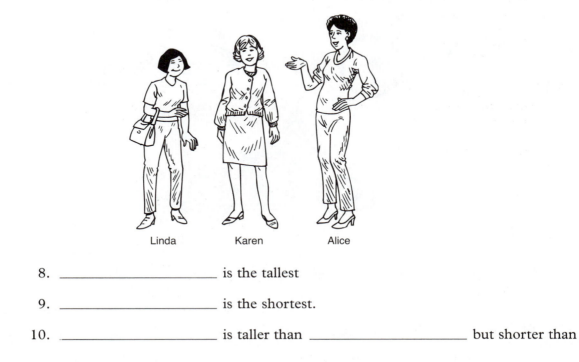

Tommy
(3 years old)

Helen
(6 years old)

Ann
(8 years old)

4. Ann is _____ Helen.

5. Helen is _____ Tommy.

6. Tommy is _____ Helen and Ann.

7. Ann is _____ of all.

C. COMPARE THE HEIGHTS OF THE THREE WOMEN.

Linda

Karen

Alice

8. _____ is the tallest

9. _____ is the shortest.

10. _____ is taller than _____ but shorter than

_____ .

D. COMPARE THE STRENGTHS OF THE THREE MEN.

Mike   Joe   Ron

11. _____

12. _____

13. _____

14. _____

E. COMPARE THE PRICES OF THE THREE VEHICLES.

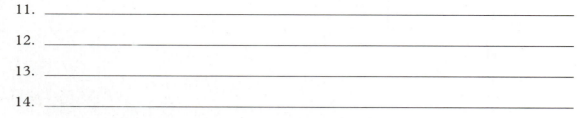

15. _____

16. _____

17. _____

18. _____

F. COMPARE THE GRADES OF THE TEST PAPERS.

19. _____

20. _____

21. _____

22. _____

G. COMPARE HOW INTERESTING (TO YOU) THE THREE BOOKS LOOK.

23. _____

24. _____

25. _____

26. _____

☐ **EXERCISE 23. Sentence practice.**

Directions: Complete the sentences. Use the correct form (comparative or superlative) of the adjectives in *italics*.

1. *long*   The Yangtze River is _____ the Mississippi River.

2. *long*   The Nile is _____ river in the world.

3. *large*   The Caribbean Sea is _____ the Mediterranean Sea.

4. *large*   The Caribbean Sea is _____ sea in the world.

5. *high*   Mt. Everest is _____ mountain in the world.

6. *high*   Mt. Everest is _____ Mt. McKinley.

7. *big*   Africa is _____ North America.

8. *small*   Europe is _____ South America.

9. *large*   Asia is _____ continent in the world.

10. *big*   Canada is _____ the United States in area.

11. *large*   Indonesia is _____ Japan in population.

12. *good*   Fruit is _____ for your health _____ candy.

13. *good*   The student cafeteria has _____ roast beef sandwiches

     in the city.

14. *comfortable*   I have a pair of boots, a pair of sandals, and a pair of running shoes.

     The sandals are _____ the

     boots, but the running shoes are _____

     _____ of all.

15. *easy*   This exercise is _____ the next one. This is

     one of _____ exercises in the book.

16. *bad*   There are over 800 million people in the world who don't get enough

     to eat. With few exceptions, poverty and hunger are _____

     in rural areas than in cities and towns.

☐ **EXERCISE 24. Listening.**

Directions: Listen to the sentences about shopping in a clothing store. Write the words you hear.

1. The blue dress is _____ the red one.

2. Well, I think the red one is _____.

3. Is it too _____, or does it look OK?

4. It's _____ of all the ones you tried on.

5. I'm not going to buy the brown shoes. They're too _____.

6. How do you like this hat? It's _____ size they have.

7. No, this hat is _____ that one.

8. I need a belt, but one that is _____ my old one.

9. Is this belt _____ enough?

10. It's perfect. And it's _____ of all of them.

16-5 USING *ONE OF* + SUPERLATIVE + PLURAL NOUN

(a) The Amazon is *one of the longest rivers* in the world.	The superlative often follows *one of*. Notice the pattern:
(b) A Rolls Royce is *one of the most expensive cars* in the world.	*one of* + *superlative* + *plural noun*
(c) Alice is *one of the most intelligent people* in our class.	See Chart 14-5, p. 419, for more information about *one of*.

☐ EXERCISE 25. Sentence practice.

Directions: Use the given phrases to make sentences. Use *one of* + *superlative* + *plural noun*.

1. a high mountain in the world
   → *Mt. McKinley is one of the highest mountains in the world.*

2. a pretty park in *(this city)*
   → *Forest Park is one of the prettiest parks in St. Louis.*

3. a tall person in our class
   → *Talal is one of the tallest people★ in our class.*

4. a big city in the world

5. a beautiful place in the world

6. a nice person in our class

7. a long river in the world

_____

★*People* is usually used instead of *persons* in the plural.

8. a good restaurant in *(this city)*

9. a famous landmark in the world

10. an important event in the history of the world

□ **EXERCISE 26. Let's talk: class interview.**

Directions: Make questions using **one of** + *superlative* + *plural noun*. You are Speaker A. Ask two students each question. Write their first names and their answers. (Note: Try to change people with each question.) Share some of your answers with the class.

Example: a big city in Canada
SPEAKER A: What is one of the biggest cities in Canada?
SPEAKER B: Toronto is one of the biggest cities in Canada.
SPEAKER C: Vancouver is one of the biggest cities in Canada.

1. a big city in Asia		
2. a large state in the United States		
3. a beautiful city in the world		
4. a tall person in our class		
5. a good place to visit in the world		
6. a famous person in the world		
7. an important thing in life		
8. a bad restaurant in *(this city)*		
9. a famous landmark in *(name of a country)*		
10. a tall building in *(this city)*		
11. a dangerous sport in the world		
12. a serious problem in the world		

☐ **EXERCISE 27. Let's talk.**

Directions: Your teacher will ask you questions, or work in small groups and take turns asking each other these questions.

1. How many brothers and sisters do you have? Are you the oldest?
2. Who is one of the most famous movie stars in the world?
3. In your opinion, what is the most exciting sport?
4. What is one of the most interesting experiences in your life?
5. In your opinion, what is the most beautiful place in the world?
6. What is one of the most important inventions in the modern world?
7. What is one of the worst experiences of your life?
8. What are the best things in life?
9. What was the happiest day of your life—or one of the happiest days of your life?
10. Who are the most important people in your life today?

☐ **EXERCISE 28. Let's talk: small groups.**

Directions: First, take this quiz by yourself. Circle the letters of the correct answers. If you don't know an answer, guess. Second, form small groups to discuss the answers. You can figure out the correct answers by looking at the Table of Statistics on p. 474.

PART I.

1. What is the longest river in the world?
   A. the Yangtze
   B. the Amazon
   C. the Nile
   D. the Mississippi

2. Is the Amazon River longer than the Mississippi River?
   A. yes
   B. no

3. Is the Yangtze River longer than the Mississippi River?
   A. yes
   B. no

4. Which two rivers are almost the same length?
   A. the Nile and the Amazon
   B. the Amazon and the Yangtze
   C. the Nile and the Mississippi
   D. the Mississippi and the Amazon

PART II.

5. What is the largest sea in the world?

   A. the Mediterranean Sea

   B. the South China Sea

   C. the Caribbean Sea

6. Is the South China Sea the smallest of the three seas listed above?

   A. yes

   B. no

PART III.

7. What is the deepest ocean in the world?

   A. the Atlantic Ocean

   B. the Indian Ocean

   C. the Pacific Ocean

8. Is the Indian Ocean larger than the Atlantic Ocean?

   A. yes

   B. no

PART IV.

9. Below is a list of the continents in the world. List them in order according to size, from the largest to the smallest.

Africa	Europe
✓ Antarctica	North America
Asia	South America
Australia	

(1) _____ (the largest)

(2) _____

(3) _____

(4) ___ Antarctica _____

(5) _____

(6) _____

(7) _____ (the smallest)

PART V

10. Which of the following cities has the largest population in the world?
    A. New York City, U.S.A.   C. Mexico City, Mexico
    B. Seoul, Korea   D. Tokyo, Japan

11. Is the population of Sao Paulo, Brazil, larger than the population of New York City, U.S.A.?
    A. yes
    B. no

12. Is the population of Sao Paulo, Brazil, larger than the population of Seoul, Korea?
    A. yes
    B. no

13. What is the largest city in North America?
    A. Mexico City
    B. New York City

PART VI.

14. Which of the following countries has the largest area in the world?
    A. Canada   C. the United States
    B. China   D. Brazil

15. Which of the following two countries is larger in area?
    A. Canada
    B. Brazil

16. Which of the following countries has the largest population in the world?
    A. India   C. the United States
    B. China   D. Indonesia

17. Which of the following two countries has the larger population?
    A. India
    B. Indonesia

18. Which of the following two countries has the larger population?
    A. the United States
    B. Brazil

19. Which of the following two countries has the smaller population?
    A. Egypt
    B. Japan

TABLE OF STATISTICS

PART I.

RIVER	LENGTH
the Amazon River	4,000 miles
the Mississippi River	2,350 miles
the Nile River	4,160 miles
the Yangtze River	3,900 miles

PART II.

SEA	SIZE
the Caribbean Sea	970,000 square miles
the Mediterranean Sea	969,000 square miles
the South China Sea	895,000 square miles

PART III.

OCEAN	SIZE	AVERAGE DEPTH
Atlantic Ocean	31,820,000 square miles	12,100 feet
Indian Ocean	29,000,000 square miles	12,750 feet
Pacific Ocean	64,000,000 square miles	13,000 feet

PART IV.

CONTINENT	SIZE
Africa	12,000,000 square miles
Antarctica	7,000,000 square miles
Asia	17,129,000 square miles
Australia	3,000,000 square miles
Europe	3,837,000 square miles
North America	9,355,000 square miles
South America	6,886,000 square miles

PART V.

CITY	POPULATION*
Mexico City, Mexico	28 million
New York, U.S.A.	21 million
Sao Paulo, Brazil	25 million
Seoul, Korea	22 million
Tokyo, Japan	30 million

PART VI.

COUNTRY	AREA	POPULATION
Brazil	3,265,059 sq mi	175 million
Canada	3,612,187 sq mi	32 million
China	3,600,927 sq mi	1,275 million*
Egypt	384,000 sq mi	79 million
India	1,147,949 sq mi	1 billion
Indonesia	767,777 sq mi	205 million
Japan	146,000 sq mi	125 million
the United States	3,539,224 sq mi	286 million

*Approximate population in the year 2004; *1,275 million* is said as "one billion, two hundred seventy-five million."

16-6 USING *BUT*

(a) John is rich, **but** Mary is poor. (b) The weather was cold, **but** we were warm inside our house.	**But** gives the idea that "This is the opposite of that." A comma usually precedes **but**.

☐ **EXERCISE 29. Sentence practice.**

Directions: Complete the sentences with adjectives.

1. An orange is sweet, but a lemon is _____*sour*_____.

2. The weather is hot today, but it was _____ yesterday.

3. These dishes are clean, but those dishes are _____.

4. This suitcase is heavy, but that suitcase is _____.

5. My hair is light, but my brother's hair is _____.

6. These shoes are uncomfortable, but those shoes are _____.

7. This street is narrow, but that street is _____.

8. This exercise is easy, but that exercise is _____.

9. This food is good, but that food is _____.

10. A chicken is stupid, but a human being is _____.

11. Smoke is visible, but clean air is _____.

12. This answer is right, but that answer is _____.

13. This towel is dry, but that towel is _____.

14. This cup is full, but that cup is _____.

15. This sentence is confusing, but that sentence is _____.

16. My apartment is messy, but Bob's apartment is always _____.

17. A pillow is soft, but a rock is

_____.

Directions: Listen to each sentence and write an adjective with the opposite meaning.

Example:
You will hear: This exercise is easy, but that exercise is _____.
You will write: <u>hard</u> .

1. _____ .   5. _____ .

2. _____ .   6. _____ .

3. _____ .   7. _____ .

4. _____ .   8. _____ .

16-7 USING VERBS AFTER *BUT*

	AFFIRMATIVE VERB + *but* + NEGATIVE VERB		Often the verb phrase following *but* is shortened, as in the examples.
(a)	John *is* rich,	*but* Mary *isn't*.	
(b)	Balls *are* round,	*but* boxes *aren't*.	
(c)	I *was* in class,	*but* Po *wasn't*.	
(d)	Sue *studies* hard,	*but* Sam *doesn't*.	
(e)	We *like* movies,	*but* they *don't*.	
(f)	Alex *came,*	*but* Maria *didn't*.	
(g)	People *can* talk,	*but* animals *can't*.	
(h)	Olga *will* be there,	*but* Ivan *won't*.	

	NEGATIVE VERB + *but* + AFFIRMATIVE VERB	
(i)	Mary *isn't* rich,	*but* John *is*.
(j)	Boxes *aren't* round,	*but* balls *are*.
(k)	Po *wasn't* in class,	*but* I *was*.
(l)	Sam *doesn't* study,	*but* Sue *does*.
(m)	They *don't* like cats,	*but* we *do*.
(n)	Maria *didn't* come,	*but* Alex *did*.
(o)	Animals *can't* talk,	*but* people *can*.
(p)	Ivan *won't* be there,	*but* Olga *will*.

□ EXERCISE 31. Sentence practice.

Directions: Complete each sentence with an appropriate verb, affirmative or negative.

1. Sara is at home, but her husband _____<u>isn't</u>_____ .

2. Hiroki isn't at home, but his wife _____ .

3. Beds are comfortable, but park benches _____ .

4. I wasn't at home last night, but my roommate _____ .

5. Kim was in class yesterday, but Anna and Linda _____.

6. I don't want to go to the movie, but my friends _____.

7. Ahmed can speak French, but I _____.

8. Amanda will be at the meeting, but Helen _____.

9. This shirt is clean, but that one _____.

10. These shoes aren't comfortable, but those shoes _____.

11. Mike doesn't write clearly, but Ted _____.

12. I ate breakfast this morning, but my roommate _____.

13. Carol has a car, but Jerry _____.

14. Jerry doesn't have a car, but Carol _____.

15. Ron was at the party, but his wife _____.

16. Ron went to the party, but his wife _____.

17. Boris can't speak Spanish, but his wife _____.

18. I won't be at home tonight, but Sue _____.

19. Ken will be in class tomorrow, but Chris _____.

20. Amy won't be here tomorrow, but Alice _____.

21. The hotel wasn't expensive, but the plane tickets _____.

□ EXERCISE 32. Listening.

Directions: Complete each sentence with an appropriate verb, affirmative or negative.

Example:

You will hear: The children wanted to play, but the teacher _____.
You will write: ___*didn't*___.

1. _____.   6. _____.

2. _____.   7. _____.

3. _____.   8. _____.

4. _____.   9. _____.

5. _____.   10. _____.

☐ EXERCISE 33. Let's talk: class activity.

Directions: Your teacher will ask you questions. Answer them using **but**. Close your book for this activity.

Example: Who in the class was at home last night? Who wasn't at home last night?
   TEACHER: Who was at home last night?
SPEAKER A: I was.
   TEACHER: Who wasn't at home last night?
SPEAKER B: I wasn't at home last night.
   TEACHER: *(to Speaker C)* Summarize, using *but*.
SPEAKER C: *(Speaker A)* was at home last night, but *(Speaker B)* wasn't.

1. Who wears glasses? Who doesn't wear glasses?

2. Who is married? Who isn't married?

3. Who didn't watch TV last night? Who watched TV last night?

4. Who will be in class tomorrow? Who won't be in class tomorrow?

5. Who has a car? Who doesn't have a car?

6. Who studied last night? Who didn't study last night?

7. Who can play *(a musical instrument)*? Who can't play *(that musical instrument)*?

8. Who is hungry right now? Who isn't hungry right now?

9. Who lives in an apartment? Who lives in a house or in a dorm?

10. Who doesn't drink coffee? Who drinks coffee?

11. Who won't be at home tonight? Who will be at home tonight?

12. Who was in class yesterday? Who wasn't in class yesterday?

13. Who can't speak *(a language)*? Who can speak *(a language)*?

14. Who didn't stay home last night? Who stayed home last night?

15. Who has *(a mustache)*? Who doesn't have *(a mustache)*?

☐ EXERCISE 34. Let's talk: pairwork.

Directions: Work with a partner. Picture A and Picture B are not the same. There are many differences between them. Can you find all of the differences? Take turns pointing out the differences.

Example:
SPEAKER A: The woman is sitting in Picture A, but she's lying down in Picture B.
             Your turn now.
SPEAKER B: There's a small fish in Picture A, but a large fish in Picture B.
             Your turn now.
Etc.

Picture A

Picture B

☐ **EXERCISE 35. Writing practice.**

Directions: Write a paragraph about one or more of the given topics. The list is a reminder of comparison words you may want to use in your paragraph.

WORDS USED IN COMPARISONS			
alike	*different (from)*	*like*	*the same (as)*
but	*-er/more*	*similar (to)*	

Topics:
1. Write about this city. Compare it to your hometown.
2. Write about your present residence. Compare it to a past residence.
3. Write about two members of your family. Compare them.
4. Write about two animals. Compare them.
5. Write about two countries. Compare them.

16-8 MAKING COMPARISONS WITH ADVERBS

	COMPARATIVE	SUPERLATIVE	
(a) Kim speaks *more fluently than* Ali (does). (b) Anna speaks *the most fluently of all*.	*more fluently* *more slowly* *more quickly*	*the most fluently* *the most slowly* *the most quickly*	Use *more* and *most* with adverbs that end in *-ly*.*
(c) Mike worked *harder than* Sam (did). (d) Sue worked *the hardest of all*.	*harder* *faster* *earlier* *later*	*the hardest* *the fastest* *the earliest* *the latest*	Use *-er* and *-est* with irregular adverbs: *hard, fast, early, late*.
(e) Rosa writes *better than* I do. (f) Kim writes *the best of all*.	*better*	*the best*	*Better* and *best* are forms of the adverb *well*.

*Exception: *early–earlier–the earliest*.

☐ **EXERCISE 36. Sentence practice.**

Directions: Complete the sentences with the correct form (comparative or superlative) of the adverbs in *italics*.

1. *late*   Karen got home _____*later than*_____ Alice (did).

2. *quickly*   I finished my work _____ Tom (did).

3. *beautifully*   Gina sings _____ Susan (does).

4. *beautifully*   Ann sings _____ of all.

5. *hard*   My sister works _____ I (do).

6. *hard*   My brother works _____ of all.

7. *carefully*   My husband drives _____ I (do).

8. *early*   We arrived at the party _____ the Smiths (did).

9. *early*   The Wilsons arrived at the party _____ of all.

10. *well*   You can write _____ I (can).

11. *well*   Ken can write _____ of all.

12. *clearly*   Anita pronounces her words _____ Tina (does).

13. *fluently* Sue speaks Spanish _____ I (do).

14. *fluently* Ted speaks Spanish _____ of all.

☐ EXERCISE 37. Sentence practice.

Directions: Use the correct form (adjective or adverb, comparative or superlative) of the words in *italics*.

1. *careful* Karen drives _____ <u>*more carefully than*</u> _____ her brother does.

2. *beautiful* A tiger is _____ a goat.

3. *neat* Paul's apartment is _____ mine.

4. *neat* Peter's apartment is _____ of all.

5. *neat* You write _____ I do.

6. *neat* Ann writes _____ of all.

7. *clear* This author explains her ideas _____

that author.

8. *good* I like rock music _____ classical music.

9. *good* My husband can sing _____ I can.

10. *good* My daughter can sing _____ of all.

11. *long* Almost universally, wives work _____ hours than their

husbands because women take primary responsibility for household

chores and child-rearing.

12. *late* Robert usually goes to bed _____ his roommate.

13. *clear* Anna pronounces her words _____ of

all the students in the class.

14. *sharp* A razor is usually _____ a kitchen knife.

15. *artistic* My son is _____ my daughter.

16. *slow* I eat _____ my husband does.

☐ EXERCISE 38. Listening: review.

Directions: Listen to each sentence. Write the words you hear.

1. I work _Faster than_ Jim does.

2. Toshi finished his work _the fastest_ of all.

3. Sue studies _harder than_ Fred.

4. Jean studies _the hardest_ of all.

5. A motorcycle is _more dangerous than_ a bicycle.

6. Ali speaks _more loudly than_ Yoko does.

7. A snail moves _more slowly than_ a crab does.

8. This suitcase is _heavier than_ that one.

9. My glasses are _clearer than_ my contact lenses.

10. I can see _more clearly_ with my glasses.

☐ EXERCISE 39. Review.

Directions: Choose the correct completions.

1. A lion is _____ a tiger.
   A. similar   B. similar with   C. similar from   D. similar to

2. Lions and tigers are _____.
   A. the same   B. similar   C. similar to   D. the same as

3. Good health is one of _____ in a person's life.
   A. best thing   C. the best things
   B. the best thing   D. best things

4. There were many chairs in the room. I sat in _____ chair.
   A. the comfortablest   C. most comfortable
   B. the most comfortable   D. more comfortable

5. Jane's story was _____ Jack's story.
   A. funnier than   C. more funnier than
   B. funny than   D. more funny

6. My last name is _____ my cousin's.
   A. same   B. same from   C. same as   D. the same as

7. I live _____ away from school than you do.
   A. far   B. farther   C. more far   D. farthest

8. Ali speaks _____ than Hamid.
      A. more clearly   C. more clear
      B. clearlier   D. more clearer

9. Robert works hard every day, but his brother _____ .
      A. is   B. isn't   C. does   D. doesn't

☐ **EXERCISE 40. Chapter review: error analysis.**
    Directions: Correct the errors.

1. Your pen is alike mine.

2. Kim's coat is similar ~~with~~ (to) mine.

3. Jack's coat is same (as) mine.

4. Soccer balls are different ~~with~~ (from) basketballs.

5. Soccer is one of (the) most popular sports in the world.

6. Green sea turtles live long more than elephants.

7. My grade on the test was worst from yours. You got a more better grade.

8. A monkey is intelligenter than a turtle.

9. Pedro speaks English more fluent than Ernesto.

10. Professor Brown teaches full-time, but her husband isn't.

11. Robert and Maria aren't same age. Robert is more young than Maria.

12. A blue whale is more large from an elephant.

13. The exploding human population is the most great threat to all forms of life on earth.

14. The Mongol Empire was the bigger land empire in the entire history of the world.

☐ EXERCISE 41. Review.

Directions: Work with a partner.
Partner A: Ask Partner B questions. Your book is open.
Partner B: Answer in complete sentences. Your book is closed.

1. What's the longest river in the world?*
2. What's the biggest continent? What's the second biggest continent?
3. What country has the largest population?
4. Is a square the same as a rectangle?
5. Name a country that is farther south than Mexico.
6. Name an animal that is similar to a horse.
7. Name a place that is noisier than a library.
8. Is a dormitory like an apartment building? How are they different? How are they similar?
9. Is (. . .)'s grammar book different from yours?
10. What is one of the most famous landmarks in the world?

Switch roles.
Partner A: Close your book.
Partner B: Open your book. Your turn now.

11. Is the population of Seoul, Korea, larger or smaller than the population of Sao Paulo, Brazil?*
12. Is the Atlantic Ocean deeper than the Indian Ocean?
13. What's the smallest continent in the world?
14. Name two students in this class who speak the same native language. Do they come from the same country?
15. Look at (. . .) and (. . .). How are they different?
16. Is a lake like a river? How are they different? How are they similar?
17. Name an insect that is smaller than a bee.
18. Name a city that is farther north than Rome, Italy.
19. What is the most popular sport in your country?
20. What is one of the most important inventions in the modern world? Why is it more important than *(name of another invention)*.

☐ EXERCISE 42. Let's write or talk.

Directions: Write or talk about things and people in this room. Look at this thing and that thing, and then compare them. Look at this person and that person, and then compare them.

———————————

*If you need to, look at the Table of Statistics on p. 474.

□ **EXERCISE 43. Writing practice.**

Directions: Write a paragraph on one or more of the given topics.

Topics:

1. Write about your family. Compare the members of your family. Include yourself in the comparisons. (Who is younger than you? Who is the youngest of all? Etc.)

2. Write about your childhood friends when you were ten years old. Compare them. Include yourself in the comparisons. (Who could run faster than you? Who could run the fastest of all? Etc.)

3. What are your three favorite places in the world? Why? Compare them.

4. What are the roles of health, money, and love in your life? Compare them.

APPENDIX
Irregular Verbs

SIMPLE FORM	SIMPLE PAST	SIMPLE FORM	SIMPLE PAST
be	was, were	keep	kept
become	became	know	knew
begin	began	leave	left
bend	bent	lend	lent
bite	bit	lose	lost
blow	blew	make	made
break	broke	meet	met
bring	brought	pay	paid
build	built	put	put
buy	bought	read	read
catch	caught	ride	rode
choose	chose	ring	rang
come	came	run	ran
cost	cost	say	said
cut	cut	see	saw
do	did	sell	sold
draw	drew	send	sent
drink	drank	shake	shook
drive	drove	shut	shut
eat	ate	sing	sang
fall	fell	sit	sat
feed	fed	sleep	slept
feel	felt	speak	spoke
fight	fought	spend	spent
find	found	stand	stood
fly	flew	steal	stole
forget	forgot	swim	swam
get	got	take	took
give	gave	teach	taught
go	went	tear	tore
grow	grew	tell	told
hang	hung	think	thought
have	had	throw	threw
hear	heard	understand	understood
hide	hid	wake up	woke up
hit	hit	wear	wore
hold	held	win	won
hurt	hurt	write	wrote

Listening Script

Chapter 1: USING *BE*

EXERCISE 2, p. 2.

Paulo is a student from Brazil. Marie is a student from France. They're in the classroom. Today is an exciting day. It's the first day of school, but they aren't nervous. They're happy to be here. Mrs. Brown is the teacher. She isn't in the classroom right now. She's late today.

EXERCISE 8, p. 6.

1. Butterflies are insects.
2. English is a country.
3. Spring is a season.
4. Canada is a city.
5. Japan is a language.
6. Roses are flowers.
7. Rabbits are machines.
8. Russian and Arabic are languages.
9. Cows are animals.

EXERCISE 13, p. 9.

1. I like my teachers. They're very nice.
2. I am at school. I'm in the classroom.
3. Yuri is not here. He's late.
4. I know you. You're a teacher.
5. I know Susan. I'm her friend.
6. Ali and I are friends. We're in the same class.
7. My sister has two children. They're young.
8. Los Angeles is a city. It's very big.
9. Anna is from Russia. She's very friendly.
10. I like soccer. It's fun.

EXERCISE 14, p. 9.

SPEAKER A: Hello. My name is Mrs. Brown. I'm the new teacher.
SPEAKER B: Hi. My name is Paulo, and this is Marie. We're in your class.
SPEAKER A: It's nice to meet you.
SPEAKER B: We're happy to meet you too.
SPEAKER A: It's time for class. Please take a seat.

EXERCISE 29, p. 22.

1. Grammar's easy.
2. My name's John.
3. My books're on the table.
4. My brother's 21 years old.
5. The weather's cold today.
6. The windows're open.
7. My money's in my wallet.
8. Mr. Smith's a teacher.
9. Mrs. Lee's at home now.
10. The sun's bright today.
11. Tom's at home right now.
12. My roommates're from Chicago.
13. My sister's a student in high school.

EXERCISE 30, p. 22.

1. The test's easy.
2. My notebook is on the table.
3. My notebooks are on the table.
4. Sue's a student.
5. The weather is warm today.
6. The windows're open.
7. My parents're from Cuba.
8. My cousins are from Cuba too.
9. My book's on my desk.
10. The teachers're in class.

Chapter 2: USING *BE* AND *HAVE*

EXERCISE 1, p. 24.

1. Are England and Canada cities?
2. Is winter a season?
3. Are bananas blue?
4. Is the weather very cold today?
5. Are airplanes slow?
6. Is a carrot a machine?
7. Are diamonds free?
8. Is the earth round?
9. Are big cities quiet?

EXERCISE 12, p. 32.

1. The boots have zippers.
2. Anna has a raincoat.
3. Her raincoat has buttons.
4. Her sweater has long sleeves.
5. She has earrings on her ears.
6. The earrings have diamonds.
7. You have long pants.
8. We have warm coats.

EXERCISE 22, p. 39.

1. This is my grammar book.
2. That is your grammar book.
3. That's your wallet.
4. This's her purse.
5. Is that your umbrella?
6. This's not my umbrella.
7. Is this your ring?
8. Yes, that's my ring.
9. This isn't my homework.
10. That's their car.

Chapter 3: USING THE SIMPLE PRESENT

EXERCISE 2, p. 55.

1. I wake up early every day. → wake
2. My brother wakes up late.
3. He gets up at 11:00.
4. I go to school at 8:00.
5. My mother does exercises every morning.
6. My little sister watches TV in the morning.
7. I take the bus to school.
8. My brother takes the bus to school.
9. My friends take the bus too.
10. We talk about our day.

EXERCISE 8, p. 59.

1. I go to work every morning. → morning
2. I celebrate my birthday every year.
3. Our son is two years old.
4. I use my computer every day.
5. Bob uses his computer five days a week.
6. I eat three times a day.
7. Anna listens to the radio every night.
8. I visit my uncle every month.

EXERCISE 13, p. 62.

1. Mrs. Miller teaches English on Saturdays. → teaches
2. Mr. and Mrs. Smith teach English in the evenings.
3. Doug fixes cars.
4. His son fixes cars too.
5. Carlos and Chris watch DVDs on weekends.
6. Their daughter watches videos.
7. I brush my hair every morning.
8. Jimmy seldom brushes his hair.

9. The Johnsons wash their car every weekend.
10. Susan rarely washes her car.

EXERCISE 18, p. 65.

Marco is a student. He has an unusual schedule. All of his classes are at night. His first class is at 6:00 P.M. every day. He has a break from 7:30 to 8:00. Then he has classes from 8:00 to 10:00.

He leaves school and goes home at 10:00. After he has dinner, he watches TV. Then he does his homework from midnight to 3:00 or 4:00 in the morning.

Marco has his own computer at home. When he finishes his homework, he usually goes on the Internet. He usually stays at his computer until the sun comes up. Then he does a few exercises, has breakfast, and goes to bed. He sleeps all day. Marco thinks his schedule is great, but his friends think it is strange.

Chapter 4: USING THE PRESENT PROGRESSIVE

EXERCISE 7, p. 96.

1. Tony is sitting in the cafeteria.
2. He is sitting alone.
3. He is wearing a hat.
4. He is eating lunch.
5. He is reading his grammar book.
6. He is looking at his computer.
7. He is studying hard.
8. He is smiling.
9. He is listening to the radio.
10. He is waving to his friends.

EXERCISE 21, p. 107.

1. I write in my grammar book . . . .
2. I am writing in my grammar book . . . .
3. It is raining outside . . . .
4. It doesn't rain . . . .
5. My cell phone rings . . . .
6. My cell phone isn't ringing . . . .
7. My friends and I listen to music in the car . . . .
8. We're not listening to music . . . .

EXERCISE 25, p. 110.

1. A: Does Tom have a black hat?
   B: Yes.
   A: Does he wear it every day?
   B: No.
   A: Is he wearing it right now?
   B: I don't know. Why do you care about Tom's hat?
   A: I found a hat in my apartment. Someone left it there. I think that it belongs to Tom.
2. A: Do animals dream?
   B: I don't know. I suppose so. Animals aren't very different from human beings in lots of ways.

A: Look at my dog. She is sleeping. Her eyes are closed. At the same time, she is barking and moving her head and her front legs. I am sure that she is dreaming right now. I'm sure that animals dream.

EXERCISE 26, p. 111.

SPEAKER A: What are you doing? Are you working on your English paper?

SPEAKER B: No, I'm not. I'm writing an e-mail to my sister.

SPEAKER A: Do you write to her often?

SPEAKER B: Yes, but I don't write a lot of e-mails to anyone else.

SPEAKER A: Does she write to you often?

SPEAKER B: Yes. I get an e-mail from her several times a week. How about you? Do you get a lot of e-mails?

SPEAKER A: Yes. I like to send e-mails to friends all over the world.

Chapter 5: TALKING ABOUT THE PRESENT

EXERCISE 1, p. 121.

1. What time is it?
2. What month is it?
3. What day is it today?
4. What year is it?
5. What's the date today?

EXERCISE 4, p. 124.

1. My birthday is in June. I was born on June 24. I have class every day at 1:00. Who am I?
2. I have class at 7:00. I go to class in the morning. I was born in 1986. Who am I?
3. I have class in the morning. I was born in July. I was born in 1990. Who am I?
4. I was born in 1989. My birthday is July 7. I go to class at night. Who am I?

EXERCISE 12, p. 130.

1. There're ten students in the classroom.
2. There's a new teacher today.
3. There're two teachers outside.
4. There's a book on the floor.
5. There's some information on the blackboard.
6. There're several papers in the wastepaper basket.
7. There're two coffee cups on the teacher's desk.
8. There's a lot of homework for tomorrow.

EXERCISE 23, p. 138.

1. There are trees behind the train.
2. A bird is under the picnic table.
3. There are butterflies in the air.
4. There is a fishing pole on top of the table.

5. There is a knife on top of the table.
6. A boat is in the water.
7. The bridge is below the water.
8. There are clouds above the hills.
9. There are flowers beside the river.
10. There are flowers next to the river.
11. The guitar is under the table.
12. One bike is under the tree.
13. The fish is on the grass.
14. The table is between the tree and the river.
15. The flowers are near the water.

EXERCISE 31, p. 145.

1. A: Where do you want to go for dinner tonight?
   B: Rossini's Restaurant.
2. A: What time do you want to go to the airport?
   B: Around five. My plane leaves at seven.
3. A: Jean doesn't want to go to the baseball game.
   B: Why not?
   A: Because she needs to study for a test.
4. A: I'm getting tired. I want to take a break for a few minutes.
   B: Okay. Let's take a break. We can finish the work later.
5. A: We don't need to come to class on Friday.
   B: Why not?
   A: It's a holiday.
6. A: Peter wants to go back to his apartment.
   B: Why?
   A: Because he wants to change his clothes before he goes to the party.
7. A: Where do you want to go for your vacation?
   B: I want to visit Niagara Falls, Quebec, and Montreal.
8. A: May I see your dictionary? I need to look up a word.
   B: Of course. Here it is.
   A: Thanks.
9. A: Do you want to go with us to the park?
   B: Sure. Thanks. I need to get some exercise.

EXERCISE 32, p. 147.

1. Tony'd like a cup of coffee.
2. He'd like some sugar in his coffee.
3. Ahmed and Anita'd like some coffee too.
4. They'd like some sugar in their coffee too.
5. A: Would you like a cup of coffee? ("Would you" can't be contracted in short answers or questions.)
   B: Yes, I would. Thank you.
6. I'd like to thank you for your kindness and hospitality.
7. My friends'd like to thank you too.
8. A: Would Robert like to ride with us?
   B: Yes, he would.

EXERCISE 34, p. 148.

1. I'd like a hamburger for dinner.
2. We like to eat in fast-food restaurants.
3. Bob'd like to go to the gym now.
4. He likes to exercise after work.
5. The teacher'd like to speak with you.
6. I think the teacher likes you.
7. We like to ride our bikes on weekends.
8. Bill and Sue like classical music.
9. They'd like to go to a concert next week.
10. I think I'd like to go with them.

Chapter 6: NOUNS AND PRONOUNS

EXERCISE 12, p. 166.

1. Sara knows Joe. She knows him ("knows 'im") very well.
2. Where does Shelley live? Do you have her ("have-er") address?
3. There's Sam. Let's go talk to him ("im").
4. There's Bill and Julie. Let's go talk to them ("em").
5. The teacher is speaking with Lisa because she doesn't have her ("have-er") homework.
6. I need to see our airline tickets. Do you have them ("have-em")?

EXERCISE 13, p. 167.

1. A: Yoko and I are ("I-er") going downtown this afternoon. Do you want to ("wanna") come with us?
   B: I don't think so, but thanks anyway. Chris and I are going to the library. We need to study for our test.
2. A: Hi, Ann. How do you like your new apartment?
   B: It's very nice.
   A: Do you have a roommate?
   B: Yes. Maria Hall is my roommate. Do you know her ("know-er")? She's from Miami.
   A: No, I don't know her ("know-er"). Do you get along with her?
   B: Yes, we enjoy living together. You must visit us sometime. Maybe you can come over for dinner soon.
   A: Thanks. I'd like that.
3. A: Do George and Mike come over to your house often?
   B: Yes, they do. I invite them to my house often. We like to play cards.
   A: Who usually wins your card games?
   B: Mike. He's a really good card player. We can't beat him.

EXERCISE 15, p. 170.

GROUP A. Final -s is pronounced /z/ after voiced sounds.

1. taxicabs	5. rooms	9. trees
2. beds	6. coins	10. cities
3. dogs	7. years	11. boys
4. balls	8. lives	12. days

GROUP B. Final -s is pronounced /s/ after voiceless sounds.

13. books	16. groups
14. desks	17. cats
15. cups	18. students

GROUP C. Final -es is pronounced /əz/.

- after "s" sounds:
  - 19. classes
  - 20. glasses
  - 21. horses
  - 22. places
  - 23. sentences
- after "z" sounds:
  - 24. sizes
  - 25. exercises
  - 26. noises
- after "sh" sounds:
  - 27. dishes
  - 28. bushes
- after "ch" sounds:
  - 29. matches
  - 30. sandwiches
- after "ge/dge" sounds:
  - 31. pages
  - 32. oranges
  - 33. bridges

EXERCISE 16, p. 171.

1. toys	6. boxes
2. table	7. package
3. face	8. chairs
4. hats	9. edge
5. offices	10. tops

EXERCISE 17, p. 172.

1. The desks in the classroom are new. → desks
2. I like to visit new places.
3. Donna wants a sandwich for lunch.
4. The teacher is correcting sentences with a red pen.
5. This apple is delicious.
6. The students are finishing a writing exercise in class.
7. I need two pieces of paper.
8. Roses are beautiful flowers.
9. Your rose bush is beautiful.
10. The college has many scholarships for students.

Chapter 7: COUNT AND NONCOUNT NOUNS

EXERCISE 6, p. 184.

1. I live in an apartment. → an
2. It's a small apartment.
3. My English class lasts an hour.

4. It's an interesting class.
5. We have a new teacher.
6. My mother has an office downtown.
7. It's an insurance office.
8. My father is a nurse.
9. He works at a hospital.
10. He has a difficult job.

EXERCISE 31, p. 204.

1. Vegetables have vitamins. → general
2. Cats make nice pets.
3. The teacher is absent.
4. I love bananas.
5. New cars are expensive.
6. I need the keys to the car.
7. Are the computers in your office working?
8. Let's feed the ducks at the park.

EXERCISE 32, p. 205.

1. A: Do you have a pen?
   B: There's one on the counter in the kitchen.
2. A: Where are the keys to the car?
   B: I'm not sure, but I have a set. You can use mine.
3. A: Shh. I hear a noise.
   B: It's just a bird outside, probably a woodpecker. Don't worry.
4. A: John Jones teaches at the university.
   B: I know. He's an English professor.
   A: He's also the head of the department.
5. A: Hurry! We're late.
   B: No, we're not. It's five o'clock, and we have an hour.
   A: No, it isn't. It's six! Look at the clock.
   B: Oh, my. I need a new battery in my watch.

Chapter 8: EXPRESSING PAST TIME, PART 1

EXERCISE 5, p. 215.

1. I wasn't at home last night. → wasn't
2. I was at the library.
3. Our teacher was sick yesterday.
4. He wasn't at school.
5. Many students were absent.
6. They weren't at school for several days.
7. There was a substitute teacher.
8. She was very patient and kind.
9. My friends and I weren't nervous on the first day of school.
10. We were very relaxed.

EXERCISE 14, p. 224.

1. Mary played the piano for the class. → played
2. She plays very well.
3. The students watched an interesting movie.

4. They enjoyed it a lot.
5. They often watch movies together.
6. The class asked the teacher many questions.
7. The teacher answered their questions clearly.
8. The students listened very carefully.
9. They like their class.
10. The class works very hard.

EXERCISE 18, p. 226.

PART I.
1. What day was it two days ago?
2. What day was it five days ago?
3. What day was it yesterday?
4. What month was it last month?
5. What year was it ten years ago?
6. What year was it last year?
7. What year was it one year ago?

PART II.
8. What time was it one hour ago?
9. What time was it five minutes ago?
10. What time was it one minute ago?

EXERCISE 22, p. 230.

1. I ate . . . .
2. We sat . . . .
3. They came . . . .
4. She had . . . .
5. He got . . . .
6. I stood . . . .

EXERCISE 30, p. 235.

1. Did we do well on the test?
2. Did you finish the assignment?
3. Did it make sense?
4. Did I answer your question?
5. Did they need more help?
6. Did he understand the homework?
7. Did I explain the project?
8. Did they complete the project?
9. Did you do well?
10. Did she pass the class?

EXERCISE 33, p. 237.

PART I.
1. Did you ("did-juh") read the paper this morning?
2. A: Tom called.
   B: Did he ("dih-de") leave a message?
3. A: Sara called.
   B: Did she ("dih-she") leave a message?
4. Did it ("dih-dit") rain yesterday?
5. A: The children are watching TV.
   B: Did they ("dih-they") finish their homework?
6. I can't find my notebook. Did I ("dih-di") leave it on your desk?

PART II.
1. Did you ("did-juh") finish the homework assignment?

2. Did it ("dih-dit") take a long time?
3. Did you ("dih-juh") hear my question?
4. Did they ("dih-they") hear my question?
5. Did I ("dih-di") speak loud enough?
6. Did he ("dih-de") understand the information?
7. Did she ("dih-she") understand the information?
8. Did you ("dih-juh") want more help?
9. Did I ("dih-di") explain it okay?
10. Did he ("dih-de") do a good job?

EXERCISE 37, p. 241.
1. She caught . . . .
2. They drove . . . .
3. We read . . . .
4. I rode . . . .
5. He bought . . . .
6. We ran . . . .

EXERCISE 41, p. 244.
I woke up with a headache this morning. I took some medicine and went back to bed. I slept all day. The phone rang. I heard it, but I was very tired. I didn't answer it. I listened to the answering machine. It was the doctor's office. The nurse said I missed my appointment. Now my headache is really bad!

EXERCISE 44, p. 247.
My mother called me early this morning. She had wonderful news for me. She had my wedding ring. I lost it many years ago. I thought someone stole it, but she told me, "No, it didn't happen that way." She told me she was outside in her garden recently with her dog. The dog brought her something. She thought it was money. Then she saw it was my ring. She put it on her finger and wore it. She didn't want to lose it again. I was so happy. I hung up the phone and began to laugh and cry at the same time.

Chapter 9: EXPRESSING PAST TIME, PART 2

EXERCISE 4, p. 255.
1. Where did Susan go?
2. Why did Susan go there?
3. Where did Nancy go?
4. When did Nancy go?
5. Why did Nancy go there?
6. Where did Tom go?
7. Why did Tom go there?
8. When did Susan go?
9. Where did Bill go?
10. When did Bill go?
11. Why did Bill go there?
12. When did Tom go?

EXERCISE 10, p. 259.
1. When did you arrive?
2. Why did you leave?
3. Where do they live?

4. What did she want?
5. What does this mean?
6. Why didn't you study?
7. Where did he go?
8. When does class end?

EXERCISE 14, p. 263.
1. Where does Sally live?
2. When did you leave?
3. What do you need?
4. Who is going with me?
5. Who came late?
6. Where are you moving to?
7. When did the movie end?
8. Why didn't you help?

EXERCISE 17, p. 266.
1. The student didn't understand . . . .
2. The woman spent . . . .
3. Did you cut . . . ?
4. The car hit . . . .
5. The man forgot . . . .

EXERCISE 20, p. 268.
1. A tree fell . . . .
2. The girls won . . . .
3. The teacher drew . . . .
4. I felt . . . .
5. My brother threw . . . .

EXERCISE 23, p. 271.
1. Mrs. Brown fed . . . .
2. Mr. and Mrs. Johnson built . . . .
3. The dog bit . . . .
4. The children hid . . . .
5. The teacher held . . . .

EXERCISE 40, p. 287.
I had a strange experience yesterday. I was reading my book on the bus when a man sat down next to me and asked me if I wanted some money. I didn't want his money. I was very confused. I stood up and walked toward the door of the bus.

While I was waiting for the door to open, the man tried to give me the money. When the door opened, I got off the bus quickly. I still don't know why he was trying to give me money.

Chapter 10: EXPRESSING FUTURE TIME, PART 1

EXERCISE 9, p. 300.
1. Look. The doctor is coming. → present
2. The doctor is coming soon.
3. Oh, no. It's raining.

4. We are leaving early in the morning.
5. Hurry. The bus is leaving.
6. Shh. Class is beginning.
7. We're going to a movie this afternoon.
8. My parents are coming over tonight.

EXERCISE 11, p. 301.

1. It's going to ("gonna") rain tomorrow.
2. I am leaving soon.
3. Our class starts at nine.
4. Anita is coming to the meeting tomorrow.
5. The doctor is going to call you.
6. Are you going to ("gonna") study tonight?
7. We are having dinner at a restaurant tomorrow.
8. We aren't going to the concert tonight.
9. Alex rides his bicycle to work.
10. Who is going to help me?

EXERCISE 15, p. 304.

1. Bob is going to finish his work → in five minutes.
2. Mary is going to school . . . .
3. Tom left . . . .
4. The Johnsons got married . . . .
5. The store is going to ("gonna") open . . . .
6. The movie started . . . .
7. Janet is going to graduate . . . .
8. We took a vacation . . . .
9. I'm going to ("gonna") buy a car . . . .
10. There was a meeting at school . . . .

EXERCISE 20, p. 307.

1. Jean is going to leave in a couple of days. → same
2. Tom is going to leave in a few weeks.
3. The doctor is going to ("gonna") call in a few minutes.
4. Tim graduated from high school a couple of years ago.
5. We sold our house a couple of years ago.
6. The mail came a couple of minutes ago.
7. The phone rang a few minutes ago.
8. John is going to ("gonna") be here in a few minutes.

EXERCISE 25, p. 310.

1. The class is working on a project today. → present
2. We are going to finish this weekend.
3. We talked about the project this morning.
4. It is going to ("gonna") rain this week.
5. It rained a lot this month.
6. I am going to graduate from college this year.
7. I am studying psychology this year.
8. The professor spoke for two hours this morning.
9. She's going to ("gonna") give us a test this week.
10. We had a lot of homework today.

EXERCISE 27, p. 312.

1. The teacher'll help you. → teacher'll
2. The teacher will help you.
3. We'll have a test tomorrow.
4. We will have a test tomorrow.
5. I'll be back in five minutes.
6. The students'll be late.
7. John will be here soon.
8. The doctor'll see you now.
9. The nurse will give you some medicine.
10. You'll feel better soon.

EXERCISE 28, p. 312.

1. Where will you go?
2. When will you go there?
3. Why will you go there?
4. Who will go with you?
5. What will you do there?

EXERCISE 31, p. 315.

1. Will Jane study more? → Yes, she will.
2. Will Jane go to more parties on weekends?
3. Will Jane begin smoking?
4. Will Jane exercise with her grandmother?
5. Will Jane graduate from a university next year?
6. Will Jane go on a diet?
7. Will Jane exercise only two times a week?
8. Will Jane spend more time with her grandmother?

EXERCISE 32, p. 316.

1. We want to see you soon. → want
2. I won't be late for class again.
3. You won't believe the news!
4. I want a new car.
5. A new car won't be cheap.
6. My car won't start.
7. Mr. and Mrs. Thomas want to retire.
8. They want to travel more.

EXERCISE 34, p. 318.

1. Bill doesn't like meat, eggs, or fish.
2. He is a vegetarian. He doesn't eat meat from animals. He didn't eat it as a child, either.
3. His wife Beth doesn't eat meat, but she isn't a vegetarian.
4. She doesn't enjoy the taste of meat.
5. They are going to ("gonna") try a new restaurant tomorrow.
6. John will probably have a dish with lots of vegetables.
7. Beth won't have vegetables for a main dish. She'll probably ask for some type of fish.
8. Are they going to ("gonna") enjoy themselves?
9. Will they go back to this restaurant?

EXERCISE 36, p. 319.

1. A: Will you be here tomorrow?
   B: Yes, I will, but I'll probably be late.
2. A: Where are your visitors from?
   B: Ali is from Kuwait, and Toshi and Hiro are from Japan.
3. A: Was everyone in class yesterday?
   B: All the students were there, but the teacher was absent.
   A: Was he sick?
   B: No, he wasn't, but his daughter was.
4. A: Let's hurry. We're going to be really late.
   B: We're not going to be late. I think your watch is fast.
   A: My watch isn't fast. Maybe your watch is slow!
   B: Let's not argue. We won't be there any sooner if we argue.

Chapter 11: EXPRESSING FUTURE TIME, PART 2

EXERCISE 6, p. 329.

1. You may be late for class tomorrow.
2. Our teacher may give a lot of homework this weekend.
3. Maybe you'll get a package in the mail tomorrow.
4. I may go to bed early tonight.
5. Maybe I'll go shopping tomorrow.
6. Maybe you will get married next year.
7. The weather may be sunny tomorrow.
8. Maybe it will rain tomorrow.

EXERCISE 11, p. 332.

1. I might be absent tomorrow. → a. Maybe I will be absent.
2. There may be a change in our plans.
3. The weather report says it'll rain tomorrow.
4. We might finish this grammar book soon.
5. John may get good news tomorrow.
6. The class'll start on time.

EXERCISE 19, p. 338.

1. What are you going to do if the weather is nice after class tomorrow?
2. What are you going to do if your teacher cancels class tomorrow?
3. What are you going to do if your teacher talks too fast?
4. What are you going to do if you're sick tomorrow?

EXERCISE 24, p. 342.

1. Before I go to bed every night, → I watch TV.
2. If I go to bed early tonight,
3. After I get to school every day,
4. If class finishes early today,

5. Before I eat breakfast every day,
6. After I finish breakfast today,
7. If I get all the answers in this exercise correct,
8. When I finish this grammar book,

EXERCISE 28, p. 347.

1. A: Did you see that?
   B: What?
   A: The man in the red shirt hit the man in the blue shirt.
   B: Are you sure?
   A: Yes, I watched the whole thing.
2. A: Were you late for the movie?
   B: No. The movie began at 7:30, and we got to the theater at 7:26.
3. A: Do you hear that noise?
   B: What noise?
   A: Listen again.
   B: Now I hear it. Is someone coming?
4. A: Do you want to ("wanna") go to the zoo this afternoon?
   B: I'd like to go, but I can't because I need to study.
   A: That's too bad.
   B: Are you going to ("gonna") go to the zoo?
   A: Yes. The weather is perfect, and I want to ("wanna") get outside and enjoy it.

Chapter 12: MODALS, PART 1: EXPRESSING ABILITY

EXERCISE 5, p. 356.

1. The students can understand their teacher. → can
2. The students can't understand their teacher.
3. I can't hear you.
4. You can help me.
5. Tom can't work today.
6. The doctor can't see you today.
7. Professor Clark can meet with you.
8. I can't find my glasses.
9. The children can't wait.
10. We can stop now.

EXERCISE 6, p. 357.

In my last job, I was an office assistant. I have good computer skills. I can do word-processing, and I can type quickly. I like talking to people and can answer the phones with a friendly voice. I also like languages. I can speak French and Chinese. I also studied English. I can read it, but I can't speak it well. I hurt my back a few years ago. I can't help guests with their suitcases. I can work both Saturdays and Sundays.

EXERCISE 10, p. 360.

1. A: (phone rings) Hello?
   B: Can I speak to Mr. Jones, please?

A: I'm sorry. He can't come to the phone right now. Can I take a message? He can return your call in about a half-hour.

B: Yes. Please tell him Bob Anderson called.

2. A: Can you help me lift this box?

B: It looks very heavy. I can try to help you, but I think we need a third person.

A: No, I'm very strong. I think we can do it together.

3. A: I can't hear the TV. Can you turn it up?

B: I can't turn it up. I'm doing my homework. If I turn it up, I can't concentrate.

A: Can you do your homework in another room?

B: Oh, all right.

EXERCISE 21, p. 367.

1. A: Were you able to talk to John last night?

B: I couldn't reach him. I can try again later today.

2. A: Do you know how to make bread?

B: Yes, I can make bread. What about you?

A: No. Can you teach me?

B: Sure, I can.

3. A: Are you able to understand the teacher?

B: I couldn't understand her in the beginning, but now I can understand most of her lectures.

A: I still can't understand her very well.

4. A: Professor Jones, when will you be able to correct our tests?

B: I began last night, but I wasn't able to finish. I'll try again tonight. I hope I will be able to hand them back to you tomorrow.

5. A: *(phone rings)* Hello?

B: Hi. This is Jan Smith. I'm wondering if I can get in to see Dr. Brown today or tomorrow.

A: Well, she can see you tomorrow morning at 11:00. Can you come in then?

B: Yes, I can. Please tell me where you are. I don't know the way to your office.

Chapter 13: MODALS, PART 2: ADVICE, NECESSITY, REQUESTS, SUGGESTIONS

EXERCISE 5, p. 383.

1. People should exercise to stay healthy.
2. People should eat a lot of candy.
3. People shouldn't steal money.
4. People should keep some money in a bank.
5. Students should study every day.
6. Students shouldn't study on weekends.
7. English students should speak English in class.
8. English teachers shouldn't translate for their students.

EXERCISE 10, p. 386.

1. I have to ("hafta") leave early today. → have to
2. You have to ("hafta") come with us.

3. Where does your friend have to ("hafta") go?
4. She has to ("hasta") go to the dentist again.
5. Why does she have to ("hafta") go there so often?
6. My teachers have to ("hafta") correct a lot of homework.
7. Do they have to ("hafta") give so much work?
8. My dog has to ("hasta") go to the animal hospital.
9. He has to ("hasta") have surgery.
10. We have to ("hafta") take good care of our pets.

EXERCISE 15, p. 390.

1. a. People must eat healthy foods.
   b. People should eat healthy foods.
2. a. People must wear clothes outdoors.
   b. People should wear clothes outdoors.
3. a. People should stop their cars for a police siren.
   b. People must stop their cars for a police siren.
4. a. People must wear coats in cool weather.
   b. People should wear coats in cool weather.
5. a. People should pay taxes to their government.
   b. People must pay taxes to their government.
6. a. People must learn how to use computers.
   b. People should learn how to use computers.
7. a. People should wear seatbelts when they're in a car.
   b. People must wear seatbelts when they're in a car.
8. a. People must be polite to one another.
   b. People should be polite to one another.
9. a. People should keep their homes clean.
   b. People must keep their homes clean.

EXERCISE 27, p. 401.

1. It might snow tomorrow. → b. It may snow.
2. Tom has to work.
3. Becky knows how to swim.
4. The teacher needed to correct papers.
5. It's a good idea to study for the test tomorrow.
6. We may go to a movie tonight.
7. We didn't have to help.
8. I couldn't go to school yesterday.

Chapter 14: NOUNS AND MODIFIERS

EXERCISE 4, p. 406.

1. The phone is on the kitchen counter.
2. The phone is in the kitchen.
3. I'm moving to a new apartment next month.
4. The apartment building has a swimming pool.
5. How do you like your music class?
6. Where are the keys to the car?
7. I'm always losing my car keys.
8. Let's have some chicken soup.
9. The soup is good, but where's the chicken?
10. This grammar book has a lot of information.

EXERCISE 13, p. 415.

1. That was delicious birthday . . . .
2. Here are the car . . . .
3. I need to buy some comfortable . . . .
4. The teacher gave the class an easy . . . .
5. The little boy is playing computer . . . .
6. I'd like to read the newspaper . . . .

EXERCISE 16, p. 418.

1. All of the coffee is gone.
2. Some of the coffee is gone.
3. Half of the coffee is gone.
4. Almost all of the coffee is gone.
5. A lot of the coffee is gone.
6. Most of the coffee is gone.

EXERCISE 21, p. 422.

1. Some of the homework is hard.
2. One of the books is missing.
3. None of the children are here yet.
4. All of the students were late.
5. Half of the class is absent.
6. Almost all of the food was vegetarian.
7. A lot of the exercises were helpful.
8. Most of the movie was scary.

EXERCISE 22, p. 422.

1. Most of the people are happy.
2. All of them are smiling.
3. One of them is mad.
4. None of them are sleeping.
5. Only half of them have hats.
6. Some of them aren't wearing hats.
7. Only one of them has sunglasses.
8. Almost all of them look happy.

Chapter 15: POSSESSIVES

EXERCISE 4, p. 438.

1. Bob's parents live in Tokyo.
2. Bob has two brothers and one sister.
3. My teacher's apartment is near mine.
4. My teacher is very funny.
5. What is your friend saying?
6. My friend's dog ran away.
7. The store manager's name is Dan.
8. My cousin studies engineering.

EXERCISE 16, p. 447.

1. Who's that?
2. Whose glasses are on the floor?
3. Who's coming?
4. Who's next?
5. Whose homework is this?

6. Whose car is outside?
7. Who's ready to begin?
8. Whose turn is it?
9. Whose work is ready?
10. Who's going to help me?

Chapter 16: MAKING COMPARISONS

EXERCISE 3, p. 450.

1. B and D are the same.
2. E is different from A.
3. G and B are similar.
4. A is similar to G.
5. F is the same as A.
6. C and G are different.
7. A and C are similar.

EXERCISE 13, p. 457.

1. It's getting cold outside.
2. The weather today is colder than yesterday.
3. The weather is getting colder outside.
4. Our teacher is happier this week than last week.
5. Professor Jones is happy every day.
6. Are you happy today?
7. Is a big car safer than a small car?
8. I want to drive a safe car.
9. I need to get a safer car.
10. The coffee is fresh and tastes delicious.
11. Maria told a very funny story in class yesterday.
12. Maria and Sami both told stories. Sami's story was funnier than Maria's story.

EXERCISE 21, p. 464.

1. Tim is older than Bob.
2. Pam looks happier than Tim.
3. Bob is the tallest of all.
4. Pam is younger than Bob.
5. Tim looks the most serious.
6. Bob is shorter than Tim.
7. Bob looks happier than Tim.
8. Tim is the youngest.
9. Pam is shorter than Bob.
10. Bob looks more serious than Pam.

EXERCISE 24, p. 468.

1. The blue dress is more expensive than the red one.
2. Well, I think the red one is prettier.
3. Is it too short, or does it look OK?
4. It's the nicest of all the ones you tried on.
5. I'm not going to buy the brown shoes. They're too small.
6. How do you like this hat? It's the biggest size they have.
7. No, this hat is bigger than that one.
8. I need a belt, but one that is longer than my old one.

9. Is this belt long enough?
10. It's perfect. And it's the cheapest of all of them.

EXERCISE 30, p. 476.

1. Linda is tall, but her sister is . . . .
2. My old apartment was small, but my new apartment is . . . .
3. First Street is noisy, but Second Street is . . . .
4. This picture is ugly, but that picture is . . . .
5. A car is fast, but a bike is . . . .
6. A kitten is weak, but a horse is . . . .
7. This watch is expensive, but that watch is . . . .
8. Tom is hard-working, but his brother is . . . .

EXERCISE 32, p. 477.

1. I like strong coffee, but my friend . . . .
2. Ellen can speak Spanish, but her husband . . . .
3. The children didn't want to go to bed early, but their parents . . . .

4. The children weren't tired, but their parents . . . .
5. Jack doesn't want to go out to eat, but his friends . . . .
6. The doctor isn't friendly, but the nurse . . . .
7. I was at home yesterday, but my roommate . . . .
8. Pablo went to the party, but Steve . . . .
9. The grocery store will be open tomorrow, but the bank . . . .
10. I won't be home tonight, but my husband . . . .

EXERCISE 38, p. 482.

1. I work faster than Jim does.
2. Toshi finished his work the fastest of all.
3. Sue studies harder than Fred.
4. Jean studies the hardest of all.
5. A motorcycle is more dangerous than a bicycle.
6. Ali speaks more loudly than Yoko does.
7. A snail moves more slowly than a crab does.
8. This suitcase is heavier than that one.
9. My glasses are clearer than my contact lenses.
10. I can see more clearly with my glasses.

AUDIO CD TRACKING SCRIPT

CD 1	TRACK	EXERCISE	CD 2	TRACK	EXERCISE
Introduction	1		**Chapter 9**	1	Exercise 4, p. 255
Chapter 1	2	Exercise 2, p. 2		2	Exercise 10, p. 259
	3	Exercise 8, p. 6		3	Exercise 14, p. 263
	4	Exercise 13, p. 9		4	Exercise 17, p. 266
	5	Exercise 14, p. 9		5	Exercise 20, p. 268
	6	Exercise 29, p. 22		6	Exercise 23, p. 271
	7	Exercise 30, p. 22		7	Exercise 40, p. 287
Chapter 2	8	Exercise 1, p. 24	**Chapter 10**	8	Exercise 9, p. 300
	9	Exercise 12, p. 32		9	Exercise 11, p. 301
	10	Exercise 22, p. 39		10	Exercise 15, p. 304
				11	Exercise 20, p. 307
Chapter 3	11	Exercise 2, p. 55		12	Exercise 25, p. 310
	12	Exercise 8, p. 59		13	Exercise 27, p. 312
	13	Exercise 13, p. 62		14	Exercise 28, p. 312
	14	Exercise 18, p. 65		15	Exercise 31, p. 315
				16	Exercise 32, p. 316
Chapter 4	15	Exercise 7, p. 96		17	Exercise 34, p. 318
	16	Exercise 21, p. 107		18	Exercise 36, p. 319
	17	Exercise 25, p. 110			
	18	Exercise 26, p. 111	**Chapter 11**	19	Exercise 6, p. 329
				20	Exercise 11, p. 332
Chapter 5	19	Exercise 1, p. 121		21	Exercise 19, p. 338
	20	Exercise 4, p. 124		22	Exercise 24, p. 342
	21	Exercise 12, p. 130		23	Exercise 28, p. 347
	22	Exercise 23, p. 138			
	23	Exercise 31, p. 145	**Chapter 12**	24	Exercise 5, p. 356
	24	Exercise 32, p. 147		25	Exercise 6, p. 357
	25	Exercise 34, p. 148		26	Exercise 10, p. 360
				27	Exercise 21, p. 367
Chapter 6	26	Exercise 12, p. 166			
	27	Exercise 13, p. 167	**Chapter 13**	28	Exercise 5, p. 383
	28	Exercise 15, p. 170		29	Exercise 10, p. 386
	29	Exercise 16, p. 171		30	Exercise 15, p. 390
	30	Exercise 17, p. 172		31	Exercise 27, p. 401
Chapter 7	31	Exercise 6, p. 184	**Chapter 14**	32	Exercise 4, p. 406
	32	Exercise 31, p. 204		33	Exercise 13, p. 415
	33	Exercise 32, p. 205		34	Exercise 16, p. 418
				35	Exercise 21, p. 422
Chapter 8	34	Exercise 5, p. 215		36	Exercise 22, p. 422
	35	Exercise 14, p. 224			
	36	Exercise 18, p. 226	**Chapter 15**	37	Exercise 4, p. 438
	37	Exercise 22, p. 230		38	Exercise 16, p. 447
	38	Exercise 30, p. 235			
	39	Exercise 33, p. 237	**Chapter 16**	39	Exercise 3, p. 450
	40	Exercise 37, p. 241		40	Exercise 13, p. 457
	41	Exercise 41, p. 244		41	Exercise 21, p. 464
	42	Exercise 44, p. 247		42	Exercise 24, p. 468
				43	Exercise 30, p. 476
				44	Exercise 32, p. 477
				45	Exercise 38, p. 482

Answer Key

Chapter 1: USING *BE*

EXERCISE 2, p. 2.

2. is a
3. They're in
4. is an
5. It's
6. aren't
7. They're happy
8. is
9. isn't
10. She's

EXERCISE 3, p. 2.

2. English is a language.
3. Tokyo is a city.
4. Australia is a country.
5. Red is a color.
6. A dictionary is a book.
7. A hotel is a building.
8. A bear is an animal.
9. A bee is an insect.
10. An ant is an insect.

EXERCISE 4, p. 3

4. Tennis is a sport.
5. Chicago is a city.
6. Spanish is a language.
7. Mexico is a country.
8. A cow is an animal.
9. A fly is an insect.
10. Baseball is a sport.
11. China is a country.
12. Russian is a language.

EXERCISE 6, p. 4.

2. Computers are machines.
3. Dictionaries are books
4. Chickens are birds.
5. Roses are flowers.
6. Carrots are vegetables.
7. Rabbits are animals.
8. Egypt and Indonesia are countries.
9. Winter and summer are seasons.

EXERCISE 7, p. 5.

1. A bear is an animal.
2. An ant is an insect.
3. London is a city.
4. Spring is a season.
5. A carrot is a vegetable.
6. September and October are months.
7. Mexico and Canada are countries.
8. A dictionary is a book.
9. Chickens are birds.
10. China is a country.
11. Winter and summer are seasons.
12. Arabic is a language.
13. A computer is a machine.
14. A fly is an insect.

EXERCISE 8, p. 6.

1. yes
2. no
3. yes
4. no
5. no
6. yes
7. no
8. yes
9. yes

EXERCISE 10, p. 7.

2. I am a student.
3. Rita is a student.
4. Rita and Tom are students.
5. You are a student.
6. You are students.

EXERCISE 12, p. 8.

2. He's in my class.
3. He's twenty years old.
4. They're students.
5. It's on my desk.
6. They're friendly.
7. They're on my desk.
8. He's married.
9. She's single.
10. They're in my class.
11. They're interesting.
12. It's easy.
13. We're roommates.
14. It's on Pine Street.
15. I'm a student.
16. You're in my English class.

EXERCISE 13, p. 9.

1. They're very nice.
2. I'm in the classroom.
3. He's late.
4. You're a teacher.
5. I'm her friend.
6. We're in the same class.
7. They're young.
8. It's very big.
9. She's very friendly.
10. It's fun.

EXERCISE 14, p. 9.

1. is
2. I'm
3. is
4. is
5. We're
6. It's
7. We're
8. It's

EXERCISE 15, p. 10.

1. Canada is a country. It is not/isn't a city.
2. Jakarta is not/isn't a country. It is/It's a city.
3. Beijing and London are cities. They are not/aren't countries.
4. Asia is not/isn't a country. It is/It's a continent.
5. Asia and South America are continents. They are not/aren't countries.

EXERCISE 16, p. 11.

PART I.

bus driver: Ms. Black
police officer: Mr. Rice
gardener: Mike
doctor: Sue
photographer: Ann.

PART II.

2. is . . . He isn't an artist.
3. isn't . . . He's a painter.
4. isn't . . . She's a doctor.
5. is . . . He isn't an artist / a bus driver / a gardener / a doctor / a photographer.
6. police officer / gardener / doctor / photographer / an artist . . . She's a bus driver.
7. *(free response)*

EXERCISE 17, p. 12.

2. He's poor.
3. It's short.
4. They're clean.
5. They're beautiful.
6. They're expensive.
7. They're fast.
8. It's easy.
9. She's tall.
10. They're old.
11. It's noisy.

EXERCISE 18, p. 13.

2. Ice and snow are cold.
3. A box is square.
4. Balls and oranges are round.
5. Sugar is sweet.
6. An elephant is large/big, but a mouse is small/little.
7. A rain forest is wet, but a desert is dry.
8. A joke is funny.
9. Good health is important.
10. They are/They're dangerous.
11. A coin is small, round, and flat.
12. A lemon is sour.

EXERCISE 20, p. 14.

3. Lemons are yellow.
4. Ripe bananas are yellow too.
5. A lemon isn't sweet. It is/It's sour.
6. My pen isn't heavy. It is/It's light.
7. This room isn't dark. It is/It's light.
8. My classmates are friendly.
9. A turtle is slow.
10. Airplanes aren't slow. They are/They're fast.

11. The floor in the classroom is/isn't clean. It isn't/is dirty.
12. The weather is/isn't cold today.
13. The sun is/isn't bright today.
14. My shoes are/aren't comfortable.

EXERCISE 21, p. 15.

Partner A:

1. The table isn't clean. It's dirty.
2. The little boy is sick. He isn't well.
3. The algebra problem isn't easy. It's difficult.
4. The cars are old. They aren't new.

Partner B:

1. The man is friendly. He isn't unfriendly.
2. The coffee isn't cold. It's hot.
3. The woman is tall. She isn't short.
4. Ken's sister isn't old. She's young.

EXERCISE 25, p. 19.

2. under
3. on
4. next to
5. above
6. behind
7. between

EXERCISE 28, p. 21.

4. are + a noun
5. is + a place
6. is + an adjective
7. are + a noun
8. am + a place
9. is + a place
10. are + an adjective

EXERCISE 30, p. 23.

1. B
2. A
3. A
4. B
5. A
6. B
7. B
8. A
9. A
10. B

Chapter 2: USING *BE* AND *HAVE*

EXERCISE 1, p. 24.

1. no
2. yes
3. no
4. yes/no
5. no
6. no
7. no
8. yes
9. no

EXERCISE 2, p. 24.

2. Is the sun a ball of fire?
3. Are carrots vegetables?
4. Are chickens birds?
5. Is Mr. Wu here today?
6. Are Sue and Mike here today?
7. Is English grammar fun?
8. Are you ready for the next grammar chart?

EXERCISE 3, p. 25.

3. A: Are you homesick?
   B: No, I'm not.
4. A: Is Bob homesick?
   B: Yes, he is.

5. A: Is Sue here today?
   B: No, she isn't.
6. A: Are the students in this class intelligent?
   B: Yes, they are.
7. A: Are the chairs in this room comfortable?
   B: No, they aren't.
8. A: Are you married?
   B: No, I'm not.
9. A: Are Tom and you roommates?
   B: Yes, we are.
10. A: Is a butterfly a bird?
    B: No, it isn't.

EXERCISE 7, p. 28.

3. Is Cairo in Egypt?
4. Where is Cairo?
5. Are the students in class today?
6. Where are the students?
7. Where is the post office?
8. Is the train station on Grand Avenue?
9. Where is the bus stop?
10. Where are Sue and Ken today?

EXERCISE 9, p. 30.

2. have	9. have
3. has . . . has	10. has . . . has
4. have	11. has
5. has	12. have
6. have . . . have	13. have
7. has	14. has
8. have . . . has	

EXERCISE 10, p. 31.

1. has a headache	5. have a cold
2. have toothaches	6. have backaches
3. have a fever	7. has a stomachache
4. has a sore throat	

EXERCISE 11, p. 31.

1. A: How are you?
   B: I have a headache.
2. A: How are you?
   B: I have a sore tooth.
3. A: How is/How's your mother?
   B: She has a sore back.
4. A: How is/How's Mr. Lee?
   B: He has a backache.
5. A: How are your parents?
   B: They have colds.
6. A: How are the patients?
   B: They have stomachaches.
7. A: How is/How's your little brother?
   B: He has a sore throat.
8. A: How is/How's Mrs. Wood?
   B: She has a fever.

EXERCISE 12, p. 32.

1. have	5. has
2. has	6. have
3. has	7. have
4. has	8. have

EXERCISE 14, p. 33.

1. your	6. their
2. her	7. your
3. their	8. our
4. her	9. his
5. my	10. her

EXERCISE 15, p. 33.

1. His . . . Palmer
2. His . . . John
3. His . . . B.
4. Their . . . 98301
5. Their . . . (888)
6. Her . . . 4/12/70
7. Her . . . April 12
8. Her . . . Ellen
9.–15. My . . . *(free response)*

EXERCISE 17, p. 36.

2. His	6. Our	10. Their
3. My	7. Your	11. His
4. Their	8. Her	12. My
5. Your	9. His	

EXERCISE 19, p. 37.

2. has . . . His	8. have . . . My
3. have . . . Your	9. have . . . Our
4. has . . . Her	10. have . . . Your
5. have . . . Their	11. has . . . Her
6. have . . . Their	12. has . . . His
7. have . . . Our	

EXERCISE 20, p. 38.

3. This	6. This	9. That
4. That	7. This	10. This
5. That	8. That	

EXERCISE 22, p. 39.

1. This	5. that	8. that
2. That	6. This	9. This
3. That	7. this	10. That
4. This		

EXERCISE 23, p. 40.

1. These	4. These
2. Those	5. Those
3. Those	6. These

EXERCISE 24, p. 40.

2. This . . . Those
3. These . . . Those
4. This . . . That
5. These . . . Those
6. This . . . Those
7. these . . . those
8. This . . . Those

EXERCISE 26, p. 42.

2. What are
3. Who is
4. What is
5. Who are
6. What is
7. Who is
8. Who are
9. What is
10. What are

EXERCISE 31, p. 47.

2. I **am not/I'm not** hungry.
3. I am/I'm **a** student. He is **a** teacher.
4. Yoko **is** not here. She **is** at school.
5. I'm from Mexico. Where **are you** from?
6. **Is** Roberto ~~he~~ a student in your class?
7. Those pictures are **beautiful**.
8. This is **your** dictionary. It **is/It's** not my dictionary.
9. Mr. Lee **has** a brown coat.
10. They **aren't** here today.
11. **These** books are expensive. OR This **book is** expensive.
12. Cuba is **an** island.

EXERCISE 32, p. 47.

1. C
2. C
3. B
4. B
5. B
6. C
7. C
8. C
9. A
10. A
11. C
12. B

EXERCISE 33, p. 48.

1. are not/aren't
2. is
3. am/am not
4. are
5. are
6. are . . . are not/aren't
7. is not/isn't . . . is
8. is
9. are
10. is not/isn't . . . is

EXERCISE 34, p. 49

1. A: is
   B: has
   A: are
   B: have
2. A: What is/What's
   B: is a
   A: Who is
   B: my
   A: Who are
3. A: this/that . . . this/that
   B: *(free response)*
4. *(free response)*
5. *(free response)*
6. A: What is/What's a . . . What is/What's a
   B: It is/It's an
   A: Is a
   B: They are/They're

EXERCISE 37, p. 51.

3. I am/I'm
4. I am/I'm
5. My
6. is
7. He is/He's
8. My
9. is
10. She is/She's
11. have
12. are
13. is
14. She is/She's
15. is
16. She is/She's
17. my
18. is
19. He is/He's
20. has
21. It is/It's
22. is
23. His
24. He is/He's
25. He is/He's
26. They are/They're
27. my
28. They are/They're

Chapter 3: USING THE SIMPLE PRESENT

EXERCISE 2, p. 55.

1. I **wake** up early every day.
2. My brother **wakes** up late.
3. He **gets** up at 11:00.
4. I **go** to school at 8:00.
5. My mother **does** exercises every morning.
6. My little sister **watches** TV in the morning.
7. I **take** the bus to school.
8. My brother **takes** the bus to school.
9. My friends **take** the bus too.
10. We **talk** about our day.

EXERCISE 3, p. 55.

2. drinks
3. take
4. takes
5. study
6. walk
7. begins
8. stops
9. eat
10. go

EXERCISE 4, p. 56.

2. usually
3. often
4. sometimes
5. seldom
6. rarely
7. never

EXERCISE 5, p. 57.

S	V	
2. I	eat	I never eat carrots
3. I	watch	I seldom watch TV
4. I	have	I sometimes have tea
5. Sonya	eats	Sonya usually eats lunch
6. Joe	drinks	Joe rarely drinks tea.
7. We	listen	We often listen to music
8. The students	speak	The students always speak English

EXERCISE 7, p. 58.

2. once . . . rarely
3. twice . . . seldom
4. six times . . . usually
5. five times . . . often
6. never
7. three times . . . sometimes

EXERCISE 8, p. 59.

1. I go to work every **morning**.
2. I celebrate my birthday every **year**.
3. Our son is two **years** old.
4. I use my computer every **day**.
5. Bob uses his computer five **days** a week.
6. I eat three **times** a day.
7. Anna listens to the radio every **night**.
8. I visit my uncle every **month**.

EXERCISE 9, p. 60.

3. Maria is **often** late for class.
4. Maria **often** comes to class late.
5. It **never** snows in my hometown.
6. It is **never** very cold in my hometown.
7. Bob is **usually** at home in the evening.
8. Bob **usually** stays at home in the evening.
9. Tom **seldom** studies at the library in the evening.
10. His classmates are **seldom** at the library in the evening.
11. I **sometimes** skip breakfast.
12. I **rarely** have time for a big breakfast.
13. I am **usually** very hungry by lunchtime.
14. Sue **never** drinks coffee.

EXERCISE 12, p. 61.

2. teaches
3. fixes
4. drinks
5. watches
6. kisses
7. wears
8. washes
9. walks
10. stretches . . . yawns

EXERCISE 13, p. 62.

1. Mrs. Miller **teaches** English on Saturdays.
2. Mr. and Mrs. Smith **teach** English in the evenings.
3. Doug **fixes** cars.
4. His son **fixes** cars too.
5. Carlos and Chris **watch** DVDs on weekends.
6. Their daughter **watches** videos.
7. I **brush** my hair every morning.
8. Jimmy seldom **brushes** his hair.
9. The Johnsons **wash** their car every weekend.
10. Susan rarely **washes** her car.

EXERCISE 14, p. 62

gets . . . cooks . . . sits . . . washes . . . turns . . . watches . . . takes . . . brushes . . . reads . . . falls

EXERCISE 15, p. 63.

1. tries
2. studies
3. says
4. worries
5. flies
6. stays
7. enjoys
8. buys
9. pays
10. plays

EXERCISE 16, p. 63.

2. seldom cries
3. studies
4. usually stays
5. flies
6. always carries
7. seldom buys
8. worries
9. enjoys

EXERCISE 17, p. 64.

3. have
4. has
5. goes
6. has
7. does
8. do
9. goes
   . . . go
10. go

EXERCISE 18, p. 65.

3. is
4. has
5. has
6. goes
7. has
8. does
9. has
10. does
11. has
12. goes
13. is
14. is

EXERCISE 20, p. 67.

2. usually studies
3. bites
4. cashes
5. worry . . . never worries . . . studies
6. teach . . . teaches
7. fly . . . have
8. flies . . . has
9. always does . . . never goes
10. always says
11. always pays . . . answers . . . listens . . . asks
12. enjoys . . . often tries . . . likes . . . invites . . . go . . . watch . . . has . . . watches . . . makes . . . washes . . . cleans . . . never cook . . . is . . . loves

EXERCISE 23, p. 69.

3. doesn't know
4. don't need
5. doesn't snow
6. don't speak
7. 'm not
8. don't live
9. doesn't have
10. isn't
11. aren't
12. don't have
13. doesn't have
14. isn't
15. doesn't rain

EXERCISE 26, p. 72.

2. don't speak
3. doesn't shave
4. don't go
5. doesn't smoke
6. don't eat
7. don't do
8. doesn't drink
9. doesn't make
10. don't do
11. doesn't put on

EXERCISE 28, p. 74.

3. A: Do you speak Chinese?
   B: No, I don't.
4. A: Does Ann speak Italian?
   B: Yes, she does.
5. A: Do Ann and Tom speak Arabic?
   B: No, they don't.

6. A: Do you exercise every morning?
   B: Yes, I do.
7. A: Does Sue have a cold?
   B: Yes, she does.
8. A: Does Jim do his homework every day?
   B: No, he doesn't.
9. A: Does it rain a lot in April?
   B: Yes, it does.
10. A: Do frogs have tails?
    B: No, they don't.

EXERCISE 32, p. 78.

3. Where does Peter work?
4. Does Peter work at the post office?
5. Do you live in an apartment?
6. Where do you live?
7. Where does Bill eat dinner every day?
8. Where do you sit during class?
9. Where does Jessica go to school?
10. Where is your book?
11. Where do you go every morning?
12. Where are the students?
13. Where do kangaroos live?

EXERCISE 34, p. 80.

3. When/What time do you get up?
4. When/What time does Maria usually get up?
5. When/What time does the movie start?
6. When/What time do you usually go to bed?
7. When/What time do you usually eat lunch?
8. When/What time does the restaurant open?
9. When/What time does the train leave?
10. When/What time do you usually eat dinner?
11. When/What time do your classes begin?
12. When/What time does the library close on Saturday?

EXERCISE 37, p. 82.

2. Do	7. Do	12. Is
3. is	8. Are	13. does
4. Are	9. Does	14. Does
5. are	10. Do	15. Are
6. do	11. Does	16. Do

EXERCISE 38, p. 84.

2. Does (no)
3. Do (yes)
4. Is (no) [It's a star.]
5. Are (no)
6. Is (yes) [Around 900 degrees Fahrenheit.]
7. Is (no) [You need a telescope.]
8. Is (yes) [The winds are stronger than the earth's winds.]
9. Do (yes)
10. Do (yes) [Saturn has at least 24; Uranus has at least 21.]

EXERCISE 40, p. 85.

(1) My friend Abdul lives in an apartment near school. (2) He walks to school almost every day. (3) Sometimes he catches a bus, especially if it's cold and rainy outside. (4) Abdul shares the apartment with Pablo. (5) Pablo comes from Venezuela. (6) Abdul and Pablo go to the same school. (7) They take English classes. (8) Abdul speaks Arabic as his first language, and Pablo speaks Spanish. (9) They communicate in English. (10) Sometimes Abdul tries to teach Pablo to speak a little Arabic, and Pablo gives Abdul Spanish lessons. (11) They laugh a lot during the Arabic and Spanish lessons. (12) Abdul enjoys having Pablo as his roommate, but he misses his family back in Saudi Arabia.

EXERCISE 42, p. 87.

1. Do you study	6. don't like
2. study	7. are you
3. studies	8. want
4. Do you spend	9. don't want
5. spend	10. think

EXERCISE 43, p. 88.

1. have	7. never washes
2. washes	8. wears
3. Do you know	9. is always
4. is	10. is always
5. doesn't change	11. says
6. keeps	12. takes

EXERCISE 46, p. 90.

Name	Where does she/he live?	What does he/she do?	Where does she/he work?	What pets does he/she have?
Peter	(on a boat)	catches fish	on his boat	a turtle
Kathy	in a cabin in the mountains	(teaches skiing)	at a ski school	ten fish
Ron	in an apartment in the city	makes jewelry	(at a jewelry store)	three cats
Lisa	in a beach cabin on an island	surfs and swims	has no job	(a snake)
Jack	in a house in the country	designs web pages	at home	a horse

EXERCISE 47, p. 91.

2. Ann **usually comes** to class on time.
3. Peter **uses** his cell phone often.
4. Amy **carries** a **computer notebook** to work every day.
5. She **enjoys** her job.
6. I **don't** know Joe.
7. Mike **doesn't** like milk. He never **drinks** it.
8. Tina doesn't **speak** Chinese. She **speaks** Spanish.
9. **Are you** a student?
10. Does your roommate **sleep** with the window open?
11. A: Do you like strong coffee?
    B: Yes, I **do**.
12. Where **do** your parents live?
13. What time **does** your English class **begin**?
14. Olga **doesn't** need a car. She **has** a bicycle.
15. **Does** Pablo **do** his homework every day?

Chapter 4: USING THE PRESENT PROGRESSIVE

EXERCISE 7, p. 96.

1. yes   5. no   8. yes
2. yes   6. no   9. no
3. no   7. no   10. no
4. no

EXERCISE 8, p. 96.

2. riding   8. counting
3. running   9. fixing
4. stopping   10. writing
5. raining   11. growing
6. sleeping   12. waiting
7. pushing

EXERCISE 9, p. 97.

2. coming   8. planning
3. dreaming   9. dining
4. biting   10. snowing
5. hitting   11. studying
6. joining   12. warning
7. hurting

EXERCISE 10, p. 98.

1. smiling   9. eating
2. flying   10. running
3. laughing   11. singing
4. sitting   12. reading
5. standing   13. drinking
6. sleeping   14. sneezing
7. clapping   15. crying
8. writing   16. cutting

EXERCISE 12, p. 99.

1. watching the news . . . talking on the phone.
2. is listening to music . . . not playing the piano.

3. is reading a magazine . . . not reading a book.
4. aren't flying . . . sitting on a telephone wire.

EXERCISE 15, p. 102.

2. Is John riding a bicycle?
3. Are you sleeping?
4. Are the students watching TV?
5. Is it raining outside?

EXERCISE 18, p. 104.

2. Why are you reading your grammar book?
3. What are you writing in your grammar book?
4. Where is Seung sitting?
5. Where are you living?
6. What is Roberto wearing today?
7. Why are you smiling?

EXERCISE 19, p. 105.

3. A: Is Anna eating lunch?
   B: she is.
4. is she eating?
5. A: Is Mike drinking a cup of coffee?
   B: he isn't.
6. is he drinking?
7. A: Are the girls playing in the street?
   B: they aren't.
8. are they playing?
9. are they playing in the park?

EXERCISE 20, p. 107.

1. . . . is talking . . . isn't talking
2. rains . . . isn't raining . . . is shining . . . Does it rain
3. sit . . . help . . . is helping
4. cooks . . . is cooking . . . Is he cooking . . .
   doesn't eat . . . Do you eat . . . Are you

EXERCISE 21, p. 107.

1. every day   5. every day
2. now   6. now
3. now   7. every day
4. every day   8. now

EXERCISE 23, p. 108.

1. Are . . . is   6. am . . . Do
2. Do   7. does
3. is . . . Does   8. is
4. do   9. do
5. Am   10. Do

EXERCISE 24, p. 109.

2. A: walk . . . don't take   5. A: are you reading
   . . . Do you take   B: am reading
3. B: is she talking   6. A: Do you want
   A: is running   B: Is this
4. A: read   A: Is hanging
   B: Do you read
   A: don't read

EXERCISE 25 p. 110.

1. A: Does . . . have
    B: (Yes.)
    A: Does he wear
    B: (No.)
    A: Is he wearing
    B: don't know
    A: think

2. A: Do . . . dream
    B: aren't
    A: is sleeping . . . are
    . . . is barking . . .
    moving . . . am . . .
    is dreaming . . .
    dream

EXERCISE 26, p. 111.

A: Are you working
B: I'm not . . . I'm writing
A: Do you write
B: don't write
A: Does she write
B: get . . . Do you get
A: like

EXERCISE 27, p. 112.

2. is snowing . . . like
3. know
4. is talking . . . understand
5. is eating . . . likes . . . tastes
6. smell . . . Do you smell
7. is telling . . . believe . . . think
8. is smoking . . . smells . . . hate
9. is holding . . . loves . . . is smiling

EXERCISE 28, p. 113.

Questions:

1. What do you like?
2. What do babies around the world like?
3. What do you want?
4. What do children around the world want?
5. What do you love?
6. What do teenagers around the world love?
7. What do you dislike or hate?
8. What do people around the world dislike or hate?
9. What do you need?
10. What do elderly people around the world need?

EXERCISE 30, p. 115.

2. speaks . . . is speaking
3. are doing . . . do
4. am looking . . . is writing . . . is looking . . . is biting
   . . . is smiling . . . is sleeping . . . is chewing
5. works . . . has . . . often eats . . . usually brings . . .
   usually sits . . . sits . . . watches . . . watches . . .
   relaxes
6. am looking . . . isn't . . . is . . . is sitting . . . is eating
   . . . is running . . . is sitting . . . is eating . . . is
   watching . . . always watches . . . are swimming . . .
   are flying . . . is riding . . . rides . . . is having . . . go

EXERCISE 34, p. 119.

2. B	5. B	8. A
3. C	6. C	9. A
4. C	7. B	10. B

EXERCISE 35, p. 119.

1. It's **raining** today. I **don't** like the rain.
2. I like New York City. I **think** that it is a wonderful city.
3. **Is** Abdul **sleeping** right now?
4. Why **are you** going downtown today?
5. I'm listening **to** you.
6. **Do** you **hear** a noise outside the window?
7. Kunio **is** at a restaurant right now. He usually **eats** at home, but today he **is eating** dinner at a restaurant.
8. I **like** flowers. They **smell** good.
9. Alex is **sitting** at his desk. He**'s writing** a letter.
10. Where **are they** sitting today?

Chapter 5: TALKING ABOUT THE PRESENT

EXERCISE 2, p. 122.

2. What's the date today?
3. What time is it?
4. What month is it?
5. What time is it?
6. What day is it?
7. What's the date today?
8. What year is it?
9. What time is it?

EXERCISE 3, p. 123.

2. from . . . to	8. on
3. in . . . in	9. on
4. in	10. on
5. at	11. from . . . to
6. in	12. at
7. in	

EXERCISE 4, p. 124.

PART I.

1. Ann	3. Ron
2. Lisa	4. Tom

PART II.

1. in . . . on . . . Tom
2. in . . . on . . . Ann
3. in . . . at . . . Lisa
4. Ron . . . in . . . on . . . in

EXERCISE 6, p. 125.

2. 0° C   cold, freezing
3. 38° C   hot
4. 24° C   warm
5. −18° C very cold, below freezing

EXERCISE 7, p. 126.

2. 34° F
3. 90° F
4. 50° F
5. 62° F
6. 7.5° C
7. 20° C
8. 14° C
9. 35° C
10. −5° C

EXERCISE 9, p. 128.

3. is (yes)
4. are (no)
5. is
6. are
7. are
8. is
9. are
10. is
11. are
12. are

} *(free response)*

EXERCISE 12, p. 130.

1. There're
2. There's
3. There're
4. There's
5. There's
6. There're
7. There're
8. There's

EXERCISE 16, p. 132.

Teacher's key:

	a swimming pool	a beach	tennis courts	horses	ocean-view rooms
Hotel 1	(yes)	yes	yes	no	yes
Hotel 2	yes	(yes)	yes	yes	no
Hotel 3	yes	yes	(yes)	yes	yes
Hotel 4	yes	yes	no	(yes)	yes
Hotel 5	no	yes	yes	yes	(yes)

EXERCISE 19, p. 134.

1. in
2. in
3. on
4. at . . . in
5. First Street
6. Miami / Florida / Miami, Florida
7. 342 First Street
8.–11. *(free response)*

EXERCISE 20, p. 136.

2. under/in front of
3. above/behind
4. beside, near, next to
5. far (away) from
6. in/inside
7. between
8. around
9. outside/next to
10. front
11. back
12. the front/inside
13. the back/inside

EXERCISE 23, p. 138.

1. yes
2. no
3. yes
4. no
5. yes
6. yes
7. no
8. yes
9. yes
10. yes
11. no
12. yes
13. no
14. yes
15. yes

EXERCISE 24, p. 139.

PART I.

1. Mary is eating at/in a restaurant.
2. I see a cup of coffee, a vase of flowers, a candle, a bowl of salad, a glass of water, a plate, and a piece of meat.
3. Mary is holding a knife in her right hand. She is holding a fork in her left hand.
4. There's some salad in the bowl.
5. There's a steak/a piece of meat on the plate.
6. There's coffee in the cup.
7. A candle is burning.
8. No, Mary isn't eating breakfast.
9. No, Mary isn't at home. She's at/in a restaurant.
10. She's cutting a steak/a piece of meat.

PART II.

11. at
12. on
13. in
14. is . . . in
15. at/in
16. isn't
17. isn't

EXERCISE 25, p. 140.

PART I.

1. John is studying.
2. I see a clock, a sign, some books, some bookshelves, a librarian, a desk, a plant, a table, three chairs, and two students.
3. No, John isn't at home. He's at the library.
4. No, John isn't reading a newspaper.
5. The librarian is standing behind the circulation desk.
6. John is right-handed.

PART II.

7. at/in
8. at
9. in/on
10. under
11. on
12. on
13. on
14. isn't
15. is . . . behind
16. beside/near/next to

EXERCISE 26, p. 141.

PART I.

1. Mary is signing/writing a check.
2. Mary's address is 3471 Tree Street, Chicago, Illinois 60565.
3. Mary's full name is Mary S. Jones.
4. Mary's middle initial is S.
5. Mary's last name is Jones.
6. Mary wants fifty dollars.

7. Mary's name and address are in the upper-left corner of the check.
8. The bank's name and address are in the lower-left corner of the check. OR Mary's bank account number is in the lower-left corner of the check.
9. The name of the bank is First National Bank.

PART II.

10. check
11. her
12. of
13. at
14. in
15. in . . . of

EXERCISE 27, p. 142.

PART I.

1. Mary is cashing a check.
2. No, Mary isn't at a store. She's at/in a bank.
3. I see a bank teller, a clock, a sign, a line of people, a check, a purse/handbag/pocketbook, a briefcase, a tie/necktie, eyeglasses, a suit, a T-shirt, a beard and a mustache, pants, jeans, and a dress.
4. A woman is standing behind Mary.
5. A man is standing at the end of the line.
6. There are three men in the picture.
7. There are two women in the picture.
8. There are five people in the picture.
9. There are four people standing in line.

PART II.

10. at/in/inside
11. are
12. at/in front of
13. behind/in back of
14. is . . . behind/in back of
15. isn't . . . at . . . of
16. is . . . at . . . of
17. is . . . between

EXERCISE 28, p. 143.

3. Linda wants **to** go to the bookstore.
4. *(no change)*
5. I need **to** make a telephone call.
6. *(no change)*
7. Do you want **to** go to the movie with us?
8. *(no change)*

EXERCISE 30, p. 144.

2. to go . . . to buy
3. to watch
4. to play
5. to call
6. to go . . . to cash
7. to do
8. to wash
9. to marry
10. to take
11. to go
12. to listen to
13. to take . . . to walk
14. to pay

EXERCISE 31, p. 145.

1. do you want to go
2. do you want to go

3. doesn't want to go . . . she needs to study
4. I want to take
5. We don't need to come
6. wants to go back . . . he wants to change
7. A: do you want to go
   B: I want to visit
8. I need to look up
9. A: Do you want to go
   B: I need to get

EXERCISE 32, p. 147.

3. Ahmed and Anita would like
4. They would like
5. A: Would you like
   B: I would
6. I would like to thank
7. My friends would like to thank
8. A: Would Robert like to ride
   B: he would

EXERCISE 34, p. 148.

1. 'd like
2. like
3. 'd like
4. likes
5. 'd like
6. likes
7. like
8. like
9. 'd like
10. 'd like

EXERCISE 37, p. 150.

PART I.

1. John/He is cooking/making dinner.
2. I see a kitchen, a stove, a pot, a salt shaker, a pepper shaker, a clock, a refrigerator, a spoon, and a shopping/grocery list.
3. John is in the kitchen./John is at the stove.
4. Yes, John/he is tasting his dinner.
5. No, John isn't a good cook. [because he doesn't like the taste of the food]
6. The refrigerator is beside/near/next to the stove. [behind John]
7. There's a shopping/grocery list on the refrigerator.
8. The food on the stove is hot.
9. The food in the refrigerator is cold.

PART II.

10. in
11. on
12. beside/near/next to
13. on
14. to go
15. on
16. on . . . of
17. in

EXERCISE 38, p. 151.

PART I.

1. John and Mary are sitting on a sofa. They're watching TV.

2. I see a TV set, a table, a fishbowl, a fish, a rug, a dog, a cat, a lamp, a clock, and a sofa.
3. No, John and Mary aren't in the kitchen. They're in the living room.
4. The lamp is on the floor. The lamp is beside/near/next to the sofa.
5. The rug is on the floor in front of the sofa.
6. The dog is on the rug.
7. The cat is on the sofa. OR The cat is beside/next to Mary.
8. No, the cat isn't walking. The cat's sleeping.
9. The dog is sleeping (too).
10. A fishbowl is on top of the TV set. OR There's a fishbowl on top of the TV set.
11. No, the fish isn't watching TV.
12. There's a singer on the TV screen. John and Mary are watching a singer on TV.

PART II.
13. are . . . to
14. are . . . on
15. aren't
16. on
17. is . . . on
18. is . . . on

EXERCISE 39, p. 152.

PART I.
1. John and Mary are talking to each other on the phone.
2. I see a clock, a refrigerator, a calendar, two phones, a table, a pen, a chair, a piece of paper, a telephone book, and a picture on the wall.
3. Yes, John/he is happy. Yes, Mary/she is happy. Yes, John and Mary/they are smiling.
4. No, they aren't sad. / No, they're not sad.
5. John is standing. Mary is sitting.
6. No, John isn't in his bedroom. He's in his kitchen.
7. Mary is drawing a heart.
8. There's a telephone book on Mary's table. OR There's a piece of paper. OR There's/are a telephone book and a piece of paper on Mary's table.
9. There's a clock on the wall next to the refrigerator. OR There's a calendar on the wall next to the refrigerator. OR A clock and a calendar are on the wall next to the refrigerator.
10. The clock is on the wall next to the refrigerator.
11. It's eight-thirty/half past eight.
12. There's a picture of a mountain on the wall above the table.

PART II.
13. are . . . on
14. is . . . to . . . is . . . to . . . are . . . each
15. in . . . in front of/near/next to/beside
16. on
17. is . . . at . . . drawing
18. talk
19. on
20. of . . . above

EXERCISE 40, p. 153.

PART I.
1. Mary is sleeping. She's dreaming about John.
2. John is sleeping. He's dreaming about Mary.
3. Mary and John are sleeping and dreaming about each other.
4. I see an alarm clock, two pillows, two heads, and two beds.
5. Yes, she is. Mary is in her bedroom.
6. No, John isn't in class. He's in his bedroom.
7. John is/He's lying down.
8. Yes, Mary is/she's dreaming.
9. Yes, Mary and John/they are dreaming about each other.
10. Yes, Mary and John/they are in love.

PART II.
11. are . . . in
12. is . . . about/of . . . is . . . about/of . . . are . . . about/of
13. on
14. aren't
15. are . . . aren't
16. in
17. to

EXERCISE 43, p. 154.

2. B	5. B	7. C
3. A	6. C	8. C
4. C		

EXERCISE 44, p. 154.

1. Do you want **to** go downtown with me?
2. There **are** many problems in big cities today.
3. I'd like **to** see a movie tonight.
4. We **need** to find a new apartment soon.
5. Mr. Rice **would like** to have a cup of tea.
6. How many students **are there** in your class?
7. Yoko and Ivan are **studying** grammar right now. They want **to** learn English.
8. I **would** like to leave now. How about you?
9. Please put the chair in **the** middle **of** the room.
10. The teacher needs to **check** our homework now.

EXERCISE 46, p. 156.

1. is sitting
2. is reading
3. is sitting
4. is studying
5. is listening to
6. hears
7. isn't listening to
8. is reading
9. is studying
10. likes
11. thinks
12. is thinking about
13. understands
14. is cooking
15. is making
16. is rising
17. doesn't like
18. knows
19. is making/makes
20. is thinking about
21. gets
22. loves

23. wants
24. take
25. is standing
26. is taking off
27. is wearing
28. is thinking about
29. wants
30. to watch
31. needs
32. to go
33. is eating
34. thinks
35. tastes
36. doesn't see
37. doesn't smell
38. is sleeping
39. is dreaming about
40. is playing
41. doesn't see
42. is looking at
43. is singing
44. isn't listening to

Chapter 6: NOUNS AND PRONOUNS

EXERCISE 2, p. 159.

Nouns: dog, eyes, English, mathematics, flowers, juice, Paris

EXERCISE 3, p. 159.

3. | Children | like | candy | (none) | (none) |
   subj.   verb obj. of verb prep. obj. of prep.

4. | The teacher | is erasing | the board | with | her hand |
   subj.   verb   obj. of verb prep.   obj. of prep.

5. | Mike | lives | (none) | in | Africa |
   subj. verb obj. of verb prep. obj. of prep.

6. | The sun | is shining | (none) | (none) | (none) |
   subj.   verb   obj. of verb prep.   obj. of prep.

7. | Robert | is reading | a book | about | butterflies |
   subj.   verb   obj. of verb prep.   obj. of prep.

8. | Tom and Ann | live | (none) | with | their parents |
   subj.   verb obj. of verb prep.   obj. of prep.

9. | Monkeys | eat | fruit and insects | (none) | (none) |
   subj.   verb   obj. of verb   prep. obj. of prep.

10. | Mary and Bob | help | Sue | with | her homework |
    subj.   verb obj.of verb prep.   obj. of prep.

11. | Ships | sail | (none) | across | the ocean |
    subj. verb obj. of verb prep.   obj. of prep.

12. | Water | contains | hydrogen and oxygen | (none) | (none) |
    subj.   verb   obj. of verb   prep. obj. of prep.

EXERCISE 4, p. 161.

2. sister = *noun*
   beautiful = *adjective*
   house = *noun*
3. Italian = *adjective*
   restaurant = *noun*
4. Maria = *noun*
   favorite = *adjective*
   songs = *noun*
   shower = *noun*
5. Olga = *noun*
   American = *adjective*
   hamburgers = *noun*
6. sour = *adjective*
   apples = *noun*
   sweet = *adjective*
   fruit = *noun*

7. Political = *adjective*
   leaders = *noun*
   important = *adjective*
   decisions = *noun*
8. Heavy = *adjective*
   traffic = *noun*
   noisy = *adjective*
   streets = *noun*
9. Poverty = *noun*
   serious = *adjective*
   problems = *noun*
   world = *noun*
10. Young = *adjective*
    people = *noun*
    interesting = *adjective*
    ideas = *noun*
    modern = *adjective*
    music = *noun*

EXERCISE 6, p. 162.

2. Jack = *a noun used as the subject*
   radio = *a noun used as the object of the verb "have"*
   car = *a noun used as the object of the preposition "in"*
3. Monkeys, apes = *nouns used as the subject*
   thumbs = *a noun used as the object of the verb "have"*
4. Janet = *a noun used as the subject*
   office = *a noun used as the object of the preposition "in"*
5. Scientists = *a noun used as the subject*
   origin = *a noun used as the object of the preposition "on"*
   earth = *a noun used as the object of the preposition "of"*
6. Egypt = *a noun used as the subject*
   summers, winters = *nouns used as objects of the verb "has"*
7. farmers = *a noun used as the subject*
   villages = *a noun used as the object of the preposition "in"*
   fields = *a noun used as the object of the preposition "near"*
8. cities = *a noun used as the subject*
   problems = *a noun used as the object of the verb "face"*
9. problems = *a noun used as the subject*
   poverty, pollution, crime = *nouns used as objects of the verb "include"*
10. hour = *a noun used as the subject*
    minutes = *a noun used as the object of the preposition "of"*
    day = *a noun used as the subject*
    minutes = *a noun used as the object of the preposition "of"*
    [Yes, there are 1440 minutes in a day. 60 × 24 = 1440.]

EXERCISE 7, p. 163.

2. (Mexico)/Mexican
3.–8. *Sample answers:*
   France/French
   Egypt/Egyptian
   Indonesia/Indonesian
   Italy/Italian
   Japan/Japanese

   Korea/Korean
   Malaysia/Malaysian
   Mexico/Mexican
   America/American

EXERCISE 8, p. 164.

2. She . . . him
3. They . . . her
4. They . . . him
5. He . . . her
6. She . . . them
7. He . . . them
8. They . . . them

EXERCISE 9, p. 165.

2. them
3. it
4. He
5. him
6. her . . . She . . . I
7. them. They
8. us
9. It
10. We . . . it

EXERCISE 10, p. 165.

Questions: When do you . . .

1. do it?
2. visit them?
3. read them?
4. talk to her?
5. watch it?
6. buy them?
7. wear them?
8. use it?

EXERCISE 11, p. 166.

2. it . . . It
3. we . . . I . . . you
4. they . . . They . . . them
5. it. It
6. he . . . him

EXERCISE 13, p. 167.

1. A: I are going . . . with us
   B: I are going . . . We need to
2. B: It's . . . know her? She's from
   A: know her . . . with her
   B: we enjoy . . . visit us . . . you
   A: I'd like
3. they do . . . them . . . He's . . . him

EXERCISE 14, p. 168.

LIST A

2. countries
3. babies
4. keys
5. cities
6. parties
7. trays
8. dictionaries
9. ladies
10. Cowboys

LIST B

11. leaves
12. wives
13. lives
14. thieves
15. knives

LIST C

16. glasses
17. sexes
18. dishes
19. taxes
20. bushes
21. matches
22. tomatoes
23. potatoes
24. sandwiches
25. classes
26. zoos

EXERCISE 16, p. 171.

2. table
3. face
4. hats
5. offices
6. boxes
7. package
8. chairs
9. edge
10. tops

EXERCISE 17, p. 172.

2. places
3. sandwich
4. sentences
5. apple
6. exercise
7. pieces
8. roses
9. bush
10. college

EXERCISE 18, p. 172.

1. students /s/ . . . books /s/ . . . backpacks /z/
2. stores /z/ . . . sizes /əz/ . . . clothes /z/
3. cats /s/ . . . dogs /z/
4. teachers /z/ . . . offices /əz/
5. Engineers /z/ . . . bridges /əz/
6. tigers /z/, monkeys /z/, birds /z/, elephants /s/, bears /z/ . . . snakes /s/
7. ears /z/ . . . eyes /z/ . . . arms /z/ . . . hands /z/ . . . legs /z/
8. tables /z/ . . . tables /z/ . . . edges /əz/
9. pages /əz/
10. apples /z/, bananas /z/, strawberries /z/ . . . peaches /əz/
11. cockroaches /əz/

EXERCISE 20, p. 175.

2. two women
3. two teeth
4. two feet
5. two men
6. two mice
7. two fish
8. two pages
9. two places
10. two bananas
11. two children
12. two desks
13. two sentences
14. two men
15. two oranges
16. two feet
17. two knives
18. two sexes
19. two girls
20. two exercises
21. two teeth
22. two women
23. two boys and two women

EXERCISE 21, p. 175.

2. | Anita | carries | her books | in | her backpack |
      subj.   verb   obj.   prep.   obj. of prep.

3. | Snow | falls | *(none)* | *(none)* | *(none)* |
      subj.   verb   obj.   prep.   obj. of prep.

4. | Monkeys | sleep | *(none)* | in | trees |
      subj.   verb   obj.   prep.   obj. of prep.

5. | The teacher | is writing | words | on | the chalkboard |
      subj.   verb   obj.   prep.   obj. of prep.

6. | I | like | apples | *(none)* | *(none)* |
      subj. verb   obj.   prep.   obj. of prep.

EXERCISE 22, p. 176.

4. This class ends at two o'clock.
5. *Inc.*
6. My mother works.
7. *Inc.*
8. My mother works in an office.
9. Does your brother have a job?
10. *Inc.*
11. Rain falls.
12. My sister lives in an apartment.
13. *Inc.*
14. The apartment has two bedrooms.
15. *Inc.*
16. *Inc.*

EXERCISE 23, p. 177.

2. B	5. C	8. B
3. C	6. A	9. B
4. C	7. D	10. A

EXERCISE 24, p. 178.

2. Our teacher gives **difficult tests**.
3. Alex helps Mike and **me**.
4. **Babies** cry.
5. Mike and Tom **live** in an apartment.
6. There are seven **women** in this class.
7. There are nineteen **people** in my class.
8. Olga and Ivan **have** three **children**.
9. There **are** twenty **classrooms** in this building.
10. Mr. Jones is our teacher. I like **him** very much.

Chapter 7: COUNT AND NONCOUNT NOUNS

EXERCISE 1, p. 179.

5. s	8. x	11. x	14. x
6. x	9. s	12. s	15. s
7. x	10. s	13. x	

EXERCISE 2, p. 181.

3. coin	(count)
4. money	(noncount)
5. traffic	(noncount)
6. cars	(count)
7. fact	(count)
8. information	(noncount)
9. homework	(noncount)
10. assignment	(count)
11. music	(noncount)
12. coffee	(noncount)
13. library	(count)
14. vocabulary	(noncount)
15. advice	(noncount)
16. job	(count)
17. work	(noncount)
18. bracelets	(count)

EXERCISE 3, p. 182.

	NONCOUNT	COUNT
2.	advice	a suggestion
3.	furniture	a desk
4.	homework	an assignment
5.	information	a fact
6.	jewelry	a bracelet
7.	money	a coin
8.	music	a song
9.	weather	a cloud
10.	work	a job

EXERCISE 5, p. 183.

1. an apple		9. An hour	
2. a banana		10. A healthy person	
3. an office		11. A horse	
4. an idea		12. an honest worker	
5. a good idea		13. a math tutor	
6. a class		14. A university . . .	
7. an easy class		an educational institution	
8. an island		15. an unusual job	

EXERCISE 6, p. 184.

2. a small apartment
3. an hour
4. an interesting class
5. a new teacher
6. an office
7. an insurance office
8. a nurse
9. a hospital
10. a difficult job

EXERCISE 7, p. 185.

4. a	(sing. count)
5. some	(pl. count)
6. some	(noncount)
7. a	(sing. count)
8. some	(pl. count)
9. some	(pl. count)
10. some	(noncount)
11. some	(noncount)
12. an	(sing. count)

EXERCISE 8, p. 185.

3. a desk	6. some apples
4. some desks	7. an exercise
5. an apple	8. some exercises

EXERCISE 9, p. 186.

3. some	7. some
4. a	8. a
5. some	9. some
6. an	10. some

EXERCISE 11, p. 187.

2. some homework
3. some work
4. a job . . . a teacher
5. a table . . . a sofa . . . some chairs
6. some furniture
7. some music
8. an orange
9. some oranges . . . some fruit
10. some information
11. some advice
12. some cars . . . a bus . . . some trucks . . . some traffic

EXERCISE 12, p. 188.

Partner B's answers:

1. an apple
2. some apples
3. a child
4. some children
5. some music
6. a flower
7. a man
8. an old man
9. some men
10. an island
11. some rice
12. some advice
13. an hour
14. a horse
15. some food

Partner A's answers:

16. an animal
17. some animals
18. a chair
19. some chairs
20. some furniture
21. some homework
22. an orange
23. some bananas
24. a banana
25. some fruit
26. a university
27. an uncle
28. some people
29. a house
30. some bread

EXERCISE 13, p. 189.

4. music
5. flowers
6. information
7. jewelry
8. children
9. homework
10. advice
11. suggestions
12. help
13. sandwiches
14. animals
15. bananas
16. fruit
17. weather
18. pictures
19. rice . . . beans

EXERCISE 14, p. 190.

3. I have some coins in my pocket.
4. *(none)*
5. *(none)*
6. There are some cars on Main Street.
7. *(none)*
8. *(none)*
9. *(none)*
10. *(none)* . . . *(none)*
11. There are some dictionaries on the shelf.
12. *(none)*
13. Here are some flowers from my garden.
14. *(none)*
15. some apples
16. some potatoes . . . *(none)*

EXERCISE 15, p. 191.

2. a piece of bread
3. a cup of/a glass of water
4. a cup of coffee
5. a piece of cheese
6. a bowl of/a cup of soup
7. a piece of meat
8. a glass of wine
9. a piece of fruit
10. a bowl of/a cup of rice

EXERCISE 20, p. 194.

Partner B's answers:

1. a. some food.
   b. an apple.
   c. a sandwich.
   d. a bowl of soup.
2. a. a glass of milk.
   b. some water.
   c. a cup of tea.
3. a. some medicine.
   b. an ambulance.
4. a. a coat.
   b. a hat.
   c. some warm clothes.
   d. some heat.
5. a. some sleep.
   b. a break.
   c. a relaxing vacation.

Partner A's answers:

6. a. a snack.
   b. some fruit.
   c. an orange.
   d. a piece of chicken.
7. a. some juice.
   b. a bottle of water.
   c. a glass of ice tea.
8. a. a doctor.
   b. some help.
9. a. some boots.
   b. a blanket.
   c. a hot bath.
   d. some gloves.
10. a. some strong coffee.
    b. a break.
    c. a vacation.
    d. a nap.

EXERCISE 21, p. 195.

3. many cities
4. much sugar
5. many questions
6. much furniture
7. many people
8. much mail . . . many letters
9. many skyscrapers . . . many tall buildings
10. much work
11. much coffee
12. many friends
13. much fruit
14. much coffee
15. many letters

EXERCISE 22, p. 195.

3. many languages
4. much homework
5. much tea
6. much sugar
7. many sentences
8. much water

EXERCISE 24, p. 197.

2. a little salt
3. a few questions
4. a little help . . .
   a few problems . . .
   a little advice
5. a few clothes
6. a little homework
7. a little mail
8. a few letters
9. a little cheese
10. a few oral exercises

EXERCISE 25, p. 197.

	PARTNER A	PARTNER B
1.	many pens	a few
2.	much tea	a little
3.	much rice	a little
4.	many apples	a few

5. much money	a little
6. much help	a little
7. many toys	a few

PARTNER B	PARTNER A
1. much salt	a little
2. many bananas	a few
3. much soup	a little
4. much coffee	a little
5. many assignments	a few
6. much cheese	a little
7. many books	a few

EXERCISE 26, p. 198.

2. Leaves	14. valleys
3. sexes	15. weather
4. knives	16. Thieves
5. information	17. Strawberries
6. paper	18. trays
7. dishes	19. sizes
8. women	20. glasses
9. bushes	21. fish
10. homework	22. centimeters
11. pages	23. inches
12. pieces	24. feet
13. edges	

EXERCISE 27, p. 200.

1. (a notebook) . . . a grammar book . . .
   The notebook . . . The grammar book
2. a woman . . . a man . . .
   The woman . . . The man
3. a ring . . . a necklace . . . The ring
4. a magazine . . . a newspaper . . .
   the newspaper . . . the magazine
5. a circle . . . a triangle . . . a square . . .
   a rectangle . . . The circle . . . the triangle
   The square . . . the triangle . . . the rectangle
6. an apartment . . . an old building . . . the apartment
   . . . The building
7. a card . . . a flower . . . The card . . . the card . . .
   the flower
8. a hotel . . . The hotel

EXERCISE 28, p. 201.

1. a chair	12. a woman
2. a desk	13. The man
3. a window	14. The woman
4. a plant	15. a dog
5. the chair	16. a cat
6. The chair	17. a bird
7. the window	18. a cage
8. the plant	19. the dog
9. The plant	20. the cat
10. the chair	21. The cat
11. a man	22. the bird

EXERCISE 29, p. 202.

1. A: a coat
   B: an umbrella
2. B: The weather
   A: the coat . . . the umbrella . . . the kitchen
3. a good job . . . an office . . . a computer
4. the computer
5. a stamp
6. A: an egg
   B: a glass
7. the floor
8. the moon . . . The moon
9. a telephone
10. the telephone

EXERCISE 30, p. 203.

3. ∅	10. The coffee . . .
4. the bananas	the tea
5. ∅	11. The pages
6. The food	12. ∅ . . . ∅
7. ∅ . . . ∅	13. the fruit . . .
8. the salt . . .	the vegetables
the pepper	14. ∅ . . . ∅
9. ∅	

EXERCISE 31, p. 204.

2. general	6. specific
3. specific	7. specific
4. general	8. specific
5. general	

EXERCISE 32, p. 205.

1. A: a pen
   B: the counter . . . the kitchen
2. A: the keys . . . the car
   B: a set
3. A: a noise
   B: a bird . . . a woodpecker
4. A: a university
   B: an English professor
   A: the department
5. B: an hour
   A: the clock
   B: a new battery

EXERCISE 33, p. 206.

4. some/any help
5. any help
6. some help
7. any mail
8. any fruit . . . any apples . . . any bananas
   . . . any oranges
9. any people
10. some paper . . . some/any paper
11. any paper

12. any problems
13. some food . . . some/any groceries
14. any homework
15. any money
16. some beautiful flowers

EXERCISE 35, p. 207.
4. any new furniture
5. any children
6. any coffee . . .
    any coffee
7. a cup
8. any windows
9. any friends
10. any help
11. a comfortable chair
12. any problems
13. a car
14. any homework
15. any new clothes
16. a new suit

EXERCISE 36, p. 208.
2. I don't like hot **weather**.
3. I usually have **an** egg for breakfast.
4. **The sun** rises every morning.
5. The students in this class do a lot of **homework** every day.
6. How many **languages** do you know?
7. I don't have **much** money.
8. John and Susan don't have **any** children.
9. **The** pictures are beautiful. You're a good photographer.
10. There isn't **any** traffic early in the morning.
11. I can't find **a** bowl for my soup.

EXERCISE 38, p. 210.
3. Horses
4. (no change)
5. children
6. stories
7. minutes
8. toys
9. shelves
10. women . . . men
11. islands
12. glasses
13. Tomatoes
14. dishes, spoons, forks, knives . . . napkins
15. friends . . . enemies

Chapter 8: EXPRESSING PAST TIME, PART 1

EXERCISE 1, p. 213.
3. Mary was at the library yesterday too.
4. We were in class yesterday too.
5. You were busy yesterday too.
6. I was happy yesterday too.
7. The classroom was hot yesterday too.
8. Ann was in her office yesterday too.
9. Tom was in his office yesterday too.
10. Ann and Tom were in their offices yesterday too.

EXERCISE 3, p. 214.
3. she wasn't busy yesterday.
4. he wasn't at the library last night.
5. they weren't at work yesterday afternoon.

6. you weren't here yesterday.
7. she wasn't in her office yesterday morning.
8. it wasn't cold last week.

EXERCISE 5, p. 215.
2. was
3. was
4. wasn't
5. were
6. weren't
7. was
8. was
9. weren't
10. were

EXERCISE 7, p. 217.
2. A: Was Mr. Yamamoto absent from class yesterday?
   B: he was.
3. A: Were Oscar and Anya at home last night?
   B: they were.
4. A: Were you nervous the first day of class?
   B: I wasn't.
5. A: Was Ahmed at the library last night?
   B: he was.
6. A: Was Mr. Shin in class yesterday?
   B: he wasn't.
   A: was he?
7. A: Were you and your family in Canada last year?
   B: we weren't.
   A: were you?
8. A: Are you at the library right now?
   B: I'm not.
   A: are you?

EXERCISE 9, p. 219.
3. A: Were you tired last night?
   B: I was
4. A: Are you hungry right now?
   B: I'm not
5. A: Was the weather hot in New York City last summer?
   B: it was
6. A: Is the weather cold in Alaska in the winter?
   B: it is
7. A: Were Yoko and Mohammed here yesterday afternoon?
   B: they were.
8. A: Are the students in this class intelligent?
   B: they are
9. A: Is Mr. Tok absent today?
   B: he is.
   A: is he?
   B: He is . . . . (free response)
10. A: Were Tony and Benito at the party last night?
    B: they weren't.
    A: were they?
    B: They were . . . . (free response)
11. A: Was Amy out of town last week?
    B: she was.
    A: was she?
    B: She was . . . . (free response)

12. A: Are Mr. and Mrs. Rice in town this week?
    B: they aren't
    A: are they?
    B: They're . . . . *(free response)*

EXERCISE 10, p. 221.

1. walked	6. smiled
2. worked	7. rained
3. shaved	8. asked
4. watched	9. talked
5. cooked	10. listened

EXERCISE 11, p. 222.

2. walk . . . walked
3. asks . . . asked
4. watched . . . watch
5. cooked . . . cooks
6. stay . . . stayed
7. work . . . worked
8. dream . . . dreamed/dreamt
9. waits . . . waited
10. erased
11. smiles
12. shaved . . . shaves

EXERCISE 14, p. 224.

2. plays	7. answered
3. watched	8. listened
4. enjoyed	9. like
5. watch	10. works
6. asked	

EXERCISE 16, p. 225.

2. yesterday	9. last
3. last	10. last
4. last	11. yesterday
5. yesterday	12. last
6. last	13. last
7. last	14. last
8. yesterday	15. yesterday

EXERCISE 18, p. 226.

(Answers will vary depending on date and time.)

EXERCISE 20, p. 228.

Partner A:
1. Rita got some mail yesterday.
2. They went downtown yesterday.
3. The students stood in line at the cafeteria yesterday.
4. I saw my friends yesterday.
5. Hamid sat in the front row yesterday.
6. I slept for eight hours last night.

Partner B:
1. We had lunch yesterday.
2. I wrote e-mails to my parents last week.

3. Wai-Leng came to class late yesterday.
4. I did my homework yesterday.
5. I ate breakfast yesterday morning.
6. Roberto put his books in his briefcase yesterday.

EXERCISE 21, p. 229.

2. talked	14. had . . . dreamed/dreamt
3. is talking	. . . slept
4. talks	15. happened
5. ate	16. comes
6. eat	17. came
7. went	18. is standing
8. studied	19. stood
9. wrote	20. put
10. writes	21. puts
11. is sitting	22. sits . . . sat . . .
12. did	is . . . was
13. saw	

EXERCISE 22, p. 230.

1. some rice	5. a good grade; a new truck
2. on the floor; together	6. next to my parents;
3. late; yesterday	at the bus stop
4. an answer; a book	

EXERCISE 23, p. 230.

1. One night, John went camping.
2. He looked up at the stars.
3. They were beautiful.
4. He wrote a postcard to his girlfriend.
5. He put the postcard down and went to sleep.
6. The next morning, John sat up and rubbed his eyes.
7. He saw a bear.
8. The bear stood next to his tent. OR The bear had his postcard.
9. The bear had his postcard. OR The bear stood next to his tent.
10. *(Group story endings will vary.)*

EXERCISE 24, p. 231.

2. didn't have
3. didn't sit
4. didn't talk

EXERCISE 25, p. 231.

Partner A:
1. I don't eat breakfast every day.
   I didn't eat breakfast yesterday.
2. I don't watch TV every day.
   I didn't watch TV yesterday.
3. I don't go shopping every day.
   I didn't go shopping yesterday.
4. I don't read a newspaper every day.
   I didn't read a newspaper yesterday.
5. I don't study every day.
   I didn't study yesterday.

Partner B:
1. I don't go to the library every day.
   I didn't go to the library yesterday.
2. I don't visit my friends every day.
   I didn't visit my friends yesterday.
3. I don't see (. . .) every day.
   I didn't see (. . .) yesterday.
4. I don't do my homework every day.
   I didn't do my homework yesterday.
5. I don't get on the Internet every day.
   I didn't get on the Internet yesterday.

EXERCISE 27, p. 232.
1. (didn't come) . . . stayed
2. went . . . didn't enjoy . . . wasn't
3. is reading . . . isn't watching . . . doesn't like
4. doesn't eat . . . doesn't have . . . didn't have . . . got

EXERCISE 29, p. 234.
3. A: Did you eat lunch at the cafeteria?
   B: Yes, I did.
4. A: Did Mr. Kwan go out of town last week?
   B: No, he didn't.
5. A: Did you have a cup of tea this morning?
   B: Yes, I did.
6. A: Did you and Benito go to a party last night?
   B: Yes, we did.
7. A: Did Olga study English in high school?
   B: Yes, she did.
8. A: Did Yoko and Ali do their homework last night?
   B: No, they didn't.
9. A: Did you see Gina at dinner last night?
   B: Yes, I did.
10. A: Did you dream in English last night?
    B: No, I didn't.

EXERCISE 30, p. 235.
1. Did we
2. Did you
3. Did it
4. Did I
5. Did they
6. Did he
7. Did I
8. Did they
9. Did you
10. Did she

EXERCISE 33, p. 237.
PART II.
1. Did you
2. Did it
3. Did you
4. Did they
5. Did I
6. Did he
7. Did she
8. Did you
9. Did I
10. Did he

EXERCISE 35, p. 239.
1. ran
2. A: rode
   B: drove

3. thought
4. A: Did you go
   B: bought
5. A: Did you study
   B: read . . . went
6. drank . . . was
7. brought
8. taught . . . taught
9. caught

EXERCISE 37, p. 241.
1. a fish
2. very fast; to the store
3. books; the newspaper
4. yesterday; a horse
5. some food
6. into town; home

EXERCISE 40, p. 243.
1. broke
2. spoke
3. left
4. sent
5. met
6. heard
7. took
8. rang
9. sang
10. woke
11. flew
12. paid

EXERCISE 41, p. 244.
1. no
2. yes
3. no
4. no
5. no

EXERCISE 43, p. 245.
1. began
2. told
3. lost
4. hung
5. found
6. sold
7. said
8. stole
9. wore
10. tore

EXERCISE 44, p. 247.
1. no
2. no
3. yes
4. yes
5. yes

EXERCISE 45, p. 247.
1. Did
2. Were
3. Was
4. Were
5. Did
6. Did
7. Did
8. Was
9. Were
10. Did

EXERCISE 46, p. 247.
2. was . . . did
3. A: Was . . . Did
   B: was
4. A: Were . . . Did
   B: was . . . Were
5. A: were
   B: was
   A: Did
   B: was . . . were . . . was . . . did

EXERCISE 47, p. 248.

3. A: Do you want a roommate?
   B: No, I don't.
4. A: Did you have a roommate last year?
   B: Yes, I did.
5. A: Was he difficult to live with?
   B: Yes, he was.
6. A: Did you ask him to keep the apartment clean?
   B: Yes, I did.
7. A: Were you glad when he left?
   B: Yes, I was.

EXERCISE 49, p. 250.

1. flew	11. paid	21. left
2. brought	12. heard	22. had
3. read	13. caught	23. paid
4. told	14. found	24. met
5. stood	15. slept	25. sat
6. taught	16. thought	26. took
7. drank	17. rode	27. rang
8. wore	18. broke	28. wrote
9. bought	19. said	29. sang
10. spoke	20. got	30. woke up

EXERCISE 50, p. 250.

1. Someone **stole** my bicycle two **days** ago.
2. Did you **go** to the party **last** weekend?
3. I **heard** a really interesting story yesterday.
4. The teacher **was not/wasn't** ready for class yesterday.
5. Did **Joe come** to work last week?
6. **Last** night I **stayed** home and **worked** on my science project.
7. Several students **weren't** on time for the final exam yesterday.
8. Your fax came ten minutes **ago**. Did you **get** it?
9. Did you **invite** all your friends to your graduation party?
10. I **slept** too late this morning and ~~was~~ missed the bus.
11. The market **didn't have** any bananas yesterday. I **got** there too late.
12. **Were** you nervous about your test ~~the~~ last week?
13. I didn't **see** you at the party. **Were** you there?

Chapter 9: EXPRESSING PAST TIME, PART 2

EXERCISE 1, p. 252.

2. When did Mr. Chu arrive in Canada?
3. When/What time did your plane arrive?
4. Why did you stay home last night?
5. Why were you tired?
6. Where did Sara go for her vacation?
7. When/What time did you finish your homework?
8. When did you come to this city?
9. Why did you laugh?
10. Where is Kate?

11. When/What time does the movie start?
12. Why was Tina behind the door?
13. Why does Jim lift weights?

EXERCISE 4, p. 255.

1. (To the) City Cafe
2. (For a) business meeting
3. (To the) gym
4. (At) 1:00 P.M.
5. (For a) workout
6. (To) school
7. (For a meeting with the) teacher
8. (At) 12:00 noon
9. (To) Dr. Clark / (To the) dentist
10. (At) 10:00 A.M.
11. (For a dental) checkup
12. (At) 7:00 A.M.

EXERCISE 5, p. 256.

2. you finish your homework
3. you eat breakfast
4. you clean your apartment
5. you answer the phone

EXERCISE 7, p. 257.

3. Is Mary carrying a suitcase?
4. What is Mary carrying?
5. Do you see an airplane?
6. What do you see?
7. What did Bob eat for lunch?
8. Did Bob eat some soup for lunch?
9. What does Bob usually eat for lunch?
10. Does Bob like salads?
11. Are you afraid of snakes?
12. What is the teacher pointing to?

EXERCISE 10, p. 259.

1. When did you	5. What does this
2. Why did you	6. Why didn't you
3. Where do they	7. Where did he
4. What did she	8. When does class

EXERCISE 11, p. 260.

1. Who called Yuko?
   Who visited Yuko?
   Who studied with Yuko?
   Who did John call?
   Who did John visit?
   Who did John study with?
2. Who did Mary carry?
   Who did Mary help?
   Who did Mary sing to?
   Who carried the baby?
   Who helped the baby?
   Who sang to the baby?

3. Who talked to the children?
   Who did Ron watch?
   Who played with the children?
   Who did Ron talk to?
   Who watched the children?
   Who did Ron play with?

EXERCISE 12, p. 261.
1. Who did you see at the party?
2. Who came to the party?
3. Who lives in that house?
4. Who did Janet call?
5. Who did you visit?
6. Who visited you?
7. Who did you talk to?
8. Who helped Ann?
9. Who did Bob help?
10. Did Bob help Ann?
11. Who are you thinking about?
12. Are you confused?

EXERCISE 14, p. 263.
1. In a small town.
2. At midnight.
3. Some help.
4. I am.
5. Mary did.
6. An apartment downtown.
7. Two hours ago.
8. Because I didn't have time.

EXERCISE 16, p. 265.
1. A: does a new car cost
   B: costs
2. cost
3. gave
4. hit
5. B: forgot
   A: forgot
6. made
7. puts
8. put
9. spent
10. lent
11. cuts
12. cut

EXERCISE 17, p. 266.
1. the answer; the conversation; the teacher
2. money
3. your hair; some paper
4. a tree; an animal
5. his appointment; the question

EXERCISE 19, p. 267.
1. won
2. fell
3. kept
4. drew
5. grew
6. blew
7. knew
8. swam
9. felt
10. threw

EXERCISE 20, p. 268.
1. on a car; in the park
2. the game; a prize
3. on the paper; a picture; with some chalk
4. happy; excited
5. a ball; a pillow

EXERCISE 22, p. 270.
2. hid
3. built
4. fed
5. became
6. held
7. fought
8. bit
9. bent

EXERCISE 23, p. 271.
1. the dog; her baby
2. a new house
3. a stick; my hand
4. in the bedroom; behind a tree; their money
5. some chalk; some papers

EXERCISE 25, p. 273.
2. *main clause* = We arrived at the airport
   time clause = before the plane landed
3. *main clause* = I went to the movie
   time clause = after I finished my homework
4. *main clause* = they watched TV
   time clause = After the children got home from school
5. *main clause* = I lived at home with my parents
   time clause = Before I moved to this city

EXERCISE 26, p. 274.
4. *Inc.*
5. We went to the zoo.
6. We went to the zoo before we ate our picnic lunch.
7. The children played games after they did their work.
8. The children played games.
9. *Inc.*
10. The lions killed a zebra.
11. *Inc.*
12. They ate it.
13. After the lions killed a zebra, they ate it.

EXERCISE 27, p. 274.
1. She ate breakfast before she went to work.
   Before she went to work, she ate breakfast.
   She went to work after she ate breakfast.
   After she ate breakfast, she went to work.
2. He did his homework before he went to bed.
   Before he went to bed, he did his homework.
   He went to bed after he did his homework.
   After he did his homework, he went to bed.
3. We bought tickets before we entered the movie theater.
   Before we entered the movie theater, we bought tickets.
   We entered the movie theater after we bought tickets.
   After we bought tickets, we entered the movie theater.

EXERCISE 29, p. 276.
2. When I was in Japan, I stayed in a hotel in Tokyo.
   I stayed in a hotel in Tokyo when I was in Japan.

3. Maria bought some new shoes when she went shopping yesterday.
   When she went shopping yesterday, Maria bought some new shoes.
4. I took a lot of photographs when I was in Hawaii.
   When I was in Hawaii, I took a lot of photographs.
5. Jim was a soccer player when he was in high school.
   When he was in high school, Jim was a soccer player.
6. When the rain stopped, I closed my umbrella.
   I closed my umbrella when the rain stopped.
7. The antique vase broke when I dropped it.
   When I dropped it, the antique vase broke.

EXERCISE 30, p. 277.
3. *Inc.*
4. When were you in Iran?
5. When did the movie end?
6. *Inc.*
7. *Inc.*
8. *Inc.*
9. *Inc.*
10. When does the museum open?

EXERCISE 32, p. 279.
1. was eating . . . came
2. called . . . was watching
3. was playing

EXERCISE 34, p. 281.
2. Someone knocked on my apartment door while I was eating breakfast yesterday morning.
   While I was eating breakfast yesterday morning, someone knocked on my apartment door.
3. While I was cooking dinner yesterday evening, I burned my hand.
   I burned my hand while I was cooking dinner yesterday evening.
4. Yoko raised her hand while the teacher was talking.
   While the teacher was talking, Yoko raised her hand.
5. A tree fell on my car while I was driving home yesterday.
   While I was driving home yesterday, a tree fell on my car.
6. While I was studying last night, a mouse suddenly appeared on my desk.
   A mouse suddenly appeared on my desk while I was studying last night.

EXERCISE 35, p. 282.
2. called . . . was washing
3. came . . . was eating
4. was eating . . . came
5. came . . . was watching . . . invited
6. was watching . . . came
7. was wearing . . . saw
8. was watching . . . relaxing . . . took

EXERCISE 37, p. 284.
1. were having . . . saw . . . introduced
2. heard . . . walked . . . opened . . . opened . . . saw . . . greeted . . . asked
3. were watching . . . came . . . watched
4. was walking . . . saw . . . said . . . walked

EXERCISE 38, p. 285.
1. turned . . . was driving . . . was listening . . . heard . . . looked . . . saw . . . pulled . . . waited
2. A: was . . . were eating . . . jumped . . . didn't seem
   B: did you say . . . didn't you ask
   A: didn't want

EXERCISE 39, p. 286.
Sample sentences.
In 1955, Bill Gates was born.
In 1967, he entered Lakeside School.
While Bill Gates was studying at Lakeside School, he wrote his first computer program.
While Bill Gates was studying at Lakeside School, he started his first software company.
In 1973, he graduated from Lakeside.
While he was studying at Harvard University, he began to design programs for personal computers.
While he was studying at Harvard University, he started Microsoft.
In 1977, he left Harvard.
While he was working as Chief Executive Officer for Microsoft, he got married.
In 1996, his first child was born.

EXERCISE 40, p. 287.
I <u>had</u> a strange experience yesterday. I <u>was reading</u> my book on the bus when a man <u>sat</u> down next to me and <u>asked</u> me if I wanted some money. I <u>didn't want</u> his money. I <u>was</u> very confused. I <u>stood</u> up and <u>walked</u> toward the door.
While I <u>was waiting</u> for the door to open, the man <u>tried</u> to give me the money. When the door <u>opened,</u> I <u>got</u> off the bus quickly. I still <u>don't know</u> why he <u>was trying</u> to give me money.

EXERCISE 41, p. 287.
2. C
3. C
4. A
5. C
6. B
7. C
8. A
9. C
10. D

EXERCISE 43, p. 288.
1. Did you **go** downtown yesterday?
2. Yesterday I **spoke** to Ken before he **left** his office and **went** home.
3. I **heard** a good joke last night.
4. ~~When~~ Pablo finished his work. OR
   When Pablo finished his work, (**he went home**).

5. I **visited** my relatives in New York City last month.
6. Where **did you** go yesterday afternoon?
7. Ms. Wah ~~was~~ flew from Singapore to Tokyo last week.
8. When I **saw** my friend yesterday, he didn't **speak** to me.
9. Why **didn't Mustafa come** to class last week?
10. Where **did** you **buy** those shoes? I like them.
11. Mr. Adams **taught** our class last week.
12. I **wrote** a letter last night.
13. Who **did** you **write** a letter to?
14. Who **opened** the door? Jack **opened** it.

EXERCISE 44, p. 289.

PART I.

1. was	9. are you doing
2. saw	10. am getting
3. are you	11. is
4. am doing	12. don't trust
5. Would you like	13. do you want
6. sit	14. want
7. need	15. had
8. don't need / do not need	

PART II.

16. saw	24. are
17. love	25. aren't/are not
18. stopped	26. is it
19. reached	27. did the bee sting
20. came	28. are you doing
21. was	29. are you holding
22. don't believe / do not believe	30. am holding
23. don't believe / do not believe	31. tricked
	32. happened

PART III.

33. got	43. dropped
34. wanted	43. fooled
35. to catch	44. tricked
36. caught	45. taught
37. looks	46. learned
38. don't believe / do not believe	47. am
	48. have
39. is	49. Would you like
40. is coming	
41. don't see / do not see	

Chapter 10: EXPRESSING FUTURE TIME, PART 1

EXERCISE 4, p. 296.

2. am going to go to bed.
3. is going to get something to eat.
4. am going to take them to the laundromat.
5. am going to see a dentist.

6. am going to look it up in my dictionary.
7. is going to take it to the post office.
8. are going to take a long walk in the park.
9. are going to go to the beach.
10. am going to lie down and rest for a while.
11. am going to call the police.
12. am going to major in psychology.
13. am going to stay in bed today.
14. are going to go to an Italian restaurant.
15. is going to call the manager.

EXERCISE 8, p. 300.

1. We are flying to Athens.
2. We are spending a week there.
3. My brother is meeting us there.
4. He is taking the train.
5. We are going sightseeing together.
6. I am coming back by boat, and they are returning by train.

EXERCISE 9, p. 300.

2. future	6. present
3. present	7. future
4. future	8. future
5. present	

EXERCISE 11, p. 301.

2. am leaving	7. are having
3. starts	8. aren't going
4. is coming	9. rides
5. is going to call	10. is going to help
6. Are you going to study	

EXERCISE 12, p. 302.

3. next	8. last	13. tomorrow
4. last	9. next	14. Last
5. yesterday	10. Last	15. Tomorrow
6. Tomorrow	11. next	16. yesterday
7. next	12. last	

EXERCISE 13, p. 303.

3. an hour ago.	7. a minute ago.
4. in an hour.	8. in half an hour.
5. in two more months.	9. in one more week.
6. two months ago.	10. a year ago.

EXERCISE 14, p. 303.

2. They are going to leave for their honeymoon in six days.
3. Beth and Tom got engaged three months ago.
4. They are going to return from their honeymoon in two weeks / in fourteen days.
5. Beth and Tom met (three years ago, four years ago, etc.). *(Answers will vary.)*
6. They began dating (two years ago, three years ago, etc.). *(Answers will vary.)*

7. Tom is going to quit his job in three weeks / in twenty-one days.
8. Beth and Tom are going to open a restaurant together in three months.

EXERCISE 15, p. 304.
2. in one hour
3. two weeks ago
4. one year ago
5. in ten minutes
6. a few minutes ago
7. next spring
8. last summer
9. next weekend
10. yesterday evening

EXERCISE 17, p. 304.
2. ago
3. next
4. in
5. yesterday
6. tomorrow
7. last
8. tomorrow
9. ago
10. in
11. Tomorrow
12. Last
13. Yesterday
14. last
15. in
16. Next

EXERCISE 20, p. 307.
2. same
3. different
4. same
5. different
6. different
7. same
8. different

EXERCISE 25, p. 310.
2. future
3. past
4. future
5. past
6. future
7. present
8. past
9. future
10. past

EXERCISE 27, p. 312.
2. teacher will
3. We'll
4. We will
5. I'll
6. students'll
7. John will
8. doctor'll
9. nurse will
10. You'll

EXERCISE 29, p. 313.
4. A: Will the plane be on time?
   B: it will.
5. A: Will dinner be ready in a few minutes?
   B: it will.
6. When will dinner be ready?
7. When will you graduate?
8. Where will Mary go to school next year?
9. A: Will Jane and Mark be at the party?
   B: they won't.
10. A: Will Mike arrive in Chicago next week?
    B: he will.
11. Where will Mike be next week?

12. A: Will you be home early tonight?
    B: I won't.
13. When will Dr. Smith be back?
14. A: Will you be ready to leave at 8:15?
    B: I will.

EXERCISE 31, p. 315.
2. No, she won't.
3. No, she won't.
4. No, she won't.
5. No, she won't.
6. Yes, she will.
7. No, she won't.
8. Yes, she will.

EXERCISE 32, p. 316.
2. won't
3. won't
4. want
5. won't
6. won't
7. want
8. want

EXERCISE 33, p. 317.
2. is not doing / isn't doing . . . is writing
3. writes
4. doesn't write
5. don't expect
6. wrote . . . started
7. rang . . . was
8. didn't finish . . . talked . . . went
9. is going to write / will write
10. isn't going to write / won't write
11. Do you write
12. Did you write
13. Are you going to write / Will you write

EXERCISE 34, p. 318.
1. doesn't like
2. is . . . doesn't eat . . . didn't eat
3. doesn't eat . . . isn't
4. doesn't enjoy
5. are going to try
6. will . . . have
7. won't have . . . 'll . . . ask
8. Are they going to enjoy
9. Will they go

EXERCISE 35, p. 319.
1. am . . . wasn't / was not . . . was . . . Were you . . . Was Carmen
2. were . . . were not / weren't
3. will be / are going to be . . . will be/am going to be . . . Will you be / Are you going to be . . . Will Yuko be / Is Yuko going to be
4. isn't / is not . . . is . . . aren't / are not . . . are

EXERCISE 36, p. 319.
1. A: Will you be
   B: I will . . . I'll . . . be

2. A: are
   B: is . . . are
3. A: Was
   B: were . . . was
   A: Was he
   B: he wasn't . . . was
4. A: We're going to be
   B: We're not going to be . . . is
   A: isn't . . . is
   B: We won't be

EXERCISE 40, p. 321.

1. Is Ivan **going to go** to work tomorrow? OR
   Will Ivan go to work tomorrow?
2. When **will you** call me?
3. Will Tom ~~to~~ meet us for dinner tomorrow?
4. We went to a movie **last** night.
5. Did you **find** your keys?
6. What time **are you** going to come tomorrow?
7. My sister is going to meet me at the airport. My brother won't ~~to~~ be there.
8. Mr. Wong will **sell** his business and **retire** next year.
9. **Will you be** in Venezuela next year?
10. I'm going to return home in a couple of **months**.
11. I saw Jim three **days** ago.
12. A thief **stole** my bicycle.

EXERCISE 41, p. 321.

2. A: Did you walk
   B: didn't . . . rode
3. A: do you usually study . . . Do you go
   B: don't like
4. A: Will you be / Are you going to be
   B: will / am . . . will not be / won't be / am not going to be
5. A: Do whales breathe
   B: do
   A: Does a whale have
   B: does
   A: Is a whale
   B: isn't . . . is
6. A: Did Yuko call
   B: did . . . talked
   A: Did she tell
   B: didn't . . . didn't say
   A: was . . . ran . . . didn't want . . . tried . . . ran
   B: Is he
   A: isn't . . . is

Chapter 11: EXPRESSING FUTURE TIME, PART 2

EXERCISE 4, p. 328.

3. may go = *a verb;* **may** *is part of the verb*
4. Maybe = *an adverb*
5. may like = *a verb;* **may** *is part of the verb*

6. may be = *a verb;* **may** *is part of the verb*
   Maybe = *an adverb*

EXERCISE 5, p. 328.

3. may be
4. may be
5. Maybe
6. may be . . . Maybe

EXERCISE 6, p. 329.

1. may + verb
2. may + verb
3. maybe
4. may + verb
5. Maybe
6. Maybe
7. may + verb
8. Maybe

EXERCISE 7, p. 329.

2. Maybe the teacher will give a test.
   The teacher may give a test.
3. Janet may be home early.
   Janet might be home early.
4. She may be late.
   Maybe she will be late.
5. Maybe it will rain tomorrow.
   It might rain tomorrow.

EXERCISE 8, p. 330.

3. Maybe
4. may/might
5. Maybe
6. Maybe
7. may/might
8. Maybe . . . may/might
9. Maybe . . . maybe . . . may/might . . . may/might

EXERCISE 11, p. 332.

2. b
3. a
4. a
5. a
6. b

EXERCISE 14, p. 334.

Time clauses:
2. After I get home tonight
3. before he leaves the office today
4. when I go to the grocery store tomorrow
5. Before I go to bed tonight
6. after I graduate next year

EXERCISE 15, p. 334.

2. am going to buy / will buy . . . go
3. finish . . . am going to take / will take
4. see . . . am going to ask / will ask
5. go . . . am going to meet / will meet
6. is going to change / will change . . . works

EXERCISE 17, p. 336.

2. is . . . am going to go / will go
3. am not going to stay / will not stay . . . is

4. don't feel . . . am not going to go / will not go
5. is going to stay / will stay . . . doesn't feel
6. am going to stay / will stay . . . go
7. are . . . am going to go / will go
8. continue . . . are going to suffer / will suffer

EXERCISE 21, p. 340.

1. go . . . usually stay
2. go . . . am going to stay / will stay
3. go . . . am going to have / will have
4. go . . . usually have
5. am . . . usually stay . . . go
6. am . . . am going to stay / will stay . . .
   (am going to/will) go
7. get . . . usually sit . . . read
8. get . . . am going to sit / will sit . . .
   (am going to/will) read
9. often yawn . . . stretch . . . wake
10. walks . . . is
11. go . . . am going to stay / will stay . . . leave . . .
    am going to go / will go
12. goes . . . is . . . likes . . . takes . . . is

EXERCISE 24, p. 342.

2. I'll get a good night's sleep.
3. I do my homework.
4. I'll go shopping.
5. I exercise.
6. I'll call my parents.
7. I'll be happy.
8. I'll know a lot of grammar.

EXERCISE 25, p. 343.

2. A: did you do
   B: came
3. A: are you going to do / will you do
   B: am going to come / will come
4. A: did you do
   B: watched
5. A: do you do
   B: watch
6. A: are you going to do / will you do
   B: am going to watch / will watch
7. A: are you doing
   B: am doing
8. A: does Maria do
   B: goes
9. A: are the students doing
   B: are working
10. A: are they going to do / will they do
    B: are going to take / will take
11. A: did Boris do
    B: went
12. A: does the teacher do
    B: puts . . . looks . . . says

EXERCISE 27, p. 344.

1. am going to skip / will skip
2. took . . . flew
3. usually walk . . . take
4. A: stole
   B: is
5. A: did you meet
   B: met
6. A: did the movie begin . . . Were you
   B: made
7. A: lost
   B: forgot . . . gave . . . lost . . . stole . . . didn't have
8. A: Are you going to stay / Will you stay
   B: am going to take / will take . . . am going to visit /
      will visit
   A: are you going to be / will you be
9. A: are you wearing
   B: broke . . . stepped
10. A: Did you see
    B: spoke . . . called
11. B: isn't . . . left
    A: Is she going to be / Will she be . . . did she go
    B: went

EXERCISE 28, p. 347.

1. A: Did you see . . . hit
   B: Are you
   A: I watched
2. A: were you
   B: began . . . we got
3. A: Do you hear
   B: I hear . . . Is . . . coming
4. A: Do you want to go
   B: I'd like . . . I need to . . . Are you going to go
   A: is . . . I want to get . . . enjoy it

EXERCISE 29, p. 347.

2. B	5. A	8. C
3. C	6. B	9. A
4. B	7. C	10. D

EXERCISE 30, p. 348.

1. If it **is** cold tomorrow morning, my car won't start.
2. We **may be** late for the concert tonight.
3. What time **are you** going to come tomorrow?
4. Fatima will call us tonight when she **arrives** home safely.
5. Emily ~~may~~ will be at the party. OR **Maybe** Emily will be at the party.
6. When **I** see you tomorrow, I'll return your book to you.
7. I may **not** be in class tomorrow.

8. Ahmed puts his books on his desk when he **walks** into his apartment. OR Ahmed **put** his books on his desk when he **walked** into his apartment.
9. I'll see my parents when I **return** home for a visit next July.
10. What do you **do** all day at work?

EXERCISE 31, p. 349.

PART I.

1. are	7. went
2. are staying	8. asked
3. like	9. agreed
4. always makes	10. put
5. tells	11. brushed
6. go	12. sat

PART II.

13. are you going to tell / will you tell	24. was
14. begin	25. got
15. am going to give / will give	26. stayed
16. love	27. found
17. am going to tell / will tell	28. needed
18. was	29. to eat
19. was	30. put
20. saw	31. didn't smell
21. was	32. didn't see
22. ran	33. hopped
23. stayed	34. found
	35. saw
	36. looked

PART III.

37. heard	43. heard
38. didn't see	44. spotted
39. decided	45. flew
40. wanted	46. picked
41. to rest	47. didn't know
42. said	48. ate

PART IV.

49. are
50. expect
51. Do you understand
52. have
53. am going to go / will go
54. to get
55. is going to be / will be
56. are we going to do / will we do
57. have
58. are going to go / will go
59. are
60. are going to see / will see
61. are going to see / will see
62. see
63. are going to have / will have
64. are going to have / will have

Chapter 12: MODALS, PART 1: EXPRESSING ABILITY

EXERCISE 4, p. 356.

1. Yes. [Ostriches and penguins can't fly.]
2. No.
3. Yes. [They are very good swimmers.]
4. Yes. [They change colors when they are excited.]
5. No. [They jump.]
6. No. [It lives there until it grows up.]
7. Yes. [The Australian walking fish can climb trees.]
8. No. [Sometimes they stand for weeks.]
9. No. [Some turtles can live for 200 or more years.]
10. Yes. [They can hold their breath for a long time.]

EXERCISE 5, p. 356.

2. can't	5. can't	8. can't
3. can't	6. can't	9. can't
4. can	7. can	10. can

EXERCISE 6, p. 357.

Is John a good person for this job?   no

EXERCISE 7, p. 357.

3. A: Can Jim play the piano?
   B: No, he can't.
4. A: Can you whistle?
   B: Yes, I can.
5. A: Can you go shopping with me this afternoon?
   B: Yes, I can.
6. A: Can Carmen ride a bicycle?
   B: No, she can't.
7. A: Can elephants swim?
   B: Yes, they can.
8. A: Can the students finish this exercise quickly?
   B: Yes, they can.
9. A: Can the doctor see me tomorrow?
   B: Yes, he/she can.
10. A: Can you stand on your head?
    B: Yes, I can.
11. A: Can you have pets in the dormitory?
    B: No, we can't.

EXERCISE 10, p. 360.

1. B: Can I
   A: He can't come . . . Can I . . . He can
2. A: Can you help
   B: I can try
   A: we can do
3. A: I can't hear . . . Can you
   B: I can't . . . can't
   A: Can you do

EXERCISE 15, p. 363.

2. couldn't call you
3. couldn't watch TV
4. couldn't light the candles
5. couldn't come to class
6. couldn't listen to music
7. couldn't wash his clothes
8. couldn't go swimming
9. couldn't get into my car
10. couldn't go to the movie

EXERCISE 18, p. 364.

1. Could you ~~to~~ drive a car when you were thirteen years old?
2. If your brother goes to the graduation party, he can **meet** my sister.
3. I couldn't **open** the door because I didn't have a key.
4. Please turn up the radio. I can't ~~to~~ hear it.
5. When Ernesto arrived at the airport last Tuesday, he **couldn't** find the right gate.
6. Mr. Lo was born in Hong Kong, but now he lives in Canada. He **could not** understand spoken English before he moved to Canada, but now he **speaks** and **understands** English very well.

EXERCISE 19, p. 365.

3. Mark is bilingual. He is able to speak two languages.
4. Sue will be able to get her own apartment next year.
5. Animals aren't able to speak.
6. Are you able to touch your toes without bending your knees?
7. Jack wasn't able to describe the thief.
8. Were you able to do the homework?
9. I wasn't able to sleep last night because my apartment was too hot.
10. My roommate is able to speak four languages. He's multilingual.
11. I'm sorry that I wasn't able to call you last night.
12. I'm sorry, but I won't be able to come to your party next week.
13. Will we be able to take vacations on the moon in the 22nd century?

EXERCISE 21, p. 367.

1. A: Were you able to talk
   B: I couldn't . . . can try
2. A: Do you know how to make
   B: can make
   A: Can you teach
   B: I can
3. A: Are you able to understand
   B: couldn't understand . . . can understand
   A: can't understand
4. A: will you be able to
   B: wasn't able to . . . 'll try . . . I will be able to

5. B: I can
   A: can see . . . Can you come
   B: I can . . . don't know

EXERCISE 22, p. 368.

1. The soup is too hot. Jack can't eat it.
   The soup is very hot, but Ricardo can eat it.
2. The coat is very small, but Tom can wear it.
   The coat is too small. Susan can't wear it.
3. The shoes are too tight. Marika can't wear them.
   The shoes are very tight, but Mai can wear them.
4. The problem is too hard. Robert can't do it.
   The problem is very hard, but Talal can do it.

EXERCISE 23, p. 370.

1. eat it.
2. buy it.
3. go swimming.
4. take a break.
5. do his homework.
6. reach the cookie jar.
7. sleep.
8. lift it.

EXERCISE 24, p. 371.

1. too heavy.
2. too young.
3. too noisy.
4. too cold.
5. too tired.
6. too expensive.
7. too small.
8. too tall.

EXERCISE 25, p. 371.

3. too
4. very . . . very
5. too
6. very
7. very
8. too
9. too
10. very
11. very
12. too
13. too
14. very
15. too
16. very
17. too
18. too

EXERCISE 26, p. 373.

2. two
3. too . . . too . . . to
4. to . . . to . . . to . . . too
5. to . . . to . . . too
6. to . . . to
7. to . . . to
8. too
9. too . . . to . . . to
10. two . . . to . . . two . . . too

EXERCISE 27, p. 375.

3. at
4. in
5. in . . . at
6. in . . . in
7. in
8. in
9. at . . . at
10. in
11. in
12. in
13. at
14. in . . . in
15. in
16. at
17. at
18. At
19. in
20. in

EXERCISE 31, p. 378.

1. We will ~~can~~ go to the museum tomorrow afternoon. OR
   We ~~will~~ can go to the museum tomorrow afternoon.
2. We can't count all of the stars in the universe. There are **too** many.
3. Can you ~~to~~ stand on your head?
4. I saw a beautiful vase at a store yesterday, but I couldn't **buy** it.
5. The shirt is **very** small. I can wear it. OR
   The shirt is too small. I **can't** wear it.
6. Sam **knows** how to count to 1000 in English.
7. When I was on vacation, I **could** swim every day.
8. When we lived **in** Tokyo, we took the subway every day.
9. Honeybees **are** not able to live in very cold climates.
10. Where **can we** go in the city for an inexpensive meal?
11. James can **read** newspapers in five languages.
12. Sorry. I **wasn't** able to get tickets for the concert.
13. I can't finish my homework because I'm **too** tired.

Chapter 13: MODALS, PART 2: ADVICE, NECESSITY, REQUESTS; SUGGESTIONS

EXERCISE 1, p. 379.

2. You should go to bed and take a nap.
3. You should go to the bank.
4. You should see a dentist.
5. You should study harder.
6. You should call the manager.
7. You should go to the immigration office.
8. You should buy a new pair of shoes.

EXERCISE 3, p. 381.

3. shouldn't	9. shouldn't
4. should	10. should . . . shouldn't
5. shouldn't	11. should
6. shouldn't	12. shouldn't
7. should	13. should
8. shouldn't	14. shouldn't

EXERCISE 5, p. 383.

1. should	5. should
2. should	6. shouldn't
3. shouldn't	7. should
4. should	8. shouldn't

EXERCISE 9, p. 385.

2. A: do you have to go
   B: I have to find
3. A: does Sue have to leave
   B: She has to be
4. B: I had to buy
   A: did you have to buy
5. I have to go . . . I have to get

6. she had to study
7. do you have to be
8. Does Tom have to find
9. A: Yoko doesn't have to take
   B: Do you have to take
10. He had to stay . . . He had to finish

EXERCISE 10, p. 386.

2. have to	5. have to	8. has to
3. have to	6. have to	9. has to
4. has to	7. have to	10. have to

EXERCISE 11, p. 388.

2. must stop.
3. must have a library card.
4. must pay an income tax.
5. must study harder.
6. must listen to English on the radio and TV. OR
   must make new friends who speak English. OR
   must read English newspapers and magazines. OR
   must speak English outside of class every day. OR
   must study harder. OR must talk to myself in English.
7. must have a passport.
8. must go to medical school.
9. must close the door behind you.
10. must take one tablet every six hours.

EXERCISE 13, p. 389.

2. B	5. C	7. B
3. B	6. A	8. A
4. A		

EXERCISE 15, p. 390.

(Answers may vary.)

EXERCISE 21, p. 395.

Imperatives:
1. (Wait) . . . (Hurry) . . . Let's
2. Hold . . . Drink . . . Breathe . . . Eat
3. Don't forget
4. Walk . . . turn . . . Go . . . turn
5. Wait . . . Do (it) . . . Hang (up) . . . Make . . . Put . . . Empty

EXERCISE 24, p. 398.

3. X	7. to	11. X
4. to	8. X	12. X
5. X	9. X	13. to
6. X	10. X	14. X

EXERCISE 26, p. 400.

2. C	5. A	8. A
3. C	6. C	9. B
4. C	7. C	10. B

EXERCISE 27, p. 401.

2. b   5. c   7. b
3. a   6. b   8. c
4. b

EXERCISE 28, p. 402.

Sample completions:

2. Let's go to Florida.
3. Let's go to a seafood restaurant.
4. Let's go to the zoo.
5. Let's go to a movie.
6. Let's walk.
7. Let's eat.
8. Let's go dancing.
9. Let's get a cup of coffee.

EXERCISE 30, p. 404.

1. Would you please ~~to~~ help me?
2. I will ~~can~~ go to the meeting tomorrow. OR
   I ~~will~~ can go to the meeting tomorrow.
3. My brother wasn't able **to call** me last night.
4. Ken should **write** us a letter.
5. I **had** to **go** to the store yesterday.
6. Susie! You must not ~~to~~ play with matches!
7. **Would / Could / Can** you please hand me that book?
8. Ann couldn't **answer** my question.
9. Shelley can't **go** to the concert tomorrow.
10. Let's **go** to a movie tonight.
11. Don't ~~to~~ interrupt. It's not polite.
12. Can you ~~to~~ stand on your head?
13. I saw a beautiful dress at a store yesterday, but I couldn't **buy** it.
14. **Close** the door please. Thank you.
15. May I please ~~to~~ borrow your dictionary? Thank you.

Chapter 14: NOUNS AND MODIFIERS

EXERCISE 1, p. 405.

3. ADJ   7. ADJ   10. NOUN
4. NOUN   8. NOUN   11. ADJ
5. NOUN   9. ADJ   12. NOUN
6. NOUN

EXERCISE 2, p. 406.

	ADJ		NOUN
2.	wise	→	woman
3.	native	→	language
4.	busy	→	waitress
	empty	→	cup
5.	young	→	man
	heavy	→	suitcase
6.	uncomfortable	→	chair
7.	international	→	news
	front	→	page
8.	wonderful	→	man

EXERCISE 3, p. 406.

	ADJ		NOUN
2.	new	→	CDs
	music	→	store
3.	train	→	station
4.	Vegetable	→	soup
5.	movie	→	theater
	furniture	→	store
6.	lunch	→	menu
7.	traffic	→	light
8.	business	→	card

EXERCISE 4, p. 406.

1. ADJ   5. ADJ   8. ADJ
2. NOUN   6. NOUN   9. NOUN
3. NOUN   7. ADJ   10. ADJ
4. ADJ

EXERCISE 5, p. 407.

3. a newspaper story.   7. a computer room.
4. hotel rooms.   8. airplane seats.
5. an office worker.   9. a park bench.
6. a price tag.   10. bean soup.

EXERCISE 6, p. 407.

2. store.   6. soup.   10. tickets.
3. class.   7. program.   11. room.
4. race.   8. trip.   12. number.
5. official.   9. keys.

EXERCISE 7, p. 409.

2. good television program.
3. dangerous mountain road.
4. bad automobile accident.
5. interesting magazine article.
6. delicious vegetable soup.
7. funny birthday card.
8. narrow airplane seats.

EXERCISE 8, p. 410.

2. delicious Thai   7. beautiful long black
3. small red   8. famous old Chinese
4. big old brown   9. thin brown leather
5. narrow dirt   10. wonderful old Native
6. serious young   American

EXERCISE 9, p. 411.

2. Asian   7. an important
3. leather   8. a polite
4. an unhappy   9. coffee
5. a soft   10. Canadian
6. brick

EXERCISE 11, p. 413.

3. famous Chinese landmark
4. an honest young man
5. an interesting newspaper article
6. *(no change)*
7. cold mountain stream
8. favorite Italian food
9. *(no change)*
10. comfortable old brown leather shoes
11. tiny black insects
12. brown cardboard box
13. *(no change)*
14. handsome middle-aged man . . . short brown hair
15. an expensive hotel room

EXERCISE 13, p. 415.

1. cake
2. keys
3. jeans; shoes
4. test
5. games
6. article; story

EXERCISE 14, p. 416.

2. All of
3. Most of
4. Some of
5. Almost all of
6. Almost all of
7. Most of
8. All of
9. Some of
10.–13. *(free response)*

EXERCISE 15, p. 417.

2. are
3. was
4. were
5. are
6. is
7. are . . . are
8. is
9. is
10. are
11. arrive
12. arrives

EXERCISE 16, p. 418.

1. 100%
2. 30%
3. 50%
4. 90%
5. 70%
6. 85%

EXERCISE 17, p. 419.

2. (. . .) is one of my classmates.
3. One of my books is red.
4. One of my books has a green cover.
5. (. . .) is one of my favorite places in the world.
6. One of the students in my class always comes late.
7. (. . .) is one of my best friends.
8. One of my friends lives in (. . .) .
9. (. . .) is one of the best programs on TV.
10. (. . .) is one of the most famous people in the world.
11. One of my biggest problems is my inability to understand spoken English.
12. (. . .) is one of the leading newspapers in (. . .).
13. None of the students in my class speaks/speak (. . .).
14. None of the furniture in this room is soft and comfortable.

EXERCISE 19, p. 421.

2. are
3. is
4. are
5. is
6. is
7. have
8. has
9. live
10. lives
11. is/are
12. is

EXERCISE 20, p. 421.

2. are
3. is
4. are
5. is
6. are
7. is
8. is
9. are
10. is

EXERCISE 21, p. 422.

1. Some of the homework
2. One of the books
3. None of the children
4. All of the students
5. Half of the class
6. Almost all of the food
7. A lot of the exercises
8. Most of the movie

EXERCISE 22, p. 422.

1. yes
2. no
3. yes
4. yes
5. no
6. no
7. no
8. yes

EXERCISE 24, p. 423.

1. anything
2. nothing
3. anyone
4. no one
5. nothing
6. anything
7. anything
8. nothing
9. nothing
10. anyone
11. No one
12. nothing
13. No one
14. anyone
15. A: anything
   B: nothing

EXERCISE 25, p. 425.

2. something/anything
3. anything
4. something
5. anything
6. something/anything
7. someone
8. anyone
9. someone
10. someone/anyone
11. something
12. anything
13. something/anything
14. someone
15. anyone
16. anything
   (*also possible:* anyone)
17. anyone
18. Someone
19. someone/anyone
20. anything

EXERCISE 26, p. 426.

2. book . . . is
3. students are
4. student is
5. teacher . . . gives
6. teachers . . . give
7. child . . . likes
8. children . . . know
9. people . . . are
10. wants
11. Do . . . students
12. Does . . . person
13. Do . . . people
14. Does
15. city . . . has
16. students . . . is

EXERCISE 27, p. 427.

1. I work hard every **day**.
2. I live in an apartment with one of my **friends**.
3. We saw a pretty **flower** garden in the park.
4. Almost **all** of the students are in class today.
5. Every **person** in my class **is** studying English.
6. All of the **big cities** in North America **have** traffic problems.
7. One of my cars **is** dark green.
8. Nadia drives a **small blue** car.
9. Istanbul is one of my favorite **cities** in the world.
10. Every ~~of~~ **student** in the class **has** a grammar book.
11. The work will take a long time. We can't finish **everything** today.
12. Everybody in the world **wants** peace.

EXERCISE 32, p. 431.

3. clearly
4. clear
5. careless
6. carelessly
7. easy
8. easily
9. good
10. well

EXERCISE 33, p. 432.

1. carefully
2. correct
3. correctly
4. fast
5. quickly
6. fast
7. neat
8. neatly
9. hard
10. hard
11. honestly
12. slowly
13. quickly
14. careless
15. early
16. early
17. loudly
18. slowly . . . clearly

EXERCISE 34, p. 433.

1. well
2. fast
3. quickly
4. fast
5. softly
6. hard
7. late
8. easily
9. quietly
10. beautiful
11. good
12. good
13. fluently

EXERCISE 35, p. 434.

2. B
3. D
4. D
5. C
6. A
7. A
8. B

EXERCISE 36, p. 434.

1. Everybody **wants** to be **happy**.
2. One of the **buildings** on Main Street is the post office.
3. I didn't see **anybody** at the mall. OR **I saw** nobody at the mall.
4. At the library, you need to do your work **quietly**.
5. I walk in the park every **day**.
6. Mr. Jones teaches English very **well**.
7. The answer looks **clear**. Thank you for explaining it.
8. Every grammar test **has** a lot of difficult questions.

Chapter 15: POSSESSIVES

EXERCISE 1, p. 436.

2. Bob's
3. teachers'
4. mother's
5. parents' (two people) OR parent's (one person)
6. father's
7. girl's
8. girls'
9. Tom's
10. Anita's
11. Alex's
12. students'
13. elephant's
14. monkey's
15. Monkeys'

EXERCISE 4, p. 438.

1. Bob's
2. Bob
3. teacher's
4. teacher
5. friend
6. friend's
7. manager's
8. cousin

EXERCISE 5, p. 438.

2. brother
3. mother
4. children
5. sister
6. mother
7. wife
8. mother . . . father
9. daughter
10. son

EXERCISE 6, p. 439.

2. B
3. A
4. B
5. A
6. C
7. B
8. C
9. B
10. A

EXERCISE 7, p. 440.

2. my friend's
3. my friends'
4. the child's
5. the children's
6. the woman's
7. the women's

EXERCISE 8, p. 440.

2. girl's
3. girls'
4. women's
5. uncle's
6. person's
7. people's
8. Students'
9. brother's
10. brothers'
11. wife's
12. dog's
13. dogs'
14. men's
15. man's . . . woman's
16. children's

EXERCISE 9, p. 441.

2. Yuko's
3. classmates'
4. roommate's

5. parents' (two people) OR parent's (one person)
6. people's
7. husband's
8. men's
9. children's
10. father's
11. Rosa's
12. women's

EXERCISE 10, p. 442.

2. them . . . their . . . theirs
3. you . . . your . . . yours
4. her . . . her . . . hers
5. him . . . his . . . his
6. us . . . our . . . ours

EXERCISE 11, p. 443.

2. a. ours
   b. theirs
   c. Our
   d. Theirs
3. a. Tom's
   b. Mary's
   c. His
   d. Hers
4. a. mine
   b. yours
   c. Mine . . . my
   d. Yours . . . your
5. a. Jim's
   b. Ours
   c. His
   d. Ours
6. a. my
   b. yours
   c. Mine . . . my
   d. Yours . . . your
7. a. Our
   b. Theirs
   c. Ours
   d. Their
8. a. Ann's
   b. Paul's
   c. Hers . . . her
   d. His . . . his

EXERCISE 12, p. 444.

2. hers
3. A: your
   B: my . . . Mine
4. yours
5. theirs. Their
6. A: our . . . yours
   B: Ours
7. A: your
   B: his
8. A: your
   B: yours . . . yours
   A: Mine
9. A: your
   B: yours
   A: Yours
   B: hers
   A: My . . . His

EXERCISE 13, p. 446.

2. are those
3. is this
4. is that
5. are those
6. are these

EXERCISE 15, p. 447.

2. Whose
3. Who's
4. Who's
5. Whose
6. Who's

EXERCISE 16, p. 447.

1. Who's
2. Whose
3. Who's
4. Who's
5. Whose
6. Whose
7. Who's
8. Whose
9. Whose
10. Who's

EXERCISE 17 p. 447.

1. **Who's** that woman?
2. What are those **people's** names?
3. Mr. and Mrs. Swan like **their** apartment.
4. The two **students** study together in the library every afternoon.
5. **Whose** book is this?
6. Those shoes in the bag are **theirs**, not **ours**.
7. My **father's** sister has M.D. and Ph.D. degrees.
8. Did you meet your **children's** teacher?
9. This is **my** pillow and that one is **yours**.

EXERCISE 18, p. 448.

Engaged	Jack	Jim	Jake	John	Jill	Julie	Joan	Jan
yes			x					x
no	x	x		x	x	x	x	

2. It can't be Joan. She's already married.
3. Clues 3 and 4 work together. It can't be Jill or Jack because they met at Jill's sister's wedding one year ago. The Facts (above) say that the engaged couple met just five months ago.
4. See Clue 3. So far, the answers are "no" for Julie, Joan, Jill, and Jack. Since there is only one woman left, Jan must be the engaged woman.
5. Clues 5 and 7 work together. Jan's boyfriend is a medical student, so that rules out Jim (a computer-science student).
6. (unnecessary clue)
7. See Clue 5.
8. (unnecessary clue)
9. It can't be John, since Jan doesn't love him. The only man left is Jake. Jan and Jake are the engaged couple.

Chapter 16: MAKING COMPARISONS

EXERCISE 1, p. 449.

1. Yes.
2. No.
3. Yes.
4. Yes.
5. No.
6. Yes.

EXERCISE 2, p. 450.

3. C is different from D.
4. B is the same as D.
5. B and D are the same.
6. C and D are different.

7. A and F are the same.
8. F and G are similar.
9. F is similar to G.
10. G is similar to A and F, but different from C.

EXERCISE 3, p. 450.

1. yes   5. yes
2. yes   6. yes
3. no   7. no
4. yes

EXERCISE 4, p. 451.

1. A rectangle is similar **to** a square.
2. Pablo and Rita come from **the** same country.
3. Girls and boys are **different**. Girls are different **from** boys.
4. My cousin is the same age **as** my brother.
5. Dogs are similar **to** wolves.
6. Jim and I started to speak at **the** same time.

EXERCISE 5, p. 451.

1. Figures 1, 4, 8, and 10 are the same.
   Figures 3 and 5 are the same.
   Figures 2, 7, and 9 are the same.
2. 6 is different from all the rest.
3. (Seven.)
4. Nine.
5. Eleven.

EXERCISE 7, p. 452.

2. like . . . alike   6. alike
3. alike   7. alike
4. like   8. like
5. like

EXERCISE 9, p. 454.

2. smaller than   9. more expensive than
3. bigger than   10. sweeter than
4. more important than 11. hotter than
5. easier than   12. better than
6. more difficult than 13. worse than
7. longer than   14. farther/further than
8. heavier than

EXERCISE 10, p. 455.

2. deeper than   11. better than
3. more important than 12. longer than
4. lazier than   13. more intelligent than
5. taller than   14. shorter than
6. heavier than   15. worse than
7. more difficult than 16. farther/further . . . than
8. hotter than   17. stronger than
9. thinner than   18. curlier than
10. warmer . . . than   19. more nervous . . . than

EXERCISE 13, p. 457.

1. cold   7. safer
2. colder   8. safe
3. colder   9. safer
4. happier   10. fresh
5. happy   11. funny
6. happy   12. funnier

EXERCISE 14, p. 458.

2. sweeter than   8. higher than
3. colder/warmer/hotter than   9. brighter than
4. more comfortable than   10. more expensive than
5. cheaper than   11. easier than
6. faster than   12. more important than
7. more intelligent than

EXERCISE 19, p. 461.

COMPARATIVE	SUPERLATIVE
2. smaller (than)	the smallest (of all)
3. heavier (than)	the heaviest (of all)
4. more comfortable (than)	the most comfortable (of all)
5. harder (than)	the hardest (of all)
6. more difficult (than)	the most difficult (of all)
7. easier (than)	the easiest (of all)
8. hotter (than)	the hottest (of all)
9. cheaper (than)	the cheapest (of all)
10. more interesting (than)	the most interesting (of all)
11. prettier (than)	the prettiest (of all)
12. stronger (than)	the strongest (of all)
13. better (than)	the best (of all)
14. worse (than)	the worst (of all)
15. farther/further (than)	the farthest/the furthest (of all)

EXERCISE 20, p. 462.

2. the longest
3. the most interesting
4. the highest
5. the tallest
6. the biggest
7. the shortest
8. the farthest/the furthest
9. the most beautiful
10. the worst
11. the best
12. the most comfortable
13. fastest
14. the best
15. the largest
16. the smallest
17. the most expensive
18. the easiest
19. the most important
20. the most famous

EXERCISE 21, p. 464.

1. no
2. yes
3. yes
4. yes
5. yes
6. no
7. yes
8. yes
9. no
10. yes

EXERCISE 22, p. 464.

4. older than
5. older than
6. younger than
7. the oldest
8. Alice
9. Linda
10. Karen . . . Linda . . . Alice

Sample completions:

11. Mike is the weakest.
12. Joe is stronger than Mike.
15. A car is more expensive than a bike.
19. Carol's test/grade is the best/the highest.
20. Mary's test/grade is the worst/the lowest.
23. *Love in the Spring* is more interesting than *Introduction to Psychology* (to me).
24. *Murder at Night* is more boring than *Love in the Spring* (to me).

EXERCISE 23, p. 467.

1. longer than
2. the longest
3. larger than
4. the largest
5. the highest
6. higher than
7. bigger than
8. smaller than
9. the largest
10. bigger than
11. larger than
12. better . . . than
13. the best
14. more comfortable than . . . the most comfortable
15. easier than . . . the easiest
16. worse

EXERCISE 24, p. 468.

1. more expensive
2. prettier
3. short
4. the nicest
5. small
6. the biggest
7. bigger than
8. longer than
9. long
10. the cheapest

EXERCISE 25, p. 469.

Sample sentences:

4. New York is one of the biggest cities in the world.
5. The Grand Canyon is one of the most beautiful places in the world.
6. (. . .) is one of the nicest people in our class.
7. The Yangtze River is one of the longest rivers in the world.
8. (. . .) is one of the best restaurants in *(this city)*.
9. The Taj Mahal is one of the most famous landmarks in the world.
10. The fall of the Roman Empire was one of the most important events in the history of the world.

EXERCISE 26, p. 470.

Sample sentences:

1. Hong Kong is one of the largest cities in Asia.
2. Texas is one of the largest states in the United States.
3. Paris is one of the most beautiful cities in the world.
4. (. . .) is one of the tallest people in our class.
5. San Francisco is one of the best places to visit in the world.
6. (. . .) is one of the most famous people in the world.
7. Good health is one of the most important things in life.
8. (. . .) is one of the worst restaurants in *(this city)*.
9. (. . .) is one of the most famous landmarks in (. . .).
10. (. . .) is one of the tallest buildings in *(this city)*.
11. Boxing is one of the most dangerous sports in the world.
12. Famine is one of the most serious problems in the world.

EXERCISE 28, p. 471.

PART I.
1. C
2. A
3. A
4. B

PART II.
5. C
6. A

PART III.
7. C
8. B

PART IV.
9. (1) Asia
   (2) Africa
   (3) North America
   (4) Antarctica
   (5) South America
   (6) Europe
   (7) Australia

PART V.
10. D
11. A
12. A
13. A

PART VI.
14. A
15. A
16. B
17. A
18. A
19. A

EXERCISE 29, p. 475.

2. cold
3. dirty
4. light
5. dark
6. comfortable
7. wide
8. hard/difficult
9. bad
10. smart/intelligent
11. invisible
12. wrong
13. wet
14. empty
15. clear
16. clean
17. hard

EXERCISE 30, p. 476.

1. short
2. big
3. quiet
4. pretty
5. slow
6. strong
7. cheap/inexpensive
8. lazy

EXERCISE 31, p. 476.

2. is
3. aren't
4. was
5. weren't
6. do
7. can't
8. won't
9. isn't
10. are
11. does
12. didn't
13. doesn't
14. does
15. wasn't
16. didn't
17. can
18. will
19. won't
20. will
21. were

EXERCISE 32, p. 477.

1. doesn't
2. can't
3. did
4. were
5. do
6. is
7. wasn't
8. didn't
9. won't
10. will

EXERCISE 36, p. 480.

2. more quickly than
3. more beautifully than
4. the most beautifully
5. harder than
6. the hardest
7. more carefully than
8. earlier than
9. the earliest
10. better than
11. the best
12. more clearly than
13. more fluently than
14. the most fluently

EXERCISE 37, p. 481.

2. more beautiful than
3. neater than
4. the neatest
5. more neatly than
6. the most neatly
7. more clearly than
8. better than
9. better than
10. the best
11. longer
12. later than
13. the most clearly
14. sharper than
15. more artistic than
16. more slowly than

EXERCISE 38, p. 482.

1. faster than
2. the fastest
3. harder than
4. the hardest
5. more dangerous than
6. more loudly than
7. more slowly than
8. heavier than
9. clearer than
10. more clearly

EXERCISE 39, p. 482.

2. B
3. C
4. B
5. A
6. D
7. B
8. A
9. D

EXERCISE 40, p. 483.

1. Your pen is **like** mine.
2. Kim's coat is similar **to** mine.
3. Jack's coat is **the** same **as** mine.
4. Soccer balls are different **from** basketballs.
5. Soccer is one of **the** most popular sports in the world.
6. Green sea turtles live **longer** than elephants.
7. My grade on the test was **worse than** yours. You got a ~~more~~ better grade.
8. A monkey is **more intelligent** than a turtle.
9. Pedro speaks English more **fluently** than Ernesto.
10. Professor Brown teaches full-time, but her husband **doesn't**.
11. Robert and Maria aren't **the** same age. Robert is **younger** than Maria.
12. A blue whale **is larger than** an elephant.
13. The exploding human population is the **greatest** threat to all forms of life on earth.
14. The Mongol Empire was the **biggest** land empire in the entire history of the world.

Index

A/**an**, 2, 4, 183 *(Look on pages 2, 4, and 183.)*	The numbers following the words listed in the index refer to page numbers in the text.
Consonants, 2*fn.* *(Look at the footnote on page 2.)*	The letters *fn.* mean "footnote." Footnotes are at the bottom of a chart or the bottom of a page.

NOTES

NOTES